A Curious Peril

UNIVERSITY PRESS OF FLORIDA

Florida A&M University, Tallahassee
Florida Atlantic University, Boca Raton
Florida Gulf Coast University, Ft. Myers
Florida International University, Miami
Florida State University, Tallahassee
New College of Florida, Sarasota
University of Central Florida, Orlando
University of Florida, Gainesville
University of North Florida, Jacksonville
University of South Florida, Tampa
University of West Florida, Pensacola

A Curious Peril

H.D.'s Late Modernist Prose

LARA VETTER

UNIVERSITY PRESS OF FLORIDA

Gainesville / Tallahassee / Tampa / Boca Raton
Pensacola / Orlando / Miami / Jacksonville / Ft. Myers / Sarasota

COPYRIGHT 2017 BY LARA VETTER
All rights reserved
Published in the United States of America

This book may be available in an electronic edition.

First cloth printing, 2017
First paperback printing, 2019

24 23 22 21 20 19   6 5 4 3 2 1

A record of cataloging-in-publication data is available from the Library of Congress.
ISBN 978-0-8130-5456-8 (cloth)
ISBN 978-0-8130-6441-3 (pbk.)

The University Press of Florida is the scholarly publishing agency for the State University System of Florida, comprising Florida A&M University, Florida Atlantic University, Florida Gulf Coast University, Florida International University, Florida State University, New College of Florida, University of Central Florida, University of Florida, University of North Florida, University of South Florida, and University of West Florida.

UNIVERSITY PRESS OF FLORIDA
2046 NE Waldo Road
Suite 2100
Gainesville, FL 32609
http://upress.ufl.edu

Contents

Acknowledgments vii
H.D.'s Post–World War II Writings: A Chronology xi

Introduction 1

PART I. DE-FORMATIONS: TRAUMA, GENRE,
AND *THE SWORD WENT OUT TO SEA*

1. Autobiography and Ghost Story 33
2. Mysticism and Time Travel 54
3. *Märchen* and Historical Fiction 79

PART II. CRITIQUE: GENDERED NARRATIVES
OF NATION AND IMPERIALISM

4. *By Avon River*, Arranged Marriage, and Shakespeare's Empire 105
5. Disappearing Bodies in *White Rose and the Red* 125

INTERLUDE

6. *The Mystery* 141

PART III. RE-FORMATIONS: POSTWAR ETHICS
AND IDENTITY

7. Facing the Past, Becoming *l'autre* 157
8. The Invisible Other: The Psychoanalyst as Spy 173

Coda 193
Notes 199
Works Cited 235
Works Mentioned that H.D. Owned and/or Read 249
Index 255

Acknowledgments

There is a sense in which I began writing this book in the second term of my M.A. program. The late Dabney Hart had convinced me as an undergraduate that I wanted to study modernism, but it was Randy Malamud's illuminating graduate course in modern poetry that first introduced me to H.D.'s writings. I have been grappling with notions of history, gender, spirituality, and memory in H.D.'s work ever since. This is, then, in many ways the book that I have always wanted to write.

So many scholars have supported this project in myriad ways. Jane Augustine, Annette Debo, Madelyn Detloff, Cynthia Hogue, and Demetres Tryphonopoulos each encouraged me to write what initially felt like a self-indulgent project. They believed that this would be an important book even before I had conceived of it as such. I will be forever grateful to Madelyn and to Miranda Hickman, who read the manuscript carefully and perceptively, and made invaluable suggestions. Gregory Castle's meticulous reading of a version of Chapter 7 was immensely helpful to me as I began to conceive Part III of this book. Matte Robinson and Susan Friedman shared unpublished materials with me that were crucial at various stages in this manuscript's composition, and both Elizabeth Anderson and Christina Walter invited me to deliver parts of the book as keynote talks. This book would not exist without the work of those H.D. scholars who laid the groundwork for my own, including foundational work by Susan Friedman, Rachel DuPlessis, Dee Morris, and countless others. The collaborative ethos that guides the community that comprises the H.D. International Society makes it a superlative model of feminist scholarship, and I am privileged to be a part of it. Finally, Shannon McCarthy at the University Press of Florida championed this book years before its completion, and I am grateful for her steadfast support of my work. The manuscript benefitted greatly from the superbly attentive eye of its copyeditor, Kel Pero.

Acknowledgments

I was fortunate to receive a great deal of institutional support that was essential to the project's completion as well. I was awarded the H.D. Fellowship at the Beinecke Rare Book and Manuscript Library in 2012, where I had the privilege of working with Nancy Kuhl and the outstanding staff of librarians there. Grant monies and a sabbatical leave from the Department of English and the College of Liberal Arts and Sciences at the University of North Carolina at Charlotte afforded me more time at the Beinecke to complete the research for the book. The Department also funded research assistants at various stages, and work by my graduate students—Cassandra Chaney, Lyndsey Cobb, and especially Jacqueline Plante—is gratefully acknowledged.

My father, Fred Vetter, remains my greatest fan, for which I am ever appreciative. Kirk Melnikoff's encouragement and love, as always, is a constant source of inspiration, in my work and in my life.

The Schaffner family has always been tremendously generous to H.D. scholars, and H.D.'s grandson, Val Schaffner, was kind enough to allow me access to Bryher's library at his home in East Hampton, New York. For permission to quote from H.D.'s and Bryher's unpublished writings, I would like to thank the Schaffner Family Foundation and Declan Spring at New Directions, agent for H.D.'s estate, 2017 by the Schaffner Family Foundation. For permission to quote from H.D.'s published writings, I thank Declan Spring and the Schaffner Family Foundation: *Between History and Poetry: The Letters of H.D. and Norman Holmes Pearson* (U of Iowa P, 1997), *Bid Me to Live* (UP of Florida, 2011), *By Avon River* (UP of Florida, 2014), *Collected Poems* (New Directions, 1986), *End to Torment* (New Directions, 1979), "H.D. by Delia Alton" (*Iowa Review*, 1986), *Helen in Egypt* (New Directions, 1961), *Hermetic Definition* (New Directions, 1972), *HERmione* (New Directions, 1981), *Hirslanden Notebooks* (ELS, 2015), "A Letter from England" (*Bryn Mawr Alumnae Bulletin*, 1941), *Magic Mirror, Compassionate Friendship, Thorn Thicket: A Tribute to Erich Heydt* (ELS, 2012), *Majic Ring* (UP of Florida, 2009), *The Mystery* (UP of Florida, 2009), *Narthex & Other Stories* (BookThug, 2013), *Nights* (New Directions, 1986), "A Note on Poetry" (*Agenda*, 1987), *Notes on Thought and Vision* (Peter Owen, 1982), *Paint It To-day* (New York UP, 1992), *Palimpsest* (Southern Illinois UP, 1968), *Pilate's Wife* (New

Directions, 2000), *The Sword Went Out to Sea: Synthesis of a Dream*, by Delia Alton (UP of Florida, 2007), *Tribute to Freud* (New Directions, 1984), *Trilogy* (New Directions, 1998), *Vale Ave* (New Directions, 2013), *White Rose and the Red* (UP of Florida, 2009), *Within the Walls* (UP of Florida, 2014). For permission to quote from Bryher's published work, I again thank Declan Spring and the Schaffner Family Foundation: *Days of Mars: A Memoir, 1940–1946* (Harcourt Brace, 1972).

A version of Chapter 5 appeared in an article in *Review of English Studies* in 2016; a version of Chapter 7 appeared in *The History of the Modernist Novel*, edited by Gregory Castle (Cambridge University Press, 2015); and a version of Chapter 4 appears in the introduction to my edition of H.D.'s *By Avon River* (University Press of Florida, 2014).

H.D.'s Post–World War II Writings

A Chronology

1945–1946　H.D. writes *By Avon River* in London, England, and at Klinik Brunner, in Küsnacht, near Zürich, Switzerland. Part I, "Good Frend," is a poem based on Claribel from Shakespeare's *The Tempest*. Part II, "The Guest," is an essay on English literary history and Renaissance lyric poets.

1946–1947　H.D. writes *The Sword Went Out to Sea: Synthesis of a Dream (by Delia Alton)* in Lausanne and Lugano, Switzerland. Part I of the book, "Wintersleep," recounts Delia Alton's experience with séances in London during World War II, and her memories of World War I and a thwarted teenage romance. Part II, "Summerdream," consists of a series of vignettes largely set in ancient Greece and Rome, Medieval Normandy, and Elizabethan England.

1947–1948　H.D. writes *White Rose and the Red* in Lausanne and Lugano. Set in Victorian England, the book is a fictionalized account of Pre-Raphaelite artists William Morris, Dante Gabriel Rossetti, and Elizabeth Siddall. In 1948, H.D. finalizes "Advent," which becomes part of *Tribute to Freud*.

1948–1951　H.D. writes *The Mystery* in Lausanne and Lugano. The novel, set in eighteenth-century Prague, concerns two siblings, Elizabeth de Watteville and Henry Dohna, who encounter a magician, Count Saint-Germain, while researching Moravian history. In 1950, H.D. finishes final editing of *Bid Me to Live*, a novel drafted before the war.

1952–1955　H.D. writes *Helen in Egypt* in Lausanne, Lugano, and Küsnacht.

1955–1956   H.D. writes the memoir *Compassionate Friendship* and the novel *Magic Mirror*. These closely related texts recount her experiences at the Klinik Brunner, her analysis with existential psychotherapist Erich Heydt, and reflections on her writings.

1957–1959   H.D. begins a dream journal, *Hirslanden Notebooks*, in 1957 at Klinik Hirslanden in Zürich, where she recovers from a broken leg; the journal is finished in Küsnacht in 1959. H.D. writes *Vale Ave* and *Sagesse* in 1957. In 1958, she writes *End to Torment*, a memoir of Ezra Pound. *Winter Love* is written in 1959.

1960–1961   In 1960, H.D. writes *Thorn Thicket (Bosquet)* in Küsnacht, Switzerland; the memoir consists largely of reflections on her writings. *Hermetic Definition* is written between August 1960 and February 1961. In the spring of 1961, Klinik Brunner is sold, and H.D. moves to Hotel Sonnenberg in Zürich. She begins a journal in May. After suffering a stroke, she dies at Klinik Hirslanden on September 27.

Introduction

> The heavy sea-mist stifles me.
> I choke with each breath—
> a curious peril, this—
> the gods have invented
> curious torture for us.
>
> —H.D., "Loss"

The modernist writer known as H.D. (Hilda Doolittle) spent both world wars in London. When World War II appeared imminent, she declined offers of refuge and remained in the city throughout the war, with only a few respites in the English countryside.[1] She endured the relentless bombings of the Blitz that overtook London from the fall of 1940 to the spring of 1941, the food rationings that left her sick and malnourished, and a second wave of doodlebug and V2 bombings near the close of the war. H.D.'s reasons for voluntarily staying in a perilous war zone are difficult to disentangle, and at various points—to various friends and family members—she offers several. The day after the second wave of bombings occurred in 1944—featuring the fly-bomb, new German weaponry—H.D. emphatically resists the urging of her lifelong companion Bryher that they go immediately to Cornwall, reportedly declaring that Hitler would not scare her away: "'Leave Lowndes now because of That Man? Never!'"[2] Aside from a bombastic (perhaps foolish) defiance in the face of Nazism, it seems clear that the American-born British citizen H.D. felt then that London was her home, and she felt loyal to it. "If one has taken joy and comfort from a country," she explains in 1941, "one does not want to leave it when there is trouble about."[3] Indeed, H.D. writes her friend George Plank as early as 1938 that she could quite easily heed Bryher's advice and "with a turn of the wrist" use her birth certificate to flee Europe for the States, "[b]ut all my memories and my emotional status seem here."[4] The following year she tells her former husband, Richard Aldington, that she is "desperately home-sick" for London and is making rapid plans to return from Switzerland before the war begins.[5] As Susan Stanford Friedman has argued, "To flee the war would be desertion, betrayal of the city that set her free."[6] A brief but profound sense of patriotism was evidently a compelling factor in her decision to stay in England. In a memoir of the war experience, Bryher speculates that "[i]t was the Puritan element, a matter of conscience and principle, that had now kept Hilda in London. 'It was here that people first read my poetry,' she said, 'I am staying with them.' . . . She could have left us easily, but she stayed."[7]

But I will argue that there are other reasons for her refusal to leave this "beleaguered rock—'this England.'"[8] First, for all of its tragedy, the war offered Londoners a sense of community. "I was a misfit," she wrote of her life before the Second World War, but "[n]ot now. I had stepped into the war, I had taken my place with a million others."[9] During the war, H.D. felt her faith in humanity restored, as we see in the hopeful tones of her epic *Trilogy*; it was only after the war ended that this faith began to falter. She writes passionately to an American relation in 1940 that "there has been a fine resurgence of real heroic life and will to live, in this country and in this city. We are really beautifully watched over—all a large family."[10] "I am glad to have had the time here," she tells her American cousin Gretchen Wolle Baker of the Blitz year, "It has all been most revealing and exciting and people have been so wonderful."[11] Though she does express weariness and dejection at some points, her correspondence also contains numerous instances of this more optimistic strain.

Moreover, H.D. perceived the second war as therapeutic in what had become a lifelong struggle to come to terms with the trauma of the Great War. In a letter written late in the Second World War, H.D. explains to Baker that the experience had been a psychological necessity: "You must remember that I have had TWO wars and the first one rather cut me away from family etc. and now in my ripe middle-age, I have begun to go back and weave in the jagged ends."[12] Paul Saint-Amour has usefully documented the extent to which the trauma of the Second World War was, for Londoners, embedded in post-traumatic responses to the aerial bombardment of the first, characterizing that trauma as an "interruption of mourning by a panic that forcibly returns the mourner to the originary scene of loss."[13] In her postwar *The*

Sword Went Out to Sea: (Synthesis of a Dream) by Delia Alton, and other 1940s and 1950s prose works, H.D. repeatedly links the two wars; in a 1955 memoir she observes that "I am not alone in finding that those years between wars seemed almost to be marking time."[14] World wars served as significant benchmarks for H.D. as she neared the end of her life.

Significantly for this project, though, there may well have been yet another reason for her to stay in London. H.D. had learned during the First World War how tremendously prolific she could be during periods of war. As her friend and literary executor Norman Holmes Pearson observed in a 1969 interview, "Her writing had received a new stimulus through the war and its excitement, so that in a sense a new career opened for her."[15] Throughout the early 1940s, she stayed in her South Kensington flat, and she wrote, penning *Trilogy* and several other works, even as she lived under unremitting anxiety, mental strain, and deprivation. Though we typically associate her analysis with Freud with the resolution of her early 1930s case of writers' block, the Second World War is in fact the more immediate catalyst for the incredible outpouring of fiction, nonfiction, and poetry of the 1940s and 1950s—a moment in her career that has been aptly termed a "renaissance" by Elizabeth Willis.[16] The trauma of the war birthed a body of work strikingly different from that of her earlier career. It was after the war's end that she began to produce a flood of historical novels, memoirs, and long poems that would comprise her later career. In the *Hirslanden Notebooks*, among her last writings, H.D. recollects that "[m]y life was enriched, my creative energy was almost abnormal, after I got over the first shock of leaving London. I wrote the *Avon*, I wrote three 'novels' (unpublished) on my unparalleled experiences. I wrote the long *Helen* sequence, did the recordings for the *Helen*. I wrote, on another level, *Majic Mirror*."[17]

Though my epigraph is derived from a poem penned in the World War I era, the Second World War, too, proved to be a "curious peril" for H.D., a "curious torture" wrought not by the gods but by bombs plummeting from the heavens. London denizens were "imminently exposed" to danger in the early 1940s. But H.D. was also aware that the *Siege Perilous* was the seat at King Arthur's round table reserved for the sole survivor of the Quest. Survival of the war guaranteed both earthly and divine rewards. The "peril" itself is "curious"—carefully wrought, painstakingly designed—the latter term bearing a rich etymological history, its Latin root indicating not just inquisitiveness but diligence. To be curious is to be artistic, clever, detailed, attentive, intricate, skillful. It is to be erotic, to be queer or strange. It is a term associated with the occult, with creativity, with surprise.[18] In *Sword*, one of H.D.'s autobiographically based personae observes of the "dream" that it "is so—curious"; as H.D. explains in a reflective essay some years later, "The dream is the creative imagination, the actual personal dream of the narrator, or the still more curious, astonishing or miraculous dream of those 'in that sleep of Death,' to whom we wonder with Hamlet, 'what dreams may come.'... Perhaps the most curious thing about this transcendental dream is that it appears so natural."[19] The dream appears to be natural, but it manifests as supernatural. The peril of World War II felt apocalyptic, but it was also tremendously inspirational. It is at once tragic and generative, its effects material and spiritual. It is from such a crucible that H.D.'s works of the late 1940s emerge.

This book looks closely at the critically neglected prose work produced in the years immediately following the "curious peril" of the Second World War, concluding with a consideration of her fiction and nonfiction of the 1950s. Though we tend to think of H.D. as uninterested in politics—aside from her well-documented concerns with gender and sexuality, of course—and though we have viewed much of her late prose as wholly concerned with spiritual themes, I argue that our collective neglect of this period of her career has bolstered an incomplete portrait of her *oeuvre*. In fact, this late, postwar work brings together the material, political world with the realm of the immaterial, the mystical, the otherworldly. Her postwar work marks a definitive shift from the modernist to the late modernist, gesturing, at crucial points, to the postmodern.

H.D.'s work changes dramatically over the course of her career. Though her Imagist poems of the 1910s were never as static as advertised, there is no question that they had a "crystallized" quality. The "crystalline" Imagist poem, ideally, tends toward stasis—a glimpse, a snapshot, a moment in time, apparitions of faces at a metro station. The subject of the Imagist poem is an object. H.D.'s poems of the early volume *Sea Garden*, published in 1916, do not really fit Ezra Pound's prescriptions, but their objects are often portrayed as subject to the forces of the environments that surround them, their verbs often cast in the passive voice. Her "Sea Rose," for instance, is "caught in the drift," "[s]tunted," "flung on the sand," "lifted"; her "Sea Lily" "slashed and torn," "shattered / in the wind," "flecked," "dashed," "cut," and "cover[ed]"...

with froth."[20] In fact, it is the passivity of the object that is often the focus of these poems, as H.D. explores the tension between movement and stillness. Famously, H.D. was ready to move on from Imagism even before Amy Lowell edited the last Imagist anthology in 1917, but the transition did not prove easy. "They squeal that H.D. is no longer the pure crystalline," she complained to Bryher in 1936 of unreceptive readers.[21] H.D. believed that publishers refused her novels because "H.D." shouldn't do prose, and by the time she began to write her late epic poems, she felt that much of her audience was still unwilling to relinquish the label: "they had to sniff a bit because our old H.D. had not stayed 'pure Greek,'" she writes of herself in the third person about a negative review of *Trilogy*, but "[w]hy she must write at 60 . . . what one wrote at 16, must remain a mystery!"[22]

We can trace a tension between movement and passivity in her early prose as well, which begins to depart from Imagist precepts. In her 1919 aesthetic manifesto *Notes on Thought and Vision* and her 1921 novel *Paint It To-day*, H.D. theorizes sculpture from the point of view of the audience rather than the artist or the statue, for "[t]here is no trouble about the art, it is the appreciators we want." The statue, in these texts, is "a means of approach," a "receiving station, capable of storing up energy" that can be "transmitted only to another body or another mind that is in sympathy with it."[23] It is an inanimate and inexpressive object from which a viewer can garner power and with which a viewer can "fall in love."[24] Isolating the statue of the charioteer at Delphi, H.D. admits it has "an almost hypnotic effect on me," as she focuses exclusively on its cold mathematical, "geometrical precision"—its emission of telegraphic messages in "dots and dashes"—rather than its expressivity.[25] Likewise, in *Paint It To-day*, we find a passive model of the relationship between statue and viewer: "We measure, or should measure, our capacity for life . . . not by our power of attraction but by our power or possibilities of being attracted." "We should be able, more easily, to fall in love with a statue than with any other work of art," she continues, because "[t]he dynamic strength of [the sculptor's] original impulse should . . . reach us less encumbered (as in the other arts) with our own impulses." In other words, in the "other arts," "our own emotions are apt to intrude, to cloud over the original impulse (or as commonly called, inspiration) of the artist."[26] Paradoxically, then, as viewers we experience more emotion—truer emotion, real love—if it is that which emanates from the static art object itself.

The art object, then, seduces us with a coldness that renders us numb.[27] In

Paint It To-day, her autobiographically based character Midget spends hours and days in the Louvre gazing at statues. The problem, though, is that she is not entirely comfortable, nor content, with the utter passivity of the cold, inexpressive, mathematically perfect statue. She desires the statue to move, to breathe, to have agency. She recoils from the Louvre's *Hermaphroditus*, describing it as "not modeled even with living fingers, but poured into a set mold." But in Rome, Midget encounters a variant of the statue lying not on a cold stone pedestal but on a blanket of rich black velvet (a variant that H.D. bought in replica for her home). This *Hermaphroditus* "was the same Hermaphroditus, but no little monster. . . . This was a gentle breathing image, modeled in strange, soft, honey-colored stone. The small head lay on the perfect childlike arm."[28] Unlike the utterly lifeless version in the Louvre, this statue appears to be moving and breathing.

The statue in H.D.'s "Pygmalion," first printed in 1917, is, likewise, far from lifeless. Indeed, the artist Pygmalion fears "my work is for naught" because "[e]ach from his marble base / has stepped into the light." His creations resist fixity, stepping down from their pedestals and abandoning their creator. "Each one departs," Pygmalion sounds his lament.[29] That H.D. was becoming entranced with this image of the living statue after the Great War is clear, for she named her daughter, Perdita, for the character in Shakespeare's *Winter's Tale* whose mother is a statue-come-to-life. By the turn of the twentieth century, in fact, living statues were in vogue among women. Genevieve Stebbins, a disciple of the famous performance theorist François Delsarte, originated and popularized statue-posing, a practice that, in essence, injected movement into *tableaux vivants*, itself a phenomenon dating to the early nineteenth century. According to dance historian Ann Daly, living statues "were much the same as tableaux vivants, only they moved, and their models were exclusively classical Greek sculptures."[30] H.D. and Bryher engaged in a form of statue-posing in 1920 in the woods of northern California when they posed nude for one another, producing photographs of themselves in the mode of Greek statuary. These photographs do not depict frozen statues, however. The ivory starkness of their bodies against a darker backdrop suggests a marble statue, but bodies are caught mid-movement—the tentative gesture of an arm upstretched, a head bowed, a leg raised to step into the water. The inclusion of these nudes in a scrapbook several years later, artistically arranged among images of Greek ruins and art, stresses even more the dynamic mode they attempted to capture.[31]

Pygmalion's statues walk away, declaring that *"no marble can bind me,"* and H.D.'s vision at Corfu in 1920 begins as a series of static images but becomes "a moving-picture."³² The character based on Bryher in *Paint It To-day*, Althea, poses for Midget as a statue, but Midget stresses that "Althea was not like a statue, not like a statue in a museum, that is."³³ Elsewhere I have argued that H.D. was made uncomfortable by stillness and passivity. In *Majic Ring* (completed during the Second World War), H.D.'s protagonist enters an altered state and creates a series of moving *tableaux vivants*. She struggles, moving in and out of active and passive states.³⁴ A vision of the statue of a lady "was not a statue. . . . she was alive, she was not-alive, she certainly was alive, she did not move but she could move."³⁵ Bringing a statue to life, infusing a work of art with agency—these are acts that shift H.D. further from the static objects of the Imagist poem and closer to more dynamic modes of representation. At this point in her career, though still primarily a poet, she is beginning to experiment with prose and with film, itself a medium of oscillation between stasis and movement, with its series of static stills and the illusory movement of those stills made possible by the projector. H.D.'s growing dislike of the inanimate statue mirrors her dissatisfaction with Imagism. In the last chapter of *Paint It To-day*, Midget and Althea debate aesthetics. Midget argues passionately, "Nothing is static. All things change."³⁶

Cheryl Hindrichs has hypothesized that it was World War I that offered H.D. an initial push away from Imagism.³⁷ *A Curious Peril* contends that this gradual shift away from the static culminates and peaks in the more dynamic modes of epic poetry and historical fiction written during and after World War II. While H.D. had written historical fiction in the past, the historical had served as backdrop, the thinly veiled autobiographical as foreground. Those earlier novels, she writes in 1950, are different in that they are "dressed up," stories true to life and merely adorned in historical splendor.³⁸ I will argue that this dynamic is reversed in the late 1940s, that the autobiographical ends up being merely a device for working through trauma and launching political critique. The autobiographical recedes into the background because the public sphere so persistently intrudes, interrupting irrevocably the events of the private sphere, which begin to seem trivial in the face of global crises. It is war that moves to center stage. Bryony Randall is undoubtedly right that H.D.'s autobiographical fiction of World War I is about the "'uncurability' of a trauma."³⁹ H.D.'s fiction immediately following World War II is even more emphatically pessimistic about the possibility of recovering from such trauma.⁴⁰ In *Sword* and *White Rose and the Red*, the space between public and private conflict dissipates, utterly destroying her war-worn protagonists.

Marina Mackay has argued persuasively that World War II is central to understanding late modernism, that "the correlation between late modernism in England and the world-changing circumstances with which it overlapped amounts to more than a historical coincidence."⁴¹ There is no question that the Second World War was a crucial event in H.D.'s later life. We know that it engendered her epic *Trilogy*—which was written during the middle and at the end of the war—and that it led to her permanent exile from England. Both world wars spawned a burst of creative activity that resulted in new poetry and fiction. The First World War serves, I would contend, as backdrop to the psychological drama being enacted in H.D.'s post-World War I-era fiction. Indeed, in the first of these novels, *Paint It To-day*, the war is tersely summarized in just three brief sentences, disappearing into an abyss: "There was a war. A cloud. Five Years."⁴² The war serves amply as metaphor for the personal turmoil of her characters, a means to an end. *A Curious Peril* aims to show a striking reversal in the postwar fiction of the 1940s. Drawing on Robert Caserio's observations about modernist approaches to autobiography, I will argue that after the war H.D. increasingly produces "records of selves impersonally distanced from selfhood."⁴³ The personal story matters less than the greater realities of the public sphere: war, imperialism, and political corruption. The self "is in danger of collapsing"⁴⁴ in the face of such atrocity.

I do not mean to overstate the case. This reversal is not absolute; some of H.D.'s 1920s historical fiction, such as "Hipparchia" (the subject of Chapter 7), clearly begins to take on the very issues that dominate her late 1940s fiction, and Kathy Phillips's illuminating discussion of H.D.'s "The Ear-Ring" shows that she had begun thinking seriously about the dangers of capitalism and imperialism by the 1930s. I also do not mean to paint her as a political radical. H.D. abhorred firm stances in private and public matters, embracing instead the liminal or dialectical position, and at times this may well be to her discredit. She was not Woolf, who declared "I have no country," or Loy, who wrote pacifist and feminist manifestos. H.D. may never be the radical we long for her to be not because of her spiritual beliefs or because she shared with her compatriots some of the less-enlightened views of her time—though she unfortunately did—but because her mode of being in the world was always interrogative and exploratory. For the mature H.D., it was the quest itself, not the destination, that mattered. If her characters seek truth, they will not find it, but the process of searching for it is what facilitates some degree of enlightenment. And here the form of her later writings can be as revealing as the content: form is process.

That said, we can still track a decisive shift in trajectory if we compare the prose of the 1920s to that of the 1940s. As her letters and prose writings attest, H.D. becomes more interested in the contemporary political scene than ever before, responding to the rise of Hitler and the Second World War. In *Sword*, in *White Rose*, in *By Avon River*, the political encroaches on the personal. H.D.'s protagonist fails in her efforts to block out the devastation of war in the former text; Elizabeth Siddall's mental stability is progressively and irrevocably eroded by war and violence in *White Rose*; and in *By Avon River*, Shakespeare's interior monologue cannot dislodge the political realities in which he is embedded, or detract from the life stories of his fellow poets, victims of political persecution and corruption. In the brief period following World War II, the autobiographical recedes to the background, functioning metaphorically to suggest the issues that dominate the public sphere. If "[l]arge, epic pictures bored her" in *Paint It To-day*,[45] they absorb her intellectual and creative energies in the years immediately following the Second World War.

"Is it true, I wonder," Ellen Glasgow muses near the end of her memoir *The Woman Within*, "that the only way to escape war is to be in it?" Completed just before her death in 1945, Glasgow's autobiography was written during the Second World War, and this question appears in a dispirited epilogue bemoaning the inevitable self-destructiveness of humankind. H.D. was so taken with this passage that she transcribed it in her 1955 memoir, *Compassionate Friendship*.[46] H.D. struggled with finding respite from the war, within the war. Bryher admitted to H.D.'s cousin Francis Wolle that "[i]t was always amazing to me how anyone as sensitive as Hilda, managed to survive the war in London," and she records in her memoir of the period that H.D. was particularly sensitive to the "terrible" noise of the war, a problem H.D. described to many friends and family.[47] "[T]he NOISE is the thing that finally does wear one out," H.D. writes to one friend, and she declares to another, "We do not wish to HEAR and God knows, we do not wish to SEE the horrors all around us."[48] To friends and family, H.D. wrote of the relentless "traffic" in and out of her Kensington flat, which had become a central home base—a "bee-hive" or "canteen" or "telephone-booth or box or post-office counter or medical consulting clinic"—for so many of their friends and acquaintances.[49] As she recounts in *Sword*, through her autobiographically based protagonist Delia, escaping the war was a near impossible task.

Though she held up well throughout its duration, H.D. suffered psychologically and physically at war's end.[50] Her delayed but dramatic reaction to trauma was another form of "curious torture" and is key to understanding her postwar prose. In the spring of 1946, H.D. was involuntarily committed to a hospital in Switzerland, and she never returned to England. Based on letters between her friends and family, it is possible to reconstruct only a murky picture of what actually led to the incident. In March, their close friend Robert Herring confesses to their friend and erstwhile analyst Walter Schmideberg that H.D. had begun acting "odd" in late February, excessively "hostile" and "excitable."[51] He reports that on February 27 she became psychologically ill, a date confirmed by Bryher in a letter to H.D. after the fact: "Last February you were taken very ill and for a time I think you did not know any of us."[52] A March letter from Bryher to Francis Wolle explains that H.D. is suffering from meningitis and malnutrition and that she wishes to get her to Switzerland, where the postwar living conditions are superior; about London, Bryher writes, "[c]onditions here are dreadful, most of our food is stale, there isn't much of it and there is a dreadful monotony. For years we could never go out at night on account of the black out and to go anywhere means a terrible struggle to get on the bus or subway. Also during the raids terrible things happened round us." A follow-up letter to Wolle in April specifies that H.D. "suffers from an intense lassitude" and that the doctor has prescribed what sounds very like a nineteenth-century rest cure, forbidding H.D. from doing anything, even writing, though she wanted very much to be able to go on with her work: "She is hoping very much to get back to her work but the doctor says she must not do anything for another month at least requiring any mental effort."[53] Silvia Dobson's unpublished memoir of H.D. confirms that she had heard from H.D.'s doctor that H.D. had meningitis, but Dobson claims that he also describes a possible suicide attempt. If true, this chilling incident must surely recall Virginia Woolf's reaction to the Second World War, which H.D. and Bryher discussed with friends.[54]

H.D. was airlifted from London to Zürich in May and placed in the care of doctors at the Klinik Brunner in Küsnacht.[55] Bryher writes Wolle from

Switzerland in June to relate that H.D. was "making excellent progress." The "rest cure" was continuing, and Bryher reminds Wolle again of the stress of the war: "You must remember that bombs fell on either side of us, not once or twice but continuously in the big blitz and even worse, during the flying bomb period. They want her not to write, read or do anything but lie or walk in the sun and eat until the end of the summer."[56] Dobson's papers include a June letter from H.D. that is quite lucid, excited about her regular walks in the lovely gardens surrounding the clinic.[57] In late June, H.D. tells Wolle that she is happily writing again, and her daughter, Perdita, and Pearson, too, were receiving letters from H.D. that summer and into early September.[58] H.D.'s health must have declined suddenly, however, because on September 5 she was given electroshock treatment, which induced a temporary bout of paranoia that is described at greater length in Chapter 8.[59]

H.D.'s account of her own illness is telling. H.D. did characterize it as "a 'flight from reality'" to a friend, though in the fictionalized version Delia complains in *Sword* that "I didn't gibber and hurl things at people. I didn't mind if [Howell] thought me a little crazy. But I didn't think I was." Following electroshock treatment, H.D. writes a few angry letters to Bryher then shifts her tone abruptly, perhaps because she realized that being freed from incarceration was dependent upon her acquiescence to the doctors and the treatment. In one such letter, fearful that she will be declared legally insane, H.D. enumerates the reasons for her illness: "(1) ... anxiety as to your welfare (2) bomb repercussion & possible percussion (3) famine neurosis (4) superimposition of last war illness & anxiety about birth & future of Perdita (5) infiltration of poisonous gas (6) injections to induce hysteria (7) after-effects of the same." To her confidante George Plank, H.D. adds the constant traffic in and out of her flat during the war as a key factor.[60] In a 1961 diary, she writes of another, the postwar revelation of concentration camps: "I anguished during my fever over the last reports of the Nazi atrocities the 11,000,000 men, women & alas children, sacrificed to Molluch."[61] With Pearson, she is perhaps most frank, describing both a diagnosis of meningitis and her shock at discovering Bryher unconscious: "[Bryher] had talked of suicide from the earliest days, when she came to see me, before Perdita was born. She tried it, Spring 1920 in Zermatt. . . . I was always afraid she would make away with herself, during the Blitz. Then, one terrible night, she injected herself & lay moaning on the same bed."[62] The fictionalized version in *Sword* attributes Delia's illness to meningitis, "nerve strain," and malnutrition. Dowding's repudiation of H.D.'s experiences with spiritualism has widely been seen as the cause of her "breakdown," though Delia writes that she doubts that "Lord Howell" had anything to do with it.[63]

H.D.'s letter to Pearson focuses, understandably, on her anger at the treatment she endured: "There is no doubt that we were both a little crazy but I do not yet fully know why I was brought to this place. I was here for 5 months, enduring *shock treatment* of a most pernicious nature. My papers were taken away, I was locked up without food or water & injected with—I don't know what." To Bryher, she writes of the experience, "They locked me in the bed-room, with window & shutters barred. There were 5 of us, 3 hefty men and a nurse. One of the men left with the nurse, when I refused an injection. I thought they were trying to kill me. I suppose this is 'dementia praecox.' I begged for a few minutes. An enormous prize-fighter, weighing a ton, ordered me to lie down on the bed. I refused & tried to dodge them. . . . I have been severely shocked; if that is what they wanted to do, they succeeded." She insists that she was misdiagnosed with "'paranoia' or 'schiz'" because she had refused to eat. "I am perfectly well," she writes, then adds drily, "I am also apparently mad."[64]

I detail the episode at some length because we often refer without specifics to the "breakdown"—itself a dubious term urgently in need of historicizing, though H.D. herself employs it.[65] While it seems clear that H.D. suffered from a depressive episode in 1946, it is not at all clear that her "breakdown" was not also induced by meningitis and the drugs prescribed for it. When questioned about H.D.'s involuntary commitment, Bryher tells her that "[a]ll your friends have been told that you had meningitis and that you are recovering."[66] While some have interpreted this to mean that the explanation of meningitis was fabricated, it is again not clear that this is necessarily the case. It could very well be that meningitis was just one of the factors contributing to the illness, but that friends were not told of others. Arguing that malnutrition was probably the most profound cause of H.D.'s illness, Annette Debo cites a letter from Bryher to Pearson attributing the illness to "acute malnutrition and shock."[67] Whatever the causes, the experience in Klinik Brunner in the fall of 1946 was part of the trauma of war that undergirds her postwar literary production.

Despite her "rest cure," H.D. found a way to write throughout 1946, just as she had during the war; much of *By Avon River* was completed in the fall of that year, written in pencil because the doctors had forbidden the use of a pen. In fact, H.D. was also energized by the war and wanted to write about it throughout its duration and even in its aftermath. "I never came near feeling the old war, as I felt this, quite personally," she tells Bryher in 1940, and later in the decade she describes the experience of writing *Sword* as having "a gattling-gun in my hands."[68] H.D.'s rarely read experimental prose memoir, *Within the Walls*, stands as one of the only modernist literary efforts to depict the Blitz directly, and she later expressed the desire to write even more about it: "I wanted to write about our raids, but never more than lightly touched on them."[69] Though we have seen H.D. as largely unconcerned with modern global politics, this was most certainly not true of her between the late 1930s and the late 1940s. She had become acutely aware of the threat implicit in the rise of Nazism as early as 1934 when she stepped over swastikas written on sidewalks in Vienna on the way to Freud's home-office.[70]

In fact, H.D. set aside her anti-war stance during the Second World War, writing in 1941 an open letter to the *Bryn Mawr Alumnae Bulletin* calling on Americans to join the war effort. Though she admits that "I hate war, having the violent personal experience of it," she nonetheless argues forcefully that the "brute force" of the German threat—the "persecution of all intellectual thought by Fascism"—outweighs her pacifist sentiments.[71] In this change of heart, H.D. joins many of her compatriots, for, as Marina Mackay observes, "all major British writers of the mid-century made the guilty compromise, knowing it to be exactly that, of supporting the Second World War."[72] Even for those who had lived through the Great War, the menacing figure of Hitler proved more terrifying than ominous visions of another devastating world war. Attending specifically to women writers of the period—such as Stevie Smith, Storm Jameson, and Elizabeth Bowen—Phyllis Lassner draws a similar conclusion: "Many British women writers resisted policies of making peace with Hitler by insisting that this war, unlike others, was the only way to save the führer's victims."[73]

H.D. was also very well-informed, having become fairly obsessed with the wireless news reports before and during the war, and for several years afterward, secluded in Switzerland, she continued to ask Bryher for reports of Churchill, postwar reconstruction, and other political topics, constantly seeking American and British newspapers and magazines so that she could keep current. She began listening to regular broadcasts and reading daily newspapers for news of Germany in 1938, but by early 1940 she thanked Bryher for the radio because she can "listen in two or three times a day." When they were apart, her daily correspondence with Bryher was filled with references to the news, often in some detail. "[T]he news keeps us all on the jump," she writes, "I read paper and papers daily." She even shifted her schedule in order to accommodate radio news programs, commenting to Bryher about everything from Churchill's speeches to sea battles to Hitler's military maneuvers: "I listen-in to everything now." "I seem to be turning into a military expert," she informs Bryher in 1940. Indeed, she referred to the radio as an addiction, calling it "dope." [74]

H.D. has been accused of escapism—more interested in ancient, mythic worlds than modern-day realities—but she scoffed at the claim. "Ivory tower?" she asks sarcastically in a reflective letter written to Pearson. "In order to speak adequately of my poetry and its aims, I must, you see, drag in a whole deracinated epoch," she laments. "Perhaps specifically, I might say that the house next door was struck another night. We came home and simply waded through glass, while wind from now unshuttered windows, made the house a barn, an unprotected dug-out."[75] H.D. was dismissive of allegations of escapism, for she did not believe that the only way to write about a war was to describe its battlefields. It is clear from her library and correspondence that the late 1930s and early 1940s witnessed a spike in her interest in modern politics on both sides of the Atlantic, for she was reading a wide range of books about war and politics. In 1938, for instance, H.D. was reading Leane Zugsmith's account of civil rights violations in a Southern town, *Summer Soldier*. She owned E. M. Forster's 1940 transcripts of anti-Nazi BBC broadcasts entitled *Nordic Twilight,* and in 1940 she read both Sergei Chakhotin's *The Rape of Masses: The Psychology of Totalitarian Political Propaganda* and Toni Sender's *Autobiography of a German Rebel*. In the late 1940s, she notes that she is reading Nicholas Powell's war novel *The Hills Remain* and Nigel Balchin's *A Sort of Traitors*. Indeed, for years after World War II she remained interested in accounts of it. Bryher helped her collect books and pamphlets on the subject, and H.D. noted and commemorated Battle of Britain Day well into the 1950s. H.D. obtained Max Beerbohm's *Mainly on the Air* (which reprinted war-era radio broadcasts), Leonardo Blake's *The Last Year of War and After,* Kay Boyle's *Primer for Combat,* Dorothy Burlingham and Anna Freud's *Young Children in War-time,* Negley Farson's *Bomber's*

Moon, Robert Henrey's *The Incredible City*, Ninetta Jucker's *Curfew in Paris*, Clarence Reed's *Great Prophecies about the War*, Ian Reid's *Prisoner at Large*, Rebecca West's *The Meaning of Treason*, and a pamphlet called *Front Line, 1940–1941* printed by the Ministry of Home Security. Bryher herself became a "news junkie" in the period, her politics leaning increasingly more conservative as the war years receded.[76] Her near-daily correspondence with H.D. from the late 1930s to the early 1950s (whenever they were apart) inevitably recounts an update on British political affairs.

The trauma of the war is manifest in the work H.D. produced during and immediately after the war. In addition to *Trilogy*, H.D. begins to write poetry, compiled in the slim volume *What Do I Love?*, that is strikingly different from that of previous decades. Not embedded in myth or set in the ancient world, these poems feature modern-day London—in references as far-ranging as the rubble after a night of bombing, the orangery at Kensington Palace, dead canteen drivers following a bombing—but it is the prose of the postwar period that departs most definitively from her earlier work. In *Trilogy*, she had asked, "how can you scratch out // indelible ink of the palimpsest / of past misadventure?"[77] After the war, she is intent in her prose on excavating and exposing this "past misadventure," not erasing it. H.D.'s constant monitoring of the wireless undoubtedly fed a newfound interest in modern Europe, for it is both war and imperialism that emerge as subjects of the postwar prose. Sparked perhaps by wartime patriotism, this is a period of H.D.'s writing that attends for the first time to the United Kingdom, decades after she had become a British citizen.

"While not homeless," Annette Debo has recently observed of H.D., "she was placeless."[78] H.D. thought of herself as British . . . and American. "She is always trying to balance her two nationalities,'" Bryher observed in her memoir of the war era.[79] H.D.'s rather convoluted response to a Viennese resident is illustrative: "they called me the English lady at the hotel, so I said I was from England, which in fact I was."[80] Indeed, she writes the poet May Sarton after a 1939 visit that "[i]t is so helpful to my confused national, international, un-national consciousness, to communicate with someone who has the USA, the Continental & the English back-ground."[81] H.D. had become a British subject automatically in 1913 when she married Richard Aldington; by the laws of that time period, American women marrying Englishmen had no choice but to relinquish U.S. citizenship. "Pulled both ways," Friedman argues, "she was fully at home in neither world."[82] She resisted repatriation for decades, explaining to Bryher that "it is the sentiment of the War I and the War II romances that holds me back" from reclaiming American citizenship, referring to the postwar novels set in England that followed both world wars.[83] In letters and memoirs, she represents herself as English as often as she does American, and Bryher shared her expansive vision of nationality. She and Bryher, in fact, joked that the English Bryher was in fact the true American, H.D. "an English lady." H.D. and Bryher lived in Switzerland when they weren't in England, and Bryher casts herself as Swiss in her memoir of the early 1940s, *Days of War*, writing H.D. en route to England in 1940 that she was already "homesick for Switzerland."[84] At the end of the Second World War, H.D., Bryher, and their friend Robert Herring raised a large American flag in the window of their London flat, and then hung Greek, British, and Welsh flags alongside it.[85] In letters H.D. expressed herself at home in, variously, America, England, Switzerland, Greece, France, and Italy.[86] Moreover, as discussed in Part III, she also felt close to her German heritage, and her sudden interest in nation in the 1940s is no doubt also reflective of her attempts to come to terms with her German-ness in the wake of Nazism and the Holocaust.[87] But it is clear that in the war period, her allegiance to Britain becomes primary. She writes in *Majic Ring* that though she is "somewhat of a gad-about," she "is anchored, if anywhere, in London."[88] Her cosmopolitanism is at once rooted and rootless.

She is, moreover, as she writes of Delia Alton, "torn between anglo-philia and anglo-phobia."[89] A longtime and frequent museum-goer, H.D. was not unaware of the source of many of their collections. When the bombs of the Blitz weren't falling around her, H.D. ventured out from her South Kensington neighborhood. Just as she spent time in the British Museum during the First World War, she wandered the exhibits at what was still popularly known as the South Kensington Museum (now the Victoria and Albert Museum) between 1939 and 1946. Like the British Museum, the V&A acquired its collection largely through Britain's imperial ventures, and by the mid-nineteenth century it was already known for its extensive medieval and Renaissance collection of art and artifacts. Along with the war, this preeminent collection may well have been a creative catalyst for H.D. She may have sought exhibits at the V&A for inspiration when writing *By Avon River*, which explores the Elizabethan world and verse of Shakespeare and his contemporaries. The medieval period figures heavily in H.D.'s prose of the 1940s as well, particularly *By Avon River*—which traces the origins of English poetry to its medieval roots—and *White Rose and the Red*—which portrays the Pre-Raphaelite interest in the medieval period and the Crusades.

Another major collection at the V&A, "The Cast Courts"—filled with plaster casts of major European monuments, statues, and architectural features from the medieval period and earlier—was intact by 1873, the largest such collection of that era. Wildly popular in the Victorian era, it was a mode of appropriation that did not involve acquisition, and it permitted a mode of cultural tourism that did not involve travel. What the English did not plunder from other European nations, they created in impressive replica form for display at the V&A. Indeed, plunder is a theme at the center of this area of South Kensington known as "Albertopolis," as witnessed by the colossal monuments to colonialism and imperialism built by Victoria in the late nineteenth century with public funds and monies from the 1851 Great Exhibition of the Works of Industry of all Nations. The four corners of the Prince Albert Monument, commissioned for Kensington Gardens after his death in 1861, immortalize the four continents England had conquered: Europe, America, Asia, and Africa. A second monument to the Great Exhibition resides across Kensington Road, behind Royal Albert Hall. Inscribed on this monument is a list of the participating nations, half of which are labeled British colonies, and financial data related to the Exhibition's receipts. Just beyond this monument stands the former Royal School of Mines of Imperial College, its entrance adorned by sculptures of Alfred Beit and Julius Wernher, gold and diamond magnates who made their fortunes in South Africa's mines. Busts of Beit and Wernher rest on pedestals balanced atop the bowed backs of primitive-looking slave laborers toiling in the mines. This was, in essence, H.D.'s backyard. The V&A and the Royal Albert Hall were less than one mile from her flat.

Helen Emmitt asserts that "H.D. does not attempt 'a poem including history,'" but this is not so of the prose.[90] This book argues that, in a decade when the Axis powers had threatened to conquer and occupy much of the world, H.D.'s writings constitute a sustained confrontation with imperial history, specifically the history of the British Empire. Her work of the 1940s at once defends England in a time of war and its aftermath, and condemns sharply her adopted country for its imperialist aims—aims that in fact, over time, she suggests, promoted and cultivated the very wars the country has endured for centuries. Unlike the work of the late modernist women writers David James surveys in a recent article, H.D.'s settings were not rural and regional but global. About *Sword*, H.D. reflects in the 1950s that the book is really about empire—the Roman Empire and the British Empire—but that at the time of its composition "I did not myself realize its implications."[91] She saw it as an epic, "a sort of War and Peace cum The Last Days of Pompeii."[92]

The parallel she drew between the Roman Empire and the British Empire was, of course, not an original one, but the scenes of *Sword* featuring Julius Caesar point directly to that link. Caesar's war banner featured an eagle, as did Hitler's.[93] The eagle appears as well in *White Rose*, which is set in England and features the moment in history that cemented Britain's control over India. Both *Sword* and *By Avon River* plumb this connection. In Chapter 4 we see that Shakespeare, in the latter book, is cast as an imperialist—linked to Queen Elizabeth I and her forays into the New World—and returns again and again to Antony's lines to Cleopatra about his empire. Even *The Mystery*—set in Prague—is connected to Britain in H.D.'s work when she notes that "[i]t was the Crown of England that first sanctioned the renewed [Moravian] Brotherhood."[94] It is not just war but imperialism that dominates H.D.'s postwar prose. *By Avon River* considers Elizabethan expeditions in the New World, as well as medieval France's presence in England; *Sword* moves rapidly from ancient settings to the Battle of Hastings and Elizabethan England; and the Crimean War and the Sepoy Rebellion rest behind the action of *White Rose*. If *Sword* examines those historical moments when England was conquered, *By Avon River* and *White Rose* turn to England as conqueror—as colonizer and builder of empire. The former text considers the beginnings of English imperialism in the New World of the Americas, while the latter focuses its lens on a more recent incursion, the British occupation of India initiated by the Sepoy Rebellion, in the days following the Crimean War. The five years immediately following the Second World War were a time of heightened interest for H.D. in the politics of the modern world, a period in which she writes urgently about topics far removed from the ancient worlds for which she is best known. Though this period is brief, it culminates in a more meditative decade marked by a rethinking of ethics and her place in the world from a more mature perspective.

In *White Rose* and *By Avon River*, H.D.'s concerns about imperialism and war were not separate from her progressive views on gender and sexuality. She may not have agreed with Virginia Woolf about whether or not the U.S. and the U.K. should take up arms against Hitler, but they shared an interest in the intersection of patriarchy and imperialism. The two, Woolf claims, are "the egg of the very same worm." *Three Guineas* (1938) contends that the

Dictator, like the Patriarch, "believe[s] that he has the right, whether given by God, Nature, sex or race is immaterial, to dictate to other human beings how they shall live; what they shall do." For Woolf, a woman should "have no country" but "the whole world," because women are "foreigners" or "outsiders"—even "slaves"—in their own lands.[95] H.D., too, will come to embrace such a cosmopolitan vision from a feminist perspective. As we shall see, however, Woolf's imaginative retreat into a pre-imperial English past[96] is at odds with H.D.'s efforts to critique forms of nostalgia grounded in nationalism.

In a sense, H.D.'s prolific writing of the 1940s fits quite well within the parameters of *late modernism*, a vague term contemplated seriously by modernist scholars only relatively recently, a term that refutes claims like Terry Eagleton's that "Modernism ended on or about 1930."[97] The 1940s have been largely neglected by modernist scholars, according to Marina Mackay, because the "[t]he criteria for what constituted proper war literature had already been established by the Great War," and "the literature of the second war was judged wanting," and because nearly all of the major canonical British modernist writers were dead by 1941.[98] In late modernism—that is, in the tumultuous period of the Great Depression, the rise of Fascism and Nazism, the Second World War, the decline of the British Empire—writing becomes, most agree, less concerned with aesthetics and more concerned with politics. It becomes more communitarian and less interiorized. Writers contended with the trauma of war, with political crises, with economic woes, and with the knowledge that "whatever Britishness or Englishness could be made to mean for the future, imperial grandeur would play no part in it."[99] High modernists who had expressly eschewed politics in favor of universalism—who had defined their artistic output, in fact, against history in favor of myth—began to respond more directly to the vicissitudes of a turbulent historical moment. Their writings were "perforated and torn by their relation to history."[100] The writing of late modernism, then, is at once modernist and anti-modernist, for, as Alan Wilde observes, "we are dealing with a reaction against modernism by writers who retain a good many modernist presuppositions and strategies."[101]

Two distinct models of late modernism have been proposed in the last decade, consonant in their assertion of the remarkable ambivalence among writers caught between modernism and postmodernism, but divergent in their ultimate conclusions. Focusing on vanguard figures Wyndham Lewis, Djuna Barnes, and Samuel Beckett, Tyrus Miller's "despair[ing]" late modernists occupy a liminal, mid-century space between the –isms but ultimately lean toward postmodernism, offering satire and absurdity in the face of decay, chaos, and disunification.[102] Building on Simon Gikandi's postcolonial study of English modernism and Fredric Jameson's observations about the intersection of modernism and empire, Jed Esty, by contrast, centers his study of what he terms an aesthetic "interregnum" around aging, London-based, "mainstream" modernists—T. S. Eliot, E. M. Forster, and Virginia Woolf primarily—in a time of waning national power. He argues for a "turn" toward the homeland through "a discursive process by which English intellectuals translated the end of empire into a resurgent concept of [Anglocentric] national culture," discarding the universalist and cosmopolitan mythologizing characteristic of the 1920s to embrace (at least partly) English folk culture and history.[103]

As divergent as they are, these models have extraordinary value in opening up interpretation of a broad range of critically neglected mid-century texts. Both argue for a distinctive shift toward writing that is more politically informed and invested, that is burdened with "the pressure of historical circumstances"; as Miller quips, "late modernists took a detour into the political regions that high modernism had managed to view from the distance of a closed car."[104] Esty, in particular, has inspired scholarship on modernism, history, and nation. A focus on the particularity of the historical moment in both Esty and Miller means that we must reconceptualize how we conceive of modernism as a literary and artistic phenomenon. More recently, Marina Mackay and John Marx have extended Esty's focus on empire and nationalism. Marx reminds us that the decline of empire was accompanied by the rise of modern globalization, and Mackay's study of World War II-era literature points to the 1940s as a time "when modernists were compelled to scrutinise the political and moral claims of insular nationality at a time when allegiance was demanded as rarely before." If many were suspicious of nationalism in the early 1930s, the rise of Nazism and the outbreak of war altered the landscape even further by the 1940s.[105]

H.D.'s writing over the five-year period following the end of the Second World War treats topics with which these studies of late modernists engage: war, gender, nation, and empire. But it also complicates these frameworks in some interesting ways. Late modernists were living in a transnational world of ubiquitous contact zones, a milieu engulfed in alterity—social, cultural, sexual, gendered, ethnic, religious—and their responses were necessarily conflicted. What do we make of those subjects who, for various reasons, do not enjoy all of the rights and privileges of citizenship, who are not so comfortable with their citizenship as Forster or even Eliot, who had eagerly embraced his new nation? How do we read those English writers who felt ambivalent about their Englishness? What about women and people of color who did not yet enjoy the full rights of citizenship? As we begin to look at writers not just at the margins of the metropole but at the liminal spaces of subjecthood, the murky areas of the only partly enfranchised, we do in fact find a range of political positionalities. The writings of American-born British citizen H.D. constitute just such a test case. The mid-to-late 1940s finds H.D. excavating not ancient myth but British history. Britain is not whole by the end of *Sword*; it is splintered into stories of betrayal, bloodshed, and female sacrifice to political ends.

This approach to H.D.'s prose writing of this period is not the conventional one. We have not thought of H.D. as a political writer, but in part that is because her late prose *oeuvre* has been critically ignored, much of it only recently having appeared in print for the first time. I certainly had not conceived of her in these ways until I began to read the immediate post–World War II writings. In addition to being accessible only in manuscript for decades, these writings have been largely viewed with embarrassment, as excessively autobiographical, as impossibly formally difficult, and as immersed entirely in her decidedly unorthodox spiritual pursuits.[106] But our previous assumptions about her late corpus obscure the broad critique of nationalist politics, imperialism, and war these writings engage. While it sustains an interest in the otherworldly, much of this work of the late 1940s is just as deeply concerned with the worldly—specifically, the intersection of the politics of gender, nationalism, and imperialism. In a sense, then, this shift in H.D.'s work parallels the "anthropological turn" Esty describes—an interest in the politics of English nationalism in the face of a declining British Empire. But H.D.'s treatment of England resists the nostalgia Esty finds in works by Eliot and Woolf. Moreover, H.D. persists in locating the origins of England not in Celtic or Saxon folk culture but in ancient Greece and Rome, the basis of its literature not Chaucerian tales or Shakespearean drama but medieval French ballads. H.D.'s aim is not to rebuild and redeem a broken nation or to reconstruct a pre-imperial nation of yore, but to recover its history of imperialism and colonialism in order to indict it. For H.D. in the 1940s, nations exist simply to destroy other nations and to extend their empires. As we will see in the following chapters, H.D. does not write in the absurdist mode Miller describes, but she hardly conforms to Esty's model of the aging modernist either.

As Woolf opines in *Three Guineas*, a woman's experience of citizenship and nationalism was quite different from that of her male peers, and yet, as work by Phyllis Lassner and by the contributors to Maroula Joannou's *Women Writers of the 1930s* has revealed, women's contributions have often been discounted in discussions of late modernism. That Stevie Smith shared Woolf's view late in life is apparent in her response to an interviewer who questions the extent to which she is a "typical" British poet: "I'm alive today, therefore I'm as much part of our time as everybody else." Smith boldly continues, "The times will just have to enlarge themselves to make room for me, won't they, and for everybody else."[107] Alison Light argues of Smith, and mid-century women writers more broadly, that by dismissing women's work as wholly invested in the private sphere, we have overlooked the extent to which women writers are more likely to adopt anti-authoritarian and anti-nationalist positions. Wryly challenging an assumption that "[s]ome Englishness is more English than others," Light writes pointedly, "Any historical account worth its salt will have to look across the whole panoply of possible relations which women and men writing have had to the idea of a national voice. . . . we need to see that both the apparently private forms of verse, like the lyric, and the ostensibly public, are bound up with the meanings given to sexual difference and that these meanings in turn contribute to the ways in which the nation might be imagined and addressed."[108] H.D.'s immediate postwar fiction interrogates structures of nationalism and imperialism by exposing the impact of the public on the private sphere. She does so by deconstructing the genres we use in the West to tell our stories.

Lyndsey Stonebridge argues of wartime that "even at its most traumatic, it demands new forms of comprehension."[109] H.D.'s late-1940s prose represents another, equally important departure from these models of late modernism, a departure that engages directly with this need for a "new form of comprehension." Esty and Miller agree that experiments in modernist form were largely over by the 1930s. For Esty, late modernist writers shifted from faith in "the redemptive agency of *art*" to a belief in "the redemptive agency of *culture*." He hypothesizes that "[w]ith the arrival of a limited kind of European apocalypse circa 1940, history itself begins to have an incarnate form, so there is no longer the pressing need to use form against a meaningless, merely chronological history."[110] Phyllis Lassner concurs when she notes that, aside from Virginia Woolf, modernists writing in the 1930s and 1940s "do not invite new definitions of modernism."[111] High modernist form recedes as writers become more and more engaged in political and national issues. A shared sense of nationalism, in Esty's view, comes to replace a shared sense of innovative elements of form.[112]

But H.D.'s late novel *Sword* is perhaps her most experimental, as the next three chapters discuss at some length. In 1950, H.D. contends of her post-Imagist work that "the *how* of the writing is almost as important to us now, as the writing itself."[113] As other late modernists turned to social realism, H.D. continued to develop her modernist aesthetic into new forms more accommodating of the broader, more dynamic, historical analysis she wished to conduct. She sought formal structures that would document and express the fragmentation of faith and the dismantling of authority that peaked with the dropping of the nuclear bomb. To borrow from John Whittier-Ferguson's account of late modernism, one could well say that she was to "test the capacities of aesthetic form to express . . . loss."[114] And she turned to satire, as I argue in the next chapter, mocking the solipsistic and escapist interiority of the high modernist novel. Like Esty, Miller sees a "loosen[ing]" of "the modernist dominance of form," which "allows a more fluid, dialogic relation with the immediate historical context." Nevertheless, in terms of form, certain aspects of H.D.'s writings bear a surprising relation to the late modernist figures discussed by Miller, who observes that they "weakened the formal cohesion of the modernist novel and sought to deflate its symbolic resources, reducing literary figures at points to a bald literalness or assimilating them to the degraded forms of extraliterary discourse. They represent a world in free fall."[115] This description of a "weaken[ing]" of "formal cohesion" describes *Sword* quite well, as does the flattening of characters in "a world in free fall," a phenomenon discussed in Chapter 1. *Sword*'s pastiche of popular and high modernist genres and modes beckons toward the postmodern impulse Miller identifies in the writings he explores.

H.D.'s late prose is typically read as documents recording her lifelong mystical and spiritual pursuits. I in no way disagree with such a reading. Indeed, the work abounds in references to the Kabbalah, Hermeticism, spiritualism, Tarot, astrology, Moravian mysticism, and any number of other traditions and practices. Recent books by Elizabeth Anderson and Matte Robinson illuminate this aspect of the postwar work, building on foundations laid by Jane Augustine, Rachel Connor, Susan Stanford Friedman, Adalaide Morris, Helen Sword, Demetres Tryphonopoulos, and myself, among others. Chapter 2 of this book addresses this topic explicitly; Chapters 1 and 6 touch on it as well. As a whole, however, *A Curious Peril* suggests another, complementary interpretive lens through which to view H.D.'s spiritual explorations, by illuminating her concomitant interests in narrative, ethics, war, trauma, imperialism, and, of course, gender. It explores the prose writings of the late 1940s and early 1950s and touches on those of the late 1950s.[116]

The book consists of three parts, an interlude (between Part II and Part III), and a coda. Part I, "De-formations: Trauma, Genre, and *The Sword Went out to Sea*," is the lengthiest, and places an intensive focus on the first novel H.D. wrote after the Second World War. It is the text in which her examination of trauma and narrative is most urgent and most incisive, and it is the text that is most experimental in its form. Part I scrutinizes *Sword* in such depth because it aims to demonstrate how H.D. employs a pastiche of genres and modes to expose the unreliability of national narratives.

Completed in 1947, H.D.'s *Sword* was one of her favorite compositions, and she strove unsuccessfully to publish it. "*The Sword* traces my intellectual and emotional life to its conclusion or rather to its fulfillment," she attests vigorously in 1949. "*The Sword* is the crown of all my effort. . . . I treasure it."[117] It is not an easy read, and it is not difficult to imagine why she failed to find a publisher. One of its challenges is what Susan Stanford Friedman has called its "uncertainty of genre," which Jane Augustine fears "interferes with its success as a work of art." "What is it," Augustine asks, "novel, roman à clef, romance, disguised poem, scientific record, religious meditation, autobiography, myth?"[118] Friedman refers to it as "spiritualist séance" that "moves uneasily from journalistic reportage to hermetic dreamscapes."[119] But the novel rewards a close examination. *Sword* is about the nature of time, about how the specter of history haunts the margins of the present and the future, about the importance of combating cultural amnesia. It is about how the personal and the political overlap, how the conflicts of our individual lives can be mapped to those of others, how the realm of the private sphere radically informs social and political realities. And it is also, ultimately, about modernist aesthetics, about how narratives are spun and woven, and about how we choose to tell the stories we tell. Michel Serres, a contemporary historian of science, acknowledges the instability and unreliability of the Hermetic when he writes that "Hermes passes and disappears; makes sense and destroys it; exposes the noise, the message, and the language."[120] This tension between construction and destruction, between speech and silence, emerges in *Sword* in the form of a challenge to history, to history-makers, and to historiography.

Three chapters of Part I explore six genres or modes that *Sword* weaves into its fragmented narrative: Chapter 1 considers autobiography and the ghost story, Chapter 2 looks at mysticism and science fiction, and Chapter 3 turns to historical fiction and the fairy tale. In each pair, an inexorable tension exists between genres or modes, which constantly interrogate each other. The novel is experimental in form but relies on popular genres; as such, it merges high and low forms of narrative to a degree unprecedented in H.D.'s *oeuvre*. About genre, Ralph Cohen points out that it "does not exist independently; it arises to compete or to contrast with other genres,"[121] but in *Sword* these genres are forced to coexist within one text, an impossibility that leads to a fraying of generic edges. It employs genre fiction while denying her readers the pleasure that usually comes from reading it.

The rules of genre are made to be transgressed, Todorov submits,[122] but in *Sword*, multiple genres offer the means of multiple, overlapping transgressions that push generic boundaries to their limits. Derrida has shown that genres are categories always already exceeded by their contents, that "at the very moment that a genre or a literature is broached ... degenerescence has begun, the end begins."[123] In *Sword*, this process is not veiled. Rather, degeneresence is the point. In a world at war, genres splinter radically. To tell the story of the destruction of a nation, she alleges implicitly, one must take apart the forms of narrative that construct that nation. As the world falls apart, narrative structure crumbles. If genres are "performative structures that shape the world in the very process of putting it into speech,"[124] in *Sword* they take the world apart. According to both Thomas Beebee and Lidia Curti, postmodernism necessarily entails contamination of genres; a postmodern "effect" follows from "defeating the generic expectations of the reader." As Curti observes, "Genres become borders to cross over and over again, simulacra of a past to be resurrected and erased, palimpsests that are continually rewritten."[125] In this regard, *Sword* may not only be her least-hopeful work—the H.D. novel least-committed to a redemptive ethics of re-vision—it may well also be her first text that bends toward the postmodern.

Matte Robinson and Demetres Tryphonopoulos see the traces of H.D.'s more "political" phase beginning in the late 1920s,[126] and certainly, in works such as "Hipparchia," *Nights*, and "Mouse Island" (which refers to "octopus-England"), it is clear that H.D. had been thinking about imperialism well before the Second World War. In *Nights*, Natalia's characterization of her suffocating British lover as "Empire-building" and "Empire-making ... with that ... silly bull-dog-like stupidity" is damning.[127] But this topic moves to the center immediately following the war. Part II of the current work, "Critique: Gendered Narratives of Nation and Imperialism," consists of two chapters, "*By Avon River*, Arranged Marriage, and Shakespeare's Empire" and "Disappearing Bodies in *White Rose and the Red*." In all of her books of the late 1940s, H.D. responds to the war by reimagining the relationship between nation and story; she seems to recognize, as Edward Said famously does, that "the power to narrate, or to block other narratives from forming and emerging"[128] is key to imperialist ventures. *Sword* documents the personal and public trauma of world war by taking apart narrative structure. The other two books written in the late 1940s, though, take a different approach, inspired by H.D.'s brief but intense heightened interest in modern European history and politics, her undertaking of a plan to read the English literary canon, and an examination of her own adopted Britishness.[129] *By Avon River* is a multi-genre text that explores Shakespeare, his Elizabethan contemporaries, and his ancestors. *White Rose* is a fictionalized retelling of the story of the Pre-Raphaelites William Morris, Dante Gabriel Rossetti, and Rossetti's wife, the artist Elizabeth Siddall. Though the focus and structure of these texts are profoundly different, the volumes converge around the intersection of gender and imperialism.

In Chapter 4, I turn to H.D.'s scrutiny of the European custom of arranged monarchical marriage as a strategy by which to consolidate imperial power, and the tacit parallels she draws between Italian and British empire-building. The first half of *By Avon River* addresses Shakespeare's *The Tempest*, stressing the play's New World sources. It is a challenge in verse to the author-as-monarch, Shakespeare, who creates a female character, denies her a voice, then marries her off to an African king. Claribel, Queen of Tunis, is a mere device by which to effect another politicized union, that of Ferdinand and Miranda at the hand of a Shakespeare-like Prospero. The second half of the book interlaces fiction and nonfiction prose; it explores Shakespeare's Elizabethan and Jacobean contemporaries and ancestors against a perilous landscape of unscrupulous monarchs, constant warfare, and imperial conquest. The focus of Chapter 5 is H.D.'s *White Rose and the Red*, set in the mid-nineteenth century during the wars in Crimea and the Sepoy Rebellion of 1857. In this novel, H.D. explores the way the woman's body serves as metaphor for conquered and colonized land. One of its central figures is Elizabeth Siddall, a figure torn apart by both the public sphere—fear of the Crimean War, the Sepoy Rebellion, and a London murderer who dismembered his victim's body—and the private. Her roles as artist's model and artist's wife serve to objectify and idealize her in such a way that her identity is slowly effaced, her body withering over the course of the text until her suicide closes the novel. In different ways, these texts expose the fact that the idealization of the feminine rests at the heart of European imperialism and colonization—from the early medieval Crusades to the British occupation of India. Like Virginia Woolf, H.D. locates patriarchy not just at the center of warfare but at the very core of empire-building.

The Mystery, completed in 1951, represents an interlude in H.D.'s postwar prose. We tend to group *The Mystery* with the two previous novels, *Sword* and *White Rose*. To be sure, all three constitute experiments in historical fiction, prose studies that engage more modern eras than she had previously addressed. Likewise, Jane Augustine's introduction to the edition frames it as the culmination of her interest in spiritualism.[130] This 1951 volume does fit, to some extent, within these models. But by the 1950s, H.D. had begun to turn significantly away from the more pointedly political projects of the years immediately following the war. In its faith in a spiritual solution to the world's woes, *The Mystery* returns to a more utopic sensibility. It is more akin to *Trilogy*, in that sense, than it is to the work of the late 1940s. H.D. had been living away from England for half a decade by this point, and her correspondence exhibits a waning interest in modern politics. In an essay written in 1949 and 1950, in fact, she proposes not *The Mystery* but *Bid Me to Live* as the third volume of a trilogy with *Sword* and *White Rose*; she is indecisive about *The Mystery*'s status, for by the late 1950s, it has rejoined the first two novels to complete the prose *"Trilogy."*[131] So *The Mystery* very much straddles a divide in H.D.'s career, between the immediate postwar and the more meditative texts to come, drawing on many of the devices and themes of *Sword* and *White Rose* but from a more hopeful perspective.

Adalaide Morris and Cheryl Hindrichs have done incisive work on H.D. and ethics. Morris's study of H.D.'s conception of "the gift" has been foundational to our understanding of her work, and Hindrichs's observation that the Great War spurred H.D. to imagine new aesthetic forms to engage with ethical questions is likewise a launching pad for Part III of the current work, "Re-formations: Postwar Ethics and Identity." Even after H.D.'s interest in current affairs begins to recede, ethical considerations remain prominent in her postwar work. The rise of fascism and the revelations of the Holocaust surely shook H.D.'s faith and courage, but they also created a crisis of identity for a woman who had been proud of her Moravian heritage. How was she to deal with the "political onus" of her German-ness?[132] The postwar era sparks an examination of the self and the other, as H.D. strives to think through alterity in ways she had not in her previous writings. We find in her postwar work various configurations of self and other that produce moments of empathy between characters, rather than repudiation or narcissistic assimilation. The earlier chapters of *A Curious Peril* center around how H.D. mirrors the private and public spheres, and the chapters of Part III are no different. The examination of identity and alterity has implications for both interpersonal relationships and international alliances.

This meditation on ethics can be seen in her deployment of two characters that emerge in her postwar fiction, the "other woman" and the spy. Chapter 7 returns to *Sword*, for the traces of these re-formations are apparent even in her most pessimistic, most de-formed text. In H.D.'s early historical fiction, Ancient Rome was demonized, the colonizer of her beloved Ancient Greece; in *Sword*, however, she creates an autobiographically based Roman character, a concubine of Caesar's, an "other woman." This chapter compares the treatment of the "other woman" in *Palimpsest* and *Sword*. Chapter 8 turns to the figure of the spy, a recurrent trope in her 1956 novel *Magic Mirror* and the accompanying memoir *Compassionate Friendship*. At the level of the private sphere, H.D. uses espionage as a mode of critiquing Freudian psychoanalysis, offering in its stead the short-lived phenomenon of existential psychology, a movement that grew out of the trauma of World War II and emphasized an empathetic rather than transferential model of therapy. Shifting outward to the public sphere, her analysis of the figure of the spy becomes an examination of the politics of nationalism.

A brief coda turns to H.D.'s memoir *End to Torment*, penned three years before her death in 1961. It explores how this late prose text picks up the threads of all of her postwar prose and weaves them into a meditation on the role of memory in personal and national narrative.

It is beyond the scope of this book to include H.D.'s postwar poetry—all long poems, including her epic *Helen in Egypt*. This study will, I hope, spawn new readings of the poetry of this period in light of the prose. There is undoubtedly overlap between the genres. As Susan Stanford Friedman notes, the line between her impersonal poetry and personal prose becomes significantly blurred as H.D. ages: "Initially constructed as opposites, the impersonal poet and the personal prose writer did not remain in fixed opposition.... The poet became increasingly more personal and narrative, while the prose writer, especially the novelist, was lyric and increasingly clairvoyant."[133] But there remains a line, I think, between genres for the late-career H.D., and the prose is worth studying on its own, not simply as background for understanding the poetry or putting together the biographical puzzle pieces of her fascinating life. Prose seems to have offered H.D. an opportunity to explore a world beyond the bounds of the ancient world more directly. Poetry is part of the "business of writing" that is "sacred," she once chided William Carlos Williams,[134] but prose is perhaps not as bound to this stricture. Prose allows her to map the private to the public in much more definitive ways, and it is an exploration of the private/public borderline that I argue most absorbed her in the aftermath of the Second World War.

A Curious Peril offers a framework through which to view some of H.D.'s most difficult prose texts. As such, it asks that scholars re-envision our view of her late career. But it also asks that we rethink the ways in which late modernism as an era has been theorized. There is a broadly heterogeneous range of writing from the 1930s to the 1950s that both participates in modernism and resists it, that gestures toward postmodernism without fully committing to it. It is a body of work that is entangled in nostalgia even as it turns a curious eye to the future. It poses vexed questions about nationalism as it embraces cosmopolitanism. It is, by turns, deeply sincere and sharply satiric. It is a literature of despair, paranoia, and anxiety. It is a literature that suggests that "happiness is best forgotten," that dwells on "the moments of agony that must be resolved," "the riddles of misunderstanding and cruelty that must be solved."[135] And it is also a literature that yet retains a trace of hopefulness for a postwar future. Closer examination of writings before, during, and after the Second World War will enrich significantly perspectives of those landmark scholarly works that first drew our attention to late modernism. It is my hope that this case study will both complicate and elucidate this important work to come.

PART I

De-formations

Trauma, Genre, and *The Sword Went Out to Sea*

> We live the stories we tell; the stories we don't tell live us.
>
> —Mark Doty

> If modernist poetics are a mesh of interrelated statements, evaluations, and judgments, then late modernist writing is the product of the pressure of historical circumstances on that mesh, which threatens to fray or break at its weakest points.
>
> —Tyrus Miller

1

Autobiography and Ghost Story

> Memory is not a constantly accessible copy of the different facts of our life, but an oblivion from which, at random moments, present resemblances enable us to resuscitate dead recollections.
> —Proust, *La Prisonnière*

> I don't think anyone should write their autobiography until after they're dead.
> —Samuel Goldwyn

The first three chapters of this book look closely at how H.D. creates a new form of novel to represent the un-representable trauma of World War II and its aftershocks—the relentless bombings, the food and fuel rationings, the concentration camps, the atomic bomb. The chief focus of these three chapters is the first novel she wrote after the war's end, *The Sword Went Out to Sea: (Synthesis of a Dream) by Delia Alton* (completed in 1947). In *Sword*, her method is to assemble a patchwork of genres or modes of writing that continually destabilize one another. In these chapters, each centered around paired genres or modes, we explore the demand that H.D.'s reader confront central questions about truth and the nature of reality. In successive chapters, the focus on historical accuracy is undercut by the fantastical, ahistorical fairy tale; a scientific approach to time travel rests uncomfortably against notions of astral projection. In this chapter, the autobiographical pact between author and reader in H.D.'s fiction necessitates a paradoxical belief in the impossible. Truth claims are continually erected and dismantled in this, her most postmodern prose experiment.

Sword is oddly structured, and this undoubtedly accounts, as I note in the Introduction, for perceptions of its general inaccessibility and alleged unreadability. *Sword*'s first part, "Wintersleep," recounts Delia Alton's engagement with spiritualism in London during World War II and the dreams and memories her sessions induce, and the second part, "Summerdream," portrays a dizzying journey through time that explores the political consequences of these personal reminiscences, delving into the historical layers of a palimpsest of what has been lost and forgotten. We begin with an obvious cognate of H.D., Delia, who is doing the kinds of things that we know H.D. did during World War II. We can accept, then, the flashbacks that increasingly pervade the first half of the book, and Delia invites us to draw connections between the two world wars and between men who had betrayed her at various points in her life. This is enticingly familiar to those of us who have read H.D.'s autobiographical fiction. Indeed, she writes to Aldington of the novel that "[t]here is a great deal of myself in it," and Sir Hugh Dowding was troubled to find the novel's Lord Howell quite recognizable as himself.[1]

As readers, then, we are ill-prepared when the book shifts abruptly to a series of seemingly unfinished historical vignettes in its second half. We are offered little in the way of guideposts, and we lose nearly entirely the presence of Delia to anchor our reading experience. In correspondence with Aldington, H.D. reported her initial struggles with merging the two parts, though she clearly sees them as comprising a whole.[2] In this chapter, the focus will be chiefly on the initial chapters of the novel, in which H.D. presents a version of herself engaging in séances during the Second World War. The next chapter picks up the way in which the more realist form fragments midway through the book, and with it the narrator's identity and the London setting of the initial story. Chapter 3 turns to the discrete historical episodes that comprise the second half of the novel.

It is not, of course, surprising to find a chapter on the autobiographical mode in a book about H.D.'s prose.[3] This is a commonplace throughout decades of her career, despite so many modernists' pronounced disdain for the autobiographical, a disdain surprising given their preoccupation with character and interiority. T. S. Eliot's influential essay "Tradition and the Individual Talent" ushers in an era of impersonality and objectivity: "It is not in [the writer's] personal emotions, the emotions provoked by particular events in his life, that the poetry is in any way remarkable or interesting.... Poetry... is not the expression of personality but an escape from personality."[4] Richard

Aldington was dismissive of women writers in particular on the grounds that they lacked the imagination to write beyond the self; in an essay on H.D.'s friend Violet Hunt, he observes, "Whenever a woman goes to write a novel she first chooses herself as heroine; she then decides that she had better take someone else, and ends up by choosing herself again."[5] A recent collection of essays by Maria DiBattista and Emily Wittman, though, demonstrates that a more flexible definition of autobiography permits a rethinking of autobiographical modernism. Their contention that "modernist autobiography . . . typically challenges the established narrative practices of the genre"[6] can helpfully elucidate H.D.'s own practice. As John Paul Riquelme has pointed out, "the boundaries between fictional and nonfictional life narratives are crossed significantly in major modernist works."[7] Despite their objections, modernists wrote their own lives into their fiction. H.D. was ardently drawn to the autobiographical mode, performing these "cross[ings]" in multiple texts over four decades. Beginning in the late 1910s, it became a mainstay of her prose writing.[8] Indeed, taken as a whole, it is tempting to align H.D.'s long-term autobiographical project (particularly in her later career) with that of Proust's, as described by Roland Barthes: "instead of putting his life into his novel, as is so often said, he made his life itself a work of which his own book was the model."[9]

None of H.D.'s autobiographical writing falls neatly within the formal category of autobiography; her *romans à clef*, her novels and short stories, her memoirs—all highlight the inherently and inevitably fictional nature of the autobiographical enterprise. Louis Renza has detected "a spirit of anarchism" in the autobiographical—a genre "openly defiant" of rules or guidelines, according to Shirley Geok-lin, "a genre in trouble"—and this unruliness is evident throughout H.D.'s prose *oeuvre*.[10] This is rightfully a theme of a great deal of scholarship on H.D.'s autobiography, including a key article by Adalaide Morris, which contends that H.D.'s texts frequently eschew "conventional sequence" in favor of "superimposition, contiguity, repetition, punning, all the orders of association and obsession."[11] Importantly, Dianne Chisholm holds that H.D.'s fiction highlights the otherness of the self, and this is true even in her earliest fiction, as Sarah Dillon notes of "Murex" when she deems the line between the fictive and the autobiographical in that work to be always already "queered."[12] Eileen Gregory writes of the 1920s autobiographical fiction that "H.D. engaged not simply in biographical projection but in a complex mode of historical and cultural analysis," and that "she comes to detach herself from identification with particular figures in order to reflect upon recurrent patterns of interrelationships."[13] I am claiming that this detachment is key to her later-career prose writings.

H.D.'s later fiction is perhaps more plainly representative of her faltering faith in the factual. Admitting that she fabricated much of the account, H.D. referred to *The Gift* (completed in 1943), for instance, as "autobiographical, 'almost'" and as "autobiographical fantasy," explaining in *Majic Ring* (drafted in 1943–1944) that "I worked the story of myself and Gareth into my own family and made my grandmother reconstruct a strange psychic experience to me, a child."[14] The "gift" was not, in reality, a psychic one but the gift of music.[15] She tells Pearson that in this novel she was able to place "this phantasy world of child-hood memories, of fact and phantasy into a frame."[16] Miriam Fuchs has attempted to work through these questions in her multiple examinations of this wartime account of H.D.'s childhood. Fuchs stresses that H.D. problematizes memory, point of view, and narrative voice, and thus the whole concept of autobiography: "For H.D., the autobiographical project is fragile, not durable; a process, not a product; a private, not public, gesture."[17] Moreover, as Christopher Gavaler has noted of that text, "factual and fictional information mingle without demarcation."[18] I argue in this and successive chapters that the line between "factual and fictional" becomes even more fractured in the post–World War II writings, and the constructedness of that binary even more apparent.

Some scholars nonetheless still rely, to differing degrees, on H.D.'s autobiographical fiction as a biographical source. A related strain entails a characterization of H.D.'s autobiographical prose writing as more therapeutic than artistic.[19] This is not an entirely unwarranted approach, of course, as her prose writings are in part autobiographical. But they are also fictional, and this can get lost in an understandable quest for knowledge about a fascinating writer who, during her life, scrupulously guarded her privacy. My own approach to H.D.'s persistent deployment of the autobiographical mode in her fiction was outlined in 2003: the reader must attend vigilantly to *both* elements of her prose: "Even as her protagonists teasingly invite autobiographical readings, they just as frequently call attention to the fictive nature of the text."[20] In that article, I cite, for instance, her constant reminders in *Paint It To-day* that she is, and is not, the protagonist, Midget, but there are countless other examples I could have added, including that of *HERmione*, in which she insists that she is at once "Her" and not "Her."

The reader must, moreover, be attuned to shifts in H.D.'s writing over the course of her career.

H.D.'s 1950 reflective essay entitled "H.D. by Delia Alton" is at times consulted as a source of information about the composition and interpretation of her writing. At Norman Holmes Pearson's request, in the 1940s H.D. began the sometimes-arduous, sometimes-rewarding process of rereading all of her work, and this essay contains her musings, in diary form, on her prose and poetry since 1930. Though much of the essay suggests the compatibility of herself and the various personae she had created over the years, the ending of the essay dramatically reverses itself, deconstructing, in effect, the preceding pages. Of characters she created from the 1920s through the 1940s she ultimately insists, "We are not Margaret, we are not Julia Ashton of the [World] War I *Madrigal*. We are not one or any of those whose lovely names startle and enchant me, as I read them now as if for the first time, in my own prose and poetry, Hipparchia, Heliodora, Hedyle. We are not Hedyle . . . nor the exquisite child of Hedyle, Hedylus. . . . We are not the *Sword* Rose de Beauvais of Normandy and Brittany at the time of England's conquest, nor the earlier Stella . . . We are not Raymonde of the first 'contemporary' 'Murex' nor yet the later Raymonde of 'Narthex.'"[21] It is a statement that warns readers against searching for clues to H.D.'s life in her characters, and implicitly admonishes Pearson himself, whose strategy for establishing H.D.'s canonization relied to a great extent on her biography, specifically her connections to famous men such as Ezra Pound, D. H. Lawrence, and Sigmund Freud.[22] Characters based on H.D.—even the characters that bear the most remarkable resemblance to her, such as Her or Julia Ashton—are her and not her. "I will not let *I* creep into this story," Midget declares in *Paint It To-day*, and this purposeful avoidance of correlating characters with real-life figures extends beyond protagonists to other characters she has created: in *Helen in Egypt*, she writes that "the child's name is Hermione, / it is not Hermione."[23]

While H.D.'s earliest novels of the 1920s are unabashedly self-reflexive, they also cling more closely to historical accuracy than her later books. In the Introduction, I traced a shift from stasis to movement in H.D.'s career, and here I will argue that concomitant with that shift is a movement from recounting the private to chronicling the public in her autobiographical writings. By the 1930s, she was beginning to take generous liberties with autobiographical modes, reflecting in part, I believe, her significant engagement with film, itself an extension of her lifelong attraction to drama. Her early novellas of the 1930s meld the identities of characters to create composites, while her fiction of the 1940s and 1950s, I will argue in this chapter, makes use of excessive repetition in a way that calls into question her own earlier autobiographical efforts as well as the genre more broadly conceived.[24] Not unlike the late modernist writers John Whittier-Ferguson examines in his recent book, H.D. revisits her past *oeuvre*, "sometimes building upon, sometimes repudiating, often revising, always weighing."[25]

She performs this critique of her past writings in order to re-center the autobiographical around the public, rather than private, sphere. By this point in her life, H.D. begins to take full advantage of the possibilities offered by what might be termed *fictional memoir*, which focuses on small slices of time rather than encompassing a life; as Helen Buss notes, the memoir is particularly well-equipped to "bridge the typical strategies of historical and literary discourses in order to establish necessary connections between the private and the public, the personal and the political."[26] Bryony Randall has argued that war drives a reversal of the public and the private for noncombatant writers: "The background has come right up to the foreground."[27] I would add that the experience of World War II, so much more traumatic for Londoners than the Great War, accounts for the most dramatic shift in H.D.'s autobiographical prose, in which the background of war, history, and politics takes center stage, the autobiographical story primarily a vehicle through which to document the impact of the public sphere on the private. Indeed, this chapter will contend, her post–World War II work critiques the autobiographical, as the trauma of war had shattered her sense of reality and truth.

Certainly, an autobiography that is purely nonfictional is an impossibility: as Paul de Man observes in a key essay on the genre, "just as we seem to assert that all texts are autobiographical, we should say that, by the same token, none of them is or can be."[28] Shari Benstock suggests that "autobiography reveals the impossibility of its own dream: what begins on the presumption of self-knowledge ends in the creation of a fiction that covers over the premises of its own construction."[29] By 1950, H.D. has come to understand, in even more profound ways than her experimental autobiographical fiction of the 1920s reveals, that autobiography is not grounded in any stable sense of truth or reality. To think otherwise is to "assume that 'fact' is a valid category of knowledge, that facts have discernible meanings, and that the more facts one has, the more valuable one's interpretation of a given historical situation or individual is likely to be."³⁰ About *Sword*, she wrote to Bryher that the book contrasts "so-called 'reality' values" between the world and the dream or sleep. Is reality found in our conscious or unconscious states? she asks.³¹ The "value" of the autobiographical project for H.D. cannot be located in its historical accuracy. This book looks for that "value" elsewhere. In the autobiographical writings of the late 1940s following the war, H.D. is determined to expose rather than to "cover over the premises of its own construction." In *Sword*, in particular, adherence to historical accuracy and biographical fact would produce, paradoxically, falsehoods. As de Man concludes, "The interest of autobiography ... is not that it reveals reliable self-knowledge—it does not—but that it demonstrates in a striking way the impossibility of closure."³² *Sword*, a novel born in trauma, seeks to represent this "impossibility of closure" by doing violence to the form of the novel. H.D.'s observation that "I feel I have a gattling-gun in my hands" was about the writing of *Sword*.³³

One of the characteristics of a traumatic experience is its resistance to narration. The trauma survivor relives repeatedly an experience that cannot be represented in language. "Yet," Leigh Gilmore observes, "even as the view that one cannot speak about or represent trauma prevails, language is asserted as that which can and must heal the survivor and the community. Thus language bears a heavy burden in the theorization of trauma."³⁴ *Sword* attempts to navigate this paradox; the inability to represent the experience through conventional modes of storytelling impels a need for a form of novel that is itself disintegrating. Compounding the difficulties H.D. faces, an autobiography relies on a relatively coherent and stable self, while trauma is "self-shattering" (to employ Gilmore's term). Gilmore contends that contemporary trauma narratives "illuminate how the limits of autobiography, multiple and sprawling as they are, might conspire to prevent some self-representational stories from being told at all if they were subjected to a literal truth test or evaluated by certain objective measures."³⁵ What is perhaps most striking about *Sword* in this regard, particularly when viewed within the context of H.D.'s other work, is its utter hopelessness about the possibility of healing self and community. It all but lacks the visionary qualities for which she is best known. In her study of women's wartime autobiographies, Victoria Stewart finds this pessimism common, however: "[N]one of these texts provides evidence that the writing can have a straightforwardly cathartic or palliative effect." What she finds is precisely what we see in H.D.'s immediate postwar fiction: "a refusal to allow traditional narrative trajectories to smooth over the exigencies of individual experience."[36] Yet H.D. decides upon the autobiographical mode to tell the story of her survival of the London bombings of World War II. If the autobiographical is inherently fictional, she finds it useful as a way to comment on the impact of the public sphere on the private.

Philippe Lejeune quips that "[i]n spite of the fact that autobiography is impossible, this in no way prevents it from existing."[37] Autobiographies and biographies continue to be written and consumed, and we all have some sense of what these genres are, even if we maintain a postmodern suspicion of their veracity. H.D. herself was an avid reader of life-writing. A sizable proportion of her expansive personal library was devoted to this mode, and she and Bryher regularly exchanged autobiographical and biographical books that were part of Bryher's extensive personal library or borrowed from the London Library. H.D.'s readings in biography ranged widely. The lives of artists and writers featured frequently; she owned biographies of Charles d'Orléans, Christopher Marlowe, Dorothy Wordsworth, Lord Byron, Percy Shelley, Thomas de Quincey, Peter Ilyich Tchaikovsky, Dante Gabriel Rossetti and his wife Elizabeth Siddall, William Morris, Charles Augustus Howell, Coventry Patmore, Josepha (Pepita) Durán, Ouida, Fitz-James O'Brien, Marcel Proust, Auguste Rodin, Katherine Mansfield, Dylan Thomas, Frederick Delius, Greta Garbo, Henri Gaudier-Brzeska, Jessie Capper, Violet Hunt, and D. H. Lawrence. She also read biographies of spiritual figures, including St. John of the Cross, the Dalai Lama, Emanuel Swedenborg, François Leclerc du Tremblay, Daniel Home, Juliana of Norwich, and St. Teresa of Ávila, as well as monarchs such as Queen Mary of Teck, Henry VIII, Elizabeth I, and Elisabeth of Austria. Biographies of Freud, Ludwig Snell, and Andrew Lang could be found on her shelves. Memoirs, autobiographical novels, formal autobiographies, and *romans à clef* H.D. owned included those of Margaret Anderson, art historian Bernard Berenson, Jocelyn Brooke, socialite Diana Cooper, Muriel Draper, Daphne du Maurier, Susan Glaspell, Elinor Glyn, Katharine Butler Hathaway, Marie Belloc Lowndes, theosophist Emily Lutyens, theatre historian W. J. Macqueen-Pope, George Moore, bookseller G. Orioli, Herbert Read, the painter Francis Rose, Jewish activist Tori Sender, Stephen Spender, poet Edward Thomas's wife, journalist Nora Waln, journalist and literary critic T. Earle Welby, the writer and painter Denton Welch, socialite Dorothy Wellesley, and H.D.'s friends Sylvia

Beach, Phyllis Bottome, E. M. Butler, John Cournos, Faith Compton Mackenzie, and Ezra Pound. She consumed diaries, journals, collections of letters, and personal travel narratives. Life-writing was an object of research, not just a practice.

Taken as a whole, it seems that she was obsessed with the lives of authors and artists, and how these lives are represented in narrative form. In some cases—Frederick Rolfe, Edith Wharton, Isadora Duncan, the composer Ethel Smyth, Norman Douglas—she read both biographies and autobiographies of the same figure. She was fascinated, too, by her friend E. M. Butler's *Silver Wings*, which examines the implications of mistaking autobiography for truth; a mysterious story told in the first part of the book is pronounced true-to-life, only to be proven fraudulent.[38] That H.D. was unaware of, or uninterested in, the performative or constructed nature of these kinds of stories is unthinkable, for her own autobiographical writings are so heavily fictionalized. Remember that, even in her early career she saw her characters as not, in fact, strictly autobiographical, but rather "'dressed up.'"[39] As Sidonie Smith has observed, linking Judith Butler's concept of gender performativity to theories of autobiography, "Whatever that occasion or that audience, the autobiographical speaker becomes a performative subject."[40]

I would suggest, to extend this line of thinking, that H.D.'s interest in film, photography, and drama heightened her sense of the staging of the autobiographic scene, for references to drama and the stage appear frequently in her post-1940s writings.[41] About *The Gift*, which includes scenes from a performance of *Uncle Tom's Cabin*, she mentions to Pearson that she has been advised that "the setting, the material would be wonderful for film." The first half of *By Avon River* is about Shakespeare's drama *The Tempest*, and the second half surveys a fair number of playwrights. She refers to *Sword* as a play, and sends Pearson a "dramatis personae."[42] With Aldington, she discussed at some length the possibilities of *White Rose and the Red* for the stage. "There is such magnificent material for a PLAY," she writes to him as she begins her research into the Pre-Raphaelites, "I can SEE those people, and hear the talking." She imagines the "costume possibilities" and casting it—"I am afraid it would have to be a pretty big cast"—and considers Ralph Richardson for a part, and Olivier as Rossetti. She speculates, too, about its popularity: "a play, I think would take like anything in a year or so in London." Subsequent letters continue the theme, and several months later she is still enamored of the idea, for "I see it in scenes and the costumes fascinate me."[43] History or autobiography as drama highlights its fictionality and constructedness. *Sword* itself contains three vignettes of the staging of plays: players in *fin de siècle* Philadelphia enact a Euripidean drama, temple players in Delphi perform a play about Pericles, and Elizabethan English stagehands watch as Queen Elizabeth and Essex are seated at the playhouse. In each case, we are introduced to the characters behind the scenes, those who create the experience. We are not permitted to suspend our disbelief. As Cynthia Hogue and Julie Vandivere argue in their introduction to *Sword*, "H.D. plays with the way events and persons seem staged.... she loses a sense of the separation between theatre and life."[44]

The autobiographical writings of her later career become less transparent and more abstract. A comparison of *Majic Ring* (written during World War II) and the first half of *Sword* (written just after) illustrates well this transition. Both recount H.D.'s experiences with spiritualism during the war, but the form of the former is partly epistolary (transcriptions of actual letters between H.D. and Dowding) and partly dated diary entries, conferring a sense of immediacy on the text. *Sword* narrativizes and fictionalizes the experiences, embellishing and inventing a great deal of material. But it may be that this belief in performativity was more than a device. A memoir by H.D.'s friend Silvia Dobson recalls that H.D. thought of life as a stage on which she performed a range of dramatic and technical roles.[45] This notion of performing ourselves might be said to guide her approach to life.

For Sidonie Smith, "[i]t is as if the autobiographical subject finds him/herself on multiple stages simultaneously, called to heterogeneous recitations of identity."[46] Taken as a whole, *Sword* dramatizes Smith's characterization of the autobiographical project quite literally when Delia's identity fractures midway through the book and when the setting begins to move swiftly through historical eras. But the title page alone points to the multiplicity of identity within the autobiographical subject. There we learn that Delia Alton, not H.D., is the author of *Sword*. H.D. was insistent with Pearson, in fact, that the book is "under the absolute hard-fast nom de plume, DELIA ALTON" which is also "as it happens ... the name of the dame in the book."[47] If, as Smith argues, "the narrator is both the same and not the same as the autobiographer, and the narrator is both the same and not the same as the subject of narration," H.D.'s title page stresses the extent to which these roles are far from straightforwardly enacted. In a now well-known essay, Philippe Lejeune has argued the necessity of the "autobiographical pact" between autobiographer and reader—that the "responsibility for all enunciation is assumed by the person who is in the habit of placing his *name* on the cover of the book"[48]—but H.D. flagrantly violates this pact. The first half of the novel itself is written in first person, from Delia's perspective, but the second half employs first person as well, for a number of protagonists, including Delia. We are thus always alert to the fact that the author is someone we do know, we do not know, we can know, and we cannot know. H.D. attests on the cover page that this is not in fact an autobiography of someone called "H.D." who writes poetry and prose and translates Greek drama and verse, and not Hilda Aldington either, the name she preferred in private correspondence. Rather, this is the autobiography of someone named "Delia Alton" who writes autobiographical historical novels during World War II and its aftermath.

Indeed, autobiography is already predicated on a division of the self. Robert Folkenflik sees this division as one between self and other: "The idea of the self as other is a condition of the autobiographical narrative, for there is generally some distinction between the 'I' who is talking and the figure in the past who is described. . . . An autobiography will often take shape as a way of dealing with the otherness of the figure in the past." Thus, there is "both an assertion of difference and an assertion of identity" at the site of the authorial "I."[49] Shirley Neuman usefully outlines a number of reasons for this phenomenon. First, the author must act as biographer by viewing herself as an object of discourse; second, she recounts a past self who has evolved into the present self doing the writing, such that the "I" denotes absence, not presence; and finally, she is bound to literary and narratological conventions, which are necessarily interpretative, and thus expose the split between authorial selves.[50] Autobiography, then, paradoxically, is an apt genre with which to demonstrate not the stability but the instability of the self.

"I write myself by silencing myself," Lejeune observes, and H.D. makes it very difficult to locate the voice of "H.D." with any assurance, even as we know as readers that it must be there. By renaming the self several times in the book, H.D. urges us to confront directly the alterity of the autobiographical self. It is as if she is writing about the self from a third-person perspective, in which the content of the book is "theatricalized." Lejeune contends, rightly I think, that "[t]he articulation of two truly differing points of view concerning a single individual cannot be accomplished in autobiography,"[51] and so H.D. must do violence to the form both by sowing the seeds of a critique of the genre and by infusing it with other genres. One of the most significant differences between fiction and autobiography from the standpoint of the reader is that the author is seemingly erased in the former, but central to the latter. The author is both the subject of the narrative and the object of the reader's attention, so the reader is made constantly aware of the author's presence.[52] But who, in this case, is the author? The multiple nature of the identity of the narrator means that our awareness of this problematic is felt intensely throughout the reading of the novel. We are meant to feel uneasy about identifying H.D. with any of *Sword*'s varied personages who bear the authorial "I."

Am I making too much of this? Might Delia Alton be simply a pen name, or a "nom de guerre," as H.D. once termed it?[53] H.D. was fond of this device and wrote a great deal of her prose under different names.[54] But there are personal and artistic reasons, I think, for this wordplay. "I could not have written it as H.D.," she tells Pearson, and not just because it was "too intimate."[55] To some extent, it is perhaps not entirely clear to "Hilda Aldington" in the 1940s whether or not "H.D." survived the war, but "Delia Alton" certainly did, which may explain why, at some later point in her life, she revisited the typescripts of *Sword*, *White Rose*, and *The Mystery* and struck through the name Delia Alton, replacing it with H.D. But I think that this misdirection on the title page might also be part of a larger commentary on the autobiographical mode. *Sword* is part autobiography, part ghost story, part mystical literature, part time-travel narrative, part historical fiction, and part fairy tale. It is an autobiography that calls very much into question the autobiographical, starting with the cover of the book. What H.D. is trying to accomplish in *Sword* is fruitfully considered in terms of one of the elements of Leigh Gilmore's *autobiographics*: "the name as a potential site of experimentation rather than contractual sign of identity," in which the "I" becomes "a point of resistance in self-representation" rather than a marker of the veracity of identity.[56] *Sword*'s ever-shifting "I"s mean to highlight the fundamental instability of autobiographical narrative. *The Gift* merges past and present selves, *By Avon River* challenges biographies of prominent male figures, and *White Rose* features a woman's self as disappearing body, but it is *Sword* that launches the most radical critique of self and its representation. While the autobiographical "I" always already denotes a division of self, during a time of trauma that self is more violently fragmentary.

There are other clues that *Sword* is intended as an assault on the autobiographical mode. I suspect that, in addition to its array of characters and shifting protagonists, one of the reasons that many find *Sword* challenging is the tedious nature of "Wintersleep," the first half of the novel, set in London during and immediately after World War II. "Wintersleep" features Delia, in efforts to avoid the reality of the war being waged outside her flat, becoming increasingly addicted to the séance—she calls it a "drug"[57]—all the while distracted by an apparent fixation on a man she hardly knows, Lord Howell, a thinly disguised stand-in for Dowding, the commander who led the RAF during the Battle of Britain. Howell's rejection reminds Delia of the Aldington character's betrayal of the World War I years, a narrative that is the subject of much of H.D.'s 1920s fiction and, frankly, a much more compelling story. In that story, Aldington, the dashing poet-soldier, goes back and forth between the front and their Bloomsbury home, which housed D. H. Lawrence and an assemblage of other artist types. The Aldington figure seems genuinely torn between his lust for Dorothy Yorke and his love for his wife, and we feel the pain of the autobiographically based protagonists H.D. created in the 1920s and 1930s. *Sword*, however, lacks those elements that would draw a reader in. Why does Delia even care about this celebrity military figure? And why should we, as readers, care that she does?

I would contend that H.D.'s persistent retelling of the story of her betrayal by Aldington in her work of the 1920s is critiqued in the first half of *Sword*, "Wintersleep," in which the focus on betrayal is pushed to such an excess that the novel calls into question its importance in the face of a greater historical and political reality. As *Sword* opens, as the bombs fall outside of her flat, she is again the wronged party. The phrase the Aldington figure, Geoffrey, utters more than once—"I love you but I desire *l'autre*"—becomes a refrain that echoes explicitly and implicitly throughout Part I of the volume. But instead of her husband, Aldington, the principal soldier-lovers in this part of *Sword* are men H.D.'s autobiographical protagonist, Delia Alton, barely knows: Lord Howell, a war hero she has only met a few times; and Thomas Moore, a figure from Delia's teen years, a boy she met just once, not a military man but playing the role of one on stage.

In *Sword*, chronology is reversed: "Lord Howell added a grain of alien substance to a solution in a test-tube, and crystallized out Geoffrey and the others."[58] As Dowding paradoxically spawns Aldington, and not the other way around, it is clear that the soldier-lover icon is more important than the actual person at the center of the original trauma. I make no comment on H.D.'s feelings for Dowding, but Howell and Moore, I would contend, are empty signifiers, flat characters sketched in abstract terms. The degree to which Delia is obsessed with these phantoms—to the point, in fact, of near psychosis in the novel—becomes the measure of the absurdity of her desire. That experiences with these men begin to overlay the very real personal trauma of Aldington's betrayal points to a distancing of herself from the past tragedy and the current one, Dowding's "repudiation"—to use her term. These rejections are no longer personal; they have moved into a purely symbolic or mythic realm. In other words, the intricacies of the personal experience cease to be important, for these men serve as mere symbols, actors suspended in different guises within a larger theater of war and militaristic violence throughout the remainder of the book.[59] H.D. appears to have come to the realization Primo Levi expresses so eloquently in *The Drowned and the Saved*, that "a memory evoked too often, and expressed in the form of a story, tends to become fixed in a stereotype, in a form tested by experience, crystallized, perfected, adorned, installing itself in the place of the raw memory and growing at its expense."[60]

Indeed, her late writings are filled with references to these empty symbols of masculine repudiation that stand in for Aldington, who has likewise ceased to matter to her by the 1940s and 1950s in quite the same way: Lord Dowding, her medium Arthur Bhaduri, her analyst Erich Heydt, even the journalist Lionel Durand who died from complications suffered in a war zone. H.D. refers to Durand, for instance, as merely a "peg or bobbin on which we wind the thread." She writes that "[n]o one could help loving him" and yet "this is not quite true or half-true."[61] In *Magic Mirror*, H.D. calls these men "hieroglyphs" that "crowd in on one another," and hails this stratagem as "a new writing . . . a new way of reading."[62] Whether or not these emotions run deep, it is more important that these men serve as useful symbols—or, to use H.D.'s terms, "patterns" or "hieroglyphs" or "imagos"—that evoke themes she persistently pursues in the last phase of her career: the soldier-lover, "romantic thralldom,"[63] sexual desire and infidelity, repudiation. What she writes is "true," but only insofar as "[i]t is true as a pattern, an exact impression."[64] She needs these figures for her writing, readily superimposing one upon another in various works, but "[t]he people are the same" and "the people do not matter now."[65] When she learns of Dowding's engagement, she bows out in real life, she writes in the *Hirslanden Notebooks*, "[b]ut I still need the Air Marshall, for my story."[66] Jeffrey Twitchell-Waas, then, is right that "Dowding's rejection . . . is not personal but part of the inevitable pattern of parting that is bound up with the experience of Eros in time."[67] Whittier-Ferguson notes that both Gertrude Stein and Wyndham Lewis incline toward "puppets and shells and only partly completed models for humans"[68] in their work of the World War II era, and here we might situate, too, H.D.'s warrior-poets.

Her last novel, *Magic Mirror*, and the late memoirs *Compassionate Friendship* and *Thorn Thicket* reveal this process—this "game"—at work. At one point, Dowding is the "father" who "repudiate[es]" his RAF "boys" after their deaths in the Battle of Britain, just as Aldington had rejected his unborn child, causing a miscarriage (H.D. believed) when he shocked her with news of the sinking of the *Lusitania*.[69] At another point, all of these male figures are iterations of her half-brother Eric.[70] "Heydt has now become a composite," "Heydt is . . . Hilda's husband," Heydt is Dowding, "Durand compensated for the lost Heydt *imago*," and, later, Perdita's father Cecil Gray appears in a dream as Heydt.[71] H.D. is Astraea to Herrick's soldier-lover in the seventeenth-century poem that inspired the title of one of H.D.'s novels.[72] Various personages and characters are not real but rather abstractions, distillations of essences, she writes, employing the term "*dépouillé*" from Chaboseau's alchemical philosophy.[73] It is in the late 1950s that she fully realizes the emptiness of these "hieroglyphs," and the distance between herself and these various men: "There was a feeling of exaltation in my later discovery, it was not I personally, who was repudiated." Mapping the private to the public, she writes of her epiphany about these patterns the year before she died: "I must repeat the heart-break" because "*The war was my husband*."[74] It is this war-husband (not soldier-husband) that offers her a clear sense of identity as the one who is always already abandoned and "repudiated." When Heydt leaves town for a short while, for instance, she finds that she must look elsewhere to "sustain myself, my ego with some sort of identification."[75]

H.D., of course, employs repetition throughout her autobiographical prose when she casts and re-casts the same events of her past in remarkably different books. However, the repetition in *Sword* is pushed to an extreme. The extent of the excess in the first half of *Sword* points to a parodic relationship to the autobiographical mode that permits H.D. to do what Leigh Gilmore claims contemporary writers do in their novels of trauma: expose "the interpenetration of the private and the public."[76] She also wishes, I would suggest, to critique Freud. In *Sword*, encounters with another dimension arguably become a vehicle for what Freud called "repetition compulsion" or "traumatic neurosis." In "repetition compulsion," trauma occurs when an originary experience of shock is triggered by "seemingly trivial" later events which, through indirection, create the conditions for re-experiencing that shock. As Dominick LaCapra usefully explains, a later event stimulates memory of the original event, so trauma actually occurs "retrospectively": "one thus has a conjunction of repetition and change."[77] But, in *Sword*, world war follows world war. Not only is the repeated event not in the least "trivial," but there seems to be no possibility for escaping the cycle of repetition. Equally traumatic, originary and later events are ensnared in a cycle, one triggering the other, which in turn triggers the first, and so on. This oscillation between events affords no exit. One cannot work through the originary event by recognizing the benignity of subsequent events if the latter are also a product of war. After the "shocks and wounds we have received," Delia notes of the Second World War, we "revisit the scene of disaster . . . to relive the conflict that caused our first defeat" in the First World War.[78] H.D. implies that Freud ignores the inescapability and inevitability of world war. These are not just psychic phenomena but material realities. War creates a "temporal disruption," notes Bryony Randall, in which day after day after day is experienced as "spiraling out of human time" into a "meaninglessness": "H.D.'s novels draw attention to the provisionality of meaning through their continual returning to past (and future) scenes."[79] Freud's approach may not be effective in a world of perpetual war.

This kind of repetition—of "simultaneity"—cannot be accommodated in conventional narrative, as Madelyn Detloff astutely observes.[80] One of the principal strategies by which *Sword* dismantles itself is by setting one genre against another—and what better counter to a mode of writing based in fact than a ghost story? The reader of "Wintersleep," who has been lulled by monotonously transparent autobiographical scenes, is then asked to accept the material presence of dead people speaking from the grave. To be sure, in "Wintersleep," there are numerous metaphorical ghosts—revenants, evoked in the imagination and dreams by memories of the past—but there are also actual ghosts, and these ghosts of *Sword*'s séances are not of the type one might find in a horror story, a haunted house, or a graveyard; her novel is not meant "to scare its readers," as we expect of the genre.[81] *Sword*'s ghosts are not particularly eerie, nor uncanny. Unlike the demanding spirits who take possession of Delia's body in *Majic Ring*, *Sword*'s ghosts do not cause fear, disgust, or even unease. The living characters of the novel are, in fact, more ghostly than the actual ghosts, Delia notes: "Lord Howell looked like a ghost. We were ghosts together." *Sword*'s ghosts, rather, are ordinary people—Royal Air Force soldiers who lost their lives in the Battle of Britain—and an affable and obliging spirit guide, "Z." We are asked to accept unquestioningly their physical presence as characters in a story that has, to this point, seemed almost painfully historically accurate. Using séances to seek answers to personal questions, Delia stumbles upon spirits who want to offer information about history and the war. Rather than flee the scene, as one might expect in a ghost story, she greedily seeks them out, again and again, becoming "addicted" to the scene of the séance.[82]

The incompatibility of autobiography and ghost story registers in the reader as a sense of dissonance. An autobiography is bound to a particular time and place in the historical past. While a ghost represents the past, it travels without regard to temporal boundaries or limits. It marks "a disturbance in the symbolic, moral or epistemological order," and is expected to depart once this "disturbance has been corrected."[83] A ghost story, as any fictional story, then, offers readers a sense of completion, a sense of an ending that the autobiography necessarily cannot; a story of war cannot either, as trauma keeps the war perpetually in existence. If "all autobiographies ... are corrupted by the present," fiction dwells in a world "outside of time."[84] If virtually anything can happen within fiction—particularly fantastical fiction— there are constraints on an autobiographer's freedom and imagination.

Shirley Geok-lin Lim has perceptively observed that fiction necessarily enters autobiography to make it more interesting to the reader. Because "the art of narrative gets its power from dialogue, from an exteriorization of feelings and thoughts," autobiographers can be stymied by the challenge of representing a life mostly lived "in silence and in monologue, self speaking to its self."[85] As *Sword* recounts Delia's progressive withdrawal from society and her gradual isolation, a ghost offers her someone to talk to, albeit through a spirit board. But ghosts are much more than just a convenient device in this book.

H.D. enjoyed stories of the supernatural, including Vernon Lee's ghost stories in *The Snake Lady and Other Stories*. Her friend Violet Hunt's *Tales of the Uneasy*—a volume still appreciated among readers today—sat on her bookshelf, and she read often Algernon Blackwood's *The Centaur*, a supernaturalist story with spiritual and philosophical dimensions. Hunt's book features a device that H.D. herself used often, the double, which will be discussed at greater length in Chapter 6. Integrating her own story of the supernatural into a novel seems not to have been an accident. In *Majic Ring*, the narrator asserts that the world of ghosts is something to be studied not just by academics and scholars but by poets as well: "[A]lthough there are libraries of books open to any psychic-research worker, very little has been done by modern poets or writers. There is the occasional delightful ghost-story, it is true, and imaginative reconstructions and dream-analysis enter into much of the modern novelist's content—or did enter—in the mid-twenties and on into the early thirties. But there has been a missing link, a bridge was needed. Fiction, yes. Fact, no. But the fact indeed is stranger than the strangest fiction."[86] While she allows that ghost stories and novels are fiction, she nonetheless questions explicitly where the line between fact and fiction lies.

To be sure, the autobiography and the ghost story are not absolutely diametrically opposed. Both, after all, involve representation of the return of the past, and both genres are usually grounded in realism. As Glen Cavaliero points out, the effectiveness of a ghost story is reliant to a great extent on the realism of its setting: "The paradox is that spirit should nevertheless depend upon material embodiment if it is to be communicated as spirit. In supernaturalist literature, the more integrated with physical appearances these embodiments are, the more disquieting and memorable."[87] Its power is derived from the "clash" between two worlds—the "sensation of numbing dislocation which arises at that point of intersection . . . the material and the supernatural."[88] Still, these are not two types of narrative that we often find together, and for good reason. As readers of *Sword*, we question the presence of ghosts, which in turn makes us question the veracity of the autobiographical story. If Delia believes that she communicates with ghosts, what of her narrative can we trust? H.D., I would argue, uses the ghost story genre in this novel to force us to ask that very question. The collision of the autobiographical and the supernatural is meant to pique our suspicion of truth in a narrative of trauma.

Calling the supernatural "a rogue element in the house of fiction," Cavaliero shows how its very presence "deconstruct[s]" the novel by exposing it as an "artificial construct": "[I]t reminds us that all language is metaphorical."[89] Nicholas Paige agrees, arguing that both the modern novel and the fantastical genre defy strict realism. For Paige, "in a world obsessed about both truthful representation and the reality of the imagination, the supernatural thrived because it was a prime way of thinking about the unliteral yet not purely fanciful nature of fictional reference."⁹⁰ Though we might think of the ghost story as definitively pre-modern, or pre-modernist, Simon Hay reminds us, "There was something modernist about the ghost story from the very start: its refusal of narrative conventions, its convoluted narrative frames, its opacity and unsureness, its refusal of story, its failure to offer resolution."⁹¹ Like the ghost story, "modernism is very much haunted by the past and by a sense of cultural decline."⁹² The ghost story does not disappear at the dawn of modernism. As Helen Sword has argued compellingly, modernists were drawn to "spiritualism's ontological shiftiness; its location of authorial power in physical abjection; its subversive celebrations of alternate, often explicitly feminine, modes of writing; its transgressions of the traditional divided between high and low culture; and its self-serving tendency to privilege form over content, medium over message."⁹³ Modernist novels in fact abound in ghosts.

But *Sword* isn't just a modern, or modernist, novel. It's a text ostensibly based in fact. It is not just the world of the novel but the world of reality that is critiqued. This "clash" of the supernatural with the autobiographical is not unlike the intersection of the ghost story and historical fiction, discussed at some length by Hay. Hay remarks that both genres have to navigate a vexed relationship between the present and the past, but the former "holds to a model of history as trauma," while the latter is invested in nostalgia: "The ghost story ... narrates for us ... history ... as what hurts, what haunts, what sets limits to what we can and cannot do, what exceeds our ability to control."⁹⁴ The RAF pilots Delia constantly seeks to contact through séances are a reminder of trauma, (im)material representations of symbolic and literal sacrifice. They died protecting her and other London denizens in the Battle of Britain. Their ongoing presence is not eerie but oddly comforting to Delia, who fears the present and the future. Yet her escalating addiction to these solitary séances is a sign of her inability to escape the effects of that trauma and a precursor to her ultimate psychotic break from reality at the close of the first half of the book.

The presence of a ghost does more than upset our notion of reality because we do not believe in its existence. It also disturbs a factual narrative in that the ghost is a cipher, asking to be de-encrypted or translated. Indeed, "[o]ften the most urgent task instigated by a haunting is that it be *read* accurately."⁹⁵ We are not to accept a ghost at face value. We must try to interpret it. In this sense, the ghost is not unlike the autobiographer. As Paul John Eakin has observed, "our life stories are not merely *about* us but in an inescapable and profound way *are* us."⁹⁶ Delia is a text; H.D. is a text. Readers must interpret Delia (and H.D.) just as Delia must decipher the messages she receives from the magical séance table, spelled out painstakingly, letter by letter. The supernatural element of *Sword* reminds readers again that a "fact" still requires interpretation. We make sense of facts—and we represent facts—through language, and readers must face the necessity of failure in this task. As Susan Poznar contends, "a haunting always seems in excess of human apprehension, certainly in excess of description."⁹⁷ Delia decides that her experiences are "authentic," but she never makes sense of any of the messages of the various ghosts who emerge during séances—enigmatic words devoid of context, such as "corn" or "gale" or "oar" or "roses red." When she attempts to shape narratives to explain them, she is continually confounded. At the end of "Wintersleep," she is left still guessing at the meanings of the messages: "Perhaps Lord Howell knows the answer. I do not," she admits.⁹⁸ Convinced at one point that she has invaluable information from the pilots that will end the war, she is told irrefutably that this is not the case. In fact, as insistent as the voices are, they say very little of import. They require something from her so that they can rest, but Delia ultimately fails to decipher their messages satisfactorily. Unlike in many ghost stories, there is no resolution to their quest. The final chapter of "Wintersleep" is a meditation on possible reasons for her failure. Delia's plight is not unlike that of the reader of autobiography, who can never rely upon any barometer of objective truth. The ghosts of *Sword* appear and reappear on its pages to remind us of what we simply cannot know. They remind us that the past is as unknowable as it is unresolvable.

The first half of *Sword*—the autobiographically based narrative of Delia's repudiation by a series of soldier-lovers and her forays into spiritualism, amid the trauma of World War II London—culminates in an episode both psychotic and visionary. The narrative disintegrates under the weight of the excessively tedious autobiographical moment, itself precariously bound to a truth involving beings from another dimension. Tyrus Miller's description of the satiric nature of late modernist writing offers a useful framework for thinking through this narrative failure. When the story spirals out of control in the second book of *Sword*, we are made to see the first half of the book as mocking the solipsism of high modernism's focus on interiority and autobiography's claims to truth. More importantly, the book critiques the self-indulgence of H.D.'s own autobiographies of the 1920s by first presenting us with an autobiographical story that is excessively repetitive and inconsequential. We are not just trapped within the mind of an unreliable narrator in *Sword*. Unlike her earlier fiction, this narrative is nearly indecipherable without knowledge of H.D.'s life, and Delia is so intensely self-focused that her psyche becomes unstable. The book then turns sharply away from the autobiographical as it moves into the historical realm, moves inescapably into a traumatic past.

If the works of high modernism effect a stance situated distinctly apart from mass culture, politics, and history, the second half of *Sword* rejects that apoliticism and, instead, tells stories that plumb the impact of the political on the personal. Delia claims at the opening of the novel that she will not discuss what is going on outside of her flat, but the entire second half of the novel examines the everyday within the context of war, imperialism, and European history. Miller remarks that late modernists are moved to "despair" over a "certain inevitability to the erosion of individual subjectivity," and the utter disintegration of Delia's mental processes is surely illustrative in this regard. The war and the atomic bomb impel a horrific new understanding of "subjectivity 'at play' in the face of its own extinction."[99]

2

Mysticism and Time Travel

> Spiritual values shifting means little boxes breaking.
>
> —H.D., "Narthex"

In a series of 1940–1941 autobiographical sketches about the Blitz entitled *Within the Walls*, H.D. describes the surreal, even occult or mystical, experience of the civilian noncombatant, who can so easily lose a grasp on the difference between the worlds of imagination (the "dream-state" or "art-dimension") and reality ("the actual life dimension or actual realities of life").[1] As I have written elsewhere,[2] it is upon leaving a movie theater in the midst of the Blitz that H.D. is struck by the ironies of her experience—living in a war zone, viewing footage of a war zone before the film, watching a portrayal of a war zone in the film. She senses that the line between fiction and reality had faded, and for a moment she does not know one from the other.

In both worlds, there is war and not-war; there is reality and not-reality, dream and not-dream. In this moment, time fractures into what she calls "clock-time" and "dream-time." Between the autumn of 1940 and spring of 1941, London was subject to near-constant bombing by the Germans, and, from their South Kensington flat, H.D. and Bryher bore witness to the carnage—an "orgy of destruction"[3]—and its aftermath. Her experience of "clock-time" unravels when her universe is measured not by a timepiece but by the dropping of bombs. Having experienced the dissolution of the boundary between the real and the unreal, she immerses her immediate postwar work in the liminal space between "clock-time" and "dream-time," between the normal and the paranormal, the material and the spiritual.⁴ As Kevin Hart writes of Eliot's portrayal of the Blitz in "Little Gidding," "We are in an enchanted place where the line between the natural and the supernatural worlds is broken and equivocal."⁵

It is H.D.'s sense of living at once in the material world and another dimension—this dissolution of one time into another that occurs during a time of war—that plagues and propels her writing of the late 1940s and early 1950s. René Girard has argued that "[r]eligion in its broadest sense must be another term for that obscurity that surrounds man's efforts to defend himself by curative or preventative means against his own violence."⁶ Religion, for Girard, arises in response to violence—either before or after the fact—as a "preventative" that seeks to quell our violent impulses or a "curative" that means to treat the trauma that ensues. This chapter argues that the violence of World War II impelled a marked shift in H.D.'s thinking about mysticism and spirituality, which will be traced through a comparison of her prewar and postwar writings about the mystical experience in order to analyze a feature common to all of her immediate postwar prose, including *Sword*— that moment when the narrator transcends the bounds of the narrative and temporal frame. The preceding chapter focused on the first part of *Sword*, which relates an autobiographically based narrative about the experience of living in London during the Blitz. This chapter looks at the apocalyptic vision at the center of *Sword* that fragments not only the narrator's identity but the structure of the narrative itself.

Trying to make sense of her historical moment—of World War II, the Holocaust, the dropping of atomic bombs—H.D. creates characters who live at once in two worlds, the physical and the metaphysical. Her three long prose works from 1946 to 1951 feature protagonists who experience abrupt and radical breaks in the space-time continuum, who step outside of their narratives in order to time travel to other historical eras. The introduction traced a shift during H.D.'s long career from a poetics based in stasis to one more dynamic, and this chapter looks specifically at this shift in terms of two different—at times competing—forms of mystical or spiritual experience.

By the late 1930s, H.D. had developed an epiphanic model of fiction, in which short stories culminate in a singular moment of illumination; the fiction of the 1940s and early 1950s, however, transmutes that stillpoint into a portal to past eras—and, significantly, in a singular case, an imagined future one. Her early forays into mysticism are modeled on a goal of transcendence via more traditional, apophatic forms of mysticism, in which the soul enters into an experience of the divine that is affective, enlightening, and ultimately ineffable.[7] Mystical moments occur in an altered state, in a brief moment in time, and they facilitate some understanding of the divine mystery. The trauma of the Second World War, however, brings with it a different paradigm. In the fiction of the late 1940s and early 1950s, characters achieve a form of astral projection only to find themselves cast back into historical scenes of war, violence, and imperialism. The mystical experience becomes an experience of time travel, in which characters seeking enlightenment are denied an ecstatic experience of transcendence or a union with the divine and are instead compelled repeatedly to relive past traumas in the history of Europe. These characters are trapped in the cycles of history; they *time* travel, temporally bound and subject to history. *Sword* thus brings together two genres or modes seemingly diametrically opposed—one religious and the other popular and fantastical—in ways that expose the strangeness of this union. Surveying H.D.'s models for time displacement and travel, this chapter will construct a framework for thinking about these episodes as not evidence of H.D.'s escapism—her flight into an otherworldly space free of bombings and rations and other hardships—but rather as a mode of political commentary and critique.

Notoriously, H.D. read widely in religious, mystical, supernatural, and occult literature throughout her life. Without taking into account Bryher's extensive library and her access to the London Library, H.D.'s personal library contained an astounding array of books on a range of subjects, including Eastern and Western mysticism; Swedenborgianism; the Bible, the Bhagavad-Gita, tales of the Buddha, the Midrash, and the Apocrypha; theosophy; theories of Atlantis; Ancient Egyptian, Babylonian, Indian, American Indian, and Greek mythology; fortune telling; spiritualism and ghosts; reincarnation; magic, astrology; Tarot, prophecy, witchcraft, cheirognomy and cheiromancy; parapsychology; Hermeticism; angels and saints; Gnosticism; Catharism; and the Amish and Moravian sects. Not all of this makes its way into her writings, of course, but much of it does. She became interested in mystical visions at least as early as the 1910s, and her earliest representations of those experiences adhere to traditional Western models. Pre–World War II mystical experiences are passive, and they tend to culminate in a stillness located in an altered state, and in a singular life-changing moment of enlightenment or (to employ a literary term) epiphany, offering H.D. access to what she termed "the invisible world" that exists alongside the "visible" one. Like many medieval Christian mystics—some of whom H.D. read—these protagonist-mystics undergo an (at least partial) evacuation of the self and an experience of a vast, ineffable nothingness. They are passive, often reclining, transforming themselves into vehicles for the spirit to enter, much as spiritualist mediums do. These moments of illumination occur not just in nature but amidst Egyptian ruins, onboard a ship, during idle conversation with friends over coffee, among crowds of people, in the midst of a passionate argument between lovers, in the seconds before dying. Time does not elapse during these moments—it does not stretch across history; rather, time is revealed to be an illusion.

The trauma of the World War I era and its aftermath—including the deaths of her father and her brothers, Gilbert and Eric; the stillbirth of a daughter; Aldington's infidelity and the dissolution of her marriage; her near-death from the 1918 influenza outbreak—seems to have played a part in H.D.'s development of this early notion of mysticism. This period of five years—this "cloud" of darkness—impelled a "new trick of seeing" that "shut her out from life," and her pre–World War II prose about mystical experience reflects this inward turn. In *Paint It To-day*, Midget explains to Althea (based on Bryher) that the trauma of World War I produced in her a belief in parallel states of existence: "I have found since I have outgrown the period of war convalescence that the visible world exists as poignantly, as etherially as the invisible." Midget declares, too, that her sense of time has been altered: "I used to believe in the past and in what I called the future."[8] In another autobiographical novel, *HERmione* (drafted in 1926), H.D.'s narrator, Her, reacts to trauma by turning inward. When Fayne rejects Her, Her realizes that she must protect herself by dissolving the ego: "Valiantly I will keep Her under.... Her won't anymore be."[9] Published in 1928, "Narthex," too, records an experience of "loss of identity" as "[o]ccult" mysticism.[10] *Nights* (1934) presents a frustrated protagonist, Natalia, who can only achieve any kind of heightened spiritual experience when she is alone, masturbating, and not when she is in bed with her suffocating lover, David.[11] These experiences are transcendent and ahistorical, bolstered by a belief that this is a "subject which has no racial and no time-barriers."[12] It is clear even from these scattered examples that, in the inter-war period, to protect oneself from trauma, one must move inward and attempt to achieve a transcendent state outside of the chaos and pain of the "visible world." Experiencing another war, she imagines in *Tribute to Freud*, would release her finally into "another, a winged dimension."[13]

Transcendent, altered states figure prominently in her very early manifesto, *Notes on Thought and Vision* (1919). In that text, the altered state is analogized to wearing "a cap of consciousness over my head" akin to a jellyfish, though it is possible to wear this cap in the womb to access "dream" and "ordinary" vision. Increasingly, though, through the early 1940s, these are experiences more psychic than somatic.[14] This more traditional paradigm is elaborated in terms more spiritual than aesthetic in her long prose work *Palimpsest* (1926) and in the shorter unpublished fiction produced in the 1920s through the early 1940s, which she aptly entitled *The Moment*.[15] But as late as *Trilogy*, H.D. still places great emphasis on the moment of illumination. A glimpse of Mary's luxurious hair engenders just such an experience for Kaspar, for instance; it "created a sort of vacuum, / or rather a *point* in time" that affords him a "premonition."[16] Beverly Dahlen's lovely tribute to the long poem encapsulates its theory of time in this way: "as if the universe might have been condensed or contracted into a single seed or point."[17]

Emblematic of what I am calling an epiphanic mode of transcendence, Helen Fairwood's mystical experience in "Secret Name"—the third part of H.D.'s *Palimpsest*—takes place in modern Egypt, the site of some inexplicable "psycho-hysterical visionary sensations" that she compares to being "under ether." Entering a temple at night, Helen feels her chaotic, tiring day dissolve into a dream, "some excursion into some outre-mer." Helen has a revelation that the Greeks derived their divine knowledge from the Ancient Egyptians. Looking up at the African sky, she experiences an exhilarating sense of freedom and a comforting dissolution of the ego, an "assurance that she, after all, was nothing." For Helen, time collapses, "[h]er past merged. . . . Past, present, all the commutations of past and present . . . were merged at one within her. The just past, the far past."[18]

It is, though, in H.D.'s unpublished short story collection *The Moment* that we can best see her work through this conception of time and develop this epiphanic mode. Indeed, these disparate stories—set in vastly different times and places—have little in common beyond a female narrator, a revelatory moment, and a shared concept of time as illusion. Female protagonists are often presented as passive or reclining when they enter an altered state and receive a vision: in a sequel to "Secret Name" called "Hesperia," Helen stands alone in the moonlight; in another story, Myra is possessed by a spirit and Vanna's vision comes while lying on a couch; "Aegina"'s narrator lies beneath a tree. In "Aegina" and "The Last Time," the "moment" is classically extrovertive, experienced in a trance-like state while yet retaining awareness of the surroundings. In "The Last Time," the narrator loses her sense of identity in the mode of a medieval Christian mystic: "we have no existence, for a moment... we are not so much alone, as non-existent."[19]

These prewar stories typically culminate in the bare knowledge of this "truth" about time. Experiencing a moment of rebirth—in which she "was to become alive, herself resurrected," Helen in "Hesperia" learns that "'the past is nothing, the future is nothing, there is only the eternal,'" and that "the far-past vibrated, in tune with this day.... The broken rhythm, past and present have merged, become the more harmonious."[20] The epiphany of the titular story involves a vision of time collapsed into a singular point: "The past remained, would always. The future remained, would always. The past and future met in the oracle."[21] The narrator of another story, "Jubilee," sees "all life" at once, not "in any sequence" but in one instant of time.[22]

A character in "The Last Time" realizes that a woman has "had vision, illumination," that "she had seen God."[23] But in some stories, such a vision renders the visionary herself god-like, possessing omnipotence and omniscience. In "Hesperia," Helen has "learnt everything. There wasn't anything else she could learn."[24] When the narrator of "Aegina" feels her "human vibration had stopped" she has a vision of the entire world as "all God" and herself at the "heart" of it, and she feels the power of ownership over the island around her. She refers to her vision as a "revelation" in which she "was fully expressed."[25] Such an experience is life-altering: the narrator of "Jubilee" observes, for instance, that "[h]er life had been changed, its course shifted."[26]

In a departure from the other epiphanic experiences—a departure that signals a move toward the time-traveling experiences of the 1940s—the narrator of "The Last Time" is able to leave her body for a brief instant, albeit reluctantly. The two lengthy stories written last, "The Death of Martin Presser" and "The Guardians," penned in London during the war, begin to show the shift from stasis to more dynamic experiences. Set in early America, "The Death of Martin Presser" portrays Presser having a mystical experience at the very moment of his death, a moment in which he is "in out-of-time, where time does not exist": "Martin was in that state where time ceases." His epiphany affords him sacred, secret knowledge and also an insight into the nature of time, as, in one instant, time expands to infinity: "there was time for everything, there was all the time in the world—all the time literally in the world for him, all-time was now at his disposal." But, significantly, time has begun to extend rather than crystalize. Though the vision occurs in a single moment, and Martin is a passive vehicle for the experience, it does prefigure the depictions of the spiritual experience in postwar fiction: in an episode of time travel, Martin travels "back through History, to the beginning of the break or the several breaks in Christian continuity" to learn how to reconcile factions.[27]

For a "moment," Martin is both dead and alive. In "The Guardians," an old woman, Nannie, haunted by the death of her son, Edwin, recognizes his living presence in her household: "Edwin was in the past and Edwin was in the present."[28] Again, in this later story, time seems to take history into account. Edwin does not time travel in a singular moment but across decades of time. The seeds of this notion of being in two places at once can be found in a brief passage of "Hesperia," in which Helen sees Rafton as two people, "separate entities, seen separately and distorted, like two images in a badly adjusted field-glass."[29] But in "The Guardians," it is not that the main character can merely see Edwin this way; he is actually materially in two places at once. Though he has long since died, he raps persistently at the door. In these two early 1940s stories, we can see elements of the later fiction of the decade begin to emerge.

As disconcerting, as terrifying as it was to live in the world of the Blitz—this world in which the distinction between reality and fantasy no longer exists—new possibilities for spiritual existence emerge for H.D. as she comes to see that it is possible to abide in a hybrid form of physical and metaphysical existence. As she writes in *Vale Ave* some years later, "it was the war of course and threat of death / that opened doors into this spirit-life."[30] Just as the trauma of World War I had produced a particular sense of the mystical experience, the trauma of World War II produced a different notion of mysticism entirely, born in the dissolution of the boundary between the real and the dream. To some extent, the shift is from the mystical to apocalyptic model. Madelyn Detloff has argued persuasively that H.D.'s *Trilogy* and *The Gift* are problematic in their apparent embrace of apocalypse as the means through which the world can be cleansed and reborn. In apocalyptic writing, Tony Stoneburner explains, "the new can replace the old, at least at the moment in which God changes and exchanges them utterly." This impulse is clearly there in H.D.'s writings during and just after the war. But the apocalyptic mode is lodged in the present moment, beckoning toward the future, and tends towards abstraction.[31] In the immediate postwar moment, H.D.'s protagonists ultimately turn back to the material events of history.

As early as 1928, H.D. expresses some frustration with the epiphanic model through her protagonist Raymonde Ransome, who has become absorbed by the incredible psychic energy, the "electric fervour," of one of H.D.'s favorite cities. Venice is full of "[v]ibration, electric thing beneath them, throb-throb, steamer in mid-ocean, vibration, impulse toward understanding, spiritual comprehension, actual illumination." To access this power, she has been granted the dubious gift of "loss of identity": "She had given her soul to abstraction, little crystal boxes, she had given her soul to loss of identity, a snail outside an aquarium sort of window. Soul putting out feelers was lost without crystal boxes to confine it . . . soul shut in crystal boxes too long and too deliberately is in psychic danger." The implications for poetic form are obvious: Imagist "crystal boxes" are at once sanctuaries and prisons—safe but soul-numbing—but there is also a concern here about the "psychic danger" that may stem from "loss of identity." Raymonde is apprehensive about "[c]rystalized and over static identity."[32] H.D.'s postwar protagonist-mystics are not passive, empty vessels, and their identities are far from "static." In fact, H.D. had never really been entirely comfortable with a privatized and individualized paradigm, because of the threat to the integrity of the self implicit in such a model. Helen Sword has pointed out the dangers for women in particular: "to claim divine inspiration. . . . is to admit to the suppression of one's own individual voice."[33]

But, I would argue, there is another significant reason for this dramatic rethinking of the mystical. The earlier mode of mysticism pushes the soul, as she says, toward "abstraction." Michel de Certeau observes that "[t]he paradox of the mystical 'moment' refers to a history. What is asserted there is . . . something that in itself rejects the privileging of a present and refers to other indicators—those past and those to come."[34] A mystical experience is at once universal and historically contingent, and this is a paradox H.D. attempts to navigate after the war. Moreover, like the experience of trauma, the mystical experience resists narrativization, and both are reliant on the imprecision of memory. To tell the story of a mystical experience, H.D. turns to a fantastical genre nonetheless grounded in the material world. As Cynthia Hogue and Julie Vandivere have written in their Introduction to *Sword*, "The novel is positioned as a fusion of the political (or time-bound) and eternal (or out-of-time)."[35] Importantly, in H.D.'s immediate postwar fiction time is no longer conceptualized as having collapsed into a singular moment. After the Second World War, protagonists no longer try to achieve transcendence, but rather project themselves astrally into the past. In the prewar fiction, if one is in what she calls "out-of-time," one experiences a place, as she says, "where time does not exist." In the postwar fiction, "out-of-time" takes on a whole new meaning: time elapses—it progresses through a history that binds us to it—but one can enter the past at different points.

Impossibly, this view of temporality is both linear and cyclical. It is what enables the narrator of H.D.'s *Sword* to remark that, simultaneously, "the going backward and the going forward were going on together," and the narrator of *White Rose* to observe that one can "remember ... at the same time" as one can "*remember in the future.*" Moreover, time for postwar H.D. molds itself into the pleats of an accordion—a "Z-line" that resembles a bee's flight—such that historical events touch one another at points of war and imperialism, repeating cycles of violence and domination. "[I]f you understand one fold or pleat, one superimposition," her protagonist explains in *Sword,* "you understand another."[36] An experience (ostensibly) universal has been replaced by one of historical specificity that nonetheless resonates with others like it. In a discussion of another work of literature inspired by World War II, *Slaughterhouse-Five,* one critic suggests that "the transcendent is comforting because it is transhistorical and must always be the same."[37] For H.D., the transcendent seems to have ceased to be "comforting" in the years immediately following the Second World War. Her postwar writings, in fact, challenge this illusion of comfort, forcing herself, her characters, and her readers to confront history. We are compelled to experience collectively the pain of history and the impossibility of the fulfillment of desire.

Desire for an experience of union with deity can never be quenched, and in times of heightened danger the inevitable failure of such a quest is perhaps at its most apparent and most poignant. The divine enlightenment afforded her prewar characters is denied her postwar characters. She gains knowledge of the past but not knowledge of the eternal divine, and this knowledge is not uplifting and ecstatic but disheartening. Because these time-traveling quests operate within a universe bound to the terrors of history, they are frequently thwarted. These quests, in a sense, are doomed to fail. Mystical seekers attempt journeys toward a path of enlightenment, but they are continually pushed backward, into loops of time that impede their progress.

Access to the mystical realm is no longer access to divinity. Michel Serres, a contemporary historian of science, theorizes that all objects and events are "polychronic, multitemporal, and reveal a time that is gathered together, with multiple pleats." He posits a Hermetic "figure of a free mediator . . . wander[ing] through this folded time and . . . establish[ing] connections."[38] Hermes was one of H.D.'s favorite otherworldly figures, but the knowledge gained by H.D.'s Hermetic protagonists—the "establishing" of "connections"—is the revelation that there is no way out of those cycles. It is not until the 1950s that she begins to derive again a sense of optimism from her spiritual journeys.

H.D.'s changing views of mysticism—her turn outward—align with shifts in current scholarship on the phenomenon. Recent religious studies scholars have uncovered a number of ways in which mysticism in the post-medieval era has been constructed increasingly as passive, private, somatic, and feminine; in doing so, it has begun to challenge the traditional models of mysticism with which we are most familiar, emphasizing instead the public, societal, ethical, and communal functions of mysticism and spirituality.[39] The mystical experience, to borrow Mark McIntosh's words, "is not a peculiar moment that exists in a cultural vacuum." The term now enjoys a much broader usage. Joseph Keller's work has usefully linked mysticism to the sacrament of communion, defining the experience of the mystic as "an unimpeded consciousness of the plenum in which all of us have our deepest being and whose potentialities unite us all," and McIntosh has turned to the discursive aspects of mysticism, arguing that the mystical experience carries meaning only in the context of the reader or listener—the other—of the text. Bernard McGinn calls the mystical experience "a personal appropriation, but not an individualistic one, because it is rooted in the life of the Christian community and the grace mediated through that community and its sacraments and rituals." This rethinking of mysticism has been a radical one. Indeed, Grace Jantzen concludes ultimately that "there is no such thing as an 'essence' of mysticism, a single type of experience which is characterisable as mystical while others are excluded."[40] And this is profoundly important because, as Jantzen points out, rethinking mysticism as public in nature means that the mystical is directly engaged with the world. The political ramifications of these insights are key to understanding H.D.'s postwar shift on the subject. As another religious scholar, John Passmore, has observed, a privatized notion of Christian mysticism is at odds with humanitarian ethics, because one is supposed to love God only and not be distracted by the real world. H.D., during and after the war, cannot help but be distracted by the real world. Her mode of engagement with the mystical must change accordingly.

In *Sword*, mysticism and time travel uneasily converge in astral projection, or *ex-stasis*, a phenomenon found in both Eastern and Western mysticism.[41] Moreover, the notion of projecting oneself outside of the body is inherent to the experience of religious ecstasy described by so many mystics, as "that which transports one outside oneself."[42] As Hollenback notes, "Ecstasy... implies a... radical process of abstraction from the body," and one of H.D.'s favorite mystical writers, St. Teresa of Ávila, uses the term in just this sense, describing it as a process in which "the Lord gathers up the soul... and raises it till it is right out of itself."[43] The meeting of self and Self within the mystic's body alienates the self, making an other of the self. "It expels one from the self," Certeau explains, "instead of gathering one to it."[44] Hermetic writings, another mainstay of H.D.'s interests, situate ex-stasis as integral, and, closer to our time and hers, the treatises of theosophy also emphasize the importance of astral projection. For H.D., whose reading on the subject was varied and diverse, the object is always access to another dimension—the otherworldly, mystical, spiritual, paranormal, supernatural, metaphysical, divine realm—whatever one might wish to call it. Paul Harris has suggested a term that might best describe her cobbled-together philosophy—*itinerant spirituality*: "Itinerant spirituality is nomadic and contingent.... [It] could be termed an 'outsider spirituality'... in that it does not partake of any particular spiritual—let alone religious—tradition, and is created idiosyncratically by a person according to methods they develop as they go. The term 'itinerant spirituality' conjures a practice dependent on and embedded in itineraries, in the sense of both the route of the journey and the written record of the journey."[45] After the war, H.D.'s spirituality is itinerant in a number of ways: it is syncretic, but it is also dynamic, active, moving, questing, exploring.

Despite her exposure to these elements of mysticism much earlier in her career, astral bodies and projection were not significant interests for her until after the Second World War. This is perhaps in part because of her reading, begun around the time of the Blitz, in a spiritualist library in South Kensington. In the early 1940s, H.D. came across an 1872 book called *Lumen* by French astronomer and popular science writer Camille Flammarion, who is known today for his anticipation of Einstein's notion of the relative nature of time.[46] Upon his death, the main character of this odd science fiction novel is able to exceed the speed of light and thus occupy a position outside of the continuum of time. From this standpoint in the universe, he is a spectator of history, watching "the history of France from its very beginning, unrolling before me in an order inverse to the succession of events." "[B]y removing oneself to a distance in space," Lumen avers, "one can become a witness of events long past, reversing, so to speak, the flow of time." Viewed in its entirety, Lumen sees each historical event as "bound in an indissoluble manner with the past and the future." He becomes alarmed, though, when he realizes that he is forced to watch harrowing events of the past—such as the French Revolution—over and over again, as "the history of France repeats itself and passes through the same phases over and over again."[47]

Flammarion's theorizing of posthumous time travel—his idea of positioning oneself outside of time, of revisiting the past, and of experiencing and re-experiencing the trauma of foundational historical events—bears striking resemblance to the model H.D. created within a few years of her exposure to his work. Her protagonists do not have to die to project themselves astrally: in *Sword* Delia clarifies, "I still had a body. We do not have to wait till we are dead, to cast off our various bodies like old clothes."[48] But Flammarion's science fiction volume clearly suggested a paradigm that she would begin to envision at the close of the war. In *By Avon River*, H.D. writes of "history, / Unrolled further into the past, / Unrolled mysteriously / Into the future."[49] In this text, completed the year after the war's end, Claribel—the absent Queen of Tunis, whose wedding is the occasion for the shipwreck in Shakespeare's *The Tempest*—sets herself free from Shakespeare's pages to travel back to medieval Venice at the time of the Crusades, the era also visited imaginatively and psychically by figures in *White Rose and the Red*. A range of characters in *Sword* travel to a number of historical periods, and Saint-Germain of *The Mystery* is able to project astrally as well. In the latter novel, in fact, Saint-Germain is present at the scene of the French Revolution, the very event cited in *Lumen*. We see the seeds of this model earlier, however, in *Majic Ring* (drafted in the midst of the war), in which her protagonist, Delia Alton, embodies a range of figures throughout history while in a trance state, moving progressively backwards in time—"circling counter-clockwise ... making a circle or rather a semi-circle around the world or around this spirit-world"—in a quest for the origins of humanity in India.[50] In *Sword*, rather than sharing her body with others, she creates entirely autonomous characters who exist outside of herself. Moreover, the books written between 1946 and 1951 hone the model in a few ways. First, Delia's trance dance in *Majic Ring* takes her to a definitive point of origins and not, as in the later fiction, into a spiral from which she cannot return; in this sense, *Majic Ring* is more in line with *Trilogy*, which pushes further and further back to locate *ur*-deities. Second, time-travelling characters do not just appear and disappear quickly, as they do in *Majic Ring*; rather, they linger in the past, living out entire scenes from history. Third, the postwar scenes are not randomly chosen days in the life of various personages; they are scenes of trauma set during key historical moments in the history of the West. Finally, and perhaps most significantly, the difficulty for the postwar protagonists does not stem from a loss of self only, but also from being compelled to witness periods of warfare and violence.

A marriage of modernism and science fiction may seem incongruous. However, as George Slusser and Danièle Chatelain have observed, time travel and experimental modernism converge around a loss of faith in traditional theories of time. Both modes engage in narrative play with time and space, or what they term "the 'geometrizing' of narrative."[51] H.D. creates several protagonists between 1946 and 1951 who time travel in the way I am describing, though it is *Sword* that relies most heavily on this phenomenon. *Sword* took on great significance for H.D. in the last years of her life. She describes the novel as a kind of sequel to both *Palimpsest* and *The Moment*, but she identifies a critical difference between the pre- and postwar works: if "[t]he message or the 'picture' is presumably for herself alone" in the transcendent, individual mystical experience of *Palimpsest*, it is "pertinent to the thousands, the millions" in *Sword* because of the impact of the Second World War; in *Sword*, "Delia Alton is not alone." Likewise, the three women of "The Moment" are granted "a personal answer" as "the message is given by one person to one person," but in *Sword*, "the answer is given by many to the whole world." She did not see these experiences as "related to time until [she] had written *The Sword Went Out to Sea*." The division between the physical and metaphysical world depicted in the earlier works, she explains, disappears in the later one: "In our way, in our day," she reflects, "we endeavoured to relate experiences, out of time, to time. But the collection was not finally related to time until I had written *The Sword Went Out to Sea*."[52] The war is the dividing line between interiorized and public forms of mysticism. Experiencing the war caused H.D. to rethink and revise her earlier representations.

The turn, then, is outward. The personal spiritual experience has become a communal one. As Hogue and Vandivere suggest, "she was moving beyond the 'self-centered,' spinning out of the personal to a further-reaching, mystical and political sphere."[53] The two parts of the novel can be mapped neatly to what I have described as the two modes of mystical experiences, prewar and postwar. Delia's rather anguished experiments with spiritualism are painstakingly documented in the first half of the novel, "Wintersleep," but the second half, "Summerdream," abandons this model of spiritualist encounter in favor of astral projection when the stress of the war becomes too much to bear. As we saw in the preceding chapter, in "Wintersleep," Delia's world is 1940s London. In the very first chapter of the novel, she commits to remaining in the private sphere. Though there is a world war being waged all around her—though there are "rocking houses and furrowed pavements and the over-familiar wail of the sirens, fire-bells, fire-engines"—she will not, she says, "punctuate this narrative with continued cross-references to what was going on outside." Rather, she wishes only to focus on her writing. To this end, Delia employs a medium, Ben Manisi, to help her through her writers' block. When the séances begin, Delia is expressly uninterested in the images evoked in these private sessions. She is determined to block out everything that does not pertain to the immediate questions at hand. "I didn't want advice about anyone here or communications from anyone there."[54] She initially seems to find the séances frustrating because they do not address her concerns directly, and the messages she receives are, in form, rather modernist: elliptical, enigmatic, disjunctive.

In 1950, H.D. recounted her experience of the Blitz: "That outer threat and constant reminder of death, drove me inward, almost forced me to compensate, by memories of another world, an actual world where there had been security and comfort."[55] The war outside made her want to escape psychologically to another world, a safe space. The word "almost" is key, though. While her instincts are to turn inward, to focus on the personal, the private, she is unable to do so. As H.D. explained to Aldington in 1947, "the Blitz broke into the past," and an examination of the past becomes an examination of the present.[56] Delia's attempts at remaining within the private sphere, too, are decidedly unsuccessful. The devastation of constant bombings exhumes memories of the previous World War; about the bombing of nearby Hyde Park, H.D.'s narrator writes in *Sword*, "I heard the whizz-bang but I called it imagination. That was winter, 1917. Later, I heard it again but I did not call it imagination. That was winter, 1945." Her attempt to flee mentally fails in the second war, for the accordion has contracted, and the world wars have met in its folds. "[N]ow I remembered things in this war as if they had happened twenty-five years ago," Delia reports, "and I remembered things in the last war as if they had happened yesterday." What Delia learns is that it is impossible to ignore the public sphere, which is in fact deeply entangled with her private concerns. It is the war that blasts open a passageway to awareness of both the mystical and the plight of others: "The debris that cluttered the streets of London, sometimes left a half-house open, like a doll-house or a stage-set. One looked into rooms in another dimension," she observes of what she terms "this externalization of peoples' private lives."[57] Just as bombs can obliterate the facade of a house to expose rooms and walls still standing, they can push the private sphere into the public. Delia's séances are invaded by the public sphere as well, when her sessions become mired in communications with RAF pilots who died trying to protect London from German bombers. The messages the pilots offer constitute futile attempts to stop the cycle of violence of world war, as no one—namely the living soldier, Howell—is willing to heed them. Delia finds herself helpless, the situation hopeless.

Much as Delia tries to deny it initially, then, the private and the public are intricately linked, and her previous notions of the private, including an individualized notion of mysticism, are suspect, even dangerous. Personal relationships are inevitably associated with war and trauma, and spiritualism is exposed as insufficient. At the close of "Wintersleep" and the opening of "Summerdream," she tries to take refuge in imagination and the "dream." "Nor yet shall all your dreams be vain," she quotes William Morris, and "[w]e could dream in this life as well as in the other," she wistfully posits.[58] However, "Summerdream" does not confirm such a hopeful sentiment. After "Wintersleep," Delia's self is expelled from self and then rematerialized several times over in "Summerdream" as a host of very different characters—characters who are at once her and not her—who dwell simultaneously in several different eras of war and imperialism. Delia, in these manifestations, astrally projects herself into other times and other spaces. Her self splinters—explodes, one might say, like a bomb—and the shards land at various points in European history. Delia's theory of pleated time guides the formal structure of H.D.'s novel, which blends multiple genres, contemplates the theatrical nature of seeming reality and the relativity of time, and employs several embedded narrative frames with focalization through a character who is both expressly unstable and exceptionally unreliable. Spinning out centrifugally from her present day, scenes of "Summerdream" set in ancient Athens and Rome, Elizabethan England, and medieval Normandy constantly circle back to a war-ravaged London, as the accordion pleats of time contract and expand, exposing personal and historical repetitions of the same devastating impulses to commit emotional and physical violence, to conduct war and to ravage and colonize the lands and minds of one's enemies.

These scenes are the subject of the following chapter. Here I wish to look at what facilitates the proliferation of selves in exile. It is the trauma of the war that impels the process of astral projection, but in its travels through time, the narrative of "Summerdream" borrows from the genre of science fiction. Sarah Schiff observes of trauma that "[t]he fantasy of potentially healing a traumatic narrative . . . is one that requires time travel, because in order to escape the hallucinations and repetitions that are engendered post-trauma, the traumatized consciousness must have been prepared to experience the trauma in time and not out of time."[59] In science fiction, she argues, time travel is often deployed in relation to posttraumatic stress, for revisiting the scene of trauma helps characters work through the psychological ramifications of their experiences. *Sword* attempts to enact just this kind of work, but, ultimately, it exposes the extent to which this is, in fact, a "*fantasy* of potential healing." Reliving the trauma—in different guises, in different times and places—is not therapeutic but re-traumatizing. Delia's various selves remain snarled in repetition compulsion.

Sword's depiction of time travel is not smooth. It is raw, jagged, disruptive. The episodes do not even follow one another in chronological order. The unique structure of the episodic text not only mimics the civilian noncombatant experience of war but also exposes the utter futility of the narrators' attempts to step outside the London experience of World War II. In this pessimistic postwar narrative, H.D. seems to say, militarism and imperialism are inescapable. As the bounds of time crumble, so do the boundaries of the narrator's identity. The narrator does not simply step outside the narrative to visit another era, as in other fictions of the period; her identity splinters into other characters as she loses her grip on the reality of the London setting. "To experience the traumatic, whether directly, as through time travel, or indirectly, as through fiction, is to—uncannily—be estranged from oneself," Schiff warns.[60] *Sword* literalizes this radical estrangement of self from body, self from self. About late modernism, Tyrus Miller has observed, "While accepting a certain inevitability to the erosion of individual subjectivity, later modernist writers viewed it with considerable ambivalence, verging at times on despair."[61] Delia's subjectivity does not merely erode; it explodes in a desperate vision of despair.

The writer of time-travel narratives is concerned with how "to develop new narrative patterns to deal with" the problems of "spatio-temporal displacement."[62] Indeed, H.D.'s new sense of the mystical—its capacity for self-splitting and the access to history it can engender—demanded a new narrative structure for its expression. How can a narrative contain a character who refuses to abide by laws of genre, time, and space? "Wintersleep" contains a number of flashbacks but is fairly straightforward in its development and characterization. Part I is not a high modernist fiction immersed in the consciousness of an unreliable narrator. As we will see, however, "Summerdream" edges toward abandoning the semblance of a present. Moreover, Delia's voice emerges at various points, but it competes with that of multiple iterations of her character, some of which exist side-by-side within the same story. It may not be high modernism, but it is not realism, or even impressionism, either.

It may seem odd to turn, at this point, to Giorgio Agamben's influential *Homo Sacer*, which contemplates the status of those who exist in a state of exception—the sovereign monarch and the exile—who are not subject to the rule of law. In a book that has become central to understanding Western politics, Agamben notes that contemporary representative democracies retain vestiges of this monarchical power to operate outside of the laws that govern the rest of us, citing such examples as concentration camps during World War II and the Patriot Act following the 9/11 attacks. Agamben theorizes usefully the ramifications of those who exist in a state of sustained exile. In an article about Samuel Beckett's *Catastrophe*, Jim Hansen has extended this notion of sovereignty to the author, arguing that "the artist's force bears an unmistakable similarity to something like sovereign power, to he who decides upon the exception. The problems of the artist and the sovereign become analogous in that both can appropriate and erase that which they pretend to represent."[63] He terms this power of the author *lex poetica*. H.D.'s immediate postwar fiction makes use of a form of *lex poetica* in a couple of different ways. First, her narrators operate outside of the laws of time and space when they astrally project themselves into different historical eras and regions. Second, they operate outside of the law of genre, traversing not just time and space but a range of narrative forms.[64] They reside, then, in a state of exception that exempts them not from the political or institutional laws of a nation but rather from laws of narrative.

In an autobiographically based text such as this one, it is difficult to tease out who exercises this power. Is H.D.—writing as Delia Alton—the sovereign who sentences the character Delia—based on H.D.—into exile, doomed to wander through history without moorings? Or does the trauma of the war negate *lex poetica*? Is it the war that strips Delia of agency, the Blitz that "broke into the past" and condemned these tenuously constructed personae to visit and revisit sites of violence and war? At one point, one of Delia's alter egos admits, "'Perhaps, I wanted to be a dictator myself,'" but it is not at all clear that she has that power.[65] In fact, Delia's multiple personae are outsiders, on the margins of power that is inevitably held by militaristic men. They are, variously, women, young and impossibly naive, or old and neglected; they are concubines or stagehands, not wives or theatrical stars. In *Sword*, these characters consistently lack the agency of the author or the sovereign. They do not seem to be in control of where they go or when they go. They are flung into, and cast out of, a procession of vignettes. It is the stress of the war and the political landscape of the twentieth century that explodes alike generic boundaries and character identities, and that pushes those characters to wander outside of their own stories.[66] The spiritual experiences of a war-weary Delia Alton in the first half of the novel force a confrontation with history through astral projection and time travel. At the mercy of H.D.'s pen, characters defy the law of genre as well as that of temporality. In this way, mysticism is far from a personal, individual experience for H.D. Time has expanded, and history has imposed itself.

It is of the utmost importance that H.D.'s postwar mystics do not achieve union with deity, and her time travelers never visit some utopic future nor dwell in an ethereal, transcendent state. Science fiction based in time travel tends to follow one of two models: it either tantalizes readers with the possibility of a future more fulfilling than the present,[67] or it creates in readers a nostalgia for the present.[68] H.D.'s text, however, defies the pattern of most future-oriented science fiction by entrapping her narrators in the past, emphasizing the futility of any escape attempt. Written during the war, *Trilogy* re-envisions the historical figure of Mary to shape Christianity into a force of salvation and recovery from trauma, but *Sword*, written just after the war, lacks any suggestion of such a recovery. For all of its centrifugal movement, *Sword* is stuck: it obsessively spins around and around the same scenes—the same themes—never recovering a sense of direction. One must go "backward to go forward," but there is no real forward: "I was afraid to go backward. I don't think I went forward. Then I went forward, but perhaps the going forward was right off the rails" and into insanity. In fact, she writes, "We go round and round."[69]

So, while much science fiction about time travel is utopic, H.D.'s use of time travel not to the future but to the past is not; it constitutes, to borrow the language of one science fiction critic, "*a dynamic historical critique*" as it emphasizes "historical specificity over assumptions of universal historicity."[70] More precisely, as a self-reflexive "time-slip narrative," H.D.'s *Sword* can be said to "offer an openness to 'other' histories, rather than the potentially nationalistic search for roots . . . [and] it critiques empty reconstructions of the past."[71] Delia Alton searches for the origins of civilization in *Majic Ring*, and Beverly Dahlen describes the quest of *Trilogy* in similar terms: "To redeem the world means to return to that lost instant, or instance, of being to begin, for beginning, to draw these correspondences to the point of one beginning, as it was in the beginning."[72] But in *Sword,* such a quest is doomed. H.D. is intent upon interrogating the past, by exposing it as a reconstruction and by presenting it from the perspective of marginalized characters. Set in both the ancient and the recent past, the eras represented in *Sword*'s pastiche of vignettes are pointedly chosen to illustrate the history of England as conquered and as conqueror. One character of *Sword* visits the burning of Athens by the ancient Romans; another is intimately involved with Julius Caesar, who colonized what is now England for Rome; Queen Elizabeth I, who launched England's imperial project in the New World, is a character in another scene; and still another scene depicts the eve of the Norman invasion of England by William the Conqueror. Moreover, H.D. compounds her rejection of easy stories of nationalism and patriotism by focalizing these episodes through the eyes of culturally marginalized figures who suffer from war and imperialist ventures: disempowered women, and members of the working class.

Readers, likewise, cannot escape these scenes. In *Sword*, we are not meant to experience the pleasure of historical immersion so characteristic of much historical fiction. Rather, we are forced to witness one episode after another that evokes violent national or proto-national confrontation. Like the protagonists in much of H.D.'s fiction, Delia repeatedly doubts and contradicts herself, leaving the reader to piece together an interpretation that has to be constantly revised. Time-slip narratives typically make no use of a "time machine" or other technological devices; rather, characters slip into another era quickly and without scientific explanation. As *Sword*'s narrative spins out of control, readers are thrown from one violent scene to the next without a map—without a "trace of direction"[73]—only to end up in wartime London again, precisely where they started. The fragmentary episodes commence suddenly, without transition or exposition, and they end as quickly as they begin and without resolution. One character in *Sword* refers to the process as a violent "obstacle" course, which "bang[s] your head" and "whizzes you backward."[74] It is, perhaps, cold comfort when Delia tells us that "[i]t would be impossible to deal with the entire sequence," that she "didn't especially want to know" the entire stories.[75] It is by relying on the elements of astral projection and time-travel narratives that H.D. can induce suffering in the reader that aligns with that of her shattered narrator.

To narrate trauma, H.D. traumatizes, and she does so in a way that resonates with Cathy Caruth's observation that both trauma and history are characterized by the inability to remember, comprehend, and synthesize fully an event.[76] *Sword*'s stories are incomplete because they are reconstructions from memory; they are, ultimately, inaccessible. In the Elizabethan episodes and in the final chapter of *Sword*, H.D. makes liberal use of the metaphor of the play, reminding her readers that what they are witnessing is a performance, not actual history. This is not an excavation of the past designed to heal the present, but rather a confession of the futility of such a project. Greg Forter points out the inherent violence in the historical moment as Caruth describes it: "a punctual blow to the psyche that overwhelms its functioning, disables its defenses, and absents it from direct contact with the brutalizing event itself."[77] Though the historical moments are times of national or protonational crisis, the actual violence in *Sword* is offstage, implied rather than depicted: a fire raging in the background, a war to begin the following day, the Ides of March looming. The reader resides in the moment just before the violence occurs, knowing that the violence must occur because of the historical nature of the text. The experience is unsettling. From the standpoint of narrative, Teresa de Lauretis has argued that "[s]tory demands sadism, depends on making something happen, forcing a change in another person."[78] There is undoubtedly a sadistic element to *Sword* born in the helplessness—and hopelessness—H.D. experienced in early 1940s London. It coerces its characters into painful situations over which they have no control and compels bewildered readers to watch passively as one vignette after another flashes by. About the dizzying array of characters who appear in this book, Delia protests, "I did not ask them here." She desires at all costs to avoid ancient Rome, and yet she is transported there against her will. As the narrative shifts abruptly to Normandy in 1066, she again resists: "I had no intention, no desire to return to the Normandy beaches."[79] By the power of *lex poetica*, Delia is being made to relive these traumas. To the extent that the text is semi-autobiographical, this gesture might well be seen as sadomasochistic.

In these novels of the postwar period, there is only one instance of a character traveling to the future, not the past. It is that instance that is the tipping point, that catalyzes the split in Delia's psyche and the fracture in the novel's narrative. It is what sets in motion the time travel that comprises the remainder of the novel. The anxiety over the constant bombings had been building throughout the war, and the violent intersection of the public and private culminates in Delia's one foray into the future. Unable to cope, Delia attempts to escape to another plane, another psychological world, but this one attempt to transcend the present by moving forward in time proves as harrowing as her encounters with the past will be. Suffering from anxiety, exhaustion, malnutrition, meningitis, and what today would surely be diagnosed as post-traumatic stress disorder, Delia fears she has gotten stuck in the past and has contracted bubonic plague. Her hold on reality begins to slip, and she has a dark vision of World War III, "a sort of world-revolution." She imagines that she and her fellow Europeans are buried in subterranean tunnels, having been forced underground by "the irrational assaults" of nuclear bombs that reverse the polarity of hell and heaven, such that the latter now lies beneath her. If World War II had failed to "submerge England" (to borrow her language), World War III accomplishes this submersion. In the depths of the Earth, national boundaries disappear—for "[g]eographic boundaries were bombed away," "Rotterdam, Warsaw, London—it was all one"—but people yet cling to them, persistently pledging allegiance to entities that no longer exist and fighting others amid the "avenues of scaffolds" demarcating this subterranean dystopia. She "lived through the horrors of inevitable plague, slavery of women and children, imprisonment and torture, the imprecations of the damned."[80]

Delia suffers a psychotic break at war's end, and H.D. herself endured an involuntary hospitalization in 1946. In *Sword*, H.D. may offer a fictionalized version of her own experience, making public a very personal, potentially embarrassing and degrading episode. In doing so, she is willing to exploit even the most private of experiences to illuminate her position on violence. Significantly, however, Delia's vision of World War III is never discussed in H.D.'s letters or journals as one that she had actually had; it appears only in *Sword* and is thus probably a fiction.[81] Moreover, none of these autobiographical accounts depicts a vision like Delia's in *Sword*, tied as it is to modern history and politics and bound up in apocalyptic imagery and logics. The fictionalized version of the illness in *Sword* is cast as prophecy, a vision of the future of Europe that serves as warning to the warmongers of the present day.[82] The content of the vision is terrifying, and the capacity for having visions is a damaging "gift."

In *Sword* and in H.D.'s later prose, as Jane Augustine notes, visions coincide with periods when she is unconscious or physically ill.[83] In the dream journal entitled *Hirslanden Notebooks* and in a 1961 diary, H.D. references a number of these experiences. In an entry dated January 28, 1957, H.D. recalls hearing about the death of J. J. van der Leeuw, another analysand of Freud, in September 1934. She notes that van der Leeuw's death inspired "a severe illness," during which she had, "half in delirium," talked to herself, "explaining, expounding this & that to the Professor [Freud]." Given H.D.'s infirmity after breaking her leg in 1956, the journal understandably contemplates other periods of "confinement," including her pregnancies, her near-death during the 1918-1919 Influenza Pandemic, and the periods of illness that came with age. In an entry dated February 1, 1957, she links a dream of Pennsylvania with a prophecy of her own death: "Did I want to go 'home' then? Was the feverish exaltation of the February–March 1919 'confinement,' a premonition of departure?" In May of 1961, upon hearing of the death of Lionel Durand, a journalist who had recently interviewed her, she speculates in her diary that she can access his pain in death while dreaming. She relates the tendency to experience visions while ill to the "*manic*-madness" of her therapist, Erich Heydt, in which he experienced supreme happiness: "What a pity, he had said, when he had to come back to earth."[84] In *Sword*, though, we expect a religious vision but get a political one.

Delia's vision might be construed as an escape attempt from a world structured by violence, war, and domination. But the form this vision takes is not accidental. H.D. employs this episode in *Sword* to make a statement about war, and the precise content of the vision may well have been inspired by

Freud's extended essay on Daniel Schreber. Indeed, during the war, H.D. had been reviewing and finalizing for publication her notes on her two bouts of sessions with Freud, and she may well have been rereading his writings and revisiting her arguments with his work as well. To Bryher, as discussed in my Introduction, H.D. refers to the state of confusion she suffered after electroshock treatment as "paranoia," "schiz," and "dementia praecox," the latter the precursor for what is now considered schizophrenia (Freud had been instrumental in changing the term). In 1911, Freud published his account of a patient he had never seen, basing his diagnosis of paranoia on Schreber's 1903 memoir. Schreber's book had detailed his periods of commitments to psychiatric institutions for psychosis, expounding at some length upon his visions.

While this case draws a great deal of scholarly attention today because of Freud's theory that paranoia is related to homosexuality, it is a different aspect of Schreber's hallucinations that may be relevant here. Freud had hypothesized earlier that paranoia is a defense mechanism of a kind, a form of projection, such that the ego, faced with conditions that cannot be integrated, resorts to "'hallucinatory confusion'": "the ego has fended off the incompatible idea through a flight into psychosis. . . . The ego breaks away from the incompatible idea; but the latter is inseparably connected with a piece of reality, so that, in so far as the ego achieves this result, it, too, has detached itself wholly or in part from reality."[85]

Schreber's particular vision entailed the belief that he had been called upon by God to redeem the world, and Freud notes that "[t]he Redeemer delusion is a phantasy that is familiar to us through the frequency with which it forms the nucleus of religious paranoia." Schreber, like Delia Alton, had an apocalyptic vision of the future of the world: "Schreber became convinced of the imminence of a great catastrophe, of the end of the world. Voices told him that the work of the past 14,000 years had now come to nothing." Freud concludes of this fantasy, "The end of the world is the projection of this internal catastrophe; his subjective world has come to an end since his withdrawal of his love from it." In this context, strikingly, Freud quotes several lines from Goethe's *Faust*, a book that was extremely important to H.D. in the late 1940s and plays a significant role in *The Mystery*: "Thou hast it destroyed, / The beautiful world, / With powerful fist!" Faust, Freud observes, also experiences a kind of detachment of the ego. And, just as significantly, he views this "*delusional formation*" as a positive stage toward "*recovery*" and "*reconstruction*." Distinguishing schizophrenia from paranoia, Freud explains that the paranoiac "invent[s] explanatory theories" and enjoys a better prognosis.[86] A postscript discusses the mythological importance of the eagle, an image H.D. returns to repeatedly in *Sword* and *White Rose*, a symbol of war carried by Julius Caesar into England, by medieval Crusaders into the Holy Land, and by Nazi soldiers during the Second World War.[87] There are, then, a number of resonances between Freud's essay creating the diagnosis of paranoia and H.D. writing about Delia's paranoia and her visionary experience.

H.D. would surely have been keenly interested in the historical overlap between mysticism and schizophrenia, but Delia's experiences are acutely painful, even destructive, in *Sword*. In Delia's vision, it is not just geography but time that shatters, and we will watch that process unfold in the next chapter: "Past, present and future became one. The distant past and the near past merged." This phrasing is familiar. It emulates the language of the prewar mystical encounters she narrates: time does not progress as history unfolds but, rather, it condenses or crystallizes into a singular point. But this vision is what impels the time traveling of "Summerdream," in which escaping the body does not afford transcendence and divine enlightenment to the seeker, as it had in the earlier fictions. Delia's vision is not, then, the apocalyptic cleansing and rebirth we are promised in *Trilogy*. Drawing a connection between this vision of mystical time and the passive model she perceives to be lying beneath it, Delia begins to intuit the dangers of spiritualism, astounded at how "contacting entities from outside must take it out of one," and certain that she "could never face such an ordeal again." She struggles with the passive nature of the spiritualist model of access to the ethereal plane, the loss of self it necessarily entails: "I was in the tragedy. I was no longer outside things, watching. I was inside. . . . I had merged my personality in the great drama. I had lost myself."[88] Missing as well is the heroic, indefatigable worm of *Trilogy*, edging towards metamorphosis, as Delia questions the paradigm of transformation implicit in the prewar model of mysticism: "I didn't want to find myself struggling to get out of a mangled cocoon, and then wading through ash and rubble."[89]

Mysticism in the 1930s had been a vehicle for moments of transcendence and enlightenment. The war, however, destroyed that model. In this novel, there is little hope for recovery from trauma at once private and public. *Sword* ends dismally at Westminster Abbey, on the anniversary of the Battle of Britain, with a book listing the London dead.[90] Ultimately, Delia discovers that time is not eternal, in the sense that it is an illusion. But, in another sense, it may as well be eternal, for time may elapse, but it also unrelentingly circles, spiraling back to war and violence. The past and the present and the future may not be the same, but they are alike: "It was the same story." And we cannot stop it. We are held hostage to history: "We went on with the play," she writes, "we went back to London." Experiences with astral projection through time had shown her that, "like a curtain before a play, the veil was drawn aside from time to time, and one looked on scenes of the near or far past or even of the future. Ruins were all around us."[91]

Like a play, a text is a construction. As she often does in her late career, H.D., through Delia, takes refuge in language. Delia toils throughout "Summerdream" to find hope in her expansive travels. Yes, she writes, "[t]here is negation, despair, disillusion running through." But she nonetheless imagines flattening out the spiritual map that is pleated like an accordion. "I mean to hope," Delia avers paradoxically, "when I was hopeless." Even if the world has fragmented into shards—shards depicted as hybrid monsters of war, "the wings of an eagle, the head of a lion and the claws of a dragon"—the remnants "spell something. They are the clue to the final answer."[92] The knowledge granted by the mystical experience comes through the attempt at reading the fragments and writing, even if that attempt is doomed to failure. The "dream" trumps reality not because we can escape into it but because we have bitter truths to learn from it.

Her quest, in effect, comes full circle. At the opening of the book, Delia's effort to focus narrowly on the private sphere was in service to her writing. It is, in the end, the writing that does matter, but it is writing that she learns must move beyond the personal. *Sword*, H.D. explains in 1950, was written for "the millions who directly or indirectly were participants in the war." More to the point, to Aldington she writes of *Sword* that "the 'message' [is] simply, that the world was, perhaps is and possibly will be 'crashing to extinction,' if these in authority . . . no matter where or who . . . don't stop smashing up things with fly-bombs, V2 and the ubiquitous (possibly) so-called 'atom.' They could do something with the atom—better than smashing cherry-orchards . . . that is all I am trying to put over. . . . WAR had got to stop. . . . This hope is not my last will and testament but it is a will and testament."[93] It is the writer's obligation to expose the truths she learned, however bleak, to bear witness—not (or not only) as a "writing cure" for herself but as testimony to be shared with others.

3

Märchen and Historical Fiction

> Even as every nation must draw together its legends into an epic,
> so must every nation crystallize its dreams in a fairy-tale.
> —Clemence Dane

> The historical novel is, in the first place, a novel;
> in the second place, it isn't history.
> —Alfred Döblin

> The past can neither add nor take away, I said,
> but now 'before' and 'after' challenge each other.
> —H.D., *Vale Ave*

The previous chapters began to explore how H.D.'s *The Sword Went Out to Sea* does not just play with genre but shatters all of its laws. Drawing on models from autobiography and the ghost story (as discussed in Chapter 1), and mysticism and science fiction (as examined in the previous chapter), I have argued that the first half of *Sword* interrogates narratives of self and struggles to represent an arrested historical temporality. In the second half of the book, H.D. draws on fairy tales and historical fiction, as she interlaces a barrage of vignettes concerned with the history of Britain; like Virginia Woolf in the World War II era, H.D. became interested in how to tell the story of Britain. Chapter 2 sought to illustrate how H.D.'s *Sword* draws on both mysticism and time-travel fiction to fracture the narrative form in order to emulate for her readers the experience of war. It is my contention that the effect of this fragmentation is to rip the story into shards that expose the history of British war and imperialism. Like her better-known late epic poems,

Trilogy and *Helen in Egypt*, this book, then, re-maps spatial and temporal realities. Though it begins with a thinly veiled autobiographical account of H.D.'s experiences in London during the Blitz, *Sword*'s narrative becomes increasingly unstable, spinning out centrifugally into vignettes very loosely autobiographical but ultimately historical.

Genre is grounded in repetition; it is the reiteration of certain conventions that define it. In Chapter 1, I argued that the autobiographical genre in a time of war will explode under the pressure of repetition. War resuscitates prior war, prior trauma, mirroring and layering the experiences, and the first half of H.D.'s book obsesses over this kind of repetition—the First and Second World Wars, a vision of a third—until the excess of repetition spills over the containers of the autobiographical genre, demanding other genres to direct its flow. In the second chapter, I contended that the unique structure of the text not only mimics the civilian experience of war but also exposes the utter futility of the narrators' attempts to step outside the London experience of World War II—to create for themselves a state of exception that defies the law of genre. Just as the Blitz, in the words of H.D.'s narrator, "did not fall and submerge England, but it branched off into rapids, currents and whirlpools of night and day attack,"[1] the words of her initially autobiographical text are channeled through other genres.

This chapter will argue that *Sword* tells the story of a nation in a way that simultaneously unravels national narratives. H.D.'s method, in the second half of *Sword*, is to exploit features of the fairy tale and historical fiction, and this chapter will look at the ways in which she both employs and undercuts these genres. The fairy tale is the genre H.D. describes as an "incontrovertible ... miracle" in *Tribute to Freud*; indeed, she sees Freud's work as grounded in the fairy tale.[2] H.D. does return to the folk of the pre-imperial past, just as Esty observes of other aging modernists in London, but primarily to the Germanic tradition, a surprising choice in the wake of Nazism. By bringing together *Märchen*—which are intentionally ahistorical—and historical fiction—which strives for an accurate representation of the past—H.D. poses questions of truth and authenticity in her construction of a broken narrative of Britain. Ultimately, I will show, H.D. locates nationhood in language and story rather than along axes of ethnicity, race, or geography. Jean Radford notes of other women's late modernist texts that "just as there is, clearly, more than one way of representing history and historical processes, there may be more than one conception of history in question."[3] H.D. agrees. By constructing a text of generic hybridity that deconstructs the myriad genres it deploys, she demonstrates the fictionality of nationhood and the impossibility of its representation.

At a fundamental level, the novel interrogates the nature of narrative and the utter failure of linear forms of narration, challenging as well the linearity and progressiveness of history. I have argued that H.D.'s *Sword* can be contextualized within Tyrus Miller's description of the satiric nature of late modernist novels and John Whittier-Ferguson's observation about late modernists' tendency to revisit their previous works. Here, the spiraling second half of *Sword* is privileged over the first in a way that critiques modernism's approach to time. The experience of the Second World War conjures memories from the first, so the narrative rapidly and frequently shifts back and forth between time periods, such that "the going backward and the going forward were going on together." It is the extremity—the excess—of this movement that points toward parody, but there is also self-criticism that may extend to other writers of the era. In a self-reflexive moment midway through "Wintersleep," Delia explicitly critiques what she has written so far, a thinly veiled autobiographical tale. The public and private spheres, she realizes, cannot be entirely separated from one another. Reflecting on the novel's composition to date, Delia writes, "I carefully outlined the first part of this true tale, before Christmas 1946. The straight line of the narrative satisfied my mind. As far as my mind was concerned, I had found the answer. I was satisfied." But upon rereading, she realizes that "the straight line of the narrative" of the first three chapters is inadequate to tell the story she wants to tell. In fact, "the true foundation-stone curves slightly. I had made no allowance for that." Comparing the story's foundation to the foundation of the Parthenon, she notes that it may "look straight," but it is not: "in fifth-century Athens, the actual straight line was curved, in the foundation of the most famous temple of antiquity and of all time."[4] Specifically, Delia critiques her earlier approaches to narrative. More broadly, H.D.'s novel critiques itself.

Delia rejects here a mimetic approach to writing narrative—"as it was built"—and resolves to invent instead a different kind of foundation, "curved slightly." The second half of the novel thus proceeds cyclically, for, as she writes in her decidedly more optimistic war *Trilogy*, "[l]ife advances in a spiral." As discussed in the last chapter, though, the "spiral" does not "advance," as our impulses toward violence and domination recur throughout time: "It had gone on in other countries, in other periods of history," Delia writes of war and the conquering of nations and nation-states. She analogizes Western Civilization to a "proverbial murderer" who is drawn "to the scene of the crime," forgetting the past and instigating war after war.[5] Having abandoned a linear narrative early on, the novel dispenses with any sense of conventional plot in its second half. In this way, arguably, it is structured more like poetry than a novel, though the language is not particularly lyrical. Richard Aldington, in fact, commenting on "Wintersleep," fears that H.D. will have trouble finding a publisher if she does not make it "'straight' fiction" that builds toward a climax.[6] In "Summerdream," the novel becomes more and more recursive, less and less linear. The culminating episode of the novel is a story within a story divulged in nonlinear fashion, narrated by one Delia-like figure to another, a younger double.

In the first half of "Wintersleep," then, Delia writes then attempts to rewrite the story by making it curve or spiral outward, from London to Philadelphia to the Yucatan of the Aztec Empire to ancient Greece during the Trojan War. The repudiation of Delia by male figures in London and Philadelphia is directly paralleled, as are the Aztecs and the Ancient Greeks. Still dissatisfied, Delia's second attempt is found in the second part of the novel, "Summerdream," in which she abandons the autobiographically based plot of her obsession with Howell and her séances with R.A.F. pilots. The "curve" outwardly broadens, so that mere parallels are not enough and a multiplicity of stories proliferates. Its time-traveling chapters are a series of what Delia terms *Märchen*, or fairy tales, cast as historical fiction that, taken together, tell the history of England through stories of military conquest. Delia "follow[s] our fairy-tale away from and back to London,"[7] turning to such historical moments as the burning of the Acropolis; the ancient Romans who, having conquered Greece, invade Britain; and Normandy on the eve of the Battle of Hastings. Whatever the setting, characters and events of "Summerdream" mirror each other in such a way that history is cyclical and not progressive, repeating patterns of violence.

Readers know that a certain degree of indecision and metacritical commentary is common in H.D.'s work, but the Second World War, as I argued in Chapter 1, only heightened her lack of faith in truth. *Majic Ring*, written during the war, declares at one point that Delia, as author, has "been an explorer, a path-finder," that she has "made a map or tried to make a map or to give some indication . . . as to where the path might be leading." But her assertion that she has actually produced a map quickly crumbles into a vague admission that she can merely "give some indication." Indeed, in this novel and in *Sword*, she is never really certain where she has been and where she is going. To represent this unstable journey, she has to "come back again, re-trace [her] steps, re-invoke the story, add an anecdote or repeat a 'message' and say, 'This happened, the path goes that way.'"[8] Both *Majic Ring* and *Sword* build by accretion, as each story revises the one before in an effort to establish an ever-elusive "path."

In *Sword*, H.D. devises a new form of novel, one that rests not on a firm foundation but a "curved" one, one that constantly critiques and revises itself. Exposing truth as illusory, this new novel form is at war with itself, telling stories of a nation, rejecting and replacing them, then circling back to a point of origin impossible to find. "Although I threw away the story," Delia notes, "it came back. It is the same story." It is the same and yet it cannot be. Though in *Sword* she insists at one point that "[t]he true tale was founded on a rock, it was the tale of redemption and regeneration, the tale of sacrifice"— a reference to Iphigenia, who was sacrificed by her father, Agamemnon, so that Greek ships could be afforded safe passage to Troy—the novel does not in fact offer a "true tale." Iphigenia was not in fact slaughtered in the version by H.D.'s favorite Greek dramatist, Euripides—she is magically transported from the scene—so there is no sacrifice, and thus no redemption or regeneration. The story of the Greek nation depends upon a sacrifice that, in fact, never occurred. Likewise, stories of a nation—stories of Britain—are not to be trusted. In fact, Delia admits, "I did not see the actual sequence of the story, nor its real foundation." Moreover, questions of truth are immaterial, as the story has not a "false foundation" but rather "a wrong one." A story cannot be "false," though it can be "wrong." Right and wrong are terms of ethics, not truth. Her beloved Greece is built on a curve; it is the dreaded Rome that is constructed with straight lines, its "new streets cut[ting] undeviating, straight lines."[9] As Rome founded England, the story of Britain, then, Delia implies, is "wrong."

These vignettes through which Delia's consciousness travels are grounded in very specific historical eras. Susan Stanford Friedman notes that H.D. was "[a]n avid reader of popular historical fiction"[10]; indeed, both H.D. and Bryher read and wrote historical novels. One of their particular favorites among historical novelists was their friend Katharine Burdekin (also known as Murray Constantine), whose narrators typically time-travel to previous eras, including that of *Burning Ring*, about a sculptor who travels back to the past; *Rebel Passion*, set in the twelfth century; *Venus in Scorpio*, set in eighteenth-century Versailles; and *Proud Man*, who travels back to 1930s England from a future era. Other historical novels H.D. owned and read comprise a diverse collection: E. M. Almedingen's *Frossia*, set during the Russian Revolution; Helen Beauclerk's *Mountain and the Tree*, set in pagan, ancient Greek, and early Christian periods; Louis Couperus's *The Comedians*, a story of ancient Rome that H.D. particularly enjoyed; Leonard Ehrlich's *God's Angry Man*, about radical abolitionist John Brown; Iris Morley's *Proud Paladin*, a cross-dressing romance set in the fourteenth century; D. L. Murray's *Folly Bridge*, about an eighteenth-century English poet; Zoé Oldenbourg's *The World Is Not Enough*, set in the medieval period; Mary Renault's *The King Must Die*, the story of Theseus; Howard Spring's *All the Day Long*, about Cornwall in the nineteenth century; Thornton Wilder's *Woman of Andros*, set in Ancient Greece; Valentine Williams's *Crouching Beast*, set in 1915 Constantinople; Constance Wright's *Chance for Glory*, a fictionalized account of the French Revolution; and Stark Young's *So Red the Rose*, set in the antebellum U.S. south. H.D. and Bryher often exchanged recommendations for, and commentary on, a range of other historical novels.

Sword's "Summerdream" opens in the present day in Switzerland with post-war reflections on "Wintersleep." The Swiss story closes with the realization that Delia is not unlike Coleridge's Ancient Mariner, doomed to walk the earth telling her story again and again. But the stories of the present in *Sword*, she realizes, are "frozen, final, static and irrevocable," so she declares that "the scene changes and I open a new book."[11] The narrative shifts abruptly to Ancient Greece, to the Acropolis in Athens, in the fifth century B.C.E., but the promise manifest in "a new book" is not realized. Athens is at war. In a scene that recalls the burning of printed books and periodicals during the Second World War, here Delia's female protagonist burns artifacts for fuel with her friend Pheidias, the sculptor of the statue of Athena around which the Parthenon was built. H.D. had fretted over the donation of paper to the war cause in the early 1940s; she memorializes this anxiety in *The Walls Do Not Fall* when she writes,

> yet give us, they still cry,
> give us books,
>
> folio, manuscript, old parchment
> will do for cartridge cases. . . .[12]

Noting that "these inviolate images belonged to the Eternal," *Sword*'s narrator suggests that war shifts our relationship to temporality; burning "the Eternal," it dooms us to live a reality bound to history. Pheidias has located a secret stash of artifacts beneath the foundation of the Parthenon. What is made visible in this secret place is the history of earlier civilizations and earlier wars: referencing landmarks nearly 1000 years old, the narrator observes, "The foundation of the old serpent temple had been levelled, but there was a still earlier temple underneath it. The earlier temple was built perhaps, at the time of the Cyclopean wall."[13] This is, of course, yet another reference to H.D.'s experience of the Blitz, in which the damage of the bombing exposes layers of architecture and history,

> ... another sliced wall
> where poor utensils show
> like rare objects in a museum. ...[14]

As the narrator feels caught in a labyrinth and unable to escape, the narrative shifts to the next setting, a playhouse at Delphi. The female protagonist of this brief episode is Day-star, who argues with the Greek leader Pericles—who built an empire—over her desire not to evacuate from Athens, a cognate for London, for safer ground. The scene morphs into another playhouse, in Renaissance England, as Day-star interacts with actors preparing for a performance with Queen Elizabeth and Essex in attendance. The time period H.D. has chosen is not marked by a devastating war; it does, however, evoke the beginnings of English imperial history, the subject of *By Avon River*.

Day-star becomes Stella, Julius Caesar's mistress, when the narrative shifts backwards in time to the "straight lines" of Ancient Rome, where we find her living in the countryside and awaiting Caesar's visit. When he arrives, she wishes to express her concerns to him about the Empire: "Rome had drained the resources of the country, taken our farmers from the fields, uprooted the old tradition."[15] Stella then moves forward in time to Normandy, on the eve of the 1066 invasion of England by William the Conqueror and the day before her wedding, events interestingly paralleled. Stella and an older woman, Rose, retreat so that Rose can instruct Stella on the politics of the historical moment through a story of lost love. The personal is the political in Rose's story within a story. The final chapter of *Sword* returns to the London of "Wintersleep," as Londoners gather in Westminster Abbey to remember the Battle of Britain. The vignettes have traced significant moments of crisis in the history of England while suggesting that there is still more to excavate. It is unclear, however, what is to come.

H.D referred to these episodes of "Summerdream" not as historical fiction, however, but as *Märchen*, the German word for fairy tale. To Aldington, she explained that *Sword* brings together the two genres: "Summerdream goes on into märchen or story-book world—with the same scene of the Round Table episode, taking place with variations, in Greece, Rome, Normandy etc."[16] H.D. was a devoted reader of the Grimm fairy tales and Andrew Lang's comprehensive anthologies of fairy tales from around the world, as well as stories of King Arthur's Camelot, W. R. Halliday's still-influential *Indo-European Folk-Tales and Greek Legends*, the French *Aucassin et Nicolette*, Denis de Rougemont's studies of Tristan and Iseult, William Morris's renditions of Icelandic folktales, and the experimental tales of Hermann Hesse. Arthurian legend plays a part in *Sword* and especially *White Rose and the Red*, which also relies upon Morris's tales. H.D. had read the Grimm tales in childhood, and expressed renewed interest in them as early as the spring of 1934; Pearson sent her an edition of the tales after the war. The Grimm tales in particular haunted H.D., as references to the stories are sprinkled throughout her correspondence over several decades.[17] In 1936, she traces her obsession to her childhood: "I have been re-working on the old Grimm saga.... Much of this is my buried Grimm consciousness, when I lay between two brothers in bed, and imbibed from a German nurse the immortal saga."[18] Her marginalia in her copy of de Rougemont's *Passion and Society* demonstrates her efforts to reconcile his discussion of Catharism and the Grimm tales.[19]

Historical fiction and fairy tale exist in an uneasy but generative dialogue in *Sword*. Many feminist scholars have noted the etymological connection between gender and genre, and fairy tales in particular have been viewed as stories more focused on women than men. As Lidia Curti observes of fantastical stories more broadly, "Mythical stories are fabulations of women, probably not created by women. In these narratives, as in other dominant discourses, they are used as metaphors.... History comes from discord, and discord comes from women."[20] Historical fiction, however, has been a male-centered genre focused on great historical figures. In George Dekker's influential account, "the historical romance was, above all, a modern version of the epic, hence a heroic and masculine genre."[21] Ruth Hoberman's study details how "[t]he requirements of the historical novel as a genre would seem to conflict with the exploration of women's roles in history" since most theorists of historical fiction demand a protagonist whose experience is perceived as representative and universal. "Bound by recorded history and their readers' notions of plausibility," she explains, "historical novelists are particularly likely to produce novels in which women are marginalized or powerless, novels that reinforce standard assumptions about women and women's role in history."[22] Perhaps for this reason, contemporary women novelists have been drawn to reimagining the genre, just as they have been attracted to rewriting the fairy tale.

Indeed, postmodernists have revitalized both genres in recent years. Horst Steinmetz has observed that, ironically, a loss of faith in history that followed the two world wars has fostered a renewed desire to tell stories of history—albeit stories that expose the failure of the genre to capture the past.[23] Linda Hutcheon's work on what she calls historiographic metafiction has spawned a great deal of scholarship on contemporary historical fiction, and two recent monographs by Cristina Bacchilega and Jessica Tiffin attest to the tremendous popularity of the postmodern fairy tale. But we do not usually think of modernists as having had much of an interest in either. Unlike myth, the fairy tale makes almost no appearances in high modernism, and the conventional narrative about modernism has writers of the period turning consciously away from the sweeping nineteenth-century historical epics, embracing instead highly experimental novels concerned more with the life of the individual mind than with the scene of cultural or political life. Recently, however, Marianne DeKoven has reminded us that we cannot easily extricate the novel form itself from history: "'The novel' is a genre that would not exist, or would not exist in the same way, without the foundational historical narratives of its rise . . . , its origins . . . , and its intimate historical connection to domesticity and gender."[24] Moreover, there does seem to be a distinction to be made between earlier and later phases of the modernist movement. Writers as diverse as Willa Cather, Virginia Woolf, Arna Bontemps, Ford Madox Ford, Laura Riding, Bryher, William Faulkner, Robert Graves, Joseph Conrad, and Mary Butts dabbled in the genre, typically late in their careers.

H.D. had been interested in historical fiction by the 1920s, and was returning to fairy tales by the 1930s. At first glance, the union of the two seems impossible. Fairy tales, after all, are distinctly ahistorical, espousing supposed universal values. "Fairy tale has no history," Jessica Tiffin states concisely; moreover, the fairy tale's universality is absolutely dependent upon "an illusion of decontextualization or lack of historicity."[25] Historical fiction, on the other hand, relies heavily on the authenticity of its illustrations of the past. Its readers and critics evaluate it on the basis of its faithfulness to historical accounts. As Fleishman insists, "the historical novel will stand in some relation to the habitual demand for truth, and it is here that a theory of the genre needs to begin."[26] However, as a genre, historical fiction navigates a precarious divide, situating a fictional narrative within a factual setting, and it is perhaps in this seeming paradox that H.D. finds a place for fairy tale. Alessandro Manzoni observes aptly and concisely in his early influential study of the genre that the historical novel "is a work impossible to achieve satisfactorily, because its premises are inherently contradictory."[27] In other words, the historical novel must be simultaneously and paradoxically true and untrue. As discussed above, autobiography similarly negotiates claims to truth and authenticity, so an autobiographical historical novel like *Sword* is doubly bound to truth claims. H.D.'s prose work in general compounds the theoretical complexities of historical fiction by interweaving two sets of factual events that are nonetheless fictionalized in order to tell what she sees as a timeless story, iterations of which recur throughout history. In the case of *Sword*, the universal quality of the fairy tale lends itself to the notion of the timeless story; the fairy tale is what offers the "symbolic universality" the historical novelist strives for but never attains.[28]

In *Sword*, each genre undercuts the other: historical fiction critiques the universalism of the fairy tale, while the fairy tale calls into question historical fiction's truth claims. "I knew the story," Delia asserts at one point, then quickly corrects herself, "I thought I knew the story."[29] The story cannot be known. The scenes of *Sword*, though entirely fictionalized, are realistic and often foreboding, but they are arranged out of chronological order, and leaps between eras are far from seamless. These vignettes do tell a kind of story of a nation as they bring together a scene from the Peloponnesian War, as Pericles pushes Athens into increasingly imperialist ventures; a dramatic portrayal of that era in which England becomes an imperial nation; and a scene in Normandy on the brink of invading England. If fairy tales efface the political,[30] *Sword*'s Märchen highlight it. And yet, as with fairy tales, there are lessons to be gleaned from "Summerdream." The second half of *Sword* defies that sense of universality fairy tales so famously invoke, even as it flies in the face of the demands of historical accuracy, blatantly fictionalizing the past and reordering its events.

In her insistence on historical setting and situation, H.D. works against one of the aspects of the fairy tale that is most inviting to readers, "the tension between the clear, transparent and easily understandable course of the story and the unexplained."[31] As Tiffin remarks, "Participation in the marvelous universe of fairy tale—the enjoyment of the wonder fairy tale can evoke— depends entirely on recognition of the artificiality of that universe." Readers must "refrain from attempting to connect the fairy-tale realm with a particular historical reality."[32] By injecting historical fiction into the genre, though, H.D. reminds readers that while the story may not be true—while stories cannot be true—horrific events of the past nonetheless did occur. When we read a vignette, we cannot "dismiss it as children's fantasy."[33] These are tales for adults. They make use of the genre only to parody it. Just as she had with the time-travel genre, then, H.D. foregrounds the specific historicity of the settings to deprive her readers of the pleasures afforded by this genre.

In approaching history through fairy tale, H.D.'s *Sword* begins to move toward the postmodern, or the late modern as Tyrus Miller defines it. Linda Hutcheon's term *historiographic metafiction* may well be the most apt, for it describes postmodern historical fiction that "refuses the view that only history has a truth claim, both by questioning the ground of that claim in historiography and by asserting that both history and fiction are discourses, human constructs, signifying systems, and both derive their major claim to truth from that identity."[34] As Naomi Jacobs argues further, postmodern historical fiction not only takes liberties with historical accuracy but introduces the fantastical, such that "no sensible reader can accept them as direct accounts of literal reality. . . . They offer not a rational reconstruction or re-creation of history but a new creation."[35] The problem with the whole notion of historical accuracy stems from ignoring the impact of what Tony Myers calls the "vertiginous thrall to the present": "without the 'otherness' of the past we have nothing against which to define the now. We are thus besieged by a 'nowness' for which we can prescribe no limits."[36] As Walter Benjamin had argued in his *Theses*, the present is viewed as a moment on a timeline—"like the beads of a rosary"—and not as having a constitutive role in our understanding of the past. "History," he contends, "is the subject of a structure whose site is not homogeneous empty time, but time filled by the presence of the now."[37]

History is an other to us, and this foreignness of the past destabilizes even traditional historical fiction, but postmodern historical fiction exposes these fissures. To accomplish a critique of how we tell stories of the past, H.D.'s *Sword* employs fictional elements such as an intrusive and unreliable narrator and stories within stories that offer alternative focalizations, as well as narrative fragmentation and disjunctive chronology; it also makes use of the features of fairy tales, the metafictional qualities of which serve to erode further any sense of reassurance. Jessica Tiffin describes in some detail how the modern fairy tale makes particular use of this facet of the genre, which troubles any lines drawn between fiction and reality: "Fairy tale itself . . . exhibits a self-awareness about narrative and a specifically problematized relationship with reality." The seemingly omniscient narrator of the fairy tale is not in fact unbiased in many postmodern fairy tales, which, as a genre, "has no real interest in human subjectivity or psychological characterization of the individual."[38] The fairy tale is not character-driven, but historical fiction is: "[t]he historical novel is pre-eminently suited to telling how individual lives were shaped at specific moments of history," according to Fleishman.[39] *Sword*'s "Summerdream" marks the shift from a focus on self in the mimetic autobiography of "Wintersleep" to a focus on the militaristic settings and situations rendered largely, like fairy tales and folktales, without the presence of an acknowledged author. What "Summerdream" has instead is "a series of narrators whose relationship to the tales is both intimate and detached."[40] *Sword* employs this device extensively throughout "Summerdream," both in the recurrent intrusions of Delia's voice that attempt to link the disparate historical narratives and in the myriad focalizers through which these narratives are filtered. The insertion of such distance between narrator and focalizers reveals the unreliability of these multiple perspectives, as Bacchilega notes of the tale.[41] Indeed, the genre as a whole is "profoundly unstable," according to Stephen Benson, because it is based in an oral culture and its text is malleable, its tales told and retold—expanded and adapted—by a range of communities.[42]

    H.D. exploits this instability. Hutcheon notes that works of historiographic metafiction "tend to fragment or at least to render unstable the traditional unified identity or subjectivity of character" by either introducing multiple points of view or making use of a hyper-controlling narrator.[43] *Sword* uses both strategies. Working against reader immersion, Delia's voice intrudes insistently between each of the historically grounded stories, reminding readers that these are fictions, that there is a present time outside of these stories, and that she is guiding us. As the narrative shifts from the initial episode with Pheidias to the temple-players at Delphi, the "I" of "Summerdream" reemerges. Delia explains what she has learned: "I had seen the end. Now I saw the beginning. It was Pheidias who helped me to remember." Traveling to Elizabethan London, Delia apologizes for our abrupt departure from ancient Greece: "It would be impossible to deal with the entire sequence.... It was difficult enough to follow the threads, disentangle and re-work them for those three panels, scenes or pictures." Chapter VIII is entirely in Delia's voice, as she lays out a theory of time and time travel that will accommodate her movements to and from ancient Greece, Renaissance England, ancient Rome, and present-day Switzerland and Italy: "We followed the Z or the bee-line in its zig-zag track or path across time. Time was conveniently pleated and the pleats lay flat under the chart or map that took us from London to Lausanne, to Lugano, to Knossos, to Athens, to Delphi... back to London, to Venice.... [T]his bee-line or Z-line has this advantage over time, time is neatly folded; the pleats are disproportionate, it is true, but under the Z-map, no-one will notice. It is very easy to understand this, if you like fairy-tales or *Märchen*." In the following chapter, though her journey is far from over, she pauses before traveling reluctantly to Rome, acknowledging that "[t]here is negation, despair, disillusion running through it." Arriving in Rome, Delia expresses her dismay before giving the narrative voice over to Stella, Caesar's mistress: "Rome—I can hardly bring myself to write it."[44]

The novel ends in Delia's voice, after Stella's time in 1066 Normandy. We are rarely afforded the opportunity to lose ourselves in a historical narrative. Delia constantly has to remind us where we are and where we have been. Moreover, in addition to Delia's voice, we have the various principal narrators of each vignette, female characters who sometimes share the same name—Stella is a character in ancient Rome and in medieval France—and sometimes do not. But there are also stories within stories, told by figures who are not the protagonists of the episodes: stewards and female characters who are not the protagonists are afforded lengthy passages, even chapters, of their own. *Sword* tells "history from below." It is not the famous men, the victors, who control the narrative of war and domination, but rather those who rarely occupy such positions in history's annals. When one "[s]hift[s] the angle of vision away from the powerful," Hoberman remarks, "history as a self-justifying organic movement into the future dissolves into an open-ended story that refuses to coalesce."[45] Characters who tell stories within stories in *Sword* are either of a lower class status or are exiles or disenfranchised outsiders to the broad historical crises in which they find themselves. In ancient Athens, Pheidias explains to the protagonist the burning of artifacts, for instance, and later a steward explains to her the political situation of the Peloponnesian War. It is a Roman steward who tells the story of Rome's colonization of Britain in Chapter XI; his concern is what kind of herbs and other flora will grow there so that he can send needed plants to the new colony.[46] In Chapter XIII, Stella's voice is ceded to another woman, Rose, who instructs Stella about the imminent Norman invasion of England. Rose's story is told out of order, but it is this story that helps readers see the thread that has connected all of these "Z-line" pathways of our travels. We and Stella can understand "Summerdream" as a history of Britain. In this way, "Summerdream" distributes and diffuses narrative authority.

Sword further fragments the narrative in its rearrangement of historical events in defiance of chronological time. The various episodes shift from scenes of the ancient world to modern Europe to the medieval period. In this way the narrative more closely resembles those of women writers Hoberman discusses who favor a model of history not as overarching metanarrative but as "a collection of disparate details," or of Richard Murphy's avant-garde modernists who use an "open, and eminently *reversible*, montage form precisely in order to oppose the strict linearity and causality of conventional narrativisation."[47] Indeed, disordering chronology disrupts the sense of causality implicit in historical narrative, such that the timeline of history comprises a series of ruptures and not a sweeping, linear upward progress. The invasion of Normandy in 1066, for instance, does not lead to the explorations of the New World by Queen Elizabeth I. Rather, these individual moments are discrete, repeating a cycle of domination and militarism regardless of what has transpired in the past or what the future holds. Though historically grounded, these vignettes are isolated in time like fairy tales. However, the individual tales told in "Summerdream" lack the beginnings and endings we associate with traditional fairy tales. Likewise, as Hutcheon notes, traditional historical fiction "imposes a meaning on the past and does so by postulating an end (and/or origin)."[48] In the final story within a story, Stella's description of Rose's tale illustrates well H.D.'s method for the second half of *Sword*: "She told me the story. She did not tell it to me all at once, and she did not tell it, straight through, from the beginning to the end. She told me different parts of the story at different times."[49]

The inevitability of violence wreaked by a nation-state, or proto-nation-state, then, casts a cloud over *Sword*. Rose's tale will not—cannot—change the outcome of the next day's battle. While the fairy tale's plot appears to be premised on free will—a character's decision determines absolutely the outcome of the story—the tales of "Summerdream" relate a world without choices. In fact, Benson contends that "the folktale, as narrative, is 'both free and controlled at the same time: free (for the narrator must at every moment choose the continuation of his story) and controlled (for the narrator's only choice, after each option, is between the two discontinuous and contradictory terms of an alternative')."[50] Characters' fates depend on their choices, and yet part of the pleasure of the tale depends on the readers' knowledge of the inevitable outcome. The choices of fairy tale characters have to be circumscribed and predictable, or the tale is no longer a fairy tale at all. Cinderella and Snow White will find their princes, the bears of Goldilocks and the wolf of "The Three Little Pigs" will enjoy success after three attempts have been made, and Red Riding Hood will uncover the wolf's identity.

In this sense, the genre resonates with historical fiction, which presents characters who only seem to have choices within a universe that is fixed historically. H.D. has chosen genres that expose free will as an illusion to represent the experience of war. It is also significant that she is not content with the time-travel genre, perhaps because time-travel narratives tend to offer choices and alternatives: a "multitude of possible parallel times, of time going at different paces or even in different directions in separate worlds."[51] The world of the fairy tale is narrow and confined. When Delia attempts escape through time travel, she becomes stuck in a series of harrowing tales of the past with no way out, no endings, only recursion. This paradox, of course, is one of the sites of incongruity between modernism as an aesthetic movement and historical fiction as a genre. Temporally bound, "true" accounts of the past seem to belong to the deterministic world of realism or naturalism, not modernism. For the modernist who has lost faith in notions of historical authenticity, "[h]istory has become a burden, from which one wishes to be and must be liberated."[52]

Both historical fiction and the fairy tale (with its origins in folklore) are genres that concern the construction of nation, and stories of nation depend upon teleology and causality, which the disordered multiple frames of *Sword* deny. Playing on several structural elements of the fairy tale, H.D. deliberately refuses mimesis as representation, even as she offers believable historical contexts that themselves seem to rely on mimesis. Using the two genres in tandem, she will tell the stories of a nation in a way that undermines the telling, and to do so she resists teleological stories of nation. As Elisabeth Wesseling has argued, there are political implications to the teleological nature of stories of nation-building: "If historical discourse tacitly depicts history as an objective process with an inherent forward motion and purpose of its own, then any particular status quo is to be regarded as the inevitable outcome of an inexorable development . . . to whose extension into the future we must accede. For this reason, the seizure and subsequent stabilization of power is often accompanied by the rewriting of history."[53] In the story of a nation, we expect a story of origins, but, as in historical fiction, the beginnings of these "Summerdream" stories are selected by the narrator. For each of *Sword*'s *Märchen*, we are dropped *in medias res*, a decision that creates confusion on the part of the reader who must figure out not only the historical setting but also the relationship between the characters and the action already taking place. We cannot easily locate the origins of nation either, she implies. We cannot look to ethnicity, race, even geographical cues, because a nation is built on story. It is not natural or inevitable. If we have origin, we have a timeline, and we can predict future possibilities, but the stories of *Sword*, in their centrifugal movement, highlight the failure of linear chronological time—the "straight line of the narrative"—to depict a nation. As many postcolonial scholars have shown, realist fiction relies upon origins and teleology in imaginatively constructing the nation; here H.D. turns to a fantastical genre for *Sword*, even while she tempers it with historical fiction. She wants historicity but not certainty; she presents not tales of the past (the tales are fictional) but representations of the past (they are also historically grounded).

Thus, there can be no "happily ever after" in *Sword*. Fairy tales traditionally "illuminated the possible fulfilment of utopian longings and wishes";[54] more specifically, though, they have an "ability to give a deeply satisfying and utopian gloss to assumptions about society, power, and gender which are often profoundly reactionary."[55] It is through utopic content and structure that fairy tales come to embody the hopes of a nation, that they define a nation by its dreams, that they identify a nation and its people as heroic or benevolent. But H.D.'s *Märchen* dispel hope for a better future, just as the postmodern tales Tiffin describes do when "the somewhat utopian notion of structure is invoked only to be explored and disrupted, either playfully or radically, or both."[56] In denying happy endings—indeed, any endings at all—H.D. is withholding from her readers any pleasure offered by conventional fairy tales. Bacchilega argues cogently that the fairy tale works because it mediates between a conservative comfort in consensus and an ending invested in transformation.[57] "Summerdream," which constantly rewrites its own story, refutes "the powers of transformation." Precious artifacts are still burned in ancient Athens, Stella reaches no resolution with Caesar, and Day-star stands up to Pericles but the war continues. It denies readers of historical fiction the pleasure of achieving closure. As Hoberman suggests, "Historical discourse... loves death because it loves endings. No matter how sad, the ending always feels good, because it is what the reader has been waiting for."[58]

In addition to the Grimm collection, H.D. owned and read seven of Lang's twelve "Fairy Books" volumes.[59] Lang was an Oxford-educated Scottish writer, translator, and folklorist. He also presided over the Society for Psychical Research for a time, so H.D. shared his interest not just in the fantastical but the paranormal. In *Sword*, Delia notes that Lang's books were at least part of the foundation of the novel: "Andrew Lang was my springboard."[60] H.D. no doubt appreciated that Lang was trying to legitimate fairy tales as a genre, just as Halliday was when he consistently referred to them as "artistic." They both aimed to revise notions of fairy tales as mere "degenerate forms of cosmological myths."[61] However, Lang's "Fairy Books"—which amassed stories from around the world—are not an ideal source for a critique of war and imperialism. As Sara Hines has argued, "The Fairy Books... effectually allow British readers to collect, possess, and display the empire through ownership of 'outlandish native stories.' They may contain stories of other places, other peoples, and other cultures, but the stories have been collected, translated, and edited specifically so that white people will like them and are meant to be read from the safety and security of the British home."[62] These are not the kinds of tales H.D. wants to tell.

Strikingly, in these chapters H.D. is tacitly critiquing her more nostalgic writings about Ancient Greece, her early poetry and her earlier historical fiction in which she casts herself as a Greek victim of Roman colonization. As she does in *Trilogy*, H.D. pushes further back in history to uncover more and more cycles of warfare. Her narrator describes the horror of the sacking of Troy by the Greeks in language that must surely recall the German V-2 bombing of London during the war: "the Greeks had descended from their head-lands, master of a new war-weapon and a new technique, and attacked a defenceless people without warning. They plundered and wantonly destroyed perhaps the most beautiful city, outside legend and mythology, the world has ever known." She then critiques not just the merciless actions of the Greeks but their later attempts to represent themselves favorably in their stories of the war: "But even the legendary Homer did not give the real facts," she avers. She offers a corrective narrative that indicts the Greeks while yet pointing out that the Trojans were not innocent either: "A city, a civilization had been destroyed. It was not Greek but it was allied to Greece—or rather, it had colonized the mainland before the so-called Greeks arrived there.... The Greeks went back, drawn like the proverbial murderer, to the scene of the crime." In the end, she grieves that "[w]e had learned nothing from the warriors of the new iron-age, the new war-age."[63] Britain, too, itself a violent colonizer of the New World, had been colonized in the past. In this initial historical vignette, Greece is also criticized for its imperialism and for its hierarchical system of slavery, practices that undermine any stable identificatory relationship to nationality. H.D.'s narrator poses a question she cannot answer definitively: "What is Greek?" The nation can only be articulated discursively, in language, as when a long speech to Pericles is described as having "summed up a nation." In like manner, *Sword* interrogates Roman identity as it focuses on Caesar's role in shifting the Roman Republic into a Roman Empire, a plan that encompassed the colonization of Britannia. "[Y]ou might say that the legions of Caesar consolidated Arthur's kingdom," Rose explains to Stella. The Normans will invade now that "Normandy's Britain had been abandoned by Rome."[64]

So it is not to Lang, a British collector, that H.D. turns primarily for a model of a fairy tale in *Sword*. Rather, it is Hermann Hesse's German-Swiss fairy tales that most resonate with the vignettes of "Summerdream." H.D. immersed herself in reading works of German Romanticism after World War II, and the German fairy tale is central to that movement.[65] As H.D. began to settle into permanent residence in Switzerland, she was excited to learn of the close proximity of Hesse—she dubs it "Hesse country"[66]—whose books she read voraciously. In the year of *Sword*'s composition, she initiated a correspondence with Hesse and his wife, visiting them later in the decade; Hesse was to review positively the German-language edition of *By Avon River*, which came out in 1955, and he is referenced briefly in *Sword* when she imagines traveling to see him. H.D.'s initial enthusiasm with Hesse is sparked late in 1946, after her hospitalization and shock treatments, when she discovers a German-language edition of his *Märchen*, written "in the great, simple, dream-tradition." "It is sheer dope to me," she writes excitedly to Bryher, gushing that "I am absorbing Hesse & find so many new-old worlds & ideas, these contemporary *Märchen* feed my soul." "The books have opened up new vistas & re-established the old," she affirms.

Reassuring Bryher, who had been acutely concerned with H.D.'s psychological health, H.D. praises Hesse's "insistence on beauty & the beautiful mountains, lakes, woods, gardens & trees, regardless of the boundaries."[67] But his tales are much darker than H.D. represents them, and, unlike Lang's or Grimm's tales, Hesse's *Märchen* pointedly critique science, war, imperialism, and commercialism.[68] H.D. appreciates, too, Hesse's complicated relationship to nationality; to Bryher, she explains that "his grand-mother was French & his grand-father connected with Ceylon, Siam & Indian affairs, in some way, & his mother was born in the East," and to Aldington she writes that "[h]e is Swiss.... mixed, one grandmother French and Russian Baltic-grand-father, I think and connections with oriental linguistics and/or missionaries in Indies."[69]

In using Hesse as a model, she employs a genre inherently nostalgic,[70] then turns it back on itself, supplanting utopic gestures with dystopic leanings. Hesse's tales are darker, more sinister, more surreal than the fairy tales to which we are more accustomed, and his frequent focus on violence and war may have appealed to her more than stories of princes and princesses did. Jack Zipes argues that Hesse was not a collector but a sincere reader of the literature of the East, and he lauds Hesse's characters as outsiders—"loners, rebels, poets, intellectuals, painters, and eccentrics": "It was in order to commemorate the struggles of such marginal types who survive on the fringes of society, alienated by the increase of industrialization and capitalism, that Hesse experimented with the fairy-tale genre." These characters exist in exile, and Hesse portrays them as victims of materialism and warfare. Zipes contends that Hesse "was convinced that the divisive forces of technology, nationalism, totalitarianism, and capitalism were most detrimental to individual freedom and peaceful coexistence." Though he does not set his tales in specific historical periods, as H.D. does, he does inject a certain degree of realism into the tales, according to Zipes.[71] Hesse's authoring of these pacifist tales just before and during World War I led to his ostracism in Germany.

There is no "happily ever after" in Hesse's tales, and his narrators experience bliss but also "ecstatic pain." Hesse's story "Faldum" warns readers of the consequences of greed. "The City" recounts the story of class revolt in a global economy. The imperializing citizens of "The City" lose everything when they realize that they "had nothing more to build and conquer," so poets, scholars, and artists revive "The City," raising it from the ashes of war and conflict. "A Dream about the Gods" depicts vividly an experience of war in which "[t]he world was sinking" and "walls were falling and splitting apart." The narrator imagines that he can "build new and more beautiful things" to replace the crass materialist urban center full of "junk." In "The European," the gods send a flood to cleanse a war-torn world, "clear[ing] away the rotting corpses, along with those people who wept for them." Only one European remains, and he is rescued by an African patriarch who instructs his people that "[y]ou all have a great deal to forgive these white men. They are the ones who ruined our poor earth and made it into a criminal court once again."[72]

"The Empire" is a parable of greed and imperialism. It narrates a story of a country that was content and culturally rich until an industrial revolution made it avaricious and imperial. When "not much more remained to rob and acquire," the victims build weapons and rise up against "The Empire." "All this came to an end in the Great War," Hesse writes, "which caused such terrible havoc and destruction in the world and among whose ruins we are now standing, bewildered by its noise, embittered by its senselessness, and sick from its streams of blood that flow through all our dreams." This story seems tied to World War I Germany, as Hesse admits sadly that "[t]he empire cannot become a child again. Nobody can. It cannot simply give away its cannons, machines, and money and once again write poems in small peaceful cities and play sonatas." Nonetheless, the narrator hopes that the devastated nation "can recall its previous past, its heritage and childhood, its maturation, its rise and all."[73] The gesture may be nostalgic in a way that H.D. may not endorse, for texts such as *The Walls Do Not Fall* and *Sword* seem to indicate that there is no moment without war, no matter how far you reach into the past. But she, too, embraced German Romanticism, and Hesse's focus on maintaining cultural memory certainly resonates with that of H.D.'s writings during and after the Second World War.

In a story that bears significant resemblance to H.D.'s "Summerdream," Hesse's "If the War Continues" tells the story of a world in a seemingly permanent state of war and a man who escapes periodically into altered states to protect his psyche from the trauma. Like H.D.'s time travelers, he "left the realm in which we live and was a guest in distant parts for a long time, speeding through people and eras," and also like her time travelers in exile, the experience only increases his sense of hopelessness. In his mental travels, he sees "nothing but the usual tribulations, trade, progress, and improvements on earth" and is forced back into the present day of war each time. His view of war is bleak, and over time "[t]he limited imagination of the generals and the technicians had led to the invention of a few more weapons of annihilation." Arrested for not carrying proper identification, the narrator is told that "[w]ar is the only thing that we still have! Pleasure and personal gain, social ambition, greed, love, intellectual work—all this no longer exists. War is the one and only activity for which we are grateful. It still gives us something like order, law, thought, and spirit in the world."[74] He again retreats grimly into the cosmos to start a new cycle.

Traditional folk and fairy tales often employ time travel in order to proffer opportunities for a narrator's spiritual enlightenment and wisdom.[75] Hesse's "Strange News from Another Star" features another protagonist who is whisked away to an alternate dimension. This protagonist, however, travels to a state of war, a war that is quite literally never-ending. His account of this foreign world is harrowing: "Everything here was like a horror story. This whole strange world of atrocity, corpses, and vultures seemed to have no meaning or order. In fact, it seemed subject to incomprehensible laws, insane laws, according to which bad, foolish, and nasty things occurred instead of beautiful and good things." The war has been going on so long that its soldiers have no sense of its origins or purpose: "The war is nobody's fault. It occurs by itself, like thunder and lightning," explains one combatant, who is also a king. "All of us who must fight wars are not the perpetrators. We are only their victims." War is truly self-perpetuating: "Nobody kills out of hate or envy. Rather, they do what society demands of them."[76] Hesse appears to leave us with a shred of hope when the king says that the narrator's presence will help him try to remember that there is a larger world outside his own reality—"I'll think of the world as a whole, and how our folly and fury and ruthlessness cannot separate us from it"—but in the end, the protagonist's memory of the horrific event is erased and nothing is learned.

In *Within the Walls*, H.D. seems to share Hesse's dark vision of the fairy tale when she remarks that the Blitz has awakened memories of past trauma: "[T]error deeply felt in childhood, submerged terror or half-submerged, is tapped by this supreme terror that is always with us. Tales in fairy-books or a chance glimpse of illustrations in The Book of Martyrs or some picture from our illustrated Gustav Doré bible or the Ancient Mariner which we spread open, before we could read, on our grandmother's carpet, seared deeply, awakened one's mind to the actual reality of death."[77] H.D., like Hesse, spins a fairy tale into a twisted, bleak, foreboding story. His tales parody those of the European tradition with which we are perhaps most familiar, those of the Grimm brothers. Perched always on the precipice of violent encounter, her tales reject utopic desires, the promise for a better future, and any nostalgia that Esty describes among late modernist "English intellectuals" who "translated the end of empire into a resurgent concept of national culture."[78] If Woolf, Forster, and Eliot attach "social and aesthetic renewal" to a revivified nationalism,[79] the narrators of H.D.'s hybrid text refuse this "anthropological turn." Hutcheon's historiographic metafiction is "willfully unencumbered by nostalgia in its critical, dialogical reviewing of the forms, contexts, and values of the past."[80] For her audience, H.D. has replaced what one fairy tale scholar as termed "access to the collective, if fictionalized past of social communing"[81] with a sense of shared responsibility and guilt for historical acts of aggression and conquest. And yet H.D. has also suggested that this kind of violence is inevitable, that humans will always commit acts of atrocity.

Genre fiction relies upon repetition. Historical fiction re-presents the past, while the fairy tale employs repetition excessively; think, for instance, of the repeated attempts of the wolf to destroy the three little pigs' house, or the succession of observations Red Riding Hood makes of the lupine features of her supposed grandmother. Fairy tales are not just repetitive across stories but repetitive within them. And repetition is at once a symptom of trauma and central to H.D.'s method of representation in *Sword*. When *Sword*'s narrative breaks apart under the weight of autobiographical excess, it spins tales excessively repetitive. As Cristina Bacchilega observes of the postmodern fairy tale, "repetition functions as reassurance within the tale, but this very same compulsion to repeat the tale explodes its coherence as well-made artifice."[82] The excess reminds us constantly that the narrative we are reading is fictive. I noted in Chapter 2 the extent to which H.D. torments her readers in efforts to help them experience the radical instability of the war; likewise, here she taunts her readers with a genre structured by reassurance only to expose that repetition as a fiction. About postmodern fairy tales, Tiffin observes that "the mixing of fairy tale with other genres is not about clash as much as it is about diffusion, reinforcement, and echo."[83] While the conventions of fairy tale and historical narrative are not the same, they work together in "Summerdream" to "reinforce" an inescapable instability.

Sword is a recursive text, rewriting stories and rewriting the self before circling back on itself. H.D. does not entirely embrace postmodernism; if postmodernists claim that "history has become irrelevant, and can teach its victors nothing more,"[84] *Sword* ultimately veers from such a position. It is the fairy tale, and its convention of teaching a life lesson or moral, that undercuts it. But *Sword* is certainly a liminal text caught between modernism and postmodernism. In that sense, it is very much a late modernist text as Tyrus Miller defines it, a parodic text that brings multiple genres and modes into dialogue with one another even as they critique one another—autobiography, mystical and spiritualist writings, ghost stories, time-travel narratives, fairy tales, historical fiction. Moreover, H.D. does not permit the comfort repetition affords to the reader of the fairy tale and other genres.[85] In *Sword*, repetition of similar traumatic events is stressed to the point of breaking, so that the narrative seems to implode under its pressure; it is Delia's obsession with overlaying specific wars and betrayals that prompts her psychotic break in the first half of the book.

Though the first part of this book has focused entirely on *Sword* as a text that exposes a dramatic shift in H.D.'s thinking about the politics of the modern world and its representation through language, this is not the only book that makes use of a "diffusion" and "echo" of genres and modes. *The Gift*, written during the war, interrupts autobiographical fiction of her childhood with a jarring present-day account of the Blitz, using the image of fire to connect the passages. *Majic Ring*, also composed in the early 1940s, moves from the epistolary mode to narrative journal entries as Delia recedes more and more into isolation. The subjects of the next two chapters, *By Avon River* and *White Rose and the Red*, also engage multiple genres: the former in its wedding of verse with literary criticism, and the latter—in which the protagonist wishes to write "a sort of fairy-tale, she supposed, but with prayers"[86]—in its union of autobiographical fiction and historical narrative. *The Mystery* (finished in 1951) brings together time travel and historical fiction. The subject of Chapter 8 is the late 1950s fiction, in which the spy genre is featured.

During and after the Second World War, H.D. employs a vast range of genres, devices, and methods to narrativize the trauma of violence and its recursive effects and to problematize narrative itself. Part II of this book examines what results from this shift in her thinking. The next two chapters address specifically her critique of European nationalism and imperialism, while the final chapters of Part III turn to how her 1950s writings reconceptualize her ethical stance in the final years of her life. If Antonius of *The Mystery* imagines that there could be "a formula that fitted history,"[87] it becomes clear that, late in life, H.D. loses faith in such an ideal. Instead, she meditates upon representations of the trauma of history and our responses to it.

PART II

Critique

Gendered Narratives of Nation and Imperialism

Frankly, I am torn between anglo-philia and anglo-phobia.
—H.D., as Delia Alton

4

By Avon River, Arranged Marriage, and Shakespeare's Empire

> [T]here is a strangeness about the fact that she here speaks of England rather than of the Greece which she has interpreted so very well.
> —A review of *By Avon River*

> Kisses bear marks of former ornament,
> as coins repeat the heads of King or Victory.
> —H.D., *Pilate's Wife*

The two books that H.D. wrote immediately before and after the devastatingly pessimistic *Sword* continue to subvert generic expectations, though not to the same extent. Alongside a distorted narrative of Britain that presents a seemingly endless series of nations conquering and colonizing one another, H.D. composed two gendered critiques of English nationalism and imperialism in the same period: *By Avon River* (completed in 1945–1946) and *White Rose and the Red* (written in 1947–1948). With *Trilogy*, H.D. had finally retired the small, sparse Imagist lyrics for which she was best known, and had turned to lengthier poetic forms. The composition of *By Avon River*, I would contend, launches a new phase of H.D.'s career, for H.D. herself considered the text a turning point. Though she had published multiple books of poetry and prose by the mid-1940s, she writes to a friend that while she is proud of her epic war poem *Trilogy*, *By Avon River* "is the first BOOK I have had": "Though our darling AVON is slim, it seems to contain really, the whole of me, not an intense cerebral ice-edge merely."[1] She is no longer only a poet of cold, crystalline lyrics. Indeed, she exclaims to Pearson that "I had crossed literally my Rubicon, albeit AVON y-clept!"[2]

Having survived the Blitz, H.D. traveled at the close of World War II from London to Stratford-upon-Avon to visit Shakespeare's tomb in Holy Trinity Church and the gardens of New Place, the lavish home he purchased in 1597. The result of this pilgrimage, *By Avon River*, is a hybrid volume of poetry about Shakespeare's *The Tempest* and prose about him and his contemporaries. Part I, entitled "Good Frend," a phrase from Shakespeare's epitaph, revives Claribel from *The Tempest*, the unfortunate daughter of Alonso whose arranged marriage to the King of Tunis instigates the action of the play; the shipwreck survivors are among those traveling home from her wedding when they are waylaid by the rage of Prospero's storm. The second part of the book, entitled "The Guest," is a mix of critical commentary on Shakespeare's contemporaries, fictionalized episodes imagining Shakespeare at home in Stratford towards the end of his life, and a brief literary history of England from the time of Richard the Lionhearted until Shakespeare's death. Once published, H.D. reportedly carried this volume around with her "for re-reading and memorizing": "I am almost 63 & have been writing for 40 years but *Avon* is the first book that really made me happy," she wrote to a friend after its publication.[3] In fact, when the book arrived, she gushed that "I am prouder than Elizabeth with young Charles!"[4]

To careful readers of *By Avon River*, these remarks—those conflations of herself with England's conqueror, Julius Caesar, and with the woman who was soon to become Queen Elizabeth II[5]—are startling, for the book is deeply concerned with the unsettling abuses of power by the English monarchy and the origins of the British Empire, which began with Elizabeth I's expeditions into the New World. H.D. is a poet of palimpsests, and a multitude of Elizabeths lies beneath what appears to be a casual comment to a friend. For H.D., Elizabeth is at once Shakespeare's Elizabeth I, the only female poet in the anthology of Renaissance poets from which H.D. is working, and Elizabeth II, on the verge of taking the throne in the late 1940s. Elizabeth is the cognate of Dido's name, Elissa, who, like Alonso's daughter Claribel of the *Tempest*, is another queen of Carthage mentioned in the play, but one who chose death over marriage to a king of Tunis. But a reference to Elizabeth may also be to Elizabeth of Bohemia (Elizabeth Stuart), whose marriage in 1613 H.D. believed was celebrated with the first performance of the *Tempest*.[6] Elizabeth Stuart, like Claribel, lived in exile for most of her life, and her daughter, Sophia, is the direct forebear of the current royal family. What links these royal women, besides their name, is their arranged marriages (fulfilled or not), and, with the abuses of the court, the politics of arranged marriage is a subject that dominates this book.

When *By Avon River* has received critical attention, the focus has invariably been a feminist one, a reading of H.D.'s recovery of Shakespeare's neglected character Claribel, a process by which H.D. rewrites literary history such that she authorizes herself as woman writer by giving this figure a voice.[7] Susan Stanford Friedman argues that "Shakespeare's reinterpreted greatness authenticates the female poet: her existence, her quest, her woman-centered vision."[8] Kate Chedgzoy agrees: "In *By Avon River* and *Tribute to Freud* she confidently rewrites a powerful male precursor as an enabling source of intertextual material and revisionary methodology, in order to create a self-authorising female voice which acknowledges its relation to cultural tradition while asserting a difference from it."[9] This focus on Claribel and female authorship is not unwarranted; indeed, her recovery of the forgotten Claribel is absolutely crucial to the text's project.

This chapter builds on these readings to push the analysis further, to plumb *By Avon River*'s commentary on the politics of English history, nationalism, and imperialism, a politics in which Shakespeare is implicated. It is in 1946 that H.D. decides to delve into these subjects, and, arguably, the Second World War informs the book as much as the Elizabethan era. Presence is past: "We stand with our flowers.... To-day? Yesterday?" the poet asks, conflating the two historical periods as she stands at Shakespeare's grave in 1946.[10] Ostensibly about Shakespeare and his fellow bards, this book has much broader territory to explore. Like the transgressive Claribel of H.D.'s poem, *By Avon River* traverses space—generic and geographical—well beyond its stated borders. Like the various female protagonists of *Sword*'s "Summerdream," the Claribel of this mixed-genre book is a time traveler.

H.D. opens the second part of the book, the prose section, "Remembering Shakespeare always, but remembering him differently."[11] Though critical assessment of the text univocally locates Shakespeare at the center, he is, in fact, hardly mentioned until the final pages, his presence sensed only at the margins; we are *by* Avon River, nearby. Instead, she treats nearly five dozen other Elizabethan lyricists, quoting her favorites among their poems and contextualizing each biographically and historically, stressing their bonds with one another, their desire to be freed from the chains that bind them to corporeal existence, and their travails at the whims of English monarchs who send them to war and who persecute and punish them.[12] But the specter of Shakespeare drifts in and out of the poem of the first part of the book and the narrative of the second, and in some sense the entire book is organized around his ephemeral presence. In the poem and in the dream-like sequences in which H.D. fictionalizes him, he appears in contexts that, taken together, frame her condemnation of the Elizabethan era: his flaws stand in for England's, as he is, as sovereign, an embodiment of the nation. He is a man consumed by his riches; he is poacher, plunderer, thief; and he is an aging man who cannot remember, perhaps the most serious criticism for H.D., who identifies cultural amnesia for most of her career as central to, and a facilitator of, continual cycles of warfare. This is, then, a far more serious critique of Shakespeare than has been realized.[13]

Before sketching out her own version of English literary history at the end of the book—an act of recovery and memory that traces English poetry to its roots in the troubadour ballads of medieval Provence—H.D. offers a multi-pronged analysis of the Elizabethan era: she critiques the imperial European state for negotiating and consolidating power and territory through arranged marriage; she chronicles the abuses of the state, as embodied in the monarchy, and the amassing of wealth; and she implicates Shakespeare in these projects. On the opening dedicatory page, H.D. parallels Shakespeare Day and St. George's Day, merging literary and national history.[14] As both Friedman and Diana Collecott note, Shakespeare embodies nation even as his plays inaugurate English nationalist identity according to G. Wilson Knight, whose 1944 study of Shakespeare's plays, *The Olive and the Sword*, was discovered by H.D. in one of her pilgrimages to Stratford. She conveys her excitement about the find to Bryher, stressing that "it shows *war* also used as background for even the light comedies—& comedy-tragedy!"[15] Declaring that "the voice of the new nation is Shakespeare," Knight's monograph traces a history in which England (not, significantly, Britain), once wracked by civil wars, emerges into a more peaceful Elizabethan era: from the sixteenth century forward, he writes, "England functions as England, with a new sense of sovereignty, a new church, a new national allegiance," and the Renaissance "create[s] . . . the England we know."[16]

Knight casts Hitler as the tyrant from whom Europe will be saved by an English "messiah," Shakespeare. Hitler, Knight argues forcefully, is "attacking the root-principles of that growing imperial and international structure, or organism, which Britain consciously or unconsciously fosters," for "*she cannot, however much she wishes it, think of herself without thinking of the whole world.*" England is, at its "root," an "imperial" power intimately embedded in a global enterprise, and it stands to lose its vast territorial holdings to another nation. Hitler-like sovereigns such as Tamburlaine and Richard III are not to be criticized because they are imperialists but because they wield their power unwisely. Knight sees Shakespeare as advocating "the more typically British approach to power; Britain's success as a colonising force having derived from some such sense of responsible authority." Distinguishing between *imperialism* and *domination*, Knight argues that the British Empire, modeled on its Roman antecedent, is committed to the former, dedicated to "a will to inclusion." While other nations show "mass military aggression," "England's expansion is certainly rooted in the soil of personal initiative." The antidote, for Knight, is a return to our "Shakespearian heritage" as a way of "re-awakening the national imagination."[17]

H.D.'s treatment of *The Tempest* reveals that her views on imperialism, and on Shakespeare, do not align neatly with Knight's. She is ambivalent about that "Shakespearian heritage," and her choice of *The Tempest*, a play very much about imperialism and about the (in)stability of sovereign power, is telling. H.D. was aware of the New World sources of the play. In her copy, she marked this line from M. R. Ridley's introduction: "By far the most interesting and certain sources are the various pamphlets describing the adventures of the expedition of nine ships and five hundred colonists which set out in May of 1609 for the new colony of Virginia. The flagship, the Sea-Adventure, carrying the leaders of the expedition, Sir Thomas Gates and Sir George Somers, was wrecked on the Bermudas."[18] And she makes ample use of the material in sections IV, V, and VII of the first part of "Good Frend." Indeed, she was so committed to these references to England's forays into the New World that she was upset that, when the poem was set up for publication in *Life and Letters Today*, the galleys had omitted her "favourite V and VII, about the *Sea Adventure*."[19]

In the poem, H.D. asks, "why did I choose / The invisible, voiceless Claribel?"[20] and in our own era Susan Stanford Friedman responds, attributing H.D.'s decision to focus on one of Shakespeare's weaker female characters to her fragile mental state in the mid-1940s. But Claribel is a far better choice for H.D.'s larger aims here. Compare, for instance, H.D.'s favorite Shakespearean drama, *As You Like It*, to *The Tempest*—both are plays in which one brother usurps the other's power, and both feature an otherworldly space ostensibly set apart from the politics of the court. *As You Like It* was one of the first plays H.D. saw staged as a young girl in Pennsylvania, and the intelligent, defiant Rosalind was her favorite character; the bisexual H.D. was inspired to perform it at home, reveling in the cross-dressing scenes. References to *As You Like It* dominate her early novel, *HERmione*, where she imagines herself a Rosalind without an Orlando, and this play haunts the second half of *By Avon River* as its lines flit in and out of the prose, remnants of Shakespeare's fractured memory. Miranda and Claribel are weak female characters, mere pawns on a chessboard—mere "marriage tokens," as H.D. dubs them[21]—no match for the fiery Rosalind. In Shakespeare's late phase—and this is the phase of his career H.D. is concerned with in *By Avon River*—H.D. finds the evolution (or devolution) from Rosalind to Claribel, from *As You Like It* to *The Tempest*, troubling.

H.D. had commented on arranged marriages in medieval England in *Sword*; as Hogue and Vandivere observe in their introduction to the volume, the final vignette of "Summerdream" makes clear the link between this aristocratic practice and the cycles of war that had plagued Europe for centuries: "Rose warns Blanchfleur that such marital alliances between territories result in unforeseen claims, and the justification to go to war, much as her marriage to a cousin of the Duke of Brittany had resulted in a war for territory that claimed her husband's life."[22] In *By Avon River*, arranged marriage is a topic raised on the opening pages of "Good Frend," the first half of the book, in which she resurrects Claribel in verse. In *Life and Letters Today*, H.D. had surely read George Garrett's 1937 irreverent invective against Prospero's self-serving plot to "stag[e] a come-back" by uniting Miranda with the king's son: "We can imagine the old schemer saying to himself: 'Be patient, girl. Daddy has a big surprise for you. A real live prince? For you're a princess, my dear.'"[23] In her copy of the play, H.D. marked passages relating to Claribel's royal status as "heir to Naples," and Miranda's marriage to Ferdinand is mirrored in Claribel's to the King of Tunis. On the very first page of "Good Frend," H.D. parallels these arranged unions with yet another associated with the play when she references a "wedding-feast," citing the popular belief that *The Tempest* was written in honor of the arranged marriage of Elizabeth, daughter of James I, to Frederick V, Elector Palatine (and briefly King of Bohemia), a marriage contrived to foster deeper associations between King James and the coalition of Protestant princes of the German states. Later, in the prose section of the book, she will explain that "*The Tempest* was written to celebrate the marriage of James' daughter, Elizabeth, later known as Elizabeth of Bohemia or the Winter Queen" and quote generously from Sir Henry Wotton's poem in tribute to her. But here in H.D.'s poem, the stage is set early in the book, as H.D. pointedly forefronts the impersonal and public function of the union between Elizabeth and the German prince:

> here we are in London—
> A new court festival, a masque?
> Elizabeth, our princess, is to wed
> The Elector Palatine—who's that?
> Frederick, I think. And where's the place—
> Bohemia? I don't think so,
> But anyhow it doesn't matter,
> A foreign fellow is to wed our princess,
> The grand-daughter of Scotland's Mary;
> Occasion—compliment—another play![24]

The subject of London gossip, Elizabeth is *our* princess; she belongs to England. "[I]t doesn't matter" whom she marries or which European nation he represents, just that he is a "foreign fellow," and thus the public is called upon to celebrate not Elizabeth but "[t]he grand-daughter of Scotland's Mary."

That alliance is referenced again in the poem with a bit of misdirection. About Claribel's marriage, H.D. creates a refrain from lines that appear to be from the Old Testament Song of Songs, but also echo a poem by Francis Quarles, cupbearer for the Winter Queen, who will figure in "The Guest."[25] On the surface, what appears to be a celebration of Claribel's love match is clouded by the reference to the unhappy Elizabeth Stuart lying beneath it. "So they say, *my beloved is mine / And I am his,*" H.D. writes, but then immediately revises it, "Our belovèd is ours, / Our belovèd is ours," changing singular to plural pronouns and adding (as Quarles does) an Elizabethan accent over the second "e" of beloved.[26] Emphasizing the public nature of the union, H.D. makes clear that these unions belong not to a *me* but an *us*, a nation, the then-emerging English nation under the reign of an earlier Elizabeth, Queen Elizabeth I.[27]

Another telling instance of revision comes when H.D. rewrites Shakespeare's line, "*in one voyage did Claribel her husband find at Tunis,*" to read instead, "The king's fair daughter / Marries Tunis."[28] Shakespeare's line grants her a name and a husband, but H.D.'s rewriting points out what Shakespeare elides, that Claribel loses her name, her identity, in the marriage; that she is defined entirely in terms of her relationship to her father, the king; and that she weds not a man but a geopolitical entity, Tunis, a pirate stronghold. Until the late 1260s, the Tunisians had carried out lucrative trade with Pisa, Venice, and Genoa, but had long been victims of Sicilian piracy. Their decision to cease paying the Normans tribute to protect them from Sicily may have been an instigating factor in the failed Eighth Crusade.[29] A marriage between a Neapolitan and a Tunisian would have strengthened this tenuous relationship by creating another "Italian" ally against Sicily. In Shakespeare's day, this alliance would have strengthened ties to the Turks who ruled Tunisia, a union invaluable for Venice, a major trading port, in consolidating power against Spain. Turkish pirates had both economic and religious motivation for their attacks on European ships: "The Turks' organization of piracy at Tunis was . . . a direct threat to the Pope and the Italian princes. It coincided with a renewal of the crusading spirit in Europe."[30] In H.D.'s period, the first major operations by Allied Forces against Germany and Italy took place in Tunisia; the British and U.S. occupation of Tunisia during the war was a cause of deep resentment among Tunisians.[31]

The opening of the second half of the book reasserts the theme of arranged marriage when H.D. recalls that Sir Philip Sidney witnessed the Massacre of St. Bartholomew, a bit of biographical data that directs the reader to contemplate the bloodshed that can stem from arranged marriages. When Catherine de Medici orchestrated a marriage between her unwilling Catholic daughter and a Protestant, the bride was physically and violently compelled to consent, sparking a revolt that ended in thousands dead. The final pages of *By Avon River* repeat lines from *Cymbeline*, a dirge sung to Imogen, who is weakened by her flight from her perfidious stepmother's plan to arrange her marriage to her rapacious stepbrother in a plot designed to steal the throne. Arranged marriages in Europe have been essential to imperialist aims, consolidating power and aiding in the amassing of territory and wealth. As Stephen Orgel's introduction to the Oxford edition of *The Tempest* notes, speculation about Queen Elizabeth's potential marital alliances, and the relentless matchmaking of James I for his progeny, form a powerful backdrop to the poetry of the period.[32] In H.D.'s poem, Shakespeare stands in for Prospero; it is ultimately, after all, Shakespeare who wrote the part, the poet's contrivance to take the stage for a world and marry off Claribel and Miranda, "marriage tokens" both, to further their fathers' appetites for power.[33] As playwright, H.D. insists, Shakespeare functions, in essence, in the role of the monarch—to borrow from Giorgio Agamben's notions of sovereignty—who exists in a state of exception that permits him to act outside the law and to exact unchecked violence upon the women of his play—in effect, sanctioned rape—just as monarchs have arranged the marriages of their heirs for centuries. Shakespeare is using what Jim Hansen has termed *lex poetica*, an unchecked, sovereign power over his characters.

Shakespeare, as monarch, embodies England in the first half of *By Avon River* as not just tyrannical sovereign but as an imperialist, a poacher, a plunderer. "Much sweet was plundered, / Stacked and stored," H.D. remarks in a stanza about Shakespeare's elaborate garden at New Place. "O, what a house he built /. . . . / O what a plesaunce, / Planed by his rule," she continues, creating a palimpsest of two otherworldly spaces set apart from the seat of the court, Prospero's island and Shakespeare's Globe, but the reference is also to his ostentatious estate and gardens at Stratford, New Place, the second largest house in Stratford at the time of its purchase, a veritable mansion by Renaissance standards.[34] Though he did not in fact build the house, H.D. imagines him throughout the second half of the book constructing its elaborate gardens. Shakespeare's apparent obsession with the garden is a persistent motif in this text, not just in the poem but in the prose, as his musings on the garden's design erratically interrupt her literary critical essay on his contemporaries, drawing her attention away from his rival poets. Friedman rightly speculates that his constant thoughts about flowers appear to feminize and thus disempower him.[35] In fact, there may be a more sinister subtext to these references as well, for H.D. may also be critiquing his materialism, as she does in the final poem of "Good Frend" when Claribel admires the dedication to poverty by the nuns of the Order of St. Clare, the "Poor Clares."

Shakespeare's grave is itself a tribute to his wealth, for he bought for himself and his family the prime sites at the very altar of Trinity Church and protected that site with verse that curses anyone who dares to move him from his exalted position. As H.D.'s speaker approaches the grave, the hallowed tone is disrupted when she sees a gravestone for the Lucy family and recalls another important story for her purposes, the tale of the young Shakespeare's theft of Sir Thomas Lucy's deer, a crime that eventually led to his flight to London. From here, H.D. moves swiftly from deer poaching to plagiarism—"He stole everything, / There isn't an original plot / In the whole lot of his plays"—locating his sources for *The Tempest* in pamphlets about the wreck of the *Sea Venture* in yet another otherworldly space, the New World, Bermuda.

Shakespeare as poacher returns in the second half of the book. What she terms "Shakespeare's indifference to originality" echoes throughout her account of his peers. While the young Ben Jonson was busy reading, she notes dryly, Shakespeare "boasted in later life of other exploits," including his theft of Lucy's deer.[36] No less than three times she indicates the links between Michael Drayton's *Nymphidia* and Shakespeare's Oberon and Queen Mab in *Midsummer Night's Dream*.[37] To emphasize further that Shakespeare lifted those characters from Drayton, she exercises some artistic license in two suggestions that intensify the links between the two poets: first, that Drayton and Sir Thomas Lucy may be cousins (in fact, it is Drayton's patron who is Lucy's cousin); and, second, that Drayton showed Shakespeare a book of pansies that inspired his construction of his garden at New Place, an event H.D.'s Shakespeare fails to remember (in fact, pansies appear importantly in both *Midsummer Night's Dream* and the *Nymphidia*). Given the intensive degree of attention that Lucy's deer and the garden receive in both halves of *By Avon River*, these suggestions cannot have been made lightly. Moreover, Drayton is not the only poet to fall victim to Shakespeare's poaching. "There are many lyrics of Shakespeare's which might well be attributed to Fletcher," H.D. writes, and John Fletcher, she claims, "had outlined [*Romeo and Juliet*] for [Shakespeare] from the Italian folio." *The Merchant of Venice*, she alleges, comes from Marlowe's *The Jew of Malta*—the latter, to her mind, the better play.[38]

Elizabeth I launched England's imperial project formally, as H.D. reminds us in "Good Frend" when she stresses *The Tempest*'s sources in narratives of England's expansion into the New World. The Elizabethan era, then, is inevitably tied to imperialism and the amassing of wealth pilfered from other parts of the world. The bad monarch of the first half of the book, embodied in both Shakespeare and Prospero, yields to the real-life monarchs of the sixteenth and early seventeenth centuries, first Elizabeth and then James.

Opening with Sir Walter Raleigh's embittered condemnation of the court, "The Guest" is unrelenting in its critique of monarchical politics, of kings and queens who compel poets to pander to their whims or risk imprisonment—like Raleigh—in the Tower.[39] That Raleigh's explorations contributed a great deal to Elizabeth's imperialist aims is not a coincidence.

Indeed, there are moments in the second half of *By Avon River* that read less like a literary critical essay on Shakespeare's contemporaries and more like a laundry list of poets wronged by the State. Sidney died fighting Elizabeth's war, Spenser's manor was burned to the ground, Raleigh and Essex were beheaded, Edward Dyer ends a life of service to the Crown in poverty, Thomas Nashe and Edmund Waller were imprisoned, Robert Southwell died a martyr, Robert Herrick is exiled, Francis Davison is disgraced. But "Shakespeare retired to Stratford." With considerable irony, H.D. remarks that "[a]n accomplished courtier is, of necessity, a poet." In the Elizabethan period, these roles are blurred. "We have imagined only one true way of recalling these, our poets," she writes,[40] but she wants to read beyond the parameters of traditional literary criticism, beyond the canonical figures she begins with—Shakespeare, Sidney, Marlowe—but also beyond the literary into the political realm. Though she quotes liberally from their poetry, her commentary consistently describes these men in their public or military function, and their poetry invariably recounts their unjust suffering in the earthly realm and their readiness for a spiritual end. She traces webs of webs of influence among literary figures that are based more in politics than in the arts. It is the court—the corrupt court associated with an imperialist state—that holds these networks together.

This focus is very much in concert with that of her chosen source text on Elizabethan poetry, an 800-page anthology compiled in 1908 by African American scholar William Braithwaite, a professor of literature.[41] Braithwaite is best known for his *Anthology of Magazine Verse*, a modernist-era annual in which H.D.'s early Imagist poems occasionally appeared. In the World War I era prefaces to his *Anthology of Magazine Verse*, he is unabashedly pro-American and pro-democracy, arguing that "[t]he world must be made safe for democracy" not with "guns" but with "music and words of the spirit, with the dream-haunted laborers of words, building an edifice of ideals for human brotherhood. . . . Armies of the soldiers of the flesh, destroying with the terrible machinery of steel, and chemical agencies, shall pass: and armies of soldiers of the spirit, will go forward with the symbols of dreams and vision building in Beauty the spirit of man's life."[42] The front matter of his Elizabethan anthology reaffirms these democratic values, attacking Queen Elizabeth as a bad poet who only disingenuously promotes the arts as just another vehicle for magnifying her own power. The only poem he selects of the Queen's demonstrates the anti-democratic, anti-immigrant insularity of her kingdom: "No foreign banished wight / Shall anchor in this port; / Our realm it brooks no stranger's force; / Let them elsewhere resort." Braithwaite finds the Elizabethan era, though, the very best of England's literary past, not, as one might think, because of Shakespeare's dominant presence, but rather because it was a period in which everyone, simply *everyone*, was a writer: "Soldiers and sea-faring adventurers, courtiers and ambassadors, barons and commons, tavern-vagabonds and play-actors, all wrote verse."[43] What he, and H.D., find in the Elizabethan era is a surfeit of poems defying monarchical authority. If Shakespeare writes "[u]neasy lies the head that wears a crown," it is those subject to that crown's capriciousness and brutality who interest H.D. and Braithwaite.

H.D. was fascinated by the English monarchy.[44] But, on the issue of state authority, H.D.'s politics in this era align much more with the patriotic Braithwaite—who invokes a "melting pot" ideal—than with the patriotic G. Wilson Knight, whose romantic appeal to state authority is linked metonymically to the "Crown": the latter writes that "[t]he Crown is ... both heart and whole of the nation, or empire; and therefore reflects at once its historic heritage, present soul-potentiality, and future destiny." In Knight's formulation, the Crown transcends time and is, essentially, egalitarian, "like the sun, soaking up and next redistributing, as a heart, the fluidities of wealth."[45] His mid-twentieth-century invocation of the monarch's crown surely bespeaks nostalgia, at best, and authoritarianism, at worst. If Braithwaite's choice is to begin his anthology with the chilling words of Queen Elizabeth, H.D.'s selection for epigraph to the second half of *By Avon River* is perhaps even more blatant: Raleigh's embittered condemnation of the court, "The Soul's Errand," penned from the Tower while awaiting execution. With death imminent, the speaker of Raleigh's poem urges the soul, the body's "guest," to abandon the body, assuring it that "The truth shall be thy warrant" and that his demise will "give the World the lie!" This poem—and Raleigh's corpse—erupt into the text that follows with the regularity of Shakespeare's idle ruminations on the flowers of New Place, offering a cutting juxtaposition of the minds of these two poets. At one point, as she relates stories of other poets punished by the monarchy,

H.D. ends abruptly with lines that set Raleigh and Shakespeare in stark opposition to each other: "Sir Walter Raleigh hurled his invective at the Court of King James: 'Say to the Court, it glows / And shines like rotten wood.' Shakespeare retired to Stratford."[46] Near the end of the book, she underscores the point when she makes the following observation: "William Shakespeare, unlike Christopher Marlowe, unlike Walter Raleigh, stands aside. We can not imagine him shut up in the Tower."[47]

Poet after poet in *By Avon River* is executed, excommunicated, exiled. Not only Raleigh but the Queen's devotee, Robert Devereux, Earl of Essex, she notes, was beheaded. In Platonic terms, the head houses the soul, the body existing merely to support it,[48] but a head is also a head of state, the site, as it were, of state authority. In fact, in Renaissance England, decapitation was reserved for the aristocracy: as one art historian observes, it "'symbolizes the taking away of rank, that is, the crown. Only members of the upper classes could wear the 'crown' in the first place.'"[49] As H.D. thinks of Elizabeth Stuart, she is reminded of Essex, "[t]he unfortunate favourite" of "[a]nother Elizabeth," and she imagines him writing, like Raleigh, from the Tower before Queen Elizabeth signs the execution order. She quotes the aristocrat decrying his status as, in effect, *homo sacer*: "Earth, sea, heaven, hell, are subject unto laws, / But I, poor I, must suffer and know no cause."[50] Neither Henry VIII, Mary I, Elizabeth I, nor James I escapes H.D.'s reproach.

Poets like Ben Jonson, who, H.D. quips darkly, never lost their heads "in any sense of the word," are subject to the court. Ben Jonson, Francis Bacon, John Lyly, Philip Sidney, and so many others were "steeped in the policies and politics of the time." In Jonson's character Cynthia, she argues, "[t]he mind of the Tudor Englishman could loyally transfer his ancestors' allegiance to the Queen of England," which played to the desires and investments of the court. H.D. traces both the abuse and corruption, and the role of the poet-courtier of Elizabeth's court, back to Elizabeth's father's court, and she sketches out a brief theatrical history as a palimpsest, in which the new Elizabethan theater is written over the theatrical spaces of Henry VIII's palaces, spaces still faintly visible in the lush fabrics, the banquets, the candelabras of Elizabethan play sets. The history of English imperialism, she avers, can be seen in these play sets. The church plundered the Orient, then "[t]he church was plundered by the palace; the palace became the background for new ritual," so the theater itself "was overlaid with the memory of secret plunder." The violence of history shifts from world to stage in this era, for "[t]he Tower had had its fill of tragedy" and so "now tragedy found a place upon the boards, new planed, of the Globe Theatre." "Why is this forgotten?" she asks.[51]

Shakespeare, though, was not a courtier. He himself "did not feel at home there." The first page of "The Guest" explains that Sidney's influence bought Sir Edmund Spenser certain advancements and grants; the ending of "The Guest" narrates a dying Shakespeare thinking with satisfaction that he had rejected Bacon's offer of a role at court for himself.[52] Friedman argues that his "refusal to pronounce dogma" is what H.D. so admired about Shakespeare,[53] but I would counter that there is, frankly, not a lot of praise here for his choice to play it safe either, to avoid the court and to produce plays not overtly critical of its politics. At the end of the book, H.D. stages the apocryphal scene at the Stratford inn where Shakespeare—dining with Drayton and Jonson—contracted the illness that resulted in his untimely death at the age of 52. Having spent much of the essay tracing the grim lives and horrific deaths of Shakespeare's contemporaries who had defied the Crown, she lingers on this scene at the inn for several pages, a choice that stresses Shakespeare's relatively peaceful end. He is not martyred for a cause but dies of a cold. His final thoughts are those of a self-satisfied, wealthy man. In this scene, Drayton and Jonson are animated, engaged in an intellectual discussion of Greek and Renaissance drama, of aesthetics, of the origins of English poetry, but Shakespeare's mind meanders. He finds his kinsmen the better poets, but he comforts himself that "taken all in all, he hadn't done so badly. There was the new house and the garden."[54] In the second half of the book, Shakespeare thinks occasionally of his mother, his children, his granddaughter, all blood relations. It is his lineage, his legacy he is obsessed with. Perhaps this is why Anne Hathaway, who outlived her husband by seven years, is never mentioned.

Shakespeare's implicit complicity with a court associated with empire and wealth can be discerned in the form of H.D.'s book. H.D.'s verse in "Good Frend" is more regularly iambic than is typical of her *oeuvre*. At times, this imitation of Shakespeare's verse appears to be a homage, but at other times the degree of excess seems parodic. Written in three parts, the first and second parts of the poem generally employ a variable iambic meter and a fair amount of end rhyme. Lines about Shakespeare, however, are frequently composed in an even tighter, more regular rhythm and rhyme scheme, rendering him, and particularly the site of his home and grave at Stratford, in a rigid form reminiscent of traditional English verse. If, as Michael Boughn has argued, much of English poetry entails a technique that mimics colonialism, in which "[t]he poet's intellect tames unruly content, imposing on it the order of a logical, ideal form,"[55] H.D. exploits this linkage, associating Shakespeare the man with a more conservative form while liberating his play (as she liberates Claribel) from those strictures.

In Part II of "Good Frend," set at Shakespeare's grave, she writes iambic verse in a tone of apparent solemnity that ultimately pushes sound repetition to an almost laughable degree; this section ends in the excessively assonant and alliterative couplet, "*Blest be the man*—that one who knows / His heart glows in the growing rose."[56] To read these lines without irony is to ignore several key contexts that undercut the apparent tone. In the preceding lines of the poem, the letters of the tombstone disappear and are reborn in the form of flowers, so Shakespeare's garden at New Place is invoked yet again. Second, England is commonly figured as a rose, which is represented here in less-than-positive terms, and here the "rose" "grow[s]," expanding its Empire. Moreover, the bloody War of the Roses ended the Plantagenet dynasty, H.D. notes, and she has located the birth of English poetry with Richard the Lionhearted, the English monarch who inherited a great deal more power than previous kings due to his father Henry II's victory over baronic rule. And finally, she has, again, rewritten Shakespeare's lines, which bless those who maintain the expensive crypts at the front and center of the altar of his parish church and curse those who would move them; here, though, H.D. blesses the "one who knows," who realizes that Shakespeare is implicated in the "growing rose," England's imperializing mission. That the line "His heart glows" recalls Raleigh's "Say to the Court, it glows / And shines like rotten wood" is surely not an accident.

So there is a marked reversal in these first two parts, in which Shakespeare's play is freed from its iambs, while Shakespeare himself, in Stratford, is ensnared in conventional form. Part III of the poem, however, shifts abruptly, as Claribel is unchained from Shakespeare's text to wander in medieval Italy. As she steps back in time to uncover the palimpsest of history, the poem's rhythm becomes that of the medieval troubadour's ballad, that radical form H.D. characterizes in "The Guest" as a threat to monarchical power. There is yet another reversal in the prose of the second half. For most of that half of the book, a literary critical style pervades, as H.D. addresses the life and verse of Shakespeare's many contemporaries, but periodically both Raleigh's lines and Shakespeare's thoughts intercede. Utterly disintegrating, the forgetful mind of Shakespeare intrudes upon, usurps we might say, textual space devoted to others with self-satisfied musings on his wealth and standing. In the end, Shakespeare finally does claim the book as his own, and more sustained renderings of his thought breach H.D.'s outline of literary history—but he claims it only to die. The literary history of England is birthed in France and culminates in death.

The defiant poets H.D. chooses for the volume are punished for their insubordination, as they uniformly assert the importance of the soul over the body and, by extension, religious authority over monarchical authority. What distinguishes Shakespeare from his contemporaries, she points out in selection after selection of their poetry, is their choice of heavenly reward over earthly treasure.[57] While Shakespeare retires to his spacious home and plans his garden, other poets remind their readers that "Heaven is our heritage, / Earth but a player's stage." In their verse, the royal crown—G. Wilson Knight's sun that warms the nation—is subjected to the crown of God, who also exists in a state of exception from the law of the state, but rules well beyond national borders and has the right to enforce law only from outside. As in *Trilogy*, it is the power of spirituality—albeit in a distinctly heterodox form—that the modernist H.D. wants to privilege: "The poet, like the Saint, has transferred his allegiance from earthly martyrdom to heavenly." H.D.'s poets see the material world as embodied by the monarchy and its insatiable desire for goods to be doled out only to those poets who please the crown. Examples abound. Like Raleigh and Essex, Thomas Nashe is imprisoned; this, from his quill: "This world uncertain is, / Fond are life's lustful joys, / Death proves them all but toys"; "Rich men, trust not in wealth"; "Queens have died young and fair"; "Swords may not fight with fate"; and "Heaven is our heritage, / Earth but a player's stage." James Shirley "capitulated" so "avoided exile"; his poem reminds the monarchy that it is accountable to God: "The glories of our blood and state / Are shadows, not substantial things"; and "Death lays his icy hand on kings: / Sceptre and Crown / Must tumble down." The music of Thomas Ford is set to a hymn H.D. selects that decries humanity for hosting monarchs to sumptuous feasts while relegating Christ to a manger.[58] Shakespeare's satisfaction at his own worldly success is set in stark contrast to the rhetoric of this verse.

And Raleigh's execution frames it all. His importance to the volume exceeds the fact of his fateful decapitation, however, for it is for his sea adventures, his imperializing efforts on behalf of the Crown, that he is best known. H.D. reminds us that Francis Bacon wrote cynically of England's propensity for unrest:

> Our own affection still at home to please,
> Is a disease;
> To cross the sea to any foreign soil,
> Peril and toil;
> Wars with their noise affright us; when they cease
> We're worse in peace.[59]

About England's participation in the Crusades, H.D. echoes Bacon, in opposition to Knight's romanticizing of English nationalism, arguing that the Crusades were colonizing missions and not religious pilgrimages. The medieval Crusades are key to this book, as they are to *White Rose and the Red*, for references to two famous participants, Richard the Lionhearted and the brutal Simon de Montfort, recur throughout the last third of "The Guest." The latter figure she charges with the extinction of Catharism during the Albigensian Crusade, about which she had first learned from Ezra Pound. In notes, H.D. transcribed Pound's characterization of the Albigensian Crusade as "a sordid robbery cloaking itself in religious pretense."[60]

In lines that recall Elizabeth's in Braithwaite's tome, H.D. theorizes, "That lure of foreign places, was really love of home, their own native boundaries. The urge would be satisfied for a time by wars in England. When a sort of transitional peace fell upon the prince and barons, it was time to leave."[61] Anticipating postcolonial theory, these lines also echo those of Timothy Brennan, when he observes that "European nationalism itself was motivated by what Europe was doing in its far-flung dominions. The 'national idea,' in other words, flourished in the soil of foreign conquest."[62] In a very real sense, England is an entity defined by its territories, but Shakespeare's otherworldly places are here laid bare as colonies. Shakespeare, H.D. intimates, tries to cast England as just such an otherworldly place, an island set apart, in the John of Gaunt speech from *Richard II*:

> This other-Eden, demi-paradise,
> This fortress built by Nature for herself
> Against infection and the hand of war,
> . . . .
> This blesséd plot, this earth, this realm, this England.[63]

But this effort is doomed, she contends. England is itself a seat of power, not a space that transcends, that stands outside, the whims of the court. It traffics in the lush treasures on which the Elizabethan stage was constructed. Shakespeare's garden is an extravagance, not a green world. "The Body's Guest," the original title of this half of the book, is to be wrested from its corporeal existence, to be liberated, like Claribel, from England's drama, set loose to roam a world beyond England's national borders.

As Ewa Ziarek has recently argued, Agamben fails to take adequate account of issues of gender in *Homo Sacer*. Claribel is a monarch but lacks agency and voice; she does not exist in a state of exception but is subject to the violence of male royalty, her father and her husband. She is like H.D.'s other wanderers and time travelers, and in the final section of the poem, H.D. uses her own poetic authority—her *lex poetica*—to set her free from her arranged marriage. Claribel exiles herself, but not to the heaven the poets of the volume desire. Unmanacled, Claribel travels to early medieval Venice, during the time of the Crusades, desperate to give up the earthly riches and the royal title Shakespeare had bestowed upon her. Freed of those trappings, she finds a new identity with the Poor Clares and as a healer who cures cultural amnesia, when she treats a fallen knight with a sprig of rosemary, rose of memory, *ros maris*, rose of Mary. A constant theme of H.D.'s late work, beginning with *Trilogy*, the poet's role is to preserve and restore cultural memory, to dredge up the traces left in the palimpsest of history. It is important that the close of "Good Frend" transports Claribel, Queen of Tunis, to medieval Italy in this particular era, for Tunisia was attacked by Crusaders in the 1270s, and the Crusaders' loss ended Christian domination in the Levant. In revoking her role as Queen and acting to remind Europe of its transgressions, Claribel usurps Shakespeare's position to write a different kind of story.

The recurrent scenes of an aging Shakespeare's forgetfulness that periodically disrupt the literary critical essay of the second half of the book indict him as a participant in the erasure of cultural memory, as one who perpetuates cultural amnesia. Indeed, if Knight's preface declares that "Shakespeare's thinking functions continually in terms of order,"[64] the mind of H.D.'s bard is emphatically disordered. In one revealing episode, Shakespeare struggles to remember lines from his *Antony and Cleopatra* in which Antony abdicates power in favor of love: "*Let Rome in Tiber melt—here is my—here is my—.*"[65] What he cannot remember of Antony's speech is extremely suggestive, for it is the references to his empire and kingdom: the lines from Shakespeare's play read, "Let Rome in Tiber melt, and the wide arch / Of the ranged empire fall! Here is my space. / Kingdoms are clay." As Knight argues, "Shakespeare, at the youth of Great Britain's imperial history, is necessarily fascinated by the accomplished imperialism of ancient Rome. He feels England now as inheriting the great destiny of Rome."[66] H.D.'s Shakespeare, however, forgets about the consequences of imperial history, comforting himself with his plans for a knotte garden.

As in *Trilogy*, it is a cognate of the Virgin Mary whom H.D. wishes to restore to cultural consciousness, the "Lady," whose religious presence has been suppressed; she aims to resurrect the goddess, a move she will critique in *White Rose and the Red*. It is the "Lady"—Claribel, in H.D.'s new quest—who promises an end to the violence. And it is the mother of the Plantagenet Richard the Lionhearted, Eleanor of Aquitaine, whom H.D. credits with bringing poetry from Provence to England, a claim that denies England its own folk literary tradition, its own myth of literary origins. That poetry is the subversive ballads, the *aubades*, of troubadours who sang of courtly love. The songs are palimpsests, H.D. alleges: "This worship [of the Lady], forced to renounce the official language of the Church, disguised itself in terms of earthly passion. But this passion was never requited. In other words, the love of the troubadour was love of the Spiritual. This love could not be satisfied on earth."[67] If, as she argues, "[t]he Inquisition had destroyed the cult of Our Lady," then "the Lady banished from the churches of Provence, found refuge elsewhere."[68] According to the code of courtly love, the medieval knight was caught between his allegiance to the lady and his allegiance to the king; this Lady, for H.D., is to be interpreted spiritually, so that the choice is really between heavenly and material desires. When Claribel encounters the Poor Clares, vowed to poverty, as the first step in her quest for identity, she is consorting, in effect, with radical heretics to secular authority, a threat to the state's wealth, to which one is supposed to aspire and by which that authority is maintained. Marlowe, Raleigh, Spenser, and Jonson she dubs "four outstanding heretics,"[69] who carry the message of the troubadours into the Elizabethan era; Shakespeare is conspicuously absent from this list.

Homi Bhabha and other postcolonial theorists have observed that self-contained, linear narratives of history are always already suspect, naturalizing stories invested in myths of origin. H.D.'s narrative—for even the poetry tells a story—counters that model of historical narrative. It refuses England the origins of its own literary history, in a book on Shakespeare no less, in a decidedly and defiantly nonlinear fashion, breaching political, generic, geographical, and temporal boundaries. While *By Avon River* does not enact the kind of self-deconstructing narrative that *Sword* does, she uses many of its elements to explore alternative ways of accessing and disseminating historical narratives. Unlike many late modernists, she does not reject experimental form but rather continues to invent new forms.

Like Claribel, the subject in H.D.'s late writings is simultaneously in and out of time, in and out of history—at once immersed in and displaced from the world. It is as if the subject is not stable enough to exist in history, but history is also not stable enough to fix the subject in its grasp. Encasing history in a set of accordion pleats suggests that the subject can and does exist on several planes at once, but none is ethereal, even if the poets of "The Guest" imagine such a destiny. Claribel does not escape from history into a heavenly, ethereal, otherworldly realm. In fact, H.D. rejects the whole notion of otherworldly spaces, such a prominent feature of so many of Shakespeare's plays. Claribel remains trapped, as we all are, in history.

5

Disappearing Bodies in *White Rose and the Red*

> Her humanity was at war with the fiction woven round her.
>
> —H.D., *White Rose and the Red*

This chapter turns to a historical novel critical of British imperialism in India set in the mid-nineteenth century, H.D.'s *White Rose and the Red*, which she began composing in the year India achieved independence from Britain. A fictionalized retelling of the stories of Pre-Raphaelites Dante Gabriel Rossetti, William Morris, and Rossetti's wife, Elizabeth Siddall, this novel is also a meditation on the intersection of gender and empire. If, as Alan Johnson has argued, the discourse of modernity posits India as simultaneously ancient and modern[1]—as having an ancient past and an imaginable future, but no present—H.D. opts instead to portray India in a specific historical moment of the recent past. By choosing the Pre-Raphaelites as the subject of her novel, H.D. can create a layered historical narrative—or, to use her metaphor of this period, a point at which three pleats of an accordion meet—of the wars and uprisings of the Pre-Raphaelites' historical moment, the mid-nineteenth century; the Crusades of the Middle Ages, an era with which the Pre-Raphaelite were obsessed; and, implicitly, the Second World War and the partitioning of India and Pakistan.

Centering this parallel narrative in part around Elizabeth Siddall—who lives physically in one era and, at times, psychically in another—affords H.D. an intersecting focus on gender.[2] An artist and artist's model, the famously unstable Siddall committed suicide at the age of 32. But, in H.D.'s telling, the source of her insanity is neither biological nor (as is the contention of one of H.D.'s sources, her friend Violet Hunt's sensationalist biography of Siddall) the result of Rossetti's abuse and neglect. Instead, her madness is socially and culturally determined, the product of a militaristic and imperialist culture. In fact, the narrative of war and imperialist aggression that serves as background—chiefly, the Crimean War and the 1857 Sepoy Rebellion in India,[3] events not depicted directly but nonetheless a palpable presence—threatens to erupt from beneath the surface of the text, creating an ominous atmosphere that is underscored by Siddall's lifelong fixation on a vicious London murderer, James Greenacre. Against this backdrop of tension, the novel subtly parallels a series of dismemberments: Greenacre's dismemberment of his fiancée's corpse, the Petrarchan treatment of Siddall's face and body by Rossetti, and the seemingly endless re-apportionment of territory within the British Empire (and by analogy to earlier times, the Middle East in the time of the Crusades; and to H.D.'s historical moment as well).

The book begins with Siddall's entrance into the world of the Pre-Raphaelites and ends with her death. H.D. commented in 1950 that the Pre-Raphaelite characters of this novel are cognates of those central to the Imagist movement and that she finds parallels both between her and the characters' "urge toward expression in art" and between her and Siddall's "emotional starvation."[4] Indeed, the novel has been read as a nostalgic and rather romanticized portrait of Imagism that absolves H.D.'s masculine cohorts of any charges of ill treatment of her.[5] While this biographical reading does illuminate aspects of the novel, there is much more to consider, as Alison Halsall points out when she observes that "H.D. returns to the nineteenth century to highlight its parallels with the political excesses of the twentieth."[6] Not simply a story of a time past, "[i]t is ultra-modern in all its implications," H.D. exclaimed to Pearson of *White Rose*, arguing that the Second World War and the dropping of the atomic bomb are essential contexts for this historical novel.[7] The novel, then, is not merely an autobiographical self-reflection, in which H.D. casts herself as the striking Siddall; it is also a contemplation of the imbrication of gender politics in the politics of war and imperialism. A reader familiar with H.D. might focus here on the Pre-Raphaelites' depiction of the Lady as manifestation of goddess in their numerous paintings devoted to female figures both beautiful and divine. But my reading of the novel maintains that, at least in the immediate post–World War II period, H.D. finds troubling this kind of glorification of the deified spiritual and erotic female. In *White Rose and the Red*, she critiques this kind of representation. She questions the portrayal of the female goddess, "Our Lady," that had dominated the second book of her *Trilogy*.

Though *White Rose and the Red* is set entirely in Europe and features only English characters and scenes, H.D. viewed the Crimean War and the Sepoy Rebellion as central to the novel, and it is from this claim that this chapter stems. Though she does not mention either in the novel's conclusion, she tells Aldington, "I finished the ROSE with Indian Mutiny."[8] In letters to Bryher confirming the date of the Sepoy Rebellion, she expresses her excitement that "the vol[ume] ends on that note," calling it a crucial "turning point."[9] That she favored the Indians in that conflict is clear in a letter to Pearson in which she compares the Indian Rebellion to the U.S. Revolutionary War.[10] When she had finished the novel and shared it with Pearson, he objected strenuously to any mention of either military conflict on the grounds that it detracted from the Pre-Raphaelite story. Writing to Bryher, she accuses Pearson, in essence, of missing the entire point of the narrative: "N[orman] wanted me to change *Rose*, but I have been re-reading and it really must stand as is. He objected to the war, but this is historical and Crimea and India came into the period."[11] "I realized or tried to realize," she explains patiently to Pearson, "what an effect [the war] must have had (and the Mutiny, of which we hear nothing)."[12]

It is important to note that before she begins work on *White Rose*, H.D.'s writings of the mid-1940s do not reference India's modern history. Rather, in *Majic Ring* and in *Sword*, she tends to mythologize it, much in the way that Meredith Miller and Susan Edmunds have argued she treats Egypt throughout her career.[13] India is the ancient cradle of civilization in those novels and a spiritual site of great importance.[14] Before that point, she had had a longstanding, if essentially casual, interest in India. H.D. read Andrew Lang's Indian fairy tales as a child,[15] and she studied Eastern religious traditions from the period of her early relationship with Ezra Pound—who shared with her "a series of Yogi books"[16]—through the 1940s, when she discovered the work of fellow Swiss denizen Hermann Hesse. But the Second World War, Indian Independence, and her brief friendship with Anglo-Indian spiritualist medium Arthur Bhaduri[17] seem to have aroused curiosity about modern India and its relationship to Britain. Her correspondence with Bryher also reveals that the two had become interested in India, for they exchanged occasional comments on India in correspondence from the mid-1930s to the late 1940s. H.D. read two accounts of Anglo-Indians, T. Earle Welby's *One Man's India*[18] and Lillian Ashby's *My India*, and studied the significance of India to the history of trade and commerce in E. H. Warmington's *The Commerce*

Between the Roman Empire and India and Robert Byron's *Byzantine Achievement*, which she annotated. She also wrote to a friend who had grown up in India, Una Cherberton, asking for details of her childhood.[19] H.D. and Bryher discussed Indian self-rule in in 1947, and it was Bryher who explained to her how the Sepoy Rebellion had come about ninety years previously.[20]

White Rose, I will argue, resists the mythologizing tendencies of her earlier thinking. On its surface, however, the novel is not about any of these historical events, but rather the Pre-Raphaelite brotherhood, and specifically, the treatment of the female body by that group. In Rossetti's mid-career art, women's faces and bodies were elevated to dizzying heights of objectification, symbols of grand abstractions and vehicles of transcendence for male artists and viewers.[21] His manifesto "Hand and Soul"—which H.D. read, and for which Siddall believed herself to be the source[22]—recounts an Annunciation-like visitation from a beautiful, divine woman who is in fact a reflection of the feminine soul of the male artist: "I am an image," she tells him, "of thine own soul within thee."[23] Rossetti painted Siddall after her death as *Beata Beatrix*, positioning himself as Dante and Siddall as Beatrice, the earthly vehicle to transcendent experience. As one art historian notes, however, the model hardly matters, as "Siddal's features have lost their particularity."[24] The words of another art historian echo this sentiment, stressing the way Rossetti viewed his models and muses: "Rossetti arranged the real world after visions of his ideal beauty. Which explains why his various models—Elizabeth Siddal, Mrs Morris, Fanny Cornforth, Alice Widing, Marie Spartali (Mrs Stillman)—all leave the impression of being the same woman, an impression caused by Rossetti's constant attempts to bridge the gulf between his ordinary existence and the ideal life of the imagination."[25] In H.D.'s novel, Siddall herself makes a bitter joke about Rossetti's penchant for painting "the same picture" of the fallen woman again and again. Even the otherwise sympathetically drawn character Morris reflects, "So he, William, had fallen in love with a picture but he knew the frail image to be a living woman. But as his way was, he abstracted her from the frame." Morris regards Siddall principally in terms of her capacity as model and muse—as a construction, something to be crafted: "I had seen her somewhere. I had written about her in my first poems and romances. She answers the description. You invent her—or imagine her—she appears."[26] Her objectification is underscored when, mid-way through, the novel shifts abruptly from Siddall's perspective to Morris's.

The identity of the woman, for Rossetti, can be found in the medieval period. In *White Rose*, this iconization of the female body finds its parallel in the medieval custom of courtly love, discussed in the previous chapter, for the characters engage avidly with medieval stories and images—unsurprising given the Pre-Raphaelite fascination with medieval and pre-Renaissance sources. As Lynne Pearce observes, Rossetti's interest in medievalism is linked to his objectification of the female: "Dante's Beatrice had little more material identity than Rossetti's heroine. Her personal attributes are, indeed, conceptual abstractions. She exists, principally, as a chain of abstract superlatives.... Love is ... the true addressee of the poet's thoughts; Beatrice the mere *object*."[27] The object is necessary to spiritual epiphany, the goal of art for Rossetti: "The Soul's appearance becomes a moment of revelation frozen outside of time and change, utterly static, an experiential plenum in which all the senses are overwhelmed."[28]

We look, too, to the medieval period for the Petrarchan conventions Rossetti's paintings invoke, for the body is not merely objectified in Rossetti's paintings. The suggestion in *White Rose* is that in its reliance on Petrarchan conventions, the body is effectively dismembered; it is seen as parts rather than as a whole. The Petrarchan poem fragments the woman's body into parts, describing and admiring each part in isolation. A significant strand of Rossetti's mid-career work focuses entirely on women's disembodied heads and busts, and one of the sources on the Pre-Raphaelites H.D. owned and annotated remarks upon Rossetti's penchant for fragmentation and pastiche: "He would isolate that ... which appealed to his poetic imagination and he would then surround it with accessories of his own"; if the others of the Brotherhood argued for a strict adherence to nature and realism, Rossetti permitted it—to quote a source H.D. owned and read—"to enter his verse ... reduced to symbols."[29] In "Hand and Soul," the apparitional woman is described in Petrarchan fashion, body part by body part: her eyes contained "the first thoughts he had ever known," her hair was "the golden veil through which he beheld his dreams," and her mouth "was supreme in gentleness."[30] This dismantling of the female body is made clear in H.D.'s text as well. Of Siddall, Rossetti sees only "the face, a shadowed cameo. There was the throat and the hands, in the darkness.... The face, the throat, the hands.... He did not believe ... that there was more to her than a face, a throat and two hands, folded upon darkness." Siddall confides to Morris that it was her hair alone that got her discovered as a model.[31] And, indeed, H.D.

illustrates the fragmentation of Siddall in the fragmented modernist style she employs, and in her portrayal of the increasingly fragmented nature of Siddall's thoughts over the course of her life.

Again, H.D.'s interest in Rossetti's depictions of the goddess figure as embodiment of the divine soul might well be seen as an extension of her presentation of the goddess (in such works as *Trilogy*) as a solution to a war-ridden culture. But the novel does not endorse Rossetti's abstract woman. Woman, in the novel, is being constantly taken apart. In fact, the text troubles any easy acceptance of an abstract objectification and deification of the feminine with repeated references to James Greenacre, an infamous London criminal who murdered and dismembered his female victim; Siddall's recurrent "nightmare" of Greenacre disrupts her emotional stability, and her thoughts about Greenacre repeatedly disturb the reader, distracting us from the plot recounting the early days of the Pre-Raphaelites. Greenacre, according to William Michael Rossetti's memoir, grew up in the Newington Butts neighborhood that was Siddall's childhood home; his memoir, in fact, fictively imagines Siddall as a toddler being helped across the street by the rapacious young man.[32] Executed for his crimes at Newgate in 1837 before thousands of onlookers, Greenacre killed his fiancée, Hannah Brown, in an apparent pique of rage when he discovered that she was not, as he had thought, a wealthy woman. He cut her legs and head from the torso, and then concealed her body parts in various sites across London. These parts were discovered, gradually, over the course of several months, inciting a frenzy in Londoners as they eagerly watched the macabre tale unfold in the press with each discovery.

The context of these textual disruptions is telling. The first mention of Greenacre appears on the second page of the novel, as Siddall imagines ritualistically "count[ing] the pieces" of Hannah Brown's body—"severed arms, legs, the head caught in the weir"—and just three pages later she associates Greenacre's violence with that of the Crimean War being waged during the novel's action. Later in the novel, a conversation between Siddall and Rossetti about his failure to finish a portrait of her sparks memories of a series of other fragmentations: "It was connecting terror of that far past," she explains, "the wrong they did Abélard... that reminded me of others.... Mr. Greenacre.... Then, I was afraid, remembering the guillotine in Paris." The medieval Abélard was castrated for his illicit affair with Heloise. "I put it all together," she continues, "Mr. Greenacre cutting her up and her head caught in the weir (which had a gate that pulled up, like ... the guillotine) and then Abélard and the wrong they did him." Another reference juxtaposes Siddall's irrational fear of Greenacre with a Parisian hospital for war veterans, *Les Invalides*, which also houses tombs of famous military figures, including that of Napoleon. When Siddall asks Rossetti, "why did he cut her up?" he mistakenly believes she is asking about the allegorical paintings championing French martial power that adorn the hospital's dome: "There's a chap splashed blood, I mean paint, all over the walls of *Les Invalides*. But he didn't paint the pieces. He left all that out, in his glory-of-battle pictures. ... [but] you couldn't stop war." A few pages later, Siddall compares the Greenacre crime to "the dead and wounded at Sebastopol,"[33] a Crimean city relentlessly under attack for nearly a year by British and French forces during the Crimean War. As Aldington explains to H.D. in a 1947 letter, it is the capture of Sebastopol in September of 1855 that marks the end of the war.[34] In one startling scene, Morris imagines himself as Greenacre holding a knife, Siddall his victim.[35]

"'One fear joins to another fear—one fear reminds one of another,'" Siddall tells Rossetti, elucidating the connection between seemingly disparate, but in fact deeply intertwined, sources. "'[O]ne shock begets another,'" the refrain reappears in the book, "'one fear is sometimes displaced on another.'"[36] Siddall fears the very dismemberment to which Rossetti's paintings subject her. Anxieties about gender, Greenacre, and war converge around the body's objectification and dismemberment. In the World War II years, H.D. would have witnessed frequently the ritual retrieval of human body parts in the streets of London following each bombing of the Blitz. It is, however, that other "world war"—the Crimean War—that offers a haunting backdrop to this novel. H.D. writes in 1948 to Pearson that she attributes Siddall's suicide to "a sort of submerged war-phobia (rather than Rossetti's actual neglect)."[37] Pointedly, as noted above, she argues with Pearson that his feelings about the atomic bomb parallel those of Morris for Crimea.[38] The Crimean War's significance to H.D.'s text is further evidenced in an exchange of letters with Aldington, who (at her request) sends her a detailed description of the conflict and its resolution, which reapportioned Eastern Europe and stripped Russia of its territorial holdings. In the novel, Siddall's father is constantly "talking about honour" and war; her "phobia" escalates when he tells her, "War is never far off—it doesn't depend on where you send your soldiers."[39]

But the war is not the only central political event of the novel, and at one point Siddall feels "the shock of the Mutiny"—the violence against Indian and British subjects alike—as it "struck at her."[40] We know from history that the Sepoy revolt against the British East India Company failed to win Indian independence; in fact, it accelerated British occupation and led directly to British Crown rule over the region. At the close of the Sepoy Rebellion, the British executed mutineers by dismembering them, tying them to the mouths of canons and exploding them into pieces. All of the threads of this elaborate metaphor are woven together in the only purely fictional character in H.D.'s text, Godfrey Lushington, who goes East to India when the Rebellion begins and never returns.[41] Lushington's first name evokes that of the leader of the first Crusade, Godfrey of Bouillon, and his surname suggests both the lushness and excess of his destination and his desire for Indian luxuries, a desire that drives and rationalizes British presence in the East. An Oxford grad and British politician, Lushington is at once Pre-Raphaelite brother, military hero, and British bureaucrat. While Godfrey Lushington is worshipped by Morris, Siddall guesses that Lushington's motives are less than honorable, just as many of the medieval Crusaders were motivated by more than religious reasons. H.D.'s reading about the historical trade with the East for luxuries—in Warmington's *The Commerce Between the Roman Empire and India* and Byron's *Byzantine Achievement*—may well have come into play here; as noted in the previous chapter, H.D., too, had taken particular note of Ezra Pound's characterization of the Albigensian Crusade as "a sordid robbery cloaking itself in religious pretense."[42] Lushington's trip to India is called a "pilgrimage," but Siddall and Rossetti are not deceived. For Lushington, Siddall prophesizes, "'There are plans and portents and a diamond. The Queen wears more jewels than she can carry. . . . The servant of the Queen is Crusader by profession. . . . Sceptre and Crown are indicated.'" And Rossetti is of the same mind when he later imagines that Lushington has "'wormed his way into the East India Company, disguised as an honest down-at-heels accountant. What these fellows won't do.'" Scathingly, he describes Lushington and his ilk as "'[s]tatesmen and authority . . . doing things across chessboards.'" Privately, Morris admits to himself that his only associations with India concern its luxuries, "rugs, the shawl his mother cherished, one of the early imported cashmeres." He remembers his father and associates talking "of 'India and the Company.' It was part of adventure, Drake, Hawkins, Raleigh."[43] Having read a great deal about the trade with the East in luxuries, and having written about Drake and Raleigh in *By Avon River*, H.D., then, further links England's commercial interests in India with the Renaissance-era settling of the West Indies, England's first real imperialist mission.

Dubbed a "Crusader" in the novel, the figure of Lushington conjoins the roles of medieval Crusader and British imperialist, a move that implies a further parallel between two historical events of violent domination and appropriation of the East. Crusaders in this novel bear images of eagles on their backs, which H.D. linked to Nazism.[44] The Pre-Raphaelites, of course, were drawn to the medieval period. In a story within the story, Siddall's unfinished medieval tale, Godfrey Lushington is a medieval knight in the courtly love tradition, but at the same time, "[s]he wanted Godfrey in the story, to belong to England."[45] The link between the British colonization of India and the Crusades of the Middle Ages is strengthened by an instance of H.D.'s wordplay typical of this time period.[46] Rossetti informs Morris, "*In-dia*, it is one of the clue words of Dante. . . . It's just one of his countless rubrics, anagrams, enigmas. *In-dia* can possibly be translated in-spirits, in and Deus, in-God."[47] Here India becomes *In-dia*, "in God," a new Jerusalem for the British imperialist "Crusaders" of the Victorian age.

Siddall herself links Dante's love of Beatrice with the Crusades.[48] Like the worship of the objectified female in the medieval courtly love tradition, a practice mirrored in Pre-Raphaelitism, the Crusades were waged around an abstraction—a "dream," as H.D. would say—but the Crusades ravaged, fragmented, and reunified material bodies and land in service to an ideal. Siddall, in fact, is "certain you could die of a dream."[49] In military action—in India or Crimea, or even the U.S. Civil War, which is briefly mentioned in the novel as well—bodies are objects. Like the unending quest for the Grail, the reach for transcendence is doomed to fail, but there is and was much material gain—in the opening of commercial markets and trade. "*In-dia*" represents a country divided—doomed perhaps to be partitioned—a holy land violently split by invaders, traffickers, colonialists, and natives. The resistance of the Sepoy Rebellion resulted from this rift, which was only widened into a chasm by the brutal British military presence that put it down.

The British Empire's forays into various lands, its martial engagements, function as a lingering and ominous presence in the text, destabilizing and fragmenting the narrative and, ultimately, Siddall's mental well-being and her life. Rossetti's character declares, "'I don't care for history myself,'"[50] and his devotion to pure aestheticism, to the worship of beauty, in the midst of the 1850s political situation, speaks volumes and recalls H.D.'s characterization of Shakespeare in *By Avon River*. India is not the setting of the text, however, and there are no Indian characters. H.D. does not portray the Rebellion or the victims of "Crusading" figures like Godfrey Lushington. On the one hand, H.D. was certainly not a political radical or activist, and it is not surprising that her characters' concerns with India seem confined to the politics of British imperialism and war and do not extend to the subjugated population of the region. It should be stated, too, that her refusal to represent India might be read—and rightly so, at least in part—as a failure of the imagination or an exploitative use of India as mere metaphor. While she challenges the politics of British imperialism, she also ignores the people rising up against it in the late 1850s. Though Gikandi suggests that "women were ideally placed to understand the ways in which alterity was constitutive of identity, of how the narrative of order and civility was predicated on the disorder and excess excluded from the big houses of Englishness," he also warns that women were often complicit in the colonialist project, and reminds readers of "the important role they play in the institutionalization of the dominant discourse of empire and the authority of colonial culture."[51] Jane Garrity, too, alleges that though British women writers of the interwar period critique imperialism, "they nonetheless remain invested in an idea of nation that is inextricably tied up in conceptions of the female body which in turn cannot be severed from their concept of empire."[52] To an extent, H.D. appropriates India as metaphor for her own ends, but unlike Garrity's subjects she does not idealize England. The figure of Siddall is mapped not to England—as the body of the woman had been mapped in *The Gift*,[53] and as Garrity observes of writings by other women—but to India. The shift, then, from woman as war-torn England to one of its colonies is significant, as England is no longer victim but perpetrator of violence.

Indeed, India in the novel is a vanishing point, a vortex into which Lushington disappears irrevocably. The ephemeral *"In-dia"* threatens to become an afterworld or heaven, a mythical space of death, and here H.D. falls into logics that had guided her earlier thinking about the country. In *White Rose*, India also threatens to become, to borrow Said's term, an "imagined geography," a fictionalized partitioning of space that distinguishes between the "civilized" and the "barbarians," a "construction that fold[s] distance into difference."[54] But India for H.D. is not, as Gikandi remarks of other modernists' writing of Africa, a space where the "subject can recode its world or even hallow a space in which it can contemplate itself"[55]; it is not an instance of "exploring the depths of the self by imagining it on exotic or fantastic travels," as David Adams alleges in his recent study of modernists writing the "Voyage In."[56] It is not, likewise, a liminal "Oriental" space that is paradoxically at once both familiar and foreign, "in which things came to be seen as neither completely novel nor thoroughly familiar."[57] It is, rather, a void; its geography and its people are simply not represented at all. Patricia Yaeger has usefully mused that "space moves out in all directions at once, and it is difficult to imagine a narrative structure capable of capturing this multiplicity."[58] India in much of modernism is just such a space that resists narration.

And, yet, if India is invisible in *White Rose*—if H.D. has refused to represent it in the often-dubious ways that her modernist comrades did—it is not entirely an unnarratable space. Siddall is, in fact, upset at the silence surrounding the 1857 tragedy: "No one ever spoke of the Indian Mutiny."[59] India is the site of a rebellion, even if the battles and atrocities are not portrayed for the reader. If specific acts of violence are not mentioned, the violence of the Sepoy Rebellion is palpable in the text because H.D. so intricately aligns it with so many other kinds and instances of violence, and it is fear of such violence that finally shatters Siddall. H.D.'s decision to reference, in the very year of India's independence, the very violence that led to its colonization cannot be an act of nostalgia for either an imperial or a pre-imperial past. It is to be read, rather, in terms of H.D.'s other late work, such as *Trilogy*; it is an act of recovering memory spurred by a desire to remember the violence of the past lest we repeat it in the future. *White Rose* lingers stubbornly in the nineteenth century and in the medieval period, and never ventures into the ancient world. In fact, what is striking about *White Rose*, in relation to the rest of H.D.'s *oeuvre*—from her ancient-Greek-inspired Imagist lyrics to the epic Euripidean *Helen in Egypt*—is just how modern it is.

Moreover, and perhaps more to the point, this broken *In-dia* is located in its recent past but haunted by its present, its paradoxical status as both newly divided and newly unified, for various regions scrambled to join India or Pakistan in the summer of 1947. And the parallel between the female body and India points to a much more complicated interpretation of this refusal of representation, for if India is an unknowable, unreadable, fragmented victim of British violence, so, too, is Siddall's body. This book, after all, is very much about the ways in which women and their bodies are not seen—not read—for what they are; they are metaphors or metonyms, icons or screens. They are idealized, romanticized, worshipped, even exoticized, in art and in life. "Her humanity was at war with the fiction woven round her," H.D. explains of Siddall,[60] and it is a battle she loses when she overdoses on laudanum in an attempt to stem the pain. Like India, Siddall's body lies constantly in peril, on the edge of disappearing altogether. H.D. read and took notes on Francis Bickley's 1932 *The Pre-Raphaelite Comedy*, which contained descriptions of the disappearing body of Siddall such as this one: "She seems to float in an alien air, a pale and lonely figure without a background." H.D. copied into her notes his melodramatized portrayal of Siddall—"looking thinner & more death-like," "consumed in the fire of [Rossetti's] own vitality."[61] Writing to Aldington about her work in progress, H.D. plays on the contradictory and ephemeral quality of Siddall when she dubs her "a possible 'not impossible she'" and she compares her to "'ghosts that crowd about life's empty day.'"[62] H.D. portrays a weakening, fading Siddall in her text. The Morris character sees Siddall as a ghost, and the Rossetti figure is even dismayed, at one point, when Siddall returns home from Paris "stronger, better."[63]

Geographer Simon Springer has theorized that the geography of the West has created spaces of alterity that are simultaneously spaces of irrationality, "a discourse that binds violence in place." In this way, a dominant nation can be construed as rational, its violent acts wholly justifiable. This categorization reproduces a particular structure of power: "Sanctioning certain acts of violence as 'rational,' while condemning others as 'irrational' can be discerned as a primary instrument of power insofar as perceived rationality becomes misconstrued with legitimacy."[64] H.D. defies this logic when she analogizes India to Siddall's body and the body of Greenacre's victim, for by doing so she contains the irrational violence *within* the borders of the major metropole of the British Empire. The invisibility of India is not, here, a source of comfort to the reader, but a source of anxiety; it destabilizes the text in much the way the vanishing body of Siddall does. "The empire," Ian Baucom has argued powerfully, "is less a place where England exerts control than the place where England loses command of its own narrative of identity."[65] This is the empire portrayed in *White Rose*.

By concluding with Siddall's untimely death, H.D.'s novel makes clear not just the spiritual but the material costs issuing from this complicated web of gender and military politics. Siddall—who almost died posing as Ophelia in John Everett Millais' well known Pre-Raphaelite painting—is ultimately as expendable to her cohorts as are those who died, mutilated, in the Middle East, in India, in Crimea, in H.D.'s World War II London. Siddall is fragmented, abstracted, and etherealized to the point of nonexistence. Invoked on the final page of the text is Rossetti's exhumation of Siddall's grave years later, to extract a part of her—his sonnet sequence devoted to her. The final words of the novel lament, from the Pre-Raphaelite Brotherhood's perspective, not the woman but the *"face we knew."*[66]

After visiting Campione d'Italia in 1947—an Italian enclave within Swiss borders—H.D. remarks of the region, "I have been very India-conscious since seeing it, and realize [Hermann] Hesse's meaning, when he speaks of things here being like Asia and the East. Campione is like a Ganges village, and I think the churches here are much more like rather painted shrines."[67] For a writer who considered her "home" to be, alternately, the U.S., England, Italy, Greece, and Switzerland, this statement extends the notion to the East, to India specifically, and in the very year it became detached from the Empire. The gesture is, of course, problematic. In comparing one of her favorite towns to the East, she envisions a transcultural world with a shared history, reminding Europeans of their engagements with the East, but in imagining in European terms an area of the world she has never seen or experienced, she also risks becoming an imperialist herself. She sees the East only in the terms of the West. She, like her modernist cohorts, seeks "an expansion of home, reflecting a desire to be at home everywhere."[68] But the gesture is also emblematic of the direction H.D.'s work takes in the years during and immediately after the Second World War. While many other late modernists took an "anthropological turn" inward, H.D. reached outward, resisting the nostalgic provincialism Esty finds in works by Eliot, Forster, and Woolf. If *Majic Ring* posits a shared heritage for the world's population, *The Mystery* (1950–1951), as we will see in the next chapter, conceptualizes world unification under a heterodox religious umbrella. H.D.'s aim is not to rebuild and redeem a broken nation—to reimagine a pre-imperial England—but to expose its history of imperialism and diagnose its penchant for war.

INTERLUDE

6

The Mystery

> It is more than family history. It is history.
>
> —H.D., *The Mystery*

H.D.'s interest in politics had begun to wane by 1950, her separation from England more definitive and final after spending almost half a decade in Switzerland. Just after her 1946 move to Switzerland, she still craved contemporary news, demanding of Bryher in October of 1946 "a summary" of "'politics,'" a request that yielded a letter about Churchill, Tory campaigns, and food rationing in postwar London.[1] In February of 1947, she was still routinely reading *Time Magazine* and British newspapers, and she complained to Bryher, "I can not tell you how ravening hungry and starved I am for the real news of London," praising Bryher's recent letter of factories closing in England for giving her the kind of news she wants.[2] She wrote to Bryher in June 1947 that she appreciated an update on striking workers in London, and she told her in August that she was excited to discover a kiosk where she could buy current newspapers: "I am afraid I am really taking a 'keen' interest in present-day affairs. I dash down to my best kiosk and grab two of the papers, they vary but I get head-line news about shipments of gold here, in the last days and tales of bank-notes, sent by air."[3] Her fervor for wanting to be in the know matches that of the war period.

No doubt concerned for H.D.'s mental stability, Bryher, for her part, began to discourage talk of politics, sending her reassuring letters that world affairs are in order and that H.D. should not fret. Over time, H.D. appears to grow less and less interested, and, by the time that she writes her novel *Magic Mirror* in 1956, she jokes about "political problems" that "she was too old, too lazy or too old-fashioned to understand."[4] This was perhaps inevitable given the extent of her isolation in Switzerland, away from London, that site of a great deal of both happiness and anguish for her. At the urging of H.D.'s Swiss doctors, Bryher had decided that moving H.D. back to London was inadvisable—that H.D. should, in fact, never return to the place where she survived two world wars, even for a short visit. As she recovers in the fall of 1946, H.D. repeatedly pleads her case for returning to England, expresses frustration that she is not being permitted to go home, writes London friends that she would be visiting soon, and insists on keeping her Kensington flat for that purpose. Bryher is discouraging, warning her of the adverse postwar conditions of London and advising her that she risks losing foreign resident status in Switzerland if she makes trips to London.[5] In February of 1947, H.D. timidly confesses to being "homesick" and begins to ask to go to Oxford or Stratford instead of London. By 1948, though, she appears to be resigned to staying in Switzerland, writing Bryher that "I do not see myself, in any way, in England for some time" and that "I am very, very firm and feel stabilized but my foot-hold seems Suisse."[6]

Completed in 1951, in the midst of this process of pulling away, H.D.'s novella *The Mystery* occupies a liminal position in her late career *oeuvre*. It represents an interlude—a "bridge," to use one of her favorite terms of this period—between the rawer, more critical texts of the late 1940s and the more contemplative prose of the 1950s, even as it draws on the optimistic vision of her writings before the close of the war. In *The Mystery*, she entertains many of the devices and motifs of *Sword* and *White Rose* discussed in previous chapters, but she puts them to alternate uses, offers different inflections of meaning, works toward building rather than tearing down. She saw *The Mystery* as a bookend to the period, a "FINIS ... to a whole processus or lifetime of experience," or so she writes to Pearson when she had completed the book. But it stands also as the beginning of the final phase of her prose. This ending is a beginning: the "serpent bites its own tail, at last."[7]

In many ways, *The Mystery* is much like the postwar prose of the late 1940s. The Moravian Elizabeth de Watteville nurses a would-be monk, Saint-Germain, back to life after a spiritual crisis, a scene reminiscent of Claribel attending a fallen soldier in the first half of *By Avon River*. Saint-Germain prepares to become a soldier by the end of the novella, and de Watteville is an incarnation of "Our Lady," a prominent figure of adoration in H.D.'s *Trilogy*, *By Avon River*, and *White Rose*.[8] But de Watteville as "Our Lady" isn't the disappearing phantom of *White Rose* who disintegrates under the objectifying gaze of her male companions. Gone is the critique of the worship of the transcendent feminine we find in *White Rose*. By 1951, H.D. has seemingly recovered her faith in a feminine ideal. As Jane Augustine's introduction to the edition notes, Elizabeth is no less than "an incarnation of the feminine Holy Spirit."[9]

Like *Sword* and *White Rose*, *The Mystery* is a work of historical fiction. As such, it blends fact and fiction—or, as H.D. writes in the epigraph to the novella, "fact and fantasy."[10] Moreover, like its immediate predecessors, its action unfolds not in the ancient world but in modern Europe. Eighteenth-century Prague is its setting, and its subject is the story of actual historical personages: the cousins Henry Dohna and Elizabeth de Watteville, grandchildren of the Moravian church leader Count Zinzendorf; the courtier and reputed magician Comte de Saint-Germain; and the nefarious Freemason Cagliostro. Various wars rage in *By Avon River* and *Sword*, while *White Rose* uses the Crimean War and the Sepoy Rebellion as backdrop. *The Mystery* begins near the eve of the American and French Revolutions. *The Mystery*, in many ways, as Augustine has argued, completes a project on the history of Moravianism begun in *The Gift*.

As in her fiction of the immediate postwar period, H.D.'s *The Mystery* is as much about the *process* of the making of story as about the story itself—and the making of historical fiction in particular. Henry Dohna, who shares H.D.'s initials, is the principal storyteller of the novella. It is he who aims to reconstruct the historical narrative of Zinzendorf's reestablishment of Moravianism. He labors in archives while de Watteville works fervently at her embroidery. His goals are ambitious: "'It is more than family history. It is history.'" But, as he complains at one point to his sympathetic cousin, "'It is not easy to write the story.'" Dohna is increasingly frustrated with historical records, which he beings to realize only tell part of the story: "'I feel there's something lost,'" he exclaims to an ever-patient de Watteville, who apparently agrees with his assessment when she argues that they should not read a stash of Zinzendorf's letters in search of the truth. De Watteville advocates an approach to creating narrative that is more aligned with embroidery. Dohna concedes that "'there is an emotional clue'" missing: "'When you get that you have everything.'" But when de Watteville argues that "'we have all the threads even if the picture isn't clear,'" Dohna believes that this "'emotional clue'" is still lurking, yet to be found in secret lore, the *Arcana*.[11]

Interestingly, as Saint-Germain joins their quest, he realizes what de

Watteville has known all along: that any history is also, necessarily, a fiction. Saint-Germain decides not to "reconstruct the entire story" because "that would make a memoir of it, not a dream, a fantasy." Moreover, he knows that story must rely on sources in legend, not just fact. "You didn't, as a rule, want to verify the Mystery," Saint-Germain warns, "If it was not true, it was better not to know it." And Dohna eventually comes to realize that de Watteville and Saint-Germain are right. Late in the novella, he admits to his cousin that "'there was no use trying to find the answer to the Mystery, in the veritable mountain of reports, records, legal documents and endless, tabulated bundles of old letters.'" Historical fiction is not just a textual project for Saint-Germain, or for de Watteville as she carefully stitches her tapestry; it is physical, one that one must "*act out* . . . for yourself." The historical narrative is part of the body, "infinite, tenuous, remote, drawn from his very belly," and it is "easy to understand, but only by those who had had experience of it." De Watteville agrees, "'If you love people, you live back into their lives.'" But it is not just physical but metaphysical, a process of alchemy. The process, Dohna decides in the end, is indeed more akin to alchemy—a process of selection, but also a magical transformation of elements into gold: "'[W]e have sifted the old matter and saved only what we felt was true gold.'" Though H.D. remains interested in the process of memory and the construction of narratives based in fact, her characters are moving away from the material world and into a realm of ideals and vision. The characters are searching for no less than a "plan of world-unity without war."[12]

In *The Mystery*, then, H.D. seems to be attempting to build something, rather than dismantle it. The cousins, with Saint-Germain, are trying to assemble and create, although the book is not a completed project of redemption or restoration. But the often-dissonant tension between the two interwoven stories—of the Moravian cousins and of Saint-Germain—mark this text as one of a transitional moment. The story of the luminous Elizabeth de Watteville is in many ways more akin to H.D.'s work before her post-traumatic reaction to World War II. As Saint-Germain's identity splinters slowly over the course of the book, de Watteville becomes a powerful and transformative spiritual presence that appears to transcend time and space. She is an incarnation of Our Lady, so prominent in *By Avon River* and *Trilogy*. Reminiscent of the latter, de Watteville is a cognate of Isis, helping her cousin to piece together and interpret a historical narrative. The goal in *The Mystery*—which was, at one stage of its composition, entitled "The Miracle"[13]—is to uncover a religious truth that will save the world from its endless cycles of warfare. As Augustine writes in her introduction to the edition, de Watteville is the object of a "transcendental love" at once erotic and spiritual.[14]

Saint-Germain, one the other hand, seems to be a character who would be more at home in H.D.'s work of the immediate postwar period. De Watteville tells Dohna that story is embroidery, and Saint-Germain's metaphor for historical reconstruction is weaving, which he sees not as a man's work but as God's. But while de Watteville brings a tapestry to life, Saint-Germain's threads are becoming loose, unraveling: "The strings had freed themselves," he realizes at one point.[15] This story, of Saint-Germain, is reminiscent of *Sword*, for he is torn between time periods and dimensions. In that story, time collapses in such a way that historical eras overlap, and periods of war and trauma are repeated.

De Watteville's divine presence stands in sharp contrast to that of Saint-Germain, her ailing "knight." Like other characters in the immediate postwar period, Saint-Germain is a time-traveller. The historical Saint-Germain was reputed to be immortal—to have appeared in various countries over the course of several centuries—and H.D.'s Saint-Germain is stuck in an unrelenting cycle of time travel. He, like Delia's myriad selves of *Sword* discussed in Chapter 2, does not choose or will his journeys. "It could happen at any time, with anybody," he explains, and his attempts to gain control over the power are futile: "He had tried in his own room, to prolong the sensation, in order to understand it, but he had no control over it. It was baffling." Moreover, he does not view this experience as spiritual in any way: "There was no particular ecstasy, exaltation or grace connected with the experiences, nor their opposite." Saint-Germain can exist outside of time at least temporarily—at one point in the novella, he is suspended dangerously between dimensions—but ultimately, he is bound to time and history. In fact, these experiences are traumatic; much of the middle of the novella portrays a grave illness that results from his inability to return from one such flight between dimensions and times. As in *Sword*, he experiences time travel as a debilitating disintegration of the self; when he finally recuperates from one such voyage, he represents his recovery as the restoration of the self: "This was that Saint-Germain. Myself again? Almost myself again? He had re-assembled that self, during his enforced retirement."[16] Crucially, though, H.D.'s narrative does not take her readers with Saint-Germain on his travels. We remain rooted in the novella's present and do not experience the trauma-inducing scenes of *Sword*.

H.D. models Saint-Germain on Faust, for he has sold his soul for the power of immortality, a gift that also proves to be his doom.[17] "He had sold his shadow," we are told in this novella in language that evokes Faustian legend, "he had bartered his soul, equally to God and Devil."[18] Saint-Germain, moreover, is a spy. Discussed at greater length in Chapter 8, the spy is a figure that preoccupies H.D. throughout the early to mid-1950s. This book prefigures that interest, though it does so without the critical distance on the paranoiac culture of espionage evident in her later work. In *The Mystery*, in eighteenth-century Prague, Saint-Germain is a double agent. Pretending and concealing allegiances to both Freemasonry and the Jesuits, he poses as Antonius, a Franciscan monk, as part of a secret plot by the real-life figure Cardinal de Rohan to root out heretics. Promising Cagliostro he will protect the Freemasons, he also promises de Rohan that he will expose them. Over the course of the book, Saint-Germain plots with Stephanus, a man posing as his servant; carries out a clandestine meeting with Cagliostro; and reflects on his secret conversations with de Rohan. As Saint-Germain suspects when he notes de Watteville's subtle deviance from traditional worship practices, de Watteville and Dohna, too, are not what they seem. They are Protestants attempting to elude the watchful eyes of the Catholics, on a quest for Zinzendorf's secret plan for a one-world religion.[19] The main characters of *The Mystery* are performing roles.

Saint-Germain is not just a spy but a magician as well, the *Bateleur* of Jean Chaboseau's kabbalistic *Le Tarot*,[20] which H.D. read repeatedly in her late career. In this context, the spy bears a strong resemblance to the magician. H.D. read widely about the magus or magician, in sources that ranged from scholarly to occult, from carefully constructed genealogies of the Faust myth to how-to manuals of magic and Tarot.[21] H.D. was fascinated by the magician as a profoundly dualistic figure who possesses genuine paranormal powers but who is just as capable of charlatanism and deceit, a phenomenon H.D.'s friend Eliza Butler, a Cambridge scholar of German literature, describes as "two souls in the magician's breast striving for supremacy."[22] Elsewhere, Butler writes of these contradictory characters that they are at once "[f]ounders and teachers of religion; sacrificed savior-gods; rebels and martyrs; sinners and saints; mystery-men and occultists; conjurers, charlatans and quacks."[23]

In *The Mystery*, the shadowy Cagliostro, who secretly visits Saint-Germain in his room, can be seen as Saint-Germain's darker self. The historical

Cagliostro, after all, was publicly exposed as a fraud, a fact recounted in all of the sources H.D. read, and Butler positions Saint-Germain as the "white" counterpart to Faust's (and perhaps Cagliostro's) black soul. But Saint-Germain himself is not the embodiment of purity. He serves simultaneously two sinister masters—de Rohan and Cagliostro—even while he struggles to free himself of their demands. "[Y]ou will be surprised 'in our next' to see what a two-faced Imago Saint-Germain turns out to be," H.D. warns Pearson, who is eagerly following her composition as it unfolds.[24] In fact, Saint-Germain in *The Mystery* bears little resemblance to the historical Saint-Germain described in Butler, Lévi, or Magre, all of whom depict a charismatic, debonair courtier who wines and dines his way into the hearts and purses of kings, queens, and wealthy ladies. H.D.'s Saint-Germain is quiet, awkward, psychologically tormented, and uncertain of his powers. While Butler's magus figure suffers a violent death and is resurrected, H.D.'s Saint-Germain is doomed to immortality, forced against his will to wander among historical periods. And while women rarely play a significant role in the legend of magicians, de Watteville serves as a potential vehicle of redemption for Saint-Germain, as a source of both spiritual and erotic love.[25]

Saint-Germain as magician, then, is significantly reimagined in *The Mystery*. If her sources portrayed him as the prototypical good magician, counterpart to the evil Cagliostro, H.D. is more interested in Saint-Germain's divided self. In the 1950s, she would go on to write of a series of magicians, her male "initiators," a group that included, variously, depending on the source, Ezra Pound, D. H. Lawrence, Richard Aldington, John Cournos, Cecil Grey, Kenneth Macpherson, Peter Rodeck, Hugh Dowding, Conrad Veidt, Arthur Bhaduri, Sigmund Freud, Walter Schmideberg, and Erich Heydt.[26] She would also stress the magician's "Protean" qualities and dub him "Hermes, musician, healer, actor, charlatan."[27] Saint-Germain is a discursive manifestation of this recurring figure.

Saint-Germain's divided self entails a doubling, ego and alter-ego. He is doubly doubled, however, in that he has the power of bi-location, appearing in two places at once. The historical Saint-Germain was reputed to have had this paranormal ability, and this is retained in H.D.'s version of the figure, who discovers that "two worlds could manifest, separately, to the same person."[28] H.D. was fascinated by bi-location. Books H.D. loved, including Violet Hunt's *Tales of the Uneasy* and Eliza Butler's *Silver Wings*, make use of the device, and H.D.'s *Majic Ring* and *Tribute to Freud* suggest that she believes she may have witnessed this phenomenon firsthand in a male companion, Peter Rodeck, who was apparently below deck on the ship *Borodino* and on deck with H.D. at the same time.[29] If, in the early *Palimpsest*, as noted in Chapter 2, the protagonist merely imagines a character in two places at once, the later prose makes this fantasy a reality.

H.D. dubs this phenomenon "the Mystery," and in *Sword* she cites her source for bi-location as Camille Flammarion's three-volume series, *Death and Its Mystery*: "It is a mystery not uncommon to folk and fairy-tales, the mystery of the appearance of a stranger or a near-stranger, at a time and in a place where he could not possibly have been. Such things have happened. Some instances of this kind have been recorded by Camille Flammarion, in *Death and Its Mystery*."[30] An astronomer and spiritualist, Flammarion uses a multitude of case studies to document a range of experiences of bi-location, arguing that "[t]he examples of phantasms, of bilocation, of apparitions, are so numerous that it is impossible to rule them all out of existence and to deny their reality," and that "we must apply to metaphysical research the same rational rules we apply to all branches of science."[31] H.D. writes in *Sword* that Delia had found his lengthy tomes in a spiritualist library, Stanford House, during the war, and that she particularly valued his rigorous approach to the topic: "I found many interesting histories or case-histories of dual personality, projection of the 'double,' telepathic and other psychic communications, messages received from the living, as well as the familiar last words of soldier sons, posted in distant colonies. The most scientific of these volumes were the accurately recorded data of Camille Flammarion."[32] Flammarion explains bi-location via the divided nature of the human, soul and body: "The body is visible and ponderable. The soul may manifest itself physically in phantasms of the living."[33]

Matte Robinson locates another source on the phenomenon of bi-location in Robert Ambelain's *Dans l'Ombre des Cathédrales*, a book H.D. read and annotated. Robinson points out that H.D. would have been drawn to Ambelain's belief that bi-location entailed an initiation into access to an otherworldly realm, and this source is particularly helpful in understanding H.D.'s poetry of the mid- to late 1950s. In an increasingly secular world, Michel de Certeau remarks, the mystical experience becomes interiorized— it "migrate[s] inward"—but in *The Mystery* the experience is very much material, of the body.[34] In *Sword*, H.D.'s astral travelers cannot escape time or space; Saint-Germain seems to be a liminal figure, one who is equally stuck, caught up in a cycle of traumatic historical periods, transitioning between times and places, as discussed above, without control over his experience. But he is also able to experience bi-location and to bear witness to it. Unlike *Sword*'s Delia, Saint-Germain does not always remain fixed in historical time and space; he can occupy an astral plane. He entertains "Visitors" seemingly outside of time, such as the Moravian leader Count Zinzendorf, who himself was rumored to have appeared simultaneously in two places at once.[35] Saint-Germain acts as a Hermetic figure, a "bridge" between worlds.[36]

The experience of seeing oneself as a double is termed autoscopy or heautoscopy in psychiatric literature, and James Grotstein, perhaps the most dedicated researcher in the field, calls autoscopy the "quintessence of self-consciousness." Seeing another person as a double—an imposter—is called Capgras syndrome, and both are typical, quite normal experiences when they occur in dreams, the realm of the unconscious. Grotstein relies on Freud's well-known essay on the uncanny for an explanation of this kind of doubling phenomena. Freud, Grotstein notes, sees doubling as both the "manifestation of primary narcissism and a denotation of its dissolution."[37] The creation of the ego, which involves the process of repression, is experienced as uncanny; the uncanny registers the ego's essential instability. The double reappears in a later phase of maturity as well, however, to signal the return of the repressed: "The idea of the 'double' does not necessarily disappear with the passing of primary narcissism, for it can receive fresh meaning from the later stages of the ego's development." Freud argues that "whatever reminds us of this inner 'compulsion to repeat' is perceived as uncanny." It is "the process of repression" that has "alienated" "something which is familiar and old-established in the mind."[38] The experience of the uncanny, then, stems from the death drive. The same repetition compulsion experienced after trauma arises here, within the context of the uncanny.

Because H.D. knew and read Freud's essay on doubling and the uncanny, it cannot be overlooked as another source on bi-location. The doppelganger, or double, is one of Freud's primary examples of the uncanny's expression. When the ego is threatened, the split within the self manifests externally and materially, the double a reminder of the crucial and precarious moment in which the ego began to take shape. Grotstein points out that the formation of the ego occurs when infants grasp object permanence and can enter the symbolic realm: "This aspect of autoscopy represents Freud's conception of the infant's capacity to hallucinate the presence of the mother in her absence and constitutes the beginning of symbolization and the capacity to represent objects in their absence."[39] In a related fashion, one figure can serve as a substitute or screen for another, and, as discussed in the previous chapter, H.D. is interested here and elsewhere with the extent to which women are symbolic. Indeed, Saint-Germain wonders of de Watteville—who he believes may share his power of bi-location—"Was she a symbol merely?" He decides that "[s]he was a screen, a veil" and thus "[s]he could appear where she was not." Thinking of Dante—as H.D. was in this time period, at work on translating *La Vita Nuova*—he puzzles through the use of Beatrice, too, as "a screen, a veil." He realizes that he himself, when he appears in two places at once, serves as a "screen."[40] Here, H.D. makes use of a psychoanalytic narrative to explain an occult phenomenon in a way that makes of Saint-Germain a text subject to interpretation. For H.D., the formation of the ego also entails the formation of the astral self.

Grotstein concludes that "[t]he phantom of autoscopy represents a special instance of the return of an outraged, disavowed self which now haunts the disavowing self. It now becomes the omniscient observer to its former disdainful observer."[41] Indeed, in some ways this "outraged, disavowed self" bears considerable resemblance to Kristeva's abject, that which is expelled from the ego and exiled to a realm beyond meaning, beyond the symbolic order, that which "disturbs identity, system, order. What does not respect borders, positions, rules. The in-between, the ambiguous, the composite." Like the doppelganger, the abject is the result of "a kind of *narcissistic crisis*." The abject conceals and reveals the trauma of loss inherent in the formation of the self. For Kristeva, "the abject appears in order to uphold 'I'"; it is, in effect, the self as other. Paradoxically, abjection is at once "a time of oblivion" and "the moment when revelation bursts forth."[42]

When Delia's identity splits multiply across a range of stories, times, and places in *Sword* in response to the war and its aftermath, her self re-experiences the trauma of ego formation even while it endures its dispersal and disintegration. Her visionary experience is irrational, delusional—the result of a brief psychotic break—and her travels defy the laws of physics. Her exiled selves wander through the annals of history and through a range of alter egos, at one point doubling within a single story. In *The Mystery*, it is not the trauma of war but the anxieties preceding an inevitable war that trigger

Saint-Germain's wanderings. The loss of identity Saint-Germain expresses when he time travels or occupies the astral plane is indicative of a similar crisis of ego stability. His experiences are consistently described as reversals, precise opposites, of the norm: he can't tell left from right; "[he]e was facing the wrong way"; "[t]he Cathedral had turned round."[43] Indeed, Augustine depicts Saint-Germain's paranormal experience as seeing a photographic negative of the world.[44] His double is the antithesis of the self. With Saint-Germain, his self-loathing is palpable. Spying makes him physically ill; in the company of Cagliostro, he feels a claustrophobic "blackness unutterable."[45] It takes the transcendent presence of de Watteville to heal his body and re-stabilize his ego.

H.D. revises the psychoanalytic narrative when she reads occultic and spiritualist texts alongside Freud's essay. The estranged double is transgressive because it is, in fact, the soul, not because it is a site of repression of what we disavow. By the time H.D. writes *The Mystery*, the abject self has become the astral self. It is situated in a site beyond logic and order because it occupies an otherworldly plane of existence. The schizophrenic or psychotic experience is desirable; as Deleuze and Guattari argue, it places the self outside of the materialist logics that govern the West. For H.D., it also permits a visionary experience, which, as I discussed in Chapter 2, accompanies periods of illness. The double can only be experienced when the self is threatened or traumatized, and thus H.D.'s rhetoric in the early 1950s is, in a sense, apocalyptic, as Madelyn Detloff has observed of the early 1940s writings. "Some of the most beautiful aesthetic forms are perhaps the most problematic," Detloff warns us, "because they transform suffering into 'terrible beauty' so successfully that we might begin seeing beauty in suffering and violence rather than seeing its repulsive effects." A text like *Trilogy*, Detloff argues persuasively, is problematic precisely because of "its redemptive turn": "the poem redescribes loss as something triumphant, character-building, transformative." War is viewed as "cleansing."[46] The melancholic pain of selfhood is necessary to the experience of doubling.

Written in the immediate wake of World War II, *Sword* resists the "redemptive turn." Delia's vision is harrowing, not instructive, and what she learns, if anything, is the hopelessness of the human condition. Her characters do not experience transformation. They are fragments of selves that never reassemble themselves. With some distance on the war and its setting,

London, *The Mystery*, however, is more akin to *Trilogy*. While Saint-Germain's paranormal experiences are difficult for him, the book concludes with a restoration of the self, at the hands of de Watteville, the embodiment of the feminine ideal, and with a visitation from a key religious figure. Hope and order are reaffirmed. There is a startling revelation for Saint-Germain: "[T]he *Plan* compelled him, a mysterious plan of world-unity without war. So Zinzendorf had seen it, but it was formula already registered, already put in practice. He had thought in the Cathedral, *it was not Mystery. It was ordered, it could be explained exactly. It was part of a Plan, so subtly presented, yet so clearly that you could not miss its meaning.*"[47] Saint-Germain's plan to return to France to participate in the coming Revolution might well be read as justifying the war.

H.D.'s exploration of bi-location in this text is also evidence of her postwar reconsideration of the relationship between self and other, which, I will argue in the remaining chapters of this book, constitutes a rethinking of ethics. The double represents a splitting of two selves that entails a necessary reconsideration of the self as other. The magician's two selves are simple opposites: the bearer of magnificent and beneficent paranormal powers is also capable of deceit. He is simultaneously magus and mountebank. The next two chapters will look at more complex figures that deconstruct this binary: the "other woman" and the spy. What makes the double particularly interesting in this regard, though, is its recurrent appearance in the texts of the late 1940s and early 1950s as the revenant or ghost, another figure evocative of the uncanny. A revenant is a screen in H.D.'s work of this period; the ghostly double is symbolic of archetypes, most frequently the soldier-lover. The ghost cannot be as easily reconciled as simply a manifestation of the self. It is other in a way that is difficult to assimilate; indeed, Grotstein makes its otherness the very criterion that distinguishes autoscopy from seeing a ghost.[48] In Levinasian terms, the ghost makes demands on the self for recognition as other. A ghost is, according to Colin Davis, "a wholly irrecuperable intrusion in our world, which is not comprehensible within our available intellectual frameworks, but whose otherness we are responsible for preserving." If the other is dead, the self is a survivor and thus the identity of the self is contingent upon the other.[49] It is, writes Julian Wolfreys, "the trace of non-identity within identity."[50] Its impossibility makes for radical otherness and relegates the ghost to permanent exile.[51]

The ghosts of RAF pilots contact Delia in *Sword*. The ghost of Zinzendorf appears at the end of *The Mystery*. The ghost represents the past—the persistence of the past in the present—and the revenant's haunting of the present is not without purpose. The RAF pilots are doubled, at once dead and alive, symbolic of the military conflict that both birthed them as soldiers and ended their lives. Temporally, their otherness is inescapable, and yet their presence is also uncanny because they are manifestations of the familiar. Fred Botting argues that it is the ghost's very "doubleness," its "dynamic interplay between convention, habituation and disruption," that makes it such a desirable feature of the modernist narrative.[52] The modern gothic is "defined and bedeviled by the figure of the double."[53] Delia and Saint-Germain may be doomed to immortality, but the ghosts of these texts survive as well, following the path of history as it unfolds, one war after another. Like the spy of the late 1950s prose, the ghostly double confounds expectations. It looks like the self, but is strangely somehow not what it appears to be; it is other.

It is the double as ghost that suggests a link between this novella and those of the late 1940s in their concern with Western history. But Zinzendorf's appearance in *The Mystery* lacks the troubling quality of that of the RAF pilots, who are quite friendly but who plague Delia with demands, remind her of the casualties of war, and seduce her into what she describes as an addiction. Zinzendorf is not the ghost of the past haunting the present; he is a screen for, a symbol of, the divine. He is not a complicated cipher to be read but rather, like de Watteville, a transcendent being who promises to restore order and establish a utopic world beyond war, xenophobia, classism, and patriarchy.[54] He is the embodiment of the narrative of history Dohna sought painstakingly to reassemble. As such, *The Mystery* marks a transition, a shift away from H.D.'s interest in modern history and her critique of global politics, and toward the more idealistic vision that had sustained her through two world wars.

PART III

Re-formations

Postwar Ethics and Identity

[N]ationalities can only be temporary dwelling places
and not permanent homes.

—Alison Light

We grow nearer as we grow further apart.

—H.D.

7

Facing the Past, Becoming *l'autre*

> the parting came
> before the greeting, it was *vale, ave*. . . .
>
> —H.D.

In *By Avon River* and *White Rose and the Red*, H.D. looks closely at British imperialism at the heart of warfare, but by the 1950s, she begins to pull away from the contemporary world. I will argue in Chapters 7 and 8, however, that she also comes away from a decade of heightened interest in international politics with a changed sense of ethics and the global. In part, what drives her is a pressing need to come to terms with her German heritage in a post-Hitler, post-Holocaust age. She had always been proud of her Moravian maternal lineage, and in the wartime novel *The Gift* she had written urgently and reverently of her Moravian childhood in Bethlehem, Pennsylvania, the first Moravian settlement in the United States. Indeed, Victoria Harrison argues that H.D. sees her Moravian "family and childhood community" as the source of "a different Germany, one filled with the sound of love" during this period.[1] But the rise of Hitler and Nazism, the experience of the Blitz, and the revelation of the crimes of the Holocaust tugged persistently at her sense of her own German identity, as did, undoubtedly, the Nazi appropriation of ancient Greek iconography. To her cousin Clifford Howard, in 1940, H.D. attempts to assuage these feelings by distinguishing sharply new from old Germany: "It is very sad but the world can't continue with that band of ill-bred deluded barbarians about, and the sooner they quietly and quickly disappear the better for us all—I had not this feeling in the last war, but now it is a clear case of survival, at stake. Surely, too, the greatness and beauty of the OLD Germany will arise once this calamity is over."[2] In a 1946 letter to Richard Aldington, she explicitly terms this concern about her Germanness a "political onus," declaring that the cure for it was to return to pre-Nazi literature by immersing herself in the works of nineteenth-century German Romanticism.[3] Germany, she would have read in Éliphas Lévi's *The History of Magic*, "is the native land of metaphysical mysticism and phantoms."[4] She looked to the pre-twentieth-century German literature that she had loved to ease her burden.

It is perhaps, then, no accident that Saint-Germain is one of the central characters of *The Mystery*, her second novel about Moravianism and her last historical novel. Jane Augustine does not remark upon the obvious etymological connection between Germain the character and German as ethnic or national identity, but she astutely observes, in her notes to the edition, that "[t]he English word *german* comes from the Old French *germain*" and that H.D. "links 'Germain' with the word *german*, meaning closely related, as in *cousin-german*, first cousin, and with the homonym *germen*, figuratively a germ or seed."[5] All of these meanings are acutely relevant—germane—to a discussion of how H.D. is rethinking ethics through a re-envisioning of the relationship between self and other.

By the 1950s, H.D. had become even more convinced that identity is performative and essentially unstable, and she thus had come to see the boundary between self and other as tenuous and permeable. Moreover, as discussed in Chapter 1, over time her autobiographical fiction began to create more and more distance between characters and their real-life counterparts. By the 1940s, characters in *The Sword Went Out to Sea* have become diffuse and shifting—composites, at times even abstractions or symbols. If the boundary between self and other is constructed and maintained through a kind of annihilatory violence, H.D. by the 1950s is deconstructing that binary, looking for ways to acknowledge and understand alterity through empathy rather than assimilation or repudiation. This project of disentangling the author from the autobiographical self, while creating empathetic moments that merge self and other, becomes the basis for an ethical system that has implications for both the personal and the political. In her late prose writings, H.D. maps a web of personal relationships to alliances between nations, seeking ultimately a world without national borders. The other, the German—as depicted in the characters that populate *The Mystery* and in the various constructions of H.D.'s German psychoanalyst, Erich Heydt—is in fact "cousin" to the self, closer to the self than might be imagined, in the same way that the destruction of Dresden in World War II comes to be seen as a mirror image of the Blitzing of London. In H.D.'s late writings, the "germ" of the other contaminates the self, opening up a liminal and fleeting space for understanding and dialogue.

This re-envisioning of self and other will be explored in this chapter and the next through examination of two recurring figures in her prose: the "other woman" and the spy, in various guises. Here, a comparison of H.D.'s 1926 short story "Hipparchia" and her later novel *Sword* illuminates this shift in thinking through the politics of identity and identification in both the public and private spheres, and I read some of her 1950s autobiographical prose in concert with *Sword* to show how this notion develops at the end of her life. On the theme of sexual betrayal, I contend, the late fiction departs strikingly from the 1920s fiction in its depiction of the "other woman." Adalaide Morris has produced the best study of ethics in H.D.'s writings to date, which she argues promote a radical, anti-capitalist economy of the gift as theorized by sociologist Marcel Mauss, though H.D. would have learned it experientially as a child in a Moravian community. In this chapter, I hope to build in important ways on Morris's understanding of H.D.'s sense of ethics by bringing into the conversation other theorists such as Emmanuel Levinas and Kaja Silverman. A gift economy, according to Mauss, relies on transience, not on permanence and accumulation. As such, it is not based in a fixed, stagnant logic. As Morris points out, the gift bears "obligations to give, receive, and reciprocate," and the act of gift-giving itself constitutes a brief space in which identity is suspended: "In the moment of transfer, the self flows toward union with others in a community constituted by reciprocal acts of giving."[6] This kind of economy is antithetical to imperialism, the subject of H.D.'s critique in the late 1940s. Levinas argues that a face-to-face confrontation between self and other entails an obligation as well, for the other makes a demand on the self that exposes the violence inherent in the relationship between self and other. For Silverman, the most productive—most ethical—encounter between self and other is one in which, temporarily, the two engage in an empathetic identification. While Morris focuses primarily on H.D.'s mid-career works, I will discuss how her later works continue to explore these issues.

Chapter 3 addressed the theoretical implications of H.D.'s merging of the fairy tale with historical fiction. In this chapter, a comparison of H.D.'s historical fiction of the 1920s and that of the 1940s demonstrates how she develops this form to explore how personal trauma is embedded in larger nationalist and imperialist narratives. A fairly straightforward treatment of the topic in her earlier phase is critiqued in the later work, I will argue, as she begins to problematize nationalist responses to war and to see the need for a more experimental style to grapple with complexities she had come to recognize in the immediate post–World War II era. Ultimately, in *Sword*, and in some of her later prose of the 1950s, she is able to contemplate an ethical system for living in a postwar world that allows her to confront private and public trauma by accepting the permeability of the boundary between self and other.

Set in early Greece, Rome, and Judea, three of H.D.'s early fictions of the 1920s examine the politics of gender and sexuality in the ancient world. As much of her early poetry and translation work strives to realize just this kind of analysis, historical fiction was undoubtedly a natural choice for her in this period of her career. To a point, H.D.'s earlier historical work—"Hipparchia," *Pilate's Wife*, and *Hedylus*—can be productively regarded within a framework Ruth Hoberman constructs to describe the work of early twentieth-century British women writers of historical fiction, who explore the "interlocking issues of power, gender, and narrative authority."[7] As noted in Chapter 3, Hoberman notes the specific pitfalls for women writers in a genre that requires, as many have theorized about historical fiction, that the protagonist be an emblematic subject of a tumultuous era whose life must be molded by events in a way that is representative of the larger populace. Because women of previous eras were rarely participants in the public sphere, they do not tend to be the subjects of historical fiction. The women writers of historical fiction in Hoberman's study devise female characters negotiating the gendered limitations of the past, or they "cross-dress," creating male protagonists who can explore the past without being subject to gendered restrictions. H.D. employs both strategies in her 1920s work. The titular character of *Hedylus* is a young man based on herself, battling his mother over his love for a girl, for instance. Alternately, *Pilate's Wife* centers around a young woman, Veronica, married to Pontius Pilate but erotically drawn to a female fortune-teller, Mnevis.

In these early works by H.D., the ancient world largely serves as backdrop in much the way Hoberman describes. The dominant themes and plots of these early historical works mirror those of H.D.'s other autobiographical novels of the 1920s: her bisexuality, her marriage to British writer Richard Aldington, his infidelity, and her initial encounters with Bryher. But the first story of H.D.'s three-part *Palimpsest*, "Hipparchia," deviates subtly from this formula. In this narrative, H.D. is not just interested in the politics of gender and sexuality but also the politics of imperialism. Set in Rome at the beginning of the third and final Mithridatic War, "Hipparchia" considers the theme of betrayal and the figure of the "other woman"—"*l'autre*"—by mapping wartime sexual betrayal onto the Roman imperialist project. H.D. transmutes herself into the Greek Hipparchia, who struggles to come to terms with an affair between her lover, the Roman soldier Marius, and another Roman, Olivia; though neither woman is married to Marius, it is clear that the Greek Hipparchia has a long-standing relationship with him that has been interrupted by his attraction to another. Here H.D. manipulates the historical situation so that she can place Hipparchia, the fictional daughter of a real-life radical female and proto-feminist Cynic philosopher of the fourth century BCE, Hipparchia of Thrace, in a postcolonial context—in a time *after* Greece has fallen to Rome. Had Hipparchia the philosopher given birth to such a child, that daughter would have lived in the Hellenistic period of Greece; it was not until 146 BCE, following the Battle of Corinth, that Rome claimed all of Greece as a Roman protectorate. By moving the fictional Hipparchia forward in time, H.D. places her in a historical moment of Roman imperialism; by setting the story in 75 BCE, as Eileen Gregory notes, she further establishes a wartime setting in a historical moment in which Rome is still embroiled in wars defending its right to expand its empire.[8]

As a Greek in this period, Hipparchia is the conquered, while Marius is the conqueror; if Greeks are grapes, Romans are "wine pressers," she avers. A remnant of a lost civilization that fell centuries before the story opens, Hipparchia is a corpse, her body the body of a defeated Greece. "[V]anished" and "vanquished," she is consistently described in terms of death. Her voice "reminded" Marius "of some dead city." Hipparchia is a "phantom," one of Niobe's children, smelling of the "death-flower" Hyacinth. He frets over how to make her flower like Hyacinth, but her resurrection is conceptualized in terms of his giving birth to her, remaking her in his image. Hipparchia haunts Marius, as traces of Greece linger in Rome; "'since when,'" he asks, "'has one been able to escape the dead?'" A soldier, he fears that Greece may be destined, after all, to "rule forever, not Rome, but prophetically, the whole world."[9] As Susan Stanford Friedman observes, Marius conceptualizes sex with Hipparchia as "reenact[ing] Rome's conquest of Greece."[10] His growing alliance with Olivia metaphorically solidifies the reality that "Greece was now lost."[11] As Marius turns from the Greek Hipparchia to the Roman Olivia, Greece recedes further and further into the past.

Self and other, in this short story, are Greek and Roman respectively. When Marius looks at Hipparchia, she does not return his gaze—"her eyes . . . had been seeing elsewhere"—and he fears that a glance from her would produce "dire memories, the long death-plunge forward." She sees only "the other." But when the Roman Olivia and Marius look at each other, they see sameness. They are physically similar, "dark browed" with "wide eyes" and "static and exact speech," and they are mentally and intellectually alike: "[e]ach knew the other perfectly. . . . [e]ach could follow each." For Hipparchia, looking at Marius or at Olivia through the mediating object of "an enchanter's mirror" entails occupying several subject positions simultaneously: "She saw with her own eyes, with the eyes of Marius, with the dark eyes of Olivia, Olivia. She saw Olivia as Olivia must see Olivia." When Marius touches her, she feels that he is touching Olivia.[12]

In response, Hipparchia staunchly rejects a demand for empathetic identification with the other, characterizing the episode as "some horrible phantasy," "false, theatrical." "No, no, no, no," she tells herself, "this way was madness."[13] In this story, moments of encounter between self and other—moments that inherently destabilize the self—are portrayed as bearing an insurmountable threat. In *Totality and Infinity* and other works, the philosopher Emmanuel Levinas has placed a great deal of emphasis on face-to-face interactions in his theories of ethics, finding them unique sites of confronting alterity. Ethics, according to Levinas, must be grounded in alterity because what he terms "the imperialism of the same"[14] entails either doing violence to the other by erasing its uniqueness or opening a door for violence towards those who cannot be seen as really the same. When self faces other, the self is exposed and vulnerable to the other, and in this vulnerability an opportunity for connection arises. The self wishes to assimilate the other, to ignore the uniqueness of the other, for, as Levinas points out, "It is easier to annihilate than to possess the other."[15] But in a face-to-face encounter, the self's wish cannot be fulfilled, and in response the other makes an implicit ethical "demand" on the self not to kill the other. "In the face of the obligation of the Other, the Ego . . . loses its sovereign coincidence with self, its identification," Levinas theorizes, and "[t]he challenge to self is precisely reception of the absolutely other. The epiphany of the absolutely other is a face in which the Other hails me and signifies to me, by its nakedness, by its destitution, an order. Its presence is this summons to respond." Face-to-face, the self is evacuated "of its imperialism and egoism."[16] Levinas, moreover, turns to hospitality as a metaphor for human connection; the self opens its home to the other, and this is an important concept in thinking through Hipparchia's homelessness. She has lost her homeland, and she is adrift in Rome, shifting uncomfortably between Marius's house and the country home of another Roman, Verrus. When she returns from the country unannounced, she surprises Marius and is unwelcome.

In response to her experience of identification with the Roman other—in which she sees through the eyes of Marius and Olivia—Hipparchia resists assimilating the other into the self, but she also staunchly rejects connection. She fears, in fact, that she has been absorbed into the Roman position. Hipparchia's confrontation with the other demonstrates that the other cannot be assimilated into her sense of self, but she repudiates the other, sensing that her ego will, rather, be absorbed into the Roman, that the Roman refuses the demand she, as other, makes. The ending of the story reestablishes and reifies the boundary between self and other. In the final pages of the story, she meets Julia Cornelia Augusta (a figure based on Bryher), who loves Greek poetry and whose father collects Greek artifacts. Hipparchia's decision to align herself with Julia, not Marius, enables her to shore up the fragments of her embattled identity, to effect a reaffirmation of Greek values in the midst of Roman civilization. "Greek must rule," Hipparchia concludes at the close of the story, "Not Rome only but the world."[17] In the late 1920s, H.D. sees as necessary a fundamentally essentialist—and proto-nationalist—stance to at once strengthen the ego and ensure that the ethos of ancient Greece is not forever lost.

As I explored in Chapter 3, historical fiction is a paradox; like autobiography, it constructs a fictional narrative within a factual setting. It is necessarily true and untrue at the same time. Bound to the demands of factual historical events and her own life's story, H.D.'s early historical fiction is doubly ensnared by demands for truth. "Hipparchia" tells the story of a specific period of Roman history, even while it recounts the story of Aldington's sexual betrayal of H.D. during the First World War. Yet this kind of story is temporally bound, creating, in effect, a deterministic universe. Characters may not act outside of strict parameters of historical accuracy and authenticity. In most Western fiction, Harry Shaw notes, "[d]evaluing history becomes a moral act that asserts human dignity, freedom, and moral responsibility."[18] If other post-Enlightenment fictional genres permit at least the illusion of agency and freedom, historical fiction—and autobiography—cannot. A closed temporal system is necessarily guided by not just a logic of teleology but a logic of determinism, conditions that might preclude any consideration of ethics or morality. How, after all, can characters confined to historically specific settings make ethical choices? And what would an ethical choice look like in a world in which the outcomes are predetermined, unaffected by a character's intervention? As discussed in Chapter 3, Linda Hutcheon proposes that what she calls postmodern "historiographic metafiction" circumvents some of these thorny problems by questioning the very idea that we can know the past and by undermining and violating conventional modes of representation: "Postmodern fiction suggests that to re-write or to re-present the past in fiction and in history is, in both cases, to open it up to the present, to prevent it from being conclusive and teleological."[19] This is a model for a historical novel that attends closely to the role of the present in the past. As Walter Benjamin astutely claims, "every image of the past that is not recognized by the present as one of its own concerns threatens to disappear irretrievably."[20]

H.D.'s "Hipparchia" uses a historical setting of war and imperialism to draw an extended metaphor between gender and imperialism—in which men are the (Roman) conquerors and women are the (Greek) conquered—but the personal narrative dominates that frame. Efforts to deconstruct these binaries falter, and a universalizing logic is upheld in both arenas—the politics of nationalism and, ultimately, heterosexuality. H.D.'s 1940s historical fiction, as I argued in Chapter 3, aims to accomplish something quite different and a great deal more complicated, more along the lines that Hutcheon describes. The universe of "Hipparchia" had been a cyclical one, in which war, imperialism, and betrayal are constant, recurring realities that cannot effectively be altered by the actions of its characters. As a translator and Greek historian, Hipparchia may choose to take a stand against Roman imperialism by recourse to a kind of proto-nationalism—by recovering, translating, and disseminating Greek knowledge and culture. But the real-life Hipparchia's writings did not survive, and the next story in *Palimpsest*, "Murex," makes clear that history remains unchanged by Hipparchia's actions, for "Murex" casts that same story of war and sexual betrayal in a modern setting, the World War I era. The artist figure at the center of "Murex" contemplates her soldier-lover's sexual betrayal as she strives to compose a poem that expresses and documents her trauma. Despite a significant difference in time and setting, the situation and the outcome remain virtually unchanged. The first of the 1940s historical novels, *Sword*, however, takes into account the notion of the present as a constitutive part of our understanding of the past instead of situating the present and the past as equal parts of a static equation. Here the personal narrative fades—evoked only to be critiqued—while the historical situation is pushed into the foreground.

In *Sword*, the personal serves as metaphor for the political. As I argued in Chapter 1, her recounting of the story of Aldington's betrayal of the 1920s is critiqued in the first half of *Sword*, where the story of infidelity is pushed to such excess that we question its importance in the face of a greater historical and political reality. This tale is not only the subject of several novels, but it is repeated in *Palimpsest*, in various historical periods and settings; however, this repetition of what Cheryl Hindrichs has fittingly termed "recurring traumas of a martial-patriarchal history"[21] in the earlier work is a repetition of real trauma, the same trauma instigated by the same individual, not the parodic commentary on obsession elucidated in *Sword*. In repetitively layering Aldington's betrayal with those of two men she barely knew, she suggests that it functions symbolically. These soldier-lovers are all one and the same, and likewise, the women who surround her in the Swiss rest home about which she writes in her 1950s prose can be superimposed on the recurrent figure of the mistress. Belinda, Romana, and especially Heydt's wife, Dori, any of these women might be the women Aldington had sex with on leave from the war.[22] In this way, *Sword* begins to take apart the trauma distilled in several autobiographical fictions of the 1920s. When Delia receives a dismissive letter from Lord Howell, her response interlaces personal and cultural trauma: "The impact of his letter left me cold, as the impact of the high explosives and the bombs had done." She reflects later that he had "struck" her with a "well-directed blow," she was "undefended" and "vanquished," her self obliterated: "I simply wasn't there, any more." She is haunted by the "shocks and wounds" she received. About a cognate of Howell, she refers to his "barbed shaft." "I felt," Delia writes, "that I had no place any longer in this world."[23] Similarly, in *Thorn Thicket*, Erich's repudiation is described as exploding landmines.[24]

In representing the experience of personal betrayal in terms of this excess, divorced increasingly from her psychic reality, H.D. puts a great deal of pressure on the parallel between the personal and the political she had established in "Hipparchia." In the second half of the book, "Summerdream,"

Delia splinters into a panoply of personages that surface in different historical periods associated with war and imperialism. As Cynthia Hogue notes of *Sword*'s multiple settings, "The world of 'Summerdream' is ... portrayed as being at war, having been at war for some time, or going to war. That world defines the hero's horizon, for he is defending, building, or conquering an empire."[25] While Delia is anchored in London during a world war, these various and varied protagonists occupy a range of subject positions representing forms of difference. She is, alternately, Greek, Roman, English, French; she is also, importantly, *l'autre*, the "other woman." Delia is the one who imagines herself in the position of mistress, when she reacts with jealousy to the news of the engagements of men based on Bhaduri and Dowding. Delia feels the betrayal of the mistress, not the wife. In the Roman chapters, she is not Caesar's wife, Calpurnia, but his paramour.

When she begins the Roman section of the book, the narrator initially recoils from becoming what Olivia had been in "Hipparchia," a Roman mistress: "I can hardly bring myself to write it. Why must I think about it? It is foreign and unfamiliar."[26] H.D. had written, over the course of her career, so many representations of imperial Rome as imperial England, casting herself as the Greek victim. But in *Sword* she moves forward, imaginatively becoming *l'autre Romain* in the Roman vignettes of the novel. In *Magic Mirror* and the late memoirs, the pattern is repeated when it is Erich Heydt's engagement that sparks feelings of betrayal. As she moves further and further away from real personages—as she mythologizes these romantic entanglements—she begins to see that "[o]ne cannot blame this if there is any 'blame' in this or any situation of its kind, on the Bella or Muriel or Dori of the moment."[27] It was not, after all, "a question of another woman," she explains to one of the Aldington figures of *Sword*.[28]

The fragmentation of Delia's identity, discussed above in Chapter 2, signals a shift in H.D.'s thinking about the tenuous line between self and other. Through Delia, H.D. makes herself vulnerable to an other she had, in the past, seen purely as a threat to her sense of personal and national identity. Judith Butler has argued that exposure to violence in political life can engender an ethics based in the shared experience of mourning because "each of us is constituted politically in part by virtue of the social vulnerability of our bodies."[29] This form of vulnerability, then, involves a recognition that the self is not autonomous but constituted relationally: the *I* and the *you* are inextricably linked in ways that can become clearer in times of trauma. As Michael

Gardiner puts it in his discussion of Levinas and ethics, "An understanding of this alterity requires that we cultivate a sense of 'exteriority,' and develop an awareness of our *relationality* to the world and other selves."[30] Kaja Silverman's terms *idiopathic* and *heteropathic identification* (adapted from Max Scheler) are particularly elucidating in this context. Silverman valorizes art that makes us "identify with bodies we would otherwise repudiate . . . excorporatively rather than incorporatively, and, thereby, respect . . . otherness."[31] Idiopathic identification is incorporative, an assimilation of the other into the self without recognition of or respect for essential alterity, while heteropathic identification is excorpative, a phenomenon in which the self and other can exist in a liminal, oscillating state of coming together and pulling apart. It might be seen, in a sense, as the *vale* and the *ave* of H.D.'s late work. It is the flexible movement of the accordion—the trope that had momentarily replaced the palimpsest in her immediate postwar work—the accordion's "pleats in time" joining, then separating, as her characters make "to-and-fro journeys and return flights" through time and space.[32]

In "Hipparchia," the protagonist fears a face-to-face confrontation with Marius and Olivia because she fears idiopathic identification, an interaction that would entail a loss of self, a total absorption of her Greek identity by the Romans. Thus, to employ Silverman's language, she "refus[es] to live in and through alien corporealities."[33] Marius, too, views the encounter idiopathically; according to Friedman, "[h]is desire for her ever-elusive body is the longing to possess the Other, a desire for conquest."[34] While he feels, "in one moment, the overpowering beauty of this conquest," Marius yet fears that Greece will consume him when he reflects that the sound of the syllables of Greek poetry "ate into him, scalded, flayed him." He has no such fear of Olivia, as he easily sees through her eyes.[35] A similar dynamic is evident in *Magic Mirror*, when H.D.'s autobiographically based protagonist Rica is concerned that her "identification" with the D. H. Lawrence or Aldington figures in *Bid Me to Live* might mean that she could "lose herself in another," and when she notes that the character based on Heydt "absorbed these people, these stories as a sponge soaks up water."[36] In *Vale Ave* she is still working through this problem, "striv[ing] to save identity" in the face of a "destroyer and creator."[37]

There are implications here for thinking through H.D.'s so-called "romantic thralldom," for thralldom might be another term for idiopathic identification, the total obliteration of self by the other. In her late career, it is not thralldom itself—which she no longer seems to experience—but the threat of this annihilatory violence that absorbs her: "the dart of love," she writes in *Helen in Egypt*, "is the dart of Death."[38] When H.D. refers to soldier-lovers in *Vale Ave*, she uses the term *semblables*, which "have the power of life and death / over each other."[39] "Identification," Freud warns, might be "an expression of tenderness" but it might also be "a wish for someone's removal."[40] The second part of *Sword* offers her another path when a multiply divided identity flows in and out of a range of selves and others, engaging in the temporary identificatory relationships Silverman terms heteropathic, in which the self respects alterity and accepts the risks inherent in temporary and partial identification with the other. Delia is, in effect, "induced to occupy a subject-position which is antithetical to ... her psychic formation."[41] H.D.'s protagonists in *Sword* respond, then, to the other's ethical demand for empathy in a series of sporadic, transitory, but meaningful moments of identification. Delia is the Roman Stella, but just for a chapter, before moving rapidly to another time period and another body, a French woman. *L'autre* becomes *les autres*.

Levinas observes, "The possibility for the home to open to the Other is as essential to the essence of the home as closed doors and windows." If the doors and windows of one's home are closed, the self "can close itself up in its egoism," effect a forgetting of the other, and ultimately make a home inhospitable even for the self. "[N]o face can be approached with empty hands and closed home," he insists.[42] Delia's attention to closed and open doors—a motif that is sustained throughout the late 1940s and 1950s prose—speaks to Levinas' metaphor of the house, the crumbling borderline between self and other, and the possibility of empathetic identification. When Delia imagines, and re-imagines, the scene of betrayal, she consistently hears doors slamming shut, delineating a clear boundary and separating unequivocally the self from the other. Geoffrey, one of the Aldington personae, is always standing next to a closing door when he delivers his crushing line about *l'autre*—"I love you but I desire *l'autre*." Memories of other men are associated with closed doors. Later, she recalls that "exact point ... when the door shut"—"when a door in a crowded room in a Flanders inn slammed shut"—as a forgotten key to resolving the trauma, and in contact with dead RAF pilots in a séance, she receives a message that constitutes another significant clue: "D-O-O-R O-P-E-N-S."[43]

But, again, this is not just a way of thinking through private trauma. In the memoirs of the 1950s, she characterizes this kind of door as "the Iron

Curtain," the postwar dividing line between the Communist Soviet Union and the West which will come into play in the next chapter's discussion of espionage. References to this symbol in the memoirs occur in two different contexts that together link the private and the public. In *Thorn Thicket*, the slamming door is synonymous with the Iron Curtain, as she revisits that same scene of repudiation: "An iron-curtain banged down between us."[44] In *Compassionate Friendship*, she writes that "[t]hat iron-curtain fell" when she married Aldington in England.[45] She means, on the one hand, that she sealed her future fate. But she also refers to the loss of American citizenship, the necessary result of a marriage to a British citizen at that time. The physical boundary that divided the world in two is compared to the separation between self and other when one repudiates the other.

It is not insignificant, then, that H.D. imagines this deconstruction of the self/other binary in a time when the world has been divided violently and decidedly between an *us* and a *them*, in a time when nations are conquering one another, arguably idiopathically, with an aggression that "conceals the reality that the self is heterogeneous, a product of its alterity with the Other."[46] Interestingly, Delia's psychotic break, from which the diffusion of her identity stems in Part II of the book, takes the form of contemplation about nation and war. Speculating that the Nuremburg Trials and Pound's incarceration spurred the content of her vision, she foresees, as discussed in Chapter 2, an apocalyptic future in which the streets are filled with people hanging from gallows. After years of nightly bombings, food rationings, and illness, Delia hallucinates a third world war in which "[g]eographic boundaries were bombed away." This experience forces her to reconsider the focus on ancient Greece in her earlier poetry and fiction: "So maybe," she muses, "this obsession with past civilizations was simply a matter of our own imminent danger and constant preoccupation with death and with dead cities."[47] Here she acknowledges the central function of the present in articulating the past, a recognition much less apparent in her early work. The psychotic break, however terrifying, also provokes a disintegration of self that is not annihilatory and absolute, but ultimately generative of a new ethical vision.[48]

In *Magic Mirror*, H.D. demonstrates how breaking down this boundary can generate new ways of seeing the larger world, not just the private sphere. She realizes that Germans—the other—are not the only enemy. Rather, "the Dragon, the Monster, the Minotaur that finally attacked her, was not German. The attack had come in both instances from England."[49] Just as

H.D.'s protagonists learn to navigate a weakened boundary between self and other, the excessive destruction of Dresden comes to be seen as a mirror of London during the Blitz. H.D. had been devastated by postwar photographs not only of the concentration camps and Holocaust survivors, but of the destruction of German cities, particularly Dresden. H.D.'s protagonists find common ground with the other in discrete moments, permitting them to explore the extent to which their own identities are functions of their own constructions of otherness. There is a similar pattern to be discerned in the mirroring of Dresden and London, as the implications of the revelation that England is also an enemy begin to emerge. In *Magic Mirror*, it is initially the figure based on Heydt, not the protagonist, who sees an isomorphic correlation between the two cities when he suggests that her war *Trilogy* should be translated into German: because of the firebombing of Dresden, "'Germans would understand it,' he said. Truly the poems might have been written, as from 'another sliced wall' in Dresden or Berlin."[50] Here a German analyst finds comforting the notion that England and Germany might occupy the same position; it undoubtedly assuages his sense of guilt. But H.D. is not (entirely) German. Having "shudder[ed]" at photographs of Dresden,[51] the character based on H.D. recognizes the aptness of this parallel—there were indeed "sliced wall[s]" in both cities—but she also notes pointedly that "she had 'felt' Dresden more than [Heydt] felt London."[52] Unlike Heydt, she permits identification but not an absolute reduction of one for the other. In "H.D. by Delia Alton," in fact, H.D. notes that she had doubled, rather, Dresden and Vienna, not Dresden and London, in *Sword*.[53] In doing so, she places the character based on Freud in heightened danger; she also strips him of his Jewish identity—von Alten is "wholly Saxon"—and thus makes him the victim of England, not Germany.[54] For a moment, Dresden is Vienna, before the disjunctive narrative shifts us quickly away.

As demonstrated in Part I of this book, where H.D.'s *Sword* departs most discernibly from the work of many other late modernists is in its form. If other writers largely turned to a new iteration of realism to articulate political interests, H.D. invents a new form to depict her shifting sense of political and personal realities, abandoning the lyric impressionism of "Hipparchia" in favor of a more experimental, highly fractured style that better captures the fragility and instability of the boundaries between present and past, but also self and other. The form of *Sword*, then, can be viewed fruitfully within the context of Silverman's contention that "[c]rucial to the encouragement and maintenance of a heteropathic identification is the designation of the scene of representation as radically discontinuous with the world of the spectator."[55] Delia's world is markedly unstable in "Summerdream," and, like Delia, readers of *Sword* are never comfortable, never sure of their bearings. Settings and characters constantly shift and bleed into one another. Delia's frequent use of theatrical discourse explored in Chapter 1, and her forays into the supernatural, only function to reinforce this sense of the unreal, the unstable, the unknowable. Both metaphors—of performance and of the otherworldly—serve to unsettle productively the integrity of the self. When H.D. writes in *Magic Mirror* of the cast of characters of an autobiographical novel that "[t]hey were all out of a play," she acknowledges the distance between "[t]he world of reality" and that "of myth or imagination."[56] It is "true" but also a "fantasy," a "whole cosmic, bloody show."[57] In *Sword*, Delia highlights the constructed nature of the text by talking self-reflexively of its composition and reception. Episodes of *Sword* are consistently referred to as scenes—a term that evokes theatrical performances as well as psychoanalysis. "We live mythology," Erica muses in *Magic Mirror*, "We fortunate ones, who can re-construct a world or re-create an epic."

In *Sword*, H.D. does not simply cast herself in an autobiographical role set in the remote past; rather, she creates distance between herself and her multiple protagonists, thinking carefully about the power of her choices as author. She seems to have moved from thinking about the relationship between herself and her autobiographically based protagonists as isomorphic to acknowledging a more heteropathic perspective on autobiographical identity. As noted in Chapter 1, H.D. sounds a note of caution to her readers about the various personae she created over the years: mentioning Hipparchia and several of *Sword*'s protagonists among others, she insists both that the characters are autobiographically based *and* that they are fictional. She is not just Hipparchia, not just Delia, but she is (and is not) a host of very different kinds of characters. In *Magic Mirror*, she returns to this interpretation of her work. At one point, she merges with her autobiographical counterparts in a passage that echoes one in "H.D. by Delia Alton": "Yes, I am Julia Ashton, she thought and I am other names in other stories. . . . I am Julia of that period, of that story, she thought. I am various other people, Stella in particular, of the second war (*Sword*, *Rose*) series. O—so many." At another point, however, she creates distance between the various selves: "Perhaps she was not Julia after all, perhaps she was someone else, quite different."[58]

Vale, ave. There are moments of identification, and moments in which H.D. and Delia and Stella and others are arrested in difference.

Though still physically bound to a world of nationalism, imperialism, and war, moreover, H.D. responds to the closed temporal systems of autobiography and historical fiction by devising innovations in the respective genres. The universe is no less sealed in *Sword* than it is in "Hipparchia." However, using the devices of time travel and multiple, variously unstable narrators, she is able to pry open a space for her characters to exercise agency—to empathize. Stella can occupy several bodies serially. She does not have to remain Greek; she can be English or Roman, too. Later, in Normandy, she can occupy two bodies at once, in dialogue. This is not the freedom typical of the Western novel, which Shaw argues "[d]evalu[es] history" and Levinas terms "an imperialism of the same"—"maintain[ing] oneself against the other . . . to ensure the autarchy of an I."[59] H.D. cannot change history, or her life story, but she can shift profoundly her relationship to that history, public and private. When she tells a version of her own story in the 1940s, she does so through a narrative voice based in a relational understanding of a vulnerable and malleable self, not a self that desires its autonomy and isolation at the expense of an acceptance of alterity. The 1940s self is shaped by history but not determined by it.

For H.D. in 1947, imaginatively embodying the position of *l'autre Romain* constitutes an attempt to understand, even embrace, the permeable and contingent nature of the relationship between self and other, to exorcise the "political onus" of German-ness. Clearly, the ramifications of such an attempt concern more than just how she learns to cope with the personal trauma surrounding her break with Aldington. It is an expressly anti-nationalist position that she contemplates, and we can see the evidence in the subjects and settings of the poetry and prose she produces after 1940, which range far beyond the borders of ancient Greece. To be clear, the narrators of *Sword* are not happy or even hopeful—they do not revel in a newly gained sense of postmodern identity—but they nonetheless perform what they see as an acutely painful but necessary task. What emerges by the 1950s is a world divided not by geographical or ethnic borders; it is a dream of a united world. Four years later, after all, H.D. finishes *The Mystery*, in which a different cast of characters works toward a world without national borders—"a unity, a world-unity without war"—sifting through old documents and letters to reconstruct some sense of the past in order better to envision the future.[60]

8

The Invisible Other
The Psychoanalyst as Spy

> he was invisible but he was there
>
> —H.D., *Vale Ave*

In this chapter, I turn to H.D.'s repeated references to espionage, focusing in particular on the psychoanalyst as spy. If the "other woman" is predicated on a position of alterity, the therapist-spy feigns an identification—and an empathetic connection—that does not in fact exist. One a figure of the private realm, the other belonging to the public, the "other woman" and the spy are subject positions based in hostility, even the threat of violence. The spy attempts to occupy simultaneously the position of (national) self and other in order to read the other, to obtain information about the other that can in turn be used to threaten the other. H.D.'s shifting treatment of the "other woman" illuminates her fears about engulfment and annihilation by the other. The treasonous spy allows, even invites, this engulfment. Treason involves an absolute dissolution of the (national) self and absorption by the other, a total loss of identity.

An oddity of H.D.'s 1950s prose is her focus on tropes related to espionage. My suspicion is that H.D. scholars have understandably shied away from this theme because it points to H.D.'s apparent real-life paranoia stemming from the 1946 illness that culminated, as discussed in the Introduction, in her receiving electroshock treatment. There has been a concern, I think, that discussion of this late prose, especially *Magic Mirror* and *Compassionate Friendship*, would be harmful to her reputation because she frankly exposes feelings of irrationality and paranoia as well as her faith in other dimensions of reality, a belief some might call spiritual but others delusional or schizophrenic. Following electroshock treatment, H.D.'s letters evidence some degree of paranoia, for her experiences in the Swiss clinic rendered her angry and distrustful, for a time, of her doctors and of Bryher, who had committed her involuntarily to the institution. What interests me in this chapter is how we see this play out in the 1950s writings, how this particular aspect of that trauma becomes material for her work. In Chapter 2, I explored dimensions of how H.D. constructs the psychotic break and spiritual experience. Here, I turn to how she made use of her own brief experience of paranoia to explore national paranoia about espionage and its relationship to ethics, which is worked out in a comparison of the theories of Sigmund Freud, with whom H.D. was in analysis in the 1930s, and Medard Boss, who trained Erich Heydt, H.D.'s analyst in the 1950s. We know from the work of Susan Stanford Friedman and others that H.D. was aware that "[t]he Professor was not always right,"[1] and in this chapter I will peer into one such critique of his understanding of the psyche. While H.D. remained loyal to Freud in many regards, her experience with Heydt, I will argue, offered her an alternative and more flexible model of identity and empathy.

There is a sense, of course, in which a focus on spying in the 1950s is not at all odd, even if we are surprised to find it in the work of a writer like H.D. After all, she lived through the period of heightened fear of Nazi spies in Britain during the Second World War and through the beginnings of the Cold War.[2] The British, Americans, and Soviets launched major campaigns during World War II warning citizens that Nazi spies were all around them and that, importantly, they were physically indistinguishable from those they surveilled. Posters warned that spies were everywhere, that "loose lips sink ships," that "the enemy is always listening," and that people should be ever mindful to speak softly about troop movements and war work. During the war, H.D. was more directly exposed to this fear of the invisible enemy spy in two ways. First, Bryher and H.D.'s daughter, Perdita, were involved in war work that involved covert intelligence. Bryher participated in helping to smuggle Jewish refugees out of Germany and the occupied countries, using her Swiss home as a way station and offering financial resources to those in need. After a stint as a canteen ambulance driver, Perdita—thanks to Pearson's intervention—performed what H.D. described as "very tricky and hard work, hush-hush, making use of her languages" for the U.S. Office of Strategic Services, or OSS (the predecessor of the CIA).[3]

Second, beginning in 1939, H.D. became acutely aware of the wartime censorship of the mail, and her missives are filled with references to it. She writes letters during the war with a heightened awareness of their public nature, and with knowledge that both friend and foe might have access to them. "I can not write as fully as I 'feel,'" she explains to her cousin Clifford Howard, "as there is of course, of necessity, strict censorship."[4] H.D. revealed to George Plank that she and Bryher had had to create a code language to establish that their wires were reaching each other.[5] Bryher reports her dismay over a bag of English mail being sent erroneously to the Germans in 1939, who "read it with much interest": "It apparently amused the Germans very much. I am less than pleased."[6] H.D. had to argue with a censor over a cable sent to her in 1940, and her letters of the period make frequent addresses to potential censors, asking their pardon and hoping for their leniency as she attempted to relay to friends and family what it was like to live in London during the war without giving away military secrets.[7] In addition to the mail, there were restrictions on sending maps, books, postcards, and photographs, about which Bryher repeatedly cautioned H.D.[8]

H.D. and Bryher had, of course, been accustomed to the concept of private and public correspondence, routinely enclosing personal letters to one another within public ones with instructions to destroy. But the ways in which correspondence was handled during the war had a great enough impact on H.D. that she compares the control over her letter-writing by doctors in the Klinik Brunner to the treatment of her letters by wartime censors. In a letter to her friend Silvia Dobson in the fall of 1946, she expresses anger and frustration over Bryher's complicity with the Klinik's suppression and surveillance of her personal mail.[9] H.D.'s initial letters after her electroshock treatments betray paranoid tendencies more generally, in part, she claimed, because she had been given limited "intelligence" about the circumstances of her commitment. This state of amnesia—which, in spy fiction, is a common trope for "public half-knowledge" of foreign policy[10]—creates a situation in which she cannot trust Bryher or her doctors, but the isolation they have jointly imposed on her offers her no other outlet.[11]

H.D. and Bryher discussed wartime and Cold War espionage in their letters to one another in the late 1940s and early 1950s. Their friend Elizabeth Bowen worked for the British Ministry of Information during the war, and her 1948 spy novel *The Heat of the Day* was a topic of much interest among their circle. H.D. speculates about the negative English reception of the novel that Bowen had not been sufficiently condemnatory of treason.[12] Moreover, H.D. and Bryher knew Monica Felton, a labor activist and apparent Communist sympathizer who was nearly brought up on treason charges when she visited POW camps in North Korea in 1951 and made public the adverse treatment of civilians by U.S. and British troops during the Korean War. Bryher warns H.D. not to tell anyone of their personal connection when she writes excitedly of Felton's defection: "[I]magine my emotion when I listened to the news this morning and heard that Monica Felton had escaped to Russia where she was broadcasting against England and America. She has been dismissed from her many positions under the Labor Gov[ernmen]t and her case given over to the Director of Public Prosecutions. She got to Korea to make a report to the Labor Gov[ernmen]t. There she got through the lines! and over to Russia and Moscow. Best not say anything about it."[13] Felton had received mention in Rebecca West's 1949 *The Meaning of Treason*, which Bryher and H.D. also read avidly, though H.D. embraced it while Bryher—increasingly conservative after the war—disavowed it on account of West's Labour Party affiliation.[14]

H.D. and Bryher also exchanged letters about the defection of Donald Maclean and Guy Burgess, members of a Communist spy ring rooted in Cambridge University known later as the "Cambridge Five." This particular incident bears a great deal of resemblance to the fictitious spy ring H.D. imagines in *Magic Mirror* and *Compassionate Friendship*. Bryher writes excitedly to H.D. of a "first class scandal on in London": "two high ranking diplomats have disappeared, they have either been kidnapped or gone freely to Russia it is thought, and one is a great friend of Stephen Spender, who has been dragged in to the business. Unfortunately one man was a Mr Mac Lean who was head of the British Foreign Office American section . . . and the other, Burgess, had a known communist record."[15] In letters written a few days later, she reports wild conjectures about the two, explaining that it may be "a sex affair rather than a spy one," and that "the French police think it is murder and suicide, the British rub their heads and the Americans think they may have got away to Buenos Aires!"[16] Though it is not until 1956 that the whole affair was exposed, Bryher relates in 1951 that Bowen had intimated to her the possible presence of this ring of spies: "what a thriller and I must say that I can't help feeling that Bowen 'knew' something or other. She told me once that Raymond Mortimer had a theory that there was an inside and intriguing group but we both discounted it."[17] While writing *Compassionate*

Friendship, H.D. is reading *The Missing Macleans*, which details the story of this spy ring.[18] As with the Felton case, Bryher is anxious that H.D will be concerned for their safety, and she attempts to reassure her by joking that "I don't think somehow that anyone is particularly out to kidnap our august selves unless we go wandering to the wrong part of Berlin."[19]

H.D. wondered, too, if Lord Dowding might be involved in espionage, and spy figures appear in H.D.'s prose immediately following the war.[20] In *By Avon River*, she notes rumors that Christopher Marlowe, Thomas Nashe, George Peele, and Robert Greene "were possibly all secret-service agents." In the draft of this manuscript, she changes "possibly" to "probably" as she describes these men as "working dangerously, as *counter*-éspionage agents."[21] Cryptology plays a major role in *The Sword Went Out to Sea*, as do the themes of treason and covert intelligence, for Delia Alton perceives messages sent to her from deceased RAF pilots to be encoded military secrets that could help Britain win the war. A secret band of government officials meets in *White Rose and the Red* before one of them leaves for India to defend British economic interests during the 1857 Sepoy Rebellion. In *The Mystery*, the protagonist, Saint-Germain, is disguised as Antonio, a monk, so that he may work as a spy in eighteenth-century Prague, rooting out freemasons and heretical members of other persecuted religious sects. But espionage is most prominently found in her novel *Magic Mirror* and the accompanying memoir, *Compassionate Friendship*, in which H.D. constructs narratives of her analyst, Erich Heydt (dubbed Eric Heller in the novel), as a member of a secret spy ring.

Much of the drama of *Magic Mirror* and *Compassionate Friendship*, in fact, surrounds Heydt's, or Heller's, possible identity as a spy. "It seems that I am afraid of Erich, terribly afraid," she confides in *Compassionate Friendship*. Her fears are heightened when "Erich said to me one day, apropros of something else, 'it's that way with spies. They start and they can't get out.'"[22] "He is certainly . . . an agent," she decides, remarking that he seems "afraid that I might prod into his secrets."[23] Both texts recount the clues from which she had deduced this hypothesis. When Heller expresses concern that she had slipped in the grass one day, she demands to know if she is being surveilled: "'Does everyone know everything?'" His response does nothing to allay her fears: "'Yes,' he said, 'everything.'"[24] "'[O]f course, you know that I have my spies everywhere,'" he cautions her.[25] She is suspicious when Heller, unsolicited, gifts her with books that, uncannily but consistently, seem to come at just the right moment in her work, and "he had seemed to have a very sketchy idea or none at all, of their contents, although he had given her the idea that he had read them."[26] She observes that Heydt lacks the facility with the English language to even understand these books—and likewise books she has written—of which he inexplicably displays comprehensive knowledge.[27] She is deeply suspicious that a German could understand English traditions and stories.[28]

H.D. (in the memoir) and Rica (in the novel) begin to speculate that "there was someone in the background" who was using Heydt/Heller as a pawn to get to her. "What did they want of her if they wanted her at all?" she wonders. Citing Pound's internment for treason after the war, she frets that she is also under suspicion.[29] Alternately, she considers the possibility that "she and her not inconsiderable circle of friends in England and America ... were listed on a sort of psychological dossier, in Zürich somewhere ... [at] some 'intelligence' bureau ... likely German."[30] Heller "knew too much about them, too much about her," she worries.[31] "I can trace now things that he said about books and people that he must have been coached to say," H.D. reports the results of her careful investigation.[32] In the memoir, she reveals to Bryher that she believes this handler managing Heydt to be either Medard Boss or G. Bally, both founders of existentialist psychotherapy; Boss had been Heydt's teacher.[33] "Can he trap me?" she wonders, frightful that Heller might "'lure'" her into what she describes as his "web of infinite *finesse*, circles going on and on."[34]

But what kind of spy is he? One possibility is that she is an unwilling subject of a psychological or parapsychological study. "[D]id they look upon her as a safe tool," she conjectures, "whose gossip of people (discreet though it might be) would offer hints of living, of life, of the reactions of strange people in strange lands whose weakness and whose strength had always been a source of wonder and a psychological problem that middle-Europe (and now perhaps, the East) found baffling, enigmatic, and fantastic?" Specifically, Rica recalls a party Heller had attended at the home of a German medium who collected valuable occult books, and she expresses "a certain curious feeling of insecurity ... about Zurich and the sets and circles there and the para-psychology that Eric spoke of."[35] Fearing that "[t]here is no doubt some sinister element in Erich's background," H.D. speculates that this home is the headquarters of an underground occult movement: "Zurich was always notorious for its spy-rings, its counter-espionage and espionage circles. If the pseudo-Boss is the head of a spy-ring and Erich one of his minions, then what? Do they think I can be of use to them?"[36]

Of course, a reference to a secret German occult group has a particular valence in this period, and H.D. is not unaware that she draws a connection between this supposed spy ring and the reputed underground Ariosophic *völkisch* movements of the 1930s and 1940s. Indeed, she is initially concerned that Heydt—with his "rather arrogant Teutonic profile"[37]—is a Nazi spy. Even her friend Eliza Butler sees "waves of blackness" when she thinks of Heydt, and H.D. and Bryher's friend, the Freudian psychoanalyst Walter Schmideberg (or "Bear," as they affectionately called him), is convinced of Heydt's Nazi past, referring frankly to Heydt as "'that Nazi, that showman.'"[38] In H.D.'s writings, Heydt's national identity is a topic of fervent conversation at the Klinik. When Rica and the other patients of *Magic Mirror* become alarmed when they learn that Heller is German, they anxiously attempt to confirm rumors that he is a "half-Jew," rumors Rica is disappointed to discover are untrue.[39] In *Compassionate Friendship*, too, the residents are abuzz with speculation: "Dr. Erich was born in 1920. 'He must have been a Nazi.'"[40] Rica reflects that it would be impossible for Heller not to have anti-Semitic sentiments: "For surely he must have hated [Jews]? Trained as a child, in the theory of intolerance, he could not have dropped it in a minute, nor even after his years of painful analytical work in Zurich."[41] "How could he have escaped the Nazi conditioning?" she reasons, and Bryher concedes that "'he wouldn't have survived'" otherwise.[42] To a London survivor of the Blitz, these conjectures about Heller's past "suggest satanic possibilities . . . all the evil they had been told existed—and undoubtedly did exist—in the S.S. mentality and in the concentration camps."[43]

"Paranoia—" she asks, "on my part?"[44] It is important to insert an aside at this point in my discussion. My detailed outlining of H.D.'s description of paranoid tendencies in the 1950s is not meant to diagnose her. In fact, I am not at all clear that she actually entertained any of these notions about Heydt. Rather, she may well be merely recycling her real-life experience of paranoia during the series of electroshock treatments she underwent in the autumn of 1946. But whether or not her paranoia had re-emerged in the 1950s, it is evident in both *Magic Mirror* and *Compassionate Friendship* that she is making use of the phenomenon of paranoia and of the figure of the spy in her writing—repurposing her experiences, as I will argue below—to explore different models of empathy, identification, and ethics. In both texts, in fact, she constantly undercuts her paranoia and suspicions by calling them "a game that Rica played . . . the story she wove from the hints that Eric dropped."[45] "This is sheer melodrama, on my part," she admits readily in *Compassionate Friendship*, but it is "very exciting, anyway." In fact, she writes, "It does not matter if I am wrong, I feel that I have a clue. I feel that this formula explains so much."[46] Like references to soldier-lovers in this late period, references to paranoia are useful for their symbolic value. In *Magic Mirror*, she reveals to her reader that "[e]verything is true there. . . . They are real people, everything is real, except the build-up of Eric's enigmatic German back-ground. Perhaps, that is actually real, too, but I made it up." "These things really happened," Rica insists, "only she had to fill in something for his background."[47] The only fictional part of this story, she alleges—this tale that traverses the pages of *Magic Mirror* and the journal that spawned it—is paranoiac speculation about her analyst's Nazi past.

H.D.'s postwar mapping of psychoanalysis to espionage is intricately wrought. In *Magic Mirror*, she draws a connection between the occultist and the psychoanalyst, aligning "the whole of the philosophy of magic" with "analysis, if you will or psycho-analysis, word-association," but notes that Heller's German heritage adds—linguistically and politically—a disturbing element of the unknown.[48] Both the occultist and the psychoanalyst, after all, engage in interpretation through careful analysis of language. She portrays the psychoanalyst as a kind of spy, who likewise scrutinizes language, searching for the key to decoding messages. At one stage, as noted in the previous chapter, Rica worries that Heller as a therapist-spy is a threatening other who employs idiopathic identification to violate and destroy his patients: "He absorbed these people, these stories as a sponge soaks up water." But what happens to the identity of the spy who has fed voraciously upon his victims, she wonders: "Could he live without them? What would he be without them?"[49] Does the pretense of occupying the position of the other entail the possibility—even the necessity—of evacuating the self? Does he become, then, the treasonous spy, who becomes the other? To begin to make sense of the critique of psychotherapy H.D. develops with this analogy, it is important to distinguish first between the two very different types of psychoanalysis she underwent as patient and analysand: Freudian psychoanalysis, with Freud in the 1930s; and existential psychoanalysis, with Heydt in the 1950s.

It is Freudian psychotherapy, for H.D., that most closely resembles political espionage, I will argue, for it is a model based in the twin functions of eliciting confession of secrets and of searching for a linguistic key to de-encryption or interpretation. For Freud, this process inevitably entails transference, in which the analysand comes to experience a "perfectly normal" "degree of affectionate feeling" for the analyst, "which is based on no real relation between them."[50] Transference is necessary to treatment, as it does "the inestimable service of making the patient's hidden and forgotten erotic impulses immediate and manifest."[51] While both men and women experience transference, Freud tends to depict the feelings of female patients in decidedly romantic terms. It is an "unavoidable" consequence of analysis that "she has fallen in love, as any other mortal woman might, with the doctor who is analysing her." "She" faces "two alternatives: either she must relinquish psycho-analytic treatment or she must accept falling in love with her doctor as an inescapable fate." The female patient becomes, he asserts, a seductive "*agent provocateur*"—a spy—set on nothing less than the downfall of her analyst: "to destroy the doctor's authority by bringing him down to the level of a lover and to gain all the other promised advantages incidental to the satisfaction of love." Freud warns young, unwitting analysts against the advances of sexually voracious women—"women of elemental passionateness"—under the spell of transference.[52]

For Freud, transference is, ideally, a one-sided affair. While transference may appear to involve a constant re-negotiation of the positions of self and other, in fact it gives merely the illusion of shifting positionalities. Freud viewed counter-transference as an obstacle to be avoided, so while the patient forms an emotional attachment to the analyst, the analyst is to guard vigilantly against developing feelings for the patient—to strive, rather, for the "emotional coldness" of a "surgeon, who puts aside all his feelings, even his human sympathy."[53] And, yet, the physician must maintain the pretense of a libidinal relationship. Freud advises physicians that "the patient's need and longing should be allowed to persist in her," emphasizing that "[h]e must take care not to steer away from the transference-love, or to repulse it or to make it distasteful to the patient."[54]

If Freud refers to the (female) patient as spy—coyly withholding, plotting to dominate the analyst—in fact it is clear that the analyst more aptly occupies that position. The analyst as spy feigns an emotional relationship with the patient, the other, in order to plumb the unconscious for clues, clues that eventually yield—if the analyst-spy is successful in deciphering those clues—a fixed and definitive interpretation. The analyst-spy plays, in effect, a game of chess with his patient, to paraphrase Freud's recommendations to new analysts on how to begin the process of treatment.[55] Freud's 1915 essay "Observations on Transference-Love," equivocates on the sensitive issue of the ethics of the process, admitting that in fact the love experienced during transference is, in essence, the same as "the love which appears in ordinary life." Though its source is the psychoanalytic relationship, "[w]e have no right to dispute that the state of being in love which makes its appearance in the course of analytic treatment has the character of a 'genuine' love," he confesses. The difference between these two types of love, he concludes uneasily, constitutes a matter of degree, not kind. In fact, the analyst must encourage the continuation of romantic and erotic feelings on the part of the patient so that she might learn how to be in love when she is cured.[56]

In the end, of course, the Freudian therapist must repudiate the patient—to borrow H.D.'s term. He must unmask the deceit, disclose his emotional detachment, and reject the intimacy the patient has been made to believe exists. Indeed, the model of Freudian analysis resembles to a startling extent the "romantic thralldom" H.D. is obsessed with late in her life.[57] In much of her late work, the female figure is enraptured with a soldier-lover who is bound by duty to choose battle over love. She is doomed for eternity to repeat the cycle of repudiation and pain. Moreover, the "thralldom" makes her complicit in his violence; after all, Allan Hepburn points out about espionage, we are asked to identify with the spy, not his quarry.[58] In effect, the Freudian therapist reveals himself to be a cognate of the soldier-lover. H.D., who could not complete her analysis with Freud because of the rise of Nazism in 1930s Vienna, was held suspended in a state of emotional attachment. His "rejection" may have been due to outside political forces, but it was nonetheless experienced as personal. Of course, whether or not H.D. harbored romantic feelings for Freud or Heydt is beside the point; she was interested in how the model of Freudian transference maps particularly well to thralldom. In her 1950s prose, I am arguing, H.D./Rica initially conceptualizes her relationship with Heydt/Heller in terms of romantic love and transference because this is the model of analysis she understands. In mirroring their names—Eric and [E]Rica—just as she had mirrored her name (Alton) and Freud's (von Alten) in *Sword*—she emphasizes the guise of identification and empathy implicit in transference and the danger of the idiopathic bond. A relationship between analyst and patient that bears no eroticism is a relationship that will not be therapeutic, according to Freud, but H.D. knows that the psychoanalytic relationship is feigned. H.D./Rica must knowingly place herself in the position of falling in love and being rejected. Her suspicion that Heydt/Heller is a spy is a fiction that embeds a critique of the Freudian process.

As Susan Stanford Friedman reports, H.D. claimed to have "'made irrevocably the "transference"'" with Freud, after failing to do so with other analysts.[59] However, H.D. frequently referred to Freud as "Papa," and *Tribute to Freud* includes extended passages in which she projects her father on to "the Professor," indicating a paternal rather than romantic relationship. This apparently frustrated Freud, who, in a dramatic outburst, accused H.D. of resisting the transferential process: "'The trouble is—I am an old man—*you do not think it worth your while to love me.*'"[60] But the Freudian paradigm is, at its foundation, incestuous. According to Freud, the analyst functions as a father-imago, a mother-imago, a brother-imago.[61] The relationship is grounded in a model of the familial, on a pretense of sameness at the level of the biological. To the extent that it is based in similitude, it denies a form of alterity. The illusion that the analyst is not other but an iteration of self creates the illusion of an idealized idiopathic relationship, a bond in which the misrecognition of sameness entails a threat of loss of identity.

Kaja Silverman's analogy to a snake who draws a willing and unwitting squirrel into its jaws illustrates viscerally the threat inherent in such a relationship. Her example "indicates that the ego consolidates itself by assimilating the corporeal coordinates of the other to its own."[62] Rica's concern about Heller as a "sponge" resonates sharply in this context. Freud, too, used metaphors of assimilation, annihilation, consumption, and devouring when discussing identification,[63] and the language of consumption and desire in these therapeutic situations is telling. The squirrel/patient is seduced by the snake/therapist with the mere facade of sameness. The identity of the analyst-spy—invested as it is in a resistance to recognizing alterity—is nonetheless bound up with the identity of the other; it is voracious and destructive. The Freudian analyst is, in fact, the other, but he must, like a spy, bear the disguise of the self and similitude. Everything depends on this disguise, this shield of invisibility. As Erin Carlston observes, spies are "invisible Others passing as the Same.... [T]hey could act like, and on behalf of, both the 'us' within the nation and the 'them' outside it."[64] Indeed, it is this invisibility that makes the real-world spy such a terrifying figure: "Popular images and fears of Communism after the Second World War owed much to the experience with Hitler's totalitarianism, and also integrated themes from previous encounters with racial and ethnic 'Others.' It had been easy to identify and single out for discriminatory treatment Blacks and ethnic minorities; how, though, might one identify 'Communists' within—men and women who might undermine the nation's safety?"[65] It is, then, perhaps not surprising that Rica fantasizes that Heller is a magician who owns and sometimes dons a red "cloak of invisibility."[66]

The spy's actions, though, are "not judged by universal laws but according to the context in which they transpire."[67] For all of the deception, the analyst-spy has a seemingly inviolable rationale: he is performing his role for a greater good. To serve that good, the Freudian analyst-spy reduces everything to definitive interpretation and identification—and I intend the pun, identification indicating both the assignation of meaning and the pretense of identification with the other. Once the Freudian psychoanalyst has identified the key, a singular interpretation unravels itself easily along a chain of linguistic and semantic associations. Freud's *Interpretation of Dreams* testifies to what he sees as a relatively reliable index of interpretation.[68] This cryptological model is that of *Sword*, in which Delia Alton struggles to locate the key to interpreting messages from dead RAF pilots with the hope of passing military intelligence to high-ranking British officials. And it is a model found in *The Mystery*, in which the protagonist insists, upon learning of "'a new set of signs and code-words,'" that "'[i]t is essential that I know them'"; Saint-Germain's "mind was trained to watch, to wait, to assemble particulars, to match like a trained worker in mosaic, the various fragments."[69] Inherent in this form of code-breaking, according to Yumma Siddiqi's work on empire and espionage, is a will to order or will to knowledge, in the Foucauldian sense. The "quest" of the ideal spy, Siddiqi observes, "is not for wealth or excitement, or at least not for these alone; his ultimate aim is to secure order and intelligibility."[70] Studies of the postwar culture of espionage and counter-espionage confirm this observation. The job of the spy is ultimately to sort all knowledge into definitive categories, to affix labels, and to ignore grey areas in favor of black-and-white designations. "In the late 1940s," Arthur Redding avers (using language of consumption and thus incorporation), "[McCarthyism] was spawned, which was designed to disarm, swallow up, and, most remarkably, render complicit oppositional discourses via a pervasive either/or logic."[71] Codes are not neutral, and the key to a code is the source of power for the spy, Hepburn argues, pointing out that the key can do as much harm as good.[72]

A seasoned analysand like Rica, however, does not actually believe in the "cloak of invisibility": "This was the trouble. One couldn't be invisible."[73] "Whatever invisibility a spy may have or may desire," Hepburn observes, "he can never disappear entirely."[74] Moreover, H.D.'s work—even in her early career—consistently resists definitive interpretation. Throughout her *oeuvre*, she conveys a strong distrust of the very existence of singular keys, even as she acknowledges a human need to search for them. She constantly makes statements, retracts statements, offers tentative guesses only to refute them; Friedman, in *Psyche Reborn,* aptly dubs her a profoundly "dialectical" thinker. What H.D. and Rica must learn is that their assumptions about Heydt and Heller are wrong, based as they are in a different psychiatric model. Heydt/Heller's existential analysis departs significantly from traditional Freudian psychoanalysis, in both its lack of commitment to universal keys to knowledge and its transferential paradigm for the analyst-patient relationship. It is a holistic approach that looks at each individual as unique—considering "the patient's actual, unadulterated subjective experience"—and not as an instance that can be classified according to a broader set of diagnoses: "In its purest form, 'the existential-phenomenological view does not construct any explanatory models but tries to understand situations by exploring the immediate experience [of the patient].'"[75] Interestingly, as a school, existential analysis grew specifically out of the same experiences that traumatized H.D. in the 1940s. The intertwined realities of technological warfare, the atom bomb, the Holocaust, and the concentration camp spurred a counter-reaction in psychology, as existential analysts sought to aid a haggard postwar generation: "A hyper-rationalism, driven by the attempt, in the era of industrialization, to make oneself machine-like, and the consequent suppression of emotion, seems to have been the cause of this cultural and personal fragmentation."[76]

Heydt's mentor, Medard Boss, was one of the co-founders of this approach. Boss's 1957 *Analysis of Dreams,* which H.D. owned, is not, like Freud's similarly titled project, a catalogue of archetypes.[77] It is, rather, an extended argument for treating each patient's dreams individually and honoring the subjective experience of the dreamer who experiences the dream as quite real, to do "justice to its immediate reality." There is no search for a universal key to interpretation. "[B]oth in my dreams and in waking life," Boss explains, "I am always involved in the behaviour of the people I meet, and I am involved in them even if I do nothing but look on and observe them indifferently . . . indeed even if I try to ward them off. If this is true there can no longer be any question of a projection of subjective content, or of a symbolic personification of a part of the dreamer."[78] In a related article, Boss objects pointedly to the treatment of the dream as an object rather than a process in the work of such theorists as Freud, Jung, and Adler. Existential psychotherapy, then, yields an interpretation tailored to a unique individual and without recourse to an overarching meta-narrative like the Oedipal Complex. In this article, Boss cites as illustrative Freud's now-famous case study of a female patient who dreams of a child being killed. Freud diagnoses castration anxiety and asserts the importance of the father. Pointing out that the father does not appear in the dream, Boss asks why the more obvious role of the mother was not part of the interpretation.[79]

An adherent of existential psychoanalysis, Boss moreover conceives of individual identity as inextricable from social identity, and thus the boundary between self and other as extremely malleable. He refutes, specifically, theories that hold that "[t]he human being is . . . defined as a precinct primarily self-contained and delimited over against the external world." These theories, he alleges—Freud's among them—assume a kind of automatic objectification of the other: "Such a notion of the ego is always arrived at, as it were, with a revolt of the being of man against a non-ego as object."[80] Boss's book on dreams confirms his objections to Freud by citing "the most impressive evidence for the inseparable belongingness of the things, animals and people encountered by the dreamer to the total pattern of relationships in which he moves and has his being. So much so that he exists *in* and *as* his relationship to them."[81] "We *are* nothing other than receptive, alert world-disclosiveness," he asserts, claiming that our identity is solely constituted socially: "if every human being always exists in this way *as* a unique, distinct, and completely non-objectifiable fabric of possibilities of alert receiving and answering, then we are always already *with* or in the presence of the givens of a shared world—viz. things which we encounter and which are significant in one way or another."[82]

In a sense, then, Boss proposes, in the wake of the devastation of world war, a more ethical approach to therapeutic relationships. As such, Boss's model of transference has the potential to be heteropathic. In other words, Boss takes as a given that the roles of doctor and of patient are always already intertwined, and he encourages analysts to form real relationships with their patients. In fact, he does not see therapeutic value to a relationship that is not genuine. As Stephen Diamond makes clear, "The existential therapist is not limited to the passive and interpretive role of the psychoanalyst, though such a stance may be taken when called for. But the *courage* and *commitment* to truly and genuinely *encounter* each unique patient is required by the therapist, who must not defensively avoid his or her own anxiety by hiding behind a rigid professional *persona* or distancing screen of therapeutic technique."[83] In other words, Boss rejects Freud's theory of transference, by which the analyst becomes a surrogate or imago for a vexed figure from the analysand's childhood, in part because Boss finds playing this enforced role too limiting, an obstacle to the patient's recovery. Moreover, though Freud sees a kind of fictive emotional relationship between analyst and analysand as key to the therapeutic process, Boss believes that it is destructive to perpetuate an imaginary relationship based in childhood desire: "Transference is always a genuine relationship between the analysand and the analyst. In each being together, the partners disclose themselves to each other as human beings. No transfer of an affect from a former love object to a present day partner is necessary for such disclosure."[84] If, in classical Freudian psychoanalysis, the therapist is the subject and the patient the object of study, in existential analysis the two engage in a "genuine" and nonhierarchical relationship.[85]

Certainly, espionage as metaphor explores shifting lines between self and other. The spy who can pretend to be self with such success—who can, in effect, mimic the (national) self—exposes the fictionality of the various hierarchical roles occupied by those caught up in this paradigm. To the extent that Rica, as Nephie Christodoulides suggests, "conducted her own analysis of [Heller],"[86] we can see H.D.'s keen interest in the instability of the relationship between analyst-spy and patient. Straddling the boundaries of self and other, the spy occupies a radically liminal position.[87] He is a Hermes-like figure, a "bridge" who must "mediate"—to borrow her terms from *The Mystery*. Espionage is, quite literally, self-fashioning: "Espionage and self-fashioning function as two interchangeable ways of explaining the biographically unexplainable. Espionage and self-fashioning . . . are two interchangeable biographical myths."[88] The spy as self is a fiction, and spies deploy fiction in their work. Former spies talk about the "exercise of imagination, and the movement of imaginative sympathy."[89] Their deception takes the form of narrative, of story: "the covert sphere is dominated by narrative fictions. . . .

The projection of strategic 'fictions,' in fact, is a primary goal of clandestine agencies."[90] But while the liminal specter of the spy may threaten to destabilize identity, the Freudian model of therapist-spy remains caught up in the same binary logic that it might at first be seen to critique. Deception is predicated on a tacit line between self and other. Heydt's model, on the other hand, pushes toward the cosmopolitan, post-nationalist, "un-national" stance H.D.'s 1950s writings had begun to embrace.

Hepburn remarks that it is violence that produces the spy as political subject,[91] and in her 1950s writings H.D. specifically casts a drama of Freudian transference as violence to the identity and integrity of the self by narrating her initial fears and assumptions about Freudian analysis as she enters analysis with Heydt. She makes use of paranoia in order to underscore the immensity of the threat she felt. Upon meeting Heydt, she had imagined her new analyst according to the model of her previous one, Freud. As such, she initially held him in great suspicion, employing tropes of paranoia to convey herself as under siege by an enemy spy. She also submitted herself to the "thralldom" of Freudian transference, going so far as to express her devastated reaction to his engagement. She discovers, though, that the existential approach departs significantly from the Freudian model in its advocacy of genuine identification and empathy between analyst and patient. The proverbial Freudian couch had been replaced by Heydt's tea table, which facilitated the very face-to-face situations requisite for an ethical exchange.[92] Her work with Freud had not been as successful as she had hoped in healing her mind and spirit. In *Tribute to Freud*, she had wanted to believe that Freud had facilitated in her, through finding a key, a real shift in her sense of self and the world. At the end of "Writing on the Wall," she decides that if anyone "knows," "it is the old Professor." "It is all there," she avers, "the lyrical interrogation and the implication that the answer is given with it." Freud, she believes, is the keeper of "that store of intimate revelation contained in his impressive volumes."[93] But what she learns in the 1950s is that she has not at all escaped the problems that plagued her in the 1930s. What she has to face is that there is no key, no secret knowledge to uncover that will cure her. The discovery is, alas, too late, as she is already embroiled in an imaginary romance with Heydt, and she stages a scene of her sense of betrayal at his engagement to another doctor.[94] Heydt, for his part, is loyal to his training, carrying on a friendship with H.D. until she died in 1961.

In one episode of *Tribute to Freud*, H.D. compares Freud to Hannibal and Caesar, conquerors whose conquests were legion.[95] She notes at several points that Freud uses "a modern business symbol"—striking oil—when he speaks of his successes at unearthing the secrets of the unconscious.[96] Her analysis of Freud does not remain strictly within the private sphere. H.D. takes this critique a step further in *Magic Mirror* and *Compassionate Friendship* when she maps the realm of the private to the public. In *Sword*, the figure of Essex—who attends a theatrical production with Queen Elizabeth I—represents the parallel betrayals of self and nation. Having posed the question "Why did Essex strike at the Queen?" the narrator posits that his ultimate betrayal at both levels stemmed from his inability to conceptualize the possibility that she could see him for what he was.[97] That she understands boundaries that do exist and those that do not is the source of her power over him. The Queen comprehends that the self is embedded within a double-layer of betrayal. Indeed, in that same novel, Delia's "house of life crumbled" because she had "super-imposed" the Ezra Pound figure (a spy, "a traitor" to the nation) on her unfaithful husband ("a hero in a small way," the embodiment of nation).[98] The walls fall away from her home, that figurative structure that isolates her from the rest of the world. While the "other woman" resides in the private sphere, the traitorous spy pushes H.D.'s thinking about ethics firmly into the public sphere. The self is the national self, and the borders of home disappear in the face of this realization.

After H.D.'s death, Heydt revealed to her biographer, Barbara Guest, that H.D. had been forbidden to utter Pound's name for years, a censorship imposed by Bryher.[99] The repression of the other—the "spy" who exists in a binary with the "hero"—can only result in a partial understanding of the self. Writing *End to Torment*, then, which brought "the whole Ezra complex out into the open," "achieves for me a balance," H.D. writes to Aldington in 1958.[100] For the late H.D., who strove to recover knowledge embedded in palimpsest, a forced state of "amnesia" is incredibly problematic; indeed, amnesia is a frequent trope in spy novels. Spies succeed—betrayals occur—because a policy of amnesia enables their deceptive, even traitorous, actions.

The extent to which narrative plays a role in the violence enacted on the national self places H.D.'s late-1940s investigation of the politics of historical narrative very much in line with her 1950s writings on her time at Klinik Brunner. Competing narratives of the analyst-spy expose a shift in her thinking. The spy's betrayal is not of a lover but of a nation, and the slippage in identity is of national identity. Just as she conflates the violence in the war and an operation she underwent—"It happened outside and it happened inside at the same time"[101]—H.D. erects parallels between personal and national identity. Freud's non-genuine model of relationships is destructive not just within the confines of the analyst's office but on a much broader level. More specifically, in her late prose texts the national identity of the other is German or Austrian. The fictionalized Freud figure and Heydt/Heller are both German in her 1950s prose.[102] Alarmed that others were speaking about her in German—a language she does not understand well—*Magic Mirror*'s Rica is nonetheless unsure that she wants to know German at all: "But did she want to break across it?"[103] "All this German and Swiss-German *kultur* . . . was alien to her," H.D. writes of Rica, but H.D.'s own German heritage makes for a much more complicated scenario. Carlston argues that the discourses of espionage indicate a "fundamental secret about the modern nation-state: that national self-understandings are always unstable."[104] The very presence of the spy is enough to destabilize our understandings of the self in relation to nation. Hepburn concurs when he writes that there is a "fundamental obscurity of identity in relation to convictions, belonging, citizenship, and agency."[105] H.D./Rica's encounter with the German other—an encounter she initially believes must involve a loss of identity and a wrenching repudiation—ends in a reevaluation of how the self relates to the other, but also in a consideration of the dangers of nationalism.

H.D.'s fellow late modernists were also interested in this phenomenon, and she read with great interest both Rebecca West's *The Meaning of Treason* and Elizabeth Bowen's *The Heat of the Day*. West lyricizes the spy's power "to put one's finger whimsically through the darkness and touch the fabric of the state, and feel the unstable structure rock."[106] The spy, according to Hepburn, "paradoxically challenges frontier mentality and reinforces nationalist interests."[107] The spy unsettles our allegiances. The spy figure in Bowen's novel defends himself to his lover, Stella, by citing the illusion of national identity in the modern world: "Country?—there are no more countries left; nothing but names." Stella, in turn, realizes, "It had been terror of the alien, then, had it, all the time?—and here it was, breathing its expiring minutes, *his* expiring minutes, along the foot of her bed."[108] The alien does not exist in isolation; the alien is inevitably close to the self—at the foot of the bed—and, in the end, part of the self.

By her late period, H.D.'s writings appear to concur with this view of national identity in flux. She has settled her "confused national, international, un-national consciousness" in favor of a destabilization of national boundaries, not in the model of the explosive, annihilatory violence of Delia's hallucinatory vision, but in a paradigm that simultaneously respects national difference and disclaims specific or singular national allegiance.[109] Indeed, much earlier in her career, H.D. had observed, "We are no longer nations. We are, or should be, *a* nation."[110] In the midst of the war, H.D. tells Plank that she is unconcerned about whether or not she has U.S. citizenship because national boundaries may be radically redefined by the war: "by the time the war is over, we may really be a sort of federation of nations and it won't matter anyhow."[111] She imagines herself not without nation but within a multitude of nations that foster connections between each other. In *Magic Mirror*, Rica refers to her story of Heller's Klinik as her own *Magic Mountain* by German author Thomas Mann.[112] Rica is American—"Am-erica," she plays with the pun on her given name, Erica—in an American novel, but she is by analogy a denizen of a German text. In the *Hirslanden Notebooks*, H.D. observes that the boundaries between herself, her friend Joan, and the other residents of Küsnacht, are illusory: "I said that Joan was a reflection of myself, but they all are at *Küsnacht*, all of 'Dr. Heydt's analysands or patients."[113] The clinic of *Magic Mirror*—with its motley group of nationally diverse clientele—constitutes a "small republic," a "microcosm."[114] The macrocosm, by extension, is the world in a cosmopolitan vision the characters of *The Mystery* maintain stubbornly as they persevere in their work toward a "world-unity without war."[115]

Freud, too, had "dared to say that it was the same ocean of universal consciousness" that "proclaimed all men one; all nations and races met in the universal world of the dream,"[116] but he also claimed to know a key that could interpret and decipher all. This is the claim in which she loses faith by the 1950s when she discovers a model of individuality within unity offered by Heydt. It should be said that the apocalyptic rhetoric of H.D.'s vision in *Sword*—to extend Madelyn Detloff's argument about H.D.'s early 1940s writings—may well attempt to justify the violence that precedes this idealized global space, as the bombs of an imagined World War III rip apart the borders that separate one nation from another.[117] While West blames imperialism for the fragility of national identity, Bowen's *The Heat of the Day* portrays the Second World War in terms similar to H.D.'s depiction of World War III, the multiple "theatres of war" rendering maps irrevocably useless: "War's being global meant it ran off the edges of maps; it was uncontainable."[118] For

H.D. just after the war, the distinction between national self and other dissolves in the annihilatory destructiveness of war, but by the 1950s her ethics has been realigned.

At the end of H.D.'s life, finally, identity is not to be conceived as fixed. It is not based in biology, nation, or race. It is, in the end, discursive: "I felt cast out, I was thrown away," H.D. declares in "Hermetic Definition," "and to recover identity, // I wrote furiously."[119] She realizes this, too, in *Bid Me to Live*, when she determines that "the story must write me, the story must create me."[120] Identity is unstable, transient, ephemeral. But it can be constructed and destroyed and re-constructed through lyric and narrative. National narratives are suspect because they purport not to be subject to this shaping. This acute awareness about the importance of language is perhaps why some of H.D.'s last written words, penned just three months before she died, concern a woman, Irmgard Rackwitz, who refuses to speak,[121] and H.D.'s own speech had been affected by a stroke. About her inability to connect with Heller, too, Rica wonders in *Magic Mirror* whether "[p]erhaps it was a question of language." The problem is "blank space . . . misunderstanding . . . misconstruction . . . untranslated, mistranslated."[122] Ultimately, it is, for H.D., language that creates catastrophe, nationalism, and troubling notions of identity, but it also fashions a space for empathy and understanding. Writing is a "compulsion."[123] A refusal to speak, a "blank space," these are unimaginable. "[W]rite," she insists in one of her final poems, "write or die."[124]

Coda

... memory has been torn ...

—Pierre Nora

... the laurel wreath of the acclaimed achievement
must be tempered, balanced, re-lived, re-focused or even sustained
by the unpredictable, the inchoate ...

—H.D.

Having survived the Second World War—and having endured electroshock treatments in its aftermath—an aging H.D. struggled with memory issues in her later life. I can only imagine that this disturbed deeply a poet who had committed herself to archaeological journeys through the palimpsest of history, to redressing Western civilization's lethal cultural amnesia. But, as is true of so much of her experience of personal trauma, the process of remembering and forgetting also interested her intellectually. From the immediate postwar period until the end of her life, H.D.'s prose explores the complicated entanglements of memory, trauma, ethics, and both personal and national narrative. One of her last prose works, *End to Torment*, takes up this web of concerns three years before her death in 1961.

Annette Debo's recent work has persuasively demonstrated that Norman Holmes Pearson convinced the typically reclusive H.D. to emerge into the spotlight late in life to accept awards and consent to be interviewed. In his efforts to establish a canon of vibrant and influential American modernists, Pearson prodded H.D. to write about her connections to famous friends.[1] An apparent chronicle of her thoughts about Ezra Pound upon his controversial release from St. Elizabeths, *End to Torment* is one such endeavor by a "lesser satellite," as she quips.² Or at least this is how it is typically read. A remembrance of young love, a musing about the place of the woman writer in modernism, a bid for her own canonization—there is, I would contend, even more to this slim volume. Indeed, the book deftly weaves together the strands of her postwar concerns about the nature of memory and its relationship to ethics, nation, and story. Revisiting her relationship with Pound is, in part, an opportunity to continue the work that she began at the close of the Second World War.

Part I of *A Curious Peril* shows how H.D.'s *Sword* devises a fragmented narrative to capture the state of trauma and instability war engenders. *End to Torment* continues this meditation on the relationships between trauma, narrative, loss, and memory. Written as a sequence of temporally bound journal entries, the book defies chronology in its attempt to piece together Pound's story. Indeed, the narrative depends upon the tension between the carefully documented chronology of its composition and the utter disorder and incompleteness of its subject. Her method is not aimlessly "rambling," as one critic has described it.³ Rather, it emphasizes the clutter and disarray of memory, which can bear but a tenuous relationship to truth.⁴ Perhaps disingenuously, Pearson tells H.D. that the process of writing about Pound will be therapeutic, even as Bryher warned strenuously against it.⁵ Pearson is concerned that the remembrance be clear, prodding her that "'[i]t is the ordering, not the data which is important,'" an admonition about order she expressly refuses. Her psychoanalyst Erich Heydt appears to possess a richer understanding of the project when he observes of the draft that "'[t]he simplicity is wonderful in face of the confusion.'"⁶

Perhaps the most interesting aspect of this strange account, though, is that memory comes not from within—as one would expect—but from without. Indeed, she is very much the magpie Pound himself is compared to in an article she reads in the *London Chronicle*, thieving and piecing together his story from other people's material. Her memoir derives less from her own memories than from a poem about Pound; newspaper and magazine articles about Pound and other poets; letters from Pearson, Aldington, and Pound's admirer Sheri Martinelli; "tea sessions" with, and an "inject[ion]" by, Heydt. H.D. explains that "if having been severed, painfully reintegrated, we want only to forget the whirlwind or the forked lightning that destroyed our human, domestic serenity and security, that is natural,"⁷ and her story of Pound resists personal memory from the beginning until the very end, constantly questioning and contradicting herself. She employs a phrase from Pearson as title, drawing on an image in Guthrie's poem for its opening, and offering as conclusion not her own meditation on Pound's release but Pearson's reporting of it.

But I do not believe that H.D. does so because she cannot face the trauma of the past. She seems, rather, to underscore the extent to which memory is purely construction, not an avenue to truth, admitting near the end that one of the central memories she uncovers—his anger at her giving birth to a child that is not his—may well be a fiction. Here the sense of being "clothed with confusion" is an inextricable part of the "*ecstasy*" of remembering.[8] The etymology of *ecstasy* entails displacement, to put something out of its place. Memory, for the late H.D., is necessarily about events out of place. Memory is events decontextualized and recontextualized. It is not possible, or even desirable, to impose order on memory. Memory is always "out-of-time."

In this so-called memoir, H.D. does not, however, fail to critique Pound's politics.[9] One of her chief sources for *End to Torment*, an article about Pound by David Rattray, does not hide its repugnance either toward his subject when he discusses Pound's postwar anti-Semitic writing and publishing ventures with white supremacist John Kasper and the Horton Square Dollar Books.[10] The article that in part inspired her own account of Pound is anything but sympathetic.[11] H.D. writes that it is difficult for her to grasp Pound's fascism: "There is no *reason* to accept, to condone, to forgive, to forget what Ezra has done ... if I dare think of Sylvia [Beach]'s confinement in a detention camp, her near-starvation, the meager rations shared with her by her friend Adrienne Monnier, during a term of hiding," adding that "[t]here is no *reason* to hope for his release" (emphasis in the original), not because his release is unlikely but because there is no acceptable rationale for it.[12] While she is told by friends that his broadcasts "had, in a way, nothing whatever to do with us and the 20,000 victims of the first big air attacks and the fires in London," she nonetheless exclaims, "No, Ezra!" to his line, "'Tudor indeed is gone and every rose.'" Her comments on European imperialism in her late 1940s prose come to mind as she associates Pound with a book of poems written from the perspective of the waifs who participated in the medieval Children's Crusade, and she notes that the name of the ship by which he will return to Italy is *Cristoforo Colombo*, a pointed reference to the New World explorer responsible for countless deaths. Her resistance to Pound mirrors her resistance to his fame, which was becoming more about the personal than the professional. She writes that she would like to see a "temper[ing]" of the "laurel wreath" with which "that gallant band" of poets sought to crown him when they supported the awarding of the 1949 Bollingen Prize to the *Pisan Cantos*. Her disdain for the ants, or *Ameisen*, that "cluster" around Pound and "clutch eagerly for the scattered grains" he sheds,[13] may likewise be read as a critique of Pearson's request that she participate in Pound's recuperation.

End to Torment also continues to contemplate some of the ethical problems that consumed H.D. in the 1950s, when she returned to the figures of the "other woman" and the spy. Pound's politics perhaps represented the greatest challenge, though, for she struggles against identification with a man who had intoned racist rants on Italian radio while she endured near-constant bombings from her London flat. Aldington's letter accompanying the Rattray article commented that the piece represented Pound "as a human being,"[14] but throughout the narrative she questions Pound's humanity. Time and again, H.D. tries to think of him as "human, humanizing," but turns instead to images of predatory animals—lions, lynxes, satyrs, panthers, wolves.

She does try to achieve some sense of identification with Pound, and even with the two women with him in Rattray's portrait, Martinelli and Pound's wife Dorothy, but her efforts mostly falter. How can she imagine that the man who saw her as a "poem," not a poet, could occupy her subject position?[15] At last, she remembers that Pound "identified with" three female writers and artists. Recalling that Pound had been in a detention camp, and that she, too, felt trapped in bed after injuring her hip after a fall, she seems for a time to soften toward him, at least abstractly, as a fellow poet: "It runs through all the poets, really, of the world. One of *us* has been trapped. Now, one of *us* is free." She later quotes from an article about T. S. Eliot, "'that the artist is a kind of prison from which the works of art escape,'" concluding that "[t]he prison actually of the Self was dramatized or materialized for our generation by Ezra's incarceration." But this book also undermines that sense of identification when she realizes that "Ezra would have destroyed me and the center they call 'Air and Crystal' of my poetry."[16]

It is death that represents liberation, she decides ultimately, just as she had in recounting the lives of martyred poets in her *By Avon River*. Pound's release does not merit a closing penned by H.D. Her final entries include an encomium of St. Thérèse; a tribute to the "authentic martyrdom" of Denton

Welch, who died young; a terse statement that her *bon voyage* letter would never reach the Pounds; and a lengthy quotation from Pearson's letter to her describing their departure. It is Dorothy who is offered a parting gift from H.D., and even that gesture is Pearson's, acting alone.[17] Pound, we must see, is not an "authentic martyr." Their mythical child, which both Pound and H.D. imagine at various points on the pages of the volume, dies as well, when she recalls weeping over Goethe's *Erlkönig*, about the death of a child caused by a supernatural creature.[18]

End to Torment shows H.D. still working through a set of themes prompted by her experience of the "curious peril" of the Second World War. In its spirit of disorder—in its rejection of chronology, its unabashed claims of radical uncertainty—the text resists "history" in the sense Pierre Nora ascribes to the term: "how our hopelessly forgetful modern societies, propelled by change, organize the past."[19] *A Curious Peril* offers a comprehensive way of understanding H.D.'s postwar outpouring of prose as an *oeuvre* that dismantles the truth claims of history, of personal and national narrative, and that confronts the enmity and conflict those narratives engender. It is my hope that this book will inspire re-readings of this difficult corpus and will inform both new explorations of the long poems of the 1950s and a reevaluation of H.D.'s place in the fragmentary, "inchoate" narrative of late modernism.

Notes

Introduction

Epigraph source: H.D., *Collected Poems*, 22.

1. H.D. did leave London a few times during the war, but she did not travel outside of London as often as Bryher did, even though they had close friends in Cornwall and Derbyshire anxious to receive them. In H.D.'s memoir of the Blitz, *Within the Walls*, Bryher urges her to leave town in the spring of 1941 when another Blitz was anticipated, but H.D. insists, "I do not want to go to Cornwall or to Eckington, for that matter," 119. Indeed, Bryher complains to May Sarton in a letter dated April 19, 1941, "I wish H. would go away, but she wont." May Sarton Papers.

2. Bryher, *Days of Mars*, 133.

3. Quoted in Zilboorg, *Richard Aldington & H.D.*, 74.

4. Letter from H.D. to Plank is dated November 24, [1938]. George Plank Papers.

5. Quoted in Zilboorg, *Richard Aldington & H.D.*, 70. Here and throughout the book, I have retained H.D.'s idiosyncratic spellings and punctuation when quoting from her writings.

6. Friedman, "Exile," 30–31.

7. Bryher, *Days of Mars*, 115–116.

8. Quoted in Hollenberg, *Between History*, 31; the date of the letter is [November 8, 1943].

9. H.D., *Hirslanden Notebooks*, 32.

10. Letter from H.D. to Clifford Howard is dated July 20, [1940]. In a later letter dated September 26, [1940], she echoes her admiration of the heroism of noncombatants when she writes that "[m]any intensely heroic and modest things occur hourly." H.D. Papers.

11. Letter from H.D. to Baker is dated February 14, [1941?]. H.D. Papers.

12. Letter from H.D. to Baker is dated February 20, [1944]. H.D. Papers.

13. Saint-Amour, "Air War Prophecy," 139.

14. H.D., *Compassionate Friendship, Magic Mirror*, 90.

15. Dembo, "Norman Holmes Pearson," 436.

16. Willis, "Public," 82.

17. H.D., *Hirslanden Notebooks*, 38.

18. Here I reference the definitions and etymologies of *peril* and *curious* found in the *Oxford English Dictionary*.

19. H.D., "H.D. by Delia Alton," 197.

20. H.D., *Collected Poems*, 5, 14.

21. Quoted in Friedman, *Penelope's Web*, 38.

22. Letter from H.D. to Doris Long is dated June 4, [1944], emphasis in the original. H.D. Papers.

23. H.D., *Notes*, 25, 46.

24. H.D., *Paint It To-day*, 61.

25. H.D., *Notes*, 24–25.

26. H.D., *Paint It To-day*, 61.

27. See Laity, *H.D.*, Chapter 3, for an argument that "statue-love" is present in H.D.'s work as a way of expressing and negotiating homoerotic desire.

28. H.D., *Paint It To-day*, 65.

29. H.D., *Collected Poems*, 50.

30. Daly, *Done into Dance*, 125.

31. See Vetter, "Representing," for a discussion of the scrapbook and photographs in the H.D. Papers, many of which are now available on the website of the Beinecke Rare Book and Manuscript Library. See Carrie Preston's *Modernism's Mythic Poses* for an illuminating reading of Delsartism, Stebbins, Isadora Duncan, and H.D.; in this poem, Preston sees the movement of statues from their pedestals as a "challenge [to] the traditional status of the (male) artist in relation to his (female) subject-muse," 202.

32. H.D., *Collected Poems*, 50, emphasis in the original; H.D., *Tribute to Freud*, 55.

33. H.D., *Paint It To-day*, 82.

34. See Vetter, *Modernist Writings*, 97–109.

35. H.D., *Majic Ring*, 56.

36. H.D., *Paint It To-day*, 84.

37. Hindrichs, "H.D.'s *Palimpsest*," 87.

38. H.D., "H.D.," 220.

39. Randall, *Modernism*, 133.

40. Here my position diverges from that of Adalaide Morris in "Relay," who argues that *Bid Me to Live* is "the last time in H.D.'s work [that] characters yield helplessly to world events," 518. I read *White Rose* and especially *Sword* as even more devastatingly pessimistic than her World War I-era fiction.

41. Mackay, *Modernism*, 1.

42. H.D., *Paint It To-day*, 45.

43. Caserio, "Abstraction, Personality, Dissolution," 197.

44. DiBattista and Wittman, Introduction to *Modernism and Autobiography*, xvii.

45. H.D., *Paint It To-day*, 11.

46. H.D., *Compassionate Friendship*, *Magic Mirror*, 92.

47. Letter from Bryher to Francis Wolle is dated June 6, 1946, Francis Wolle Papers; Bryher, *Days*, 6, 115; letter from H.D. to Baker, dated April 2, [1944], also describes the noise, H.D. Papers.

48. Letter from H.D. to Viola Jordan is dated March 30, [1941?], Viola Baxter Jordan Papers; letter from H.D. to Molly Hughes is dated August 5, [1942], H.D. Papers. H.D. expresses her exasperation at the noise to others as well, including Osbert Sitwell and May Sarton, and in H.D., "Letter from England."

49. Letter from H.D. to Plank is dated November 18, [1946], George Plank Papers; letter from H.D. to Hughes is dated August 5, [1942], H.D. Papers; letter from H.D. to Wolle is dated January 13, [1946], Francis Wolle Papers.

50. See Detloff, *Persistence of Modernism*, Chapter 3; Goodspeed-Chadwick, *Modernist Women*, Chapter 2; and Freedman, *Death Men and Modernism*, Chapter 5, for useful discussions of trauma in relation to writings H.D. produced during the war (in *The Gift*, *Trilogy*, and *Tribute to Freud*, respectively).

51. Letter from Herring to Schmideberg is dated March 6, 1946. Bryher Papers. I am grateful to Julie Vandivere for sharing the letter with me.

52. Letter from Bryher to H.D. is dated September 29, 1946. H.D. Papers.

53. Letters from Bryher to Wolle are dated March 20, 1946, and April 29, 1946. Francis Wolle Papers.

54. H.D. and Bryher discussed Woolf's suicide with Silvia Dobson (see Dobson, "Mirror for a Star," 443), and May Sarton (see Debo's introduction to *Within the Walls*, 42-43).

55. Louis Silverstein's chronology records a letter from H.D. to Ezra Pound that cites the date of her departure from London as May 13, 1946.

56. Letter from Bryher to Wolle is dated June 6, 1946. Francis Wolle Papers.

57. Letter from H.D. to Dobson is dated June 22, 1946. Silvia H. Dobson Papers.

58. Letter from H.D. to Wolle is dated June 22, 1946. Francis Wolle Papers. Perdita's letters to H.D. in June and July of 1946 indicate that she has been receiving letters from her. H.D. Papers. Letter from H.D. to Pearson is dated June 11, 1946; see Hollenberg, *Between History*, 56.

59. H.D. gives this date in a letter to Bryher dated September 29, 1946. Bryher Papers.

60. Letter from Plank to H.D. is dated November 18, [1946], George Plank Papers; H.D., *Sword*, 90; letter from H.D. to Bryher is dated September 26, 1946, Bryher Papers; letter from H.D. to Plank is dated November 18, [1946], George Plank Papers.

61. H.D., *Hirslanden Notebooks*, 68; the entry is dated June 1, 1961.

62. Letter from H.D. to Pearson is dated September 26, 1946, quoted in Hollenberg, *Between History*, 58.

63. H.D., *Sword*, 97, 46. In *Compassionate Friendship*, H.D. explains that Rica had had meningitis during the war. *Magic Mirror*, 22.

64. Letter from H.D. to Pearson is dated September 26, 1946, Norman Holmes Pearson Papers; letter from H.D. to Bryher is dated September 21[?], 1946, Bryher Papers.

65. She writes, for instance, of her "1946 breakdown" in *Hirslanden Notebooks*, 70, and her "so-called breakdown" in *Sword*, 61.

66. Letter from Bryher to H.D. is dated September 29, 1946. H.D. Papers.

67. Debo, *American H.D.*, 96. In her introduction to H.D.'s *Within the Walls*, Debo makes the argument about malnutrition even more forcefully, 66–71; she points out that

H.D. had lost 40 pounds during the war, 67. Debo also suspects that meningitis may have been part of the cause, 71.

68. Letters from H.D. to Bryher are dated May 21, [1940] and July 1, [1947]. Bryher Papers.

69. This short essay on Ezra Pound is in the Norman Holmes Pearson Papers.

70. H.D., *Tribute to Freud*, 58–59.

71. H.D., "Letter from England," 22–23.

72. Mackay, *Modernism*, 10

73. Lassner, *British Women*, 3.

74. I am quoting specifically from letters from H.D. to Bryher dated April 12, [1940]; April 14, [1940]; April 15, [1940]; May 13, [1940]; May 22, [1940]; and July 17, [1940]; but the letters from this period are filled with more references to war news. Bryher Papers.

75. H.D., "Note on Poetry," 72.

76. Though H.D. shares Bryher's enthusiasm about Churchill during the war, by the 1950s H.D. consistently sidesteps Bryher's endorsement of Tory politics, dexterously responding in vague platitudes.

77. H.D., *Trilogy*, 6.

78. Debo, *American H.D.*, 4. Debo's book demonstrates persuasively H.D.'s lingering attachment to the nation of her birth, though she had left it in 1911.

79. Bryher, *Days of Mars*, 79.

80. H.D., *Tribute to Freud*, 60.

81. Letter from H.D. to Sarton is undated. May Sarton Papers.

82. Friedman, "Exile," 32.

83. Quoted in Debo, *American H.D.*, 99.

84. Letters from Bryher to H.D. are dated November 12, 1936, and September 23, 1940. H.D. Papers.

85. On the flags, see letters from H.D. to Viola Jordan dated April 19, 1945, Viola Baxter Jordan Papers; Molly Hughes dated May 11, [1945], H.D. Papers; and Silvia Dobson dated May 16, [1945], Silvia H. Dobson Papers.

86. Expressions of her homesickness for the U.S. and England are numerous and occur throughout her life. But she also felt homesick for other countries as well. In H.D.'s *Majic Ring*, Delia visits Greece in 1920 for the first time and is surprised but invigorated to feel that she has come "home" to the country, 105–106. In a letter dated November 12, [1934], quoted in Friedman's *Analyzing Freud*, H.D. tells Bryher that she feels "terribly 'at home'" in Vienna because it reminds her of Italy and Paris, 470. This sentiment is repeated in H.D., *Tribute to Freud*, 165. In a letter dated March 31, [1947?], she writes Viola Jordan that she has "been very home-sick for Italy," Viola Baxter Jordan Papers; in letters dated [April] [1948] and August 29, [1951], she writes the same to Richard Aldington, H.D. Papers. To Francis Wolle, in a letter dated June 10, [1944], she reports being "homesick" for France. Francis Wolle Papers.

H.D.'s sense of homesickness for England heightens after her permanent remove to Switzerland in 1946, and this sense of dividedness does not end after the five-year period following the war. H.D. writes to Bryher on February 8, [1952], for instance, that "I am just now rather living in the English." Bryher Papers. As late as 1960, H.D. writes to Denise Levertov, "I miss the N.Y. tropics—now, it is cold here—really lovely, more 'English,' but I am so divided in my loyalties." Quoted in Hollenberg's "Within the World," 258.

87. In fact, Friedman's article "Exile" traces her sense of homelessness to her Moravian heritage, 47.

88. H.D., *Majic Ring*, 47.

89. H.D., *Sword*, 43.

90. Emmitt, "Forgotten," 147.

91. H.D., *Compassionate Friendship, Magic Mirror*, 86.

92. Letter from H.D. to Bryher is dated July 1, [1947]. Bryher Papers.

93. In a letter to Viola Jordan, dated March 30, [1941?], it is clear that H.D. is aware of the importance of the eagle when she calls the eagle "apt for the Nazi symbol." Viola Baxter Jordan Papers.

94. H.D., *The Mystery*, 32.

95. Woolf, *Three Guineas*, 53, 109, 108.

96. This is the thesis of Esty, *Shrinking Island* (as discussed below), but it is also that of Mackay, "Lunacy of Men," 140; Briggs, "'Almost Ashamed'"; Sarker, "Virginia Woolf"; and many others.

97. Quoted in Radford, "Late Modernism," 33.

98. Mackay, *Modernism*, 5; Mackay, "Lunacy," 124.

99. Mackay, *Modernism*, 2.

100. T. Miller, *Late Modernism*, 32.

101. Wilde, "Surfacings," 211.

102. T. Miller, *Late Modernism*, 31.

103. Esty, *Shrinking Island*, 16, 2. Though it does not align itself neatly with either model, John Whittier-Ferguson's recent book on late modernism echoes Esty in his emphasis on the process of aging; modernists in their late phases, he argues, confront their mortality and their place within history. Lyndsey Stonebridge characterizes the period as marked by an acute anxiety over the "shocks of history," agreeing in essence with Esty that modernists in mid-century turned to the past, or at least to some "versions" of the past. *Writing of Anxiety*, 5–6.

104. T. Miller, *Late Modernism*, 19, 13.

105. Mackay, *Modernism*, 2. Mackay observes about the war, "These cosmopolitan and European-minded intellectuals saw for the first time that their transnational interests could be imperial privilege as well as enlightened internationalism and that national identification could mean anything from pernicious parochialism to the freedom from totalitarian occupation."

106. That Friedman's *Penelope's Web* has declared the three novels written in the five years after the war "the least successful of H.D.'s prose texts" has undoubtedly been a factor in the lack of scholarly attention, 357.

107. Stevie Smith, *In Search*, 35.

108. Light, "Outside History," 246, 252.

109. Stonebridge, *Writing of Anxiety*, 9.

110. Esty, *Shrinking Island*, 2–3, 18.
111. Lassner, *British Women*, 5.
112. Esty, *Shrinking Island*, 12.
113. H.D., "H.D. by Delia Alton," 211.
114. Whittier-Ferguson, *Mortality*, 8.
115. T. Miller, *Late Modernism*, 31, 19.

116. H.D. completed two prose projects, the novel *Bid Me to Live* and the writings that became the memoir *Tribute to Freud*, that are outside the scope of this book because they were begun before the end of the war.

117. H.D., "H.D. by Delia Alton," 190, 212.
118. Augustine, "Preliminary Comments," 121.
119. Friedman, *Penelope's Web*, 357.
120. Serres, *Conversations*, 109.
121. Cohen, "History and Genre," 207.
122. Todorov, "Origin of Genres," 160.
123. Derrida, "Law of Genre," 66.
124. Frow, "'Reproducibles,'" 1633.
125. Beebee, *Ideology of Genre*, 9; Curti, *Female Stories, Female Bodies*, 40–41, 53.
126. See Robinson's introduction to H.D.'s *Hirslanden Notebooks*, xix.
127. H.D., "Mouse Island," *Narthex*, 33; H.D., *Nights*, 36–37.
128. Said, *Culture and Imperialism*, xiii.

129. See my introduction to H.D.'s *By Avon River*, for a discussion of H.D.'s project to read the English literary canon from the medieval to the pre-Raphaelite era, 35n40.

130. Augustine, Introduction to H.D.'s *The Mystery*, xxiv.
131. H.D., *Hirslanden Notebooks*, 39.

132. The phrase is from a letter from H.D. to Aldington dated December 13, [1946], quoted in Zilboorg, *Richard Aldington & H.D.*, 81. Given the intensity of her love of Venice, she may well have carried such a "political onus" in relation to Italy as well.

133. Friedman, *Penelope's Web*, 356.
134. Williams, *Kora in Hell*, 15.
135. H.D., *Sword*, 207.

Part I. De-formations: Trauma, Genre, and *The Sword Went Out to Sea*

Epigraph sources: Mark Doty, *Firebird*, 183; Tyrus Miller, *Late Modernism*, 19.

Chapter 1. Autobiography and Ghost Story

Epigraph sources: Proust, *A la Recherche*, 3653; Goldwyn's famous but perhaps apocryphal quip is quoted in Liz Smith, "Cartoonist's Novel Upsets Neighbors," *The Toledo Blade*, February 20, 2002, 3.

1. Letter from H.D. to Aldington is dated October 19, [1947]; letter from Dowding to H.D. is dated May 21, 1951. H.D. Papers.

2. In a letter from H.D. to Aldington dated June 22, [1947], she wonders if she might "bring them out later together" or if, rather, one might "follow on the heels of the other." Quoted in Zilboorg, *Richard Aldington & H.D.*, 98.

3. When I use the term *autobiography* in this chapter, I do not refer to formal autobiography on the model of works by St. Augustine or Benjamin Franklin, who authored the texts most often cited as foundational to the genre. I intend instead something more akin to an autobiographical mode, which might emerge in a number of genres, including novel, memoir, or *roman à clef*. Formal autobiography rarely acknowledges its own fictionality or features a self-reflective narrator to the extent that other autobiographical genres do. As Morris observes of the stock features of formal autobiography, "H.D.'s autobiographical writings stray from this schema in almost every particular." "Autobiography and Prophecy," 227.

4. Eliot, *Selected Essays*, 10.

5. Aldington, "Violet Hunt," 17.

6. DiBattista and Wittman, Introduction to *Modernism and Autobiography*, xi.

7. Riquelme, "Modernist," 462.

8. See Dembo, "Norman Holmes Pearson," 441; Pearson goes so far as to suggest that even her lyric poetry is autobiographical: "She has been so praised as a kind of Greek publicity girl that people have forgotten that she writes the most intensely personal poems using Greek myth as a metaphor. That is, she can say these things better and more frankly about herself using these other devices than she could if she simply said, 'I, I, I.'"

9. Barthes, *Image*, 144.

10. Renza, "Veto of the Imagination," 18; Lim, "Troubled," 303, 300.

11. Morris, "Autobiography and Prophecy," 228.

12. Dillon, *Palimpsest*, 115.

13. E. Gregory, *H.D. and Hellenism*, 3.

14. H.D., "H.D. by Delia Alton," 189, 190; H.D., *Majic Ring*, 69.

15. H.D., *Majic Ring*, 69.

16. Letter from H.D. to Pearson is dated October 18, [1943]. Norman Holmes Pearson Papers.

17. Fuchs, "H.D.'s *The Gift*," 89.

18. Gavaler, "'I mend,'" 96.

19. Cf. Lheisa Dustin, "'Now.'" Dustin argues that *Sword* is a failed therapeutic project. I depart from her argument in that I see H.D. as having more awareness and agency in the construction of the novel and of her autobiographically based protagonist. I do not see H.D. as confusing the personal and private, as Dustin suggests, 405, but quite consciously exposing the connection between the two. Likewise, as will be made clear in the first three chapters of this book, I do not see H.D.'s *Sword* as suggesting a belief in a transcendental signified, as Dustin contends, 419.

20. Vetter, "Representing," 160.

21. H.D., "H.D. by Delia Alton," 220.

22. Pearson began asking H.D. for an autobiography in 1947, and he continued until

her death to urge her to write memoirs centered on famous men she knew, telling her that publishers who rejected her prose were interested instead in such a volume. In Pearson's interview with L. S. Dembo in 1969, he stresses H.D.'s connections to Eliot, Yeats, and Pound. As Debo's *The American H.D.* argues cogently, Pearson was intent in "his quest to securely place H.D. in the American canon," 93. Debo documents his extraordinary efforts to shape her posthumous reputation, 93–109.

23. H.D., *Paint It To-day*, 26; H.D., *Helen in Egypt*, 290.

24. One exception to this assertion is *Bid Me to Live*, which bears more resemblance to the earlier novels though it was published in 1960. H.D. initially drafted the novel in 1939 as a final attempt at characterizing her early years in Europe. On the 1930s composite characters, see Vetter, "Representing."

25. Whittier-Ferguson, *Mortality*, 1.

26. Buss, *Repossessing the World*, 2.

27. Randall, *Modernism*, 124.

28. de Man, "Autobiography as De-facement," 922.

29. Benstock, "Authorizing the Autobiographical," 11.

30. Jacobs, *Character of Truth*, xv.

31. Letter from H.D. to Bryher is dated July 1, [1947]. Bryher Papers.

32. de Man, "Autobiography as De-facement," 922.

33. Letter from H.D. to Bryher is dated July 1, [1947]. Bryher Papers. As Hogue and Vandivere note in their introduction to *Sword*, H.D.'s pen becomes a weapon, xxi.

34. Gilmore, "Limit-Cases," 132.

35. Ibid., 137.

36. Stewart, *Women's Autobiography*, 169.

37. Lejeune, *On Autobiography*, 131–132.

38. In *Compassionate Friendship*, H.D. writes that she has read *Silver Wings* ten times. *Magic Mirror*, 94.

39. H.D., "H.D. by Delia Alton." *Magic Mirror*, 220.

40. Sidonie Smith, "Performativity," 17.

41. On H.D.'s participation in filmmaking, see especially Connor, *H.D. and the Image*; Mandel, "Redirected Image"; and McCabe, *Cinematics of Modernism*. She was also a frequent film reviewer in *Close Up*, the film magazine launched by Bryher and Kenneth Macpherson.

42. Letter from H.D. to Pearson is dated June 22, [1943], Norman Holmes Pearson Papers; letter from H.D. to Pearson is dated August 14, [1948], quoted in Hollenberg, *Between History*, 81.

43. Letters from H.D. to Aldington are dated August 24, [1947], and December 25, [1947], quoted in Zilboorg, *Richard Aldington & H.D.*, 102–103, 110.

44. Hogue and Vandivere, Introduction to H.D.'s *Sword*, xxxv.

45. This memoir is found in the Silvia H. Dobson Papers.

46. Sidonie Smith, "Performativity," 20.

47. Letter from H.D. to Pearson is dated August 5, [1948], quoted in Hollenberg, *Between History*, 112–113. In this letter and a subsequent one dated August 14th of that year,

she makes the same claim about the author of *White Rose and the Red*. Norman Holmes Pearson Papers.

48. Lejeune, *On Autobiography*, 11. He asserts that "the place assigned to this name is essential: it is linked, by a social convention, to the pledge of responsibility of a *real person*"; the reader needs this "sign of reality" to be certain of its truth value, 11–12.

49. Folkenflik, "Self as Other," 234.

50. Neuman, "Observer Observed," 317–323.

51. Lejeune, "Autobiography," 29, 31, 41. As Fuchs points out about *The Gift*, H.D. had used third person in her autobiographical writing: "'I' and 'she,' as pronominal links between H.D. the adult writer and Hilda Doolittle, the child, are unreliable indicators of the distance or proximity—either psychological or chronological—between the writer and the child. 'She' does not necessarily designate authorial distance and objectivity; nor does 'I' necessarily designate intimacy and subjectivity. Often fractured, the narrating autobiographic voice will settle into first-person, split into third-person, even swerve into the vague referentiality of a second-person address." "H.D.'s *The Gift*," 94.

52. For a helpful discussion of this aspect of autobiography, see Abbott, "Autobiography, Autography, Fiction," 603–608.

53. Letter from H.D. to Norman Holmes Pearson is dated July 31, [1948], quoted in Hollenberg, *Between History*, 76.

54. See Friedman, *Penelope's Web*, 35–46. Friedman explains that, for H.D., "[c]reating an author—a linguistically formed entity with a public presence—meant finding the right name that could materialize that author, bring her into visible existence," 36. She did not always sign her work "H.D." because "[t]he poet 'H.D.' was too rigidly defined to encompass other aspects of the self she wanted to make manifest through linguistic self-creation," 40.

55. Letter from H.D. to Pearson is dated July 31, [1948], quoted in Hollenberg, *Between History*, 76.

56. Gilmore, *Autobiographics*, 42.

57. H.D., *Sword*, 21.

58. Ibid., 155.

59. On a similar note, Matte Robinson argues that "the conversion of events from the personal, in-time dimension to the 'astral' realm ... allows H. D. the emotional distance necessary to take stock of the various figures and symbols found throughout her late prose" ("H.D.").

60. Levi, *Drowned and the Saved*, 24.

61. H.D., *Hirslanden Notebooks*, 67, 68.

62. H.D., *Magic Mirror, Magic Mirror*, 61.

63. See DuPlessis, "Romantic Thralldom."

64. H.D., *Magic Mirror, Magic Mirror*, 56.

65. H.D., *Thorn Thicket, Magic Mirror*, 165, 166.

66. H.D., *Hirslanden Notebooks*, 8.

67. Twitchell-Waas, "'Set in Eternity,'" 216. See also Rado, who argues that H.D. was not caught up in "any kind of romantic or sexual addiction" but rather sought "the power and recognition [the men] offered." *Modern Androgyne Imagination*, 62.

68. Whittier-Ferguson, *Mortality*, 6.
69. H.D., *Magic Mirror*, Magic Mirror, 47, 55.
70. H.D., *Compassionate Friendship*, Magic Mirror, 141–142.
71. H.D., *Thorn Thicket*, Magic Mirror, 164, 165, 170, 202; H.D., *Hirslanden*, 56.
72. H.D., *Sword*, 24.
73. H.D., *Magic Mirror*, Magic Mirror, 65.
74. H.D., *Hirslanden Notebooks*, 38, 173, 170, emphasis in the original.
75. H.D., *Thorn Thicket*, Magic Mirror, 163.
76. Gilmore, "Limit-Cases," 136.
77. LaCapra, "History and Psychoanalysis," 226.
78. H.D., *Sword*, 112.
79. Randall, *Modernism*, 126, 145.
80. Detloff, *Persistence of Modernism*, 107.
81. Briggs, *Night Visitors*, 11.
82. H.D., *Sword*, 84, 21.
83. Davis, *Haunted Subjects*, 2.
84. Abbott, "Autobiography, Autography, Fiction," 602, 610.
85. Lim, "Troubled," 305.
86. H.D. *Majic Ring*, 65–66.
87. Cavaliero, *Supernatural in English Fiction*, 231.
88. Messent, Introduction to *Literature of the Occult*, 2.
89. Cavaliero, *Supernatural in English Fiction*, 237.
90. Paige, "Permanent Re-enchantments," 179.
91. Hay, *History*, 55.
92. Botting, "Stories, Spectres, Screens," 103.
93. Sword, *Ghostwriting Modernism*, 9.
94. Hay, *History*, 54.
95. Poznar, "Judith Hawkes' *Julian's House*," 210.
96. Eakin, *Living Autobiographically*, x.
97. Poznar, "Judith Hawkes' *Julian's House*," 210.
98. H.D., *Sword*, 101, 124.
99. T. Miller, *Late Modernism*, 40, 64.

Chapter 2. Mysticism and Time Travel

Epigraph source: H.D., "Narthex," *Narthex*, 109.
1. H.D., *Within the Walls*, 116.
2. Vetter, Review-essay, 59–60.
3. H.D., "H.D. by Delia Alton," 192.
4. In both *Within the Walls* and "H.D. by Delia Alton," H.D. discusses this tension between reality and non-reality as a tension between "clock-time" and "dream-time." She uses the term "clock-time" in *Tribute to Freud* as well, 47.

5. Hart, "Fields of *Dharma*," 267.

6. Girard, *Violence and the Sacred*, 23; emphasis in the original.

7. For the authoritative text on the traditional view of mysticism, most contemporary religious scholars cite W. T. Stace, *Mysticism and Philosophy*. In the modernist period, Evelyn Underhill and William James were exponents of this view.

8. H.D., *Paint It To-day*, 47–48, 80.

9. H.D., *HERmione*, 216.

10. H.D., "Narthex," 101.

11. H.D., *Nights*, 51.

12. H.D., *Tribute to Freud*, 47.

13. Ibid., 56.

14. And this model is very much in keeping with H.D.'s reading in Hermeticism. As Jess Hollenback points out, "Among that collection of theurgic and philosophical writings dating from around the third century that were later attributed to the legendary pagan wise man Hermes Trismegistus one finds suggestions that the cultivation of ecstatic experiences formed an integral part of the philosopher's quest for wisdom. These Hermetic writings repeatedly stress that wisdom is only achievable when one radically casts aside the impediments to true spiritual perception and insight that the body imposes on the soul." *Mysticism*, 141.

15. H.D.'s *The Moment* (or *Seven Stories*) is in the H.D. Papers.

16. H.D. *Trilogy*, 166–167.

17. Dahlen, "Homonymous," 10.

18. H.D., *Palimpsest*, 177, 224, 218, 211, 219, 218. Elsewhere in *Palimpsest*, she expresses this notion with reference to Einstein: "The present and the actual past and the future were (Einstein was right) one," 166.

19. "The Last Time," *Moment*, 2.

20. "Hesperia," *Moment*, 13.

21. "The Moment," *Moment*, 19.

22. "Jubilee," *Moment*, 2.

23. "The Last Time," *Moment*, 15.

24. "Hesperia," *Moment*, 30.

25. "Aegina," *Moment*, 3, 4.

26. "Jubilee," *Moment*, 3.

27. "The Death of Martin Presser," *Moment*, 22, 19, 12, 21.

28. "The Guardians," *Moment*, 15.

29. "Hesperia," *Moment*, 1.

30. H.D., *Vale Ave*, 50.

31. Stoneburner, "Notes," 250, 254, 252.

32. H.D., "Narthex," 61, 115, 105.

33. Sword, *Engendering*, 1; see also Vetter, *Modernist Writings*, especially 97–109.

34. Certeau, "Mysticism," 18–19.

35. Hogue and Vandivere, Introduction to *Sword*, xix.

36. H.D., *Sword*, 39; H.D., *White Rose*, 312, emphasis in the original; H.D., *Sword*, 91.

37. Cacicedo, "'You must remember,'" 366.

38. Serres, *Conversations*, 60, 64.

39. The notion of a self autonomous from society arose in the age of the Enlightenment, Protestantism, secularization, and capitalism, and with it a much more individualized concept of religion. See Grace Jantzen's *Power* and Amy Hollywood's *Sensible Ecstasy*, on the feminization of the mystical experience from the medieval period to the present; they show how men's experiences have become the basis for the intellectual and theological, women's for the affective and mystical. Jantzen usefully points out that "if mystical experience could be delimited as private and subjective, this would be a way of ensuring that it did not have to be taken into account by those making social and political decisions: religion could be kept out of politics," 2. In fact, the experiences of medieval Christian male and female mystics varied quite widely, encompassing a range of perceptions, sensations, and encounters. Most medieval mystics would not even recognize the mystical experience as it has been defined since.

40. McIntosh, *Mystical Theology*, 31; Keller, "Mysticism," 41; McIntosh, *Mystical Theology*, Chapter 6; McGinn, "Mystical," 44; Jantzen, *Power*, 331.

41. See especially Hollenback, *Mysticism*, Chapter 8.

42. Certeau, "Mysticism," 18.

43. Hollenback, *Mysticism*, 137. H.D. also read about this saint. She owned books on St. Teresa by Henri Ghéon and Vita Sackville-West, and H.D.'s copy of Delarue-Mardrus's biography is marked in H.D.'s hand.

44. Certeau, "Mysticism," 18.

45. Harris, "Deleuze's Cinematic Universe," 115.

46. Flammarion's theory of time travel is addressed briefly in Vetter, *Modernist Writings*, 98–99. H.D. may not have read widely in science fiction, but she was a fan of time-travel fiction by her friend Katherine Burdekin (who also published under the name Murray Constantine), including *The Burning Ring*, *Proud Man*, and *Rebel Passion*. If science fiction was not a staple of H.D.'s reading, her grandson revealed to me that Bryher was an avid reader of the genre, hiding a trove of sci fi novels behind other, more "serious" books in her ample library.

47. Flammarion, *Lumen*, 42, 24, 68, 38.

48. H.D., *Sword*, 81.

49. H.D., *By Avon River*, 63.

50. H.D., *Majic Ring*, 124. In his introduction to *Majic Ring*, Tryphonopoulos points out that H.D. is involved not only in spiritualism but occultism in the early 1940s in ways that demonstrate why this text is transitional in her thinking about the spiritual or mystical experience. As Tryphonopoulos argues, initiates of the occult wander out-of-time (more characteristic of the later model, as I have described it) before achieving a degree of enlightenment (much as she sought in the earlier model), xxv-xxvi.

51. Slusser and Chatelain, "Spacetime Geometries," 162.

52. H.D., "H.D. by Delia Alton," 187, 206, 207–208.

53. Hogue and Vandivere, Introduction to *Sword*, xx.

54. H.D., *Sword*, 12, 7.

55. H.D., "H.D. by Delia Alton," 192.

56. The letter to Aldington is dated August 24, [1947], quoted in Zilboorg, *Richard Aldington & H.D.*, 103.

57. H.D., *Sword*, 60–61, 25, 57. This image continued to haunt H.D., who wrote in an unpublished essay, "It's odd to walk down a familiar street and look up into a façade open like a theatre scene—and see a room open to the sky, at the top where a friend lived, where I visited her." Norman Holmes Pearson Papers.

58. H.D., *Sword*, 133, 149.

59. Schiff, "Recovering (from) the Double," 123.

60. Ibid., 118.

61. T. Miller, *Late Modernism*, 40.

62. Slusser and Chatelain, "Conveying Unknown Worlds," 161.

63. Agamben, *Homo Sacer*, 675.

64. Derrida, "Law of Genre," 57, has remarked that the very utterance of the term *genre* evokes "norms," a "line of demarcation," a boundary, "essential purity," a "vow of obedience."

65. H.D., *Sword*, 226.

66. "Her humanity was at war with the fiction woven round her," remarks a character in one of her other books of the period. H.D., *White Rose*, 238.

67. See Burling, "Reading Time."

68. See Lindsay, "H. G. Wells."

69. H.D., *Sword*, 40.

70. Burling, "Reading Time," 12, emphasis in the original. Burling's reading of time-travel genres is specifically Marxist. I am adapting his model to argue that H.D is less concerned with capitalism *per se* than with war and imperialism. It should be noted as well that Burling restricts his analysis to time travel that involves the future, not the past, and thus escape from the present. What H.D. writes is closer to *time fantasy* or *time-slip narrative*, but I find Burling's focus on ideology helpful in thinking through *Sword* and H.D.'s other late 1940s work.

71. Cosslett, "'History from Below,'" 244. Cosslett, in fact, specifically links the device of repetition in time-slip narratives to the folk or fairy tale, a genre H.D. also employs in *Sword*, which will be discussed in the next chapter.

72. Dahlen, "Homonymous," 13.

73. This phrase is used often in H.D., *Sword*, and is the title of a chapter.

74. H.D., *Sword*, 38. The character, based on Aldington, probably refers specifically to a hurdle relay race, in which two competitors run in one direction while two others run in the opposite.

75. Ibid., 202.

76. Caruth, "Unclaimed Experience."

77. Forter, "Freud, Faulkner, Caruth," 259.

78. de Lauretis, *Alice Doesn't*, 132.

79. H.D., *Sword*, 202, 223, 242.

80. H.D., *Sword*, 51–54, 13, 62–64, 46–47.

81. Here I depart from Dustin when she writes, "For *Sword* displays symptoms of the disorder of language that Lacanian and other psychoanalytic theory calls psychosis, though H.D., drawing on occultism, considered it a spiritual exploration." "'Now,'" 419. In her article, there is at times a troubling slippage between Delia, who had an apocalyptic vision of World War III, and H.D., who probably did not. The content of Delia's vision is key. I would attribute more agency to H.D., who makes use of a brief experience of psychosis in order to illustrate the connection between public and private trauma.

82. Here, I use the term *prophecy* as Tony Stoneburner does, when he usefully distinguishes prophecy from *apocalypse*. Though there are certainly apocalyptic, or "cataclysmic," elements of Delia's vision—including its pessimistic bent—it seems to place responsibility on humankind, not just the deities, for atrocities, and as such it is inherently "political" and "a call to action" directed at the public at large, not to a segment of oppressed people who look forward to inheriting power in the future.

83. Augustine, Introduction to *The Mystery*, 127, 167, 180–181.

84. H.D., *Hirslanden Notebooks*, 18, 23, 65, 21, emphasis in the original. Though she did not know him well, van der Leeuw was important enough to H.D. that she includes him with other prominent male figures in her life, including Aldington, Pound, and Dowding, and she writes that it was the delirium that made her realize that fact.

85. Freud, *Standard*, Vol. XII, 3.

86. Ibid., 18, 69, 70, 75, 77, emphasis in the original.

87. As noted in the Introduction, H.D. is aware of the importance of the eagle to Nazism (see letter to Viola Jordan, dated March 30, [1941?]). Violet Baxter Jordan Papers.

88. H.D., *Sword*, 64, 63, 85–86. Here I disagree slightly with Jane Augustine, who has argued of spiritualism in *Sword* that "[i]t offered solace which joined her to others seeking solace for their grief and loss . . . By joining others she could both participate in history and, with them, gain a sense of an eternal refuge outside of history." "Preliminary," 126. In fact, I would say, one of the lessons she learns in the second half of *Sword* is the utter futility of escape.

89. H.D., *Sword*, 148–149.

90. Corresponding with Aldington in the midst of writing *Sword*, in a letter dated June 22, [1947], H.D. records her "shock and upset" at learning that what the British government referred to as the "few" constituted, in fact, hundreds. H.D. Papers. According to Delia Alton, there were 1,495 names in the Battle of Britain book. *Sword*, 267.

91. H.D., *Sword*, 91, 267, 64.

92. Ibid., 214, 215, 180, 215.

93. Letter to Aldington is dated June 6, [1947]. H.D. Papers.

Chapter 3. *Märchen* and Historical Fiction

Epigraph sources: Dane, "Fairy-Tale," 144; Döblin, quoted in Caserio, "James," 106–107; H.D., *Vale Ave*, 26.

1. H.D., *Sword*, 13.

2. H.D., *Tribute to Freud*, 187. Morris offers the following explanation for H.D.'s

invocation of the fairy tale in this text: "The fairy-tale scripts that fill *Tribute to Freud* work because the story H.D. is telling fits the folktale paradigm of the hero in training who asks the master for wisdom and receives a threshold gift, a gift that opens a passage from one state into another." "Relay," 501.

3. Radford, "Late Modernism," 34.

4. Ibid., 39, 95–96.

5. H.D., *Sword*, 95, 215, 172.

6. Quoted in Zilboorg, *Richard Aldington & H.D.*, 94. He also recommends that she shift to third person and abandon the layered autobiographical voices. By the time he reads the much less-traditional prose of the second half, he declares the novel "too allusive and too subtle" for publication anywhere.

7. Ibid., 214.

8. H.D, *Majic Ring*, 52.

9. H.D., *Sword*, 69, 171, 94, 95, 223.

10. Friedman, *Penelope's Web*, 72.

11. H.D., *Sword*, 155.

12. H.D., *Trilogy*, 16. To her cousin Hattie Howard, H.D. writes in a letter dated June 17, [1943]: "Books for Battle is the slogan—and I was much worried at one time that so many old MSS etc. were in danger of being pulped for battle-purposes, cartridge cases etc." H.D. Papers.

13. H.D., *Sword*, 169, 167–168.

14. H.D, *Trilogy*, 4.

15. H.D., *Sword*, 223.

16. Letter from H.D. to Aldington is dated October 10, [1947], quoted in Zilboorg, *Richard Aldington & H.D.*, 108.

17. See letters from H.D. to Bryher, dated March 1, [1938], and March 6, [1938], Bryher Papers; and letters from Bryher to H.D. dated May 12, 1934, March 9, 1938, and March 10, 1938, H.D. Papers. Silverstein's chronology records Pearson's gift.

18. Letter from H.D. to Bryher is dated February 7, [1936]. Bryher Papers.

19. See de Rougemont, *Passion and Society*, 170; H.D.'s copy is held by the Beinecke Rare Book and Manuscript Library, Yale University.

20. Curti, *Female Stories, Female Bodies*, viii.

21. Dekker, *American Historical Romance*, 28.

22. Hoberman, *Gendering Classicism*, 4–5, 6.

23. Steinmetz, "History in Fiction," 92–93.

24. DeKoven, "History," 332.

25. Tiffin, *Marvelous Geometry*, 15–16.

26. Fleishman, *English Historical Novel*, 4.

27. Manzoni, *On the Historical Novel*, 72.

28. The term is from Fleishman, *English Historical Novel*, 11. He explains, "The esthetic function of historical fiction is to lift the contemplation of the past above both the present and the past, to see it in its universal character, freed of the urgency of historical engagement," 14.

29. H.D., *Sword*, 191.

30. Tiffin observes that fairy tales typically "ignore or elide the historical and ideological processes which have created the system." *Marvelous Geometry*, 10.

31. Bausinger, "Concerning," 75.

32. Tiffin, *Marvelous Geometry*, 13–14, 17.

33. Bacchilega, *Postmodern Fairy Tales*, 5.

34. Hutcheon, *Poetics of Postmodernism*, 93. H.D.'s genuine interest in history and its bearing on the present places her work more clearly in the category of historiographic metafiction; that is, she does not appear to be creating a usable past that merely serves to legitimate her sense of the present.

35. Jacobs, *Character of Truth*, xvi.

36. Myers, "Modernity," 34.

37. Benjamin, *Illuminations*, 263, 261.

38. Tiffin, *Marvelous Geometry*, 23, 4, 14. As W. R. Halliday remarks of fairy tales in a book H.D. owned, "You will naturally look in vain for subtle delineation of character or analysis of motive. The dramatis personae are unindividualised." *Indo-European Folk-Tales*, 6–7.

39. Fleishman, *English Historical Novel*, 10. The typical character, he continues, "is one whose life is shaped by world-historical figures and other influences in a way that epitomizes the processes of change going forward in the society as a whole," 11. Shaw, however, points out that "[a]s characters become translucent to allow historical processes to shine through them more clearly, they also tend to become thinner as representations of 'inwardly complex' human beings." *Forms of Historical Fiction*, 48–49.

40. Benson, *Cycles of Influence*, 19. In this vein, Benson cites Fredric Jameson, who argues that folktale characters are from "a social world in which the psychological subject has not yet been constituted as such," 40. Thus, many modern deployments of fairy tales exploit our awareness of the instability of the subject.

41. Bacchilega, *Postmodern Fairy Tales*, 17–18.

42. Benson, *Cycles of Influence*, 20.

43. Hutcheon, *Poetics of Postmodernism*, 90, 117.

44. H.D. *Sword*, 187, 202, 214, 215, 223.

45. Hoberman, *Gendering Classicism*, 8.

46. H.D., *Sword*, 237–240.

47. Hoberman, *Gendering Classicism*, 8; Murphy, "History," 86.

48. Hutcheon, *Poetics of Postmodernism*, 97.

49. H.D., *Sword*, 254.

50. Benson, *Cycles of Influence*, 38.

51. Nikolajeva, "Fairy Tale and Fantasy," 142–143.

52. Steinmetz, "History in Fiction," 91–92.

53. Wesseling, "Historical Fiction," 205–206.

54. Zipes, *Breaking the Magic Spell*, 4. Bacchilega explains that fairy tales were once for the working classes "because they expressed the problems and desires of the underprivileged," but later became "'instrumentalized' to support bourgeois and/or conservative

interests," *Postmodern Fairy Tales*, 7. It is important to note, as Bottigheimer does, that this is one point of departure between the folktale and the fairy tale: "a large proportion of folktales have dystopic endings." "Fairy-Tale Origins," 211.

55. Tiffin, *Marvelous Geometry*, 1.

56. Ibid., 2.

57. Bacchilega, *Postmodern Fairy Tales*, 7.

58. Hoberman, *Gendering Classicism*, 8.

59. The editions of the "Fairy Books" are from the 1930s, so these were acquisitions made as an adult. H.D. also owned Roger Lancelyn Green's book-length study of Andrew Lang. In addition to Lang's fairy tale collections, H.D. was familiar with his prose translation from the Greek of the verse idylls of *Theocritus*; in *Sword*, Geoffrey reads Lang's *Theocritus* to Delia, 45.

60. H.D., *Sword*, 32.

61. Halliday, *Indo-European Folk-Tales*, 14.

62. Hines, "Collecting the Empire," 54. See also Smol, "The 'Savage,'" which documents how Lang used his fairy tales to justify his retrogressive beliefs about civilization.

63. H.D., *Sword*, 171–172.

64. Ibid., 160, 199, 257–259.

65. Ziolkowski, *Novels*, 200–201.

66. Letter from H.D. to Bryher is dated April 23, [1947]. Bryher Papers.

67. Letters from H.D. to Bryher are dated Dec 31 [[1946], January 4, [1947], and January 5, [1947]. Bryher Papers. In a letter from H.D. to Aldington dated January 20, [1947], H.D. writes of Hesse's "lovely *Märchen*": "I have found myself very happy, going on from the earlier German poets, some of which I had a slight knowledge of, to contemporary German, that is, most fortunately, HERMANN HESSE, the latest Nobel poet, though a German of the old-school and the old tradition, came before WAR I, to Switzerland ... He has the best diction I have met." Quoted in Zilboorg, *Richard Aldington & H.D.*, 83.

68. Zipes remarks that Hesse saw the modern world "as indicative of the decline of Western civilization. It was through art, especially the fairy tale, that Hesse sought to contend with what he perceived to be the sinister threat of science and commercialism." "Hermann Hesse's Fairy Tales," x.

69. Letter from H.D. to Bryher is dated January 5, [1947], Bryher Papers; letter from H.D. to Aldington is dated May 24, [1949], H.D. Papers.

70. Tiffin observes that "the structures of fairy tale operate nostalgically," *Marvelous Geometry*, 4. Tiffin's book addresses how contemporary postmodernists engage in a project I see as strikingly similar to H.D.'s: "the somewhat utopian notion of structure is invoked only to be explored and disrupted, either playfully or radically, or both," 2.

71. Zipes, "Hermann Hesse's Fairy Tales," xxii, xxvii; Zipes, *Breaking the Magic Spell*, 206.

72. Hesse, *Fairy Tales*, 202, 47, 123–124, 213, 222–223.

73. Ibid., 226, 228, 229.

74. Ibid., 205, 206, 210.

75. Moss, "Crime and Punishment," 26.

76. Hesse, *Fairy Tales*, 136, 139, 140.
77. H.D., *Within the Walls*, 10.
78. Esty, *Shrinking Island*, 2.
79. Ibid., 3.
80. Hutcheon, *Poetics of Postmodernism*, 89.
81. Bacchilega, *Postmodern Fairy Tales*, 5.
82. Ibid., 22–23.
83. Tiffin, *Marvelous Geometry*, 7.
84. Mandelbrote, "History, Narrative, and Time," 339.
85. Bacchilega writes that "repetition functions as reassurance within the tale" and notes that postmodern rewritings of fairy tales tend to exploit this feature. *Postmodern Fairy Tales*, 23.
86. H.D., *White Rose*, 205.
87. H.D., *The Mystery*, 63.

Part II. Critique: Gendered Narratives of Nation and Imperialism

Epigraph source: H.D., as Delia Alton, *Sword*, 43.

Chapter 4. *By Avon River*, Arranged Marriage, and Shakespeare's Empire

Epigraph sources: Kenneth Rockwell, review of *By Avon River*, by H.D., *Dallas Daily Times Herald*, July 17, 1949, 46; H.D., *Pilate's Wife*, 13.

1. Quoted in Friedman, "'Remembering Shakespeare,'" 55.
2. Letter from H.D. to Pearson is dated June 24, [1950]. Norman Holmes Pearson Papers.
3. This letter from H.D. to George Plank, dated July 9, [1949], is quoted in Friedman, "'Remembering Shakespeare,'" 47. Friedman notes that H.D. "liked to carry *By Avon River* in her purse or pocket for re-reading and memorizing during the period when the ideas for *Helen in Egypt* began to take shape" in the early 1950s.
4. Letter from H.D. to Plank, dated June 22, [1949]. George Plank Papers.
5. In fact, the coronation of Elizabeth II attracted a great deal of attention from H.D., who collected news clippings of the event. H.D. Papers.
6. In this period of war and postwar writing, moreover, Elizabeth is also Elizabeth Seidel, H.D.'s Moravian grandmother; and she is two Elizabeths about whom H.D. was writing novels, Elizabeth Siddall, wife of Dante Gabriel Rossetti, and Elizabeth de Watteville, granddaughter of the founder of Moravianism, Count Zinzendorf (H.D., *White Rose and the Red*, and H.D., *The Mystery*, respectively). In 1943 H.D. read for the Queen Mother, another Elizabeth, and the two princesses, one of whom would become Elizabeth II.
7. For variations on this argument, see Friedman, "'Remembering Shakespeare'"; Chedgzoy, *Shakespeare's Queer Children*; Baccolini, "Remembering and Rewriting Shakespeare"; Conilleau, "'What's in a Name'"; and Crown, "Two Judith Shakespeares."

Both Friedman and Chedgzoy place this text in the context of others like *Tribute to Freud* that address and reimagine powerful male figures.

8. Friedman, "'Remembering Shakespeare,'" 45.

9. Chedgzoy, *Shakespeare's Queer Childen*, 108.

10. H.D., *By Avon River*, 55.

11. Ibid., 75.

12. Indeed, Richard Aldington characterized the book as "a compact anthology of Tudor-Stuart lyrics with a running commentary." Quoted in Guest, *Herself Defined*, 273.

13. We can discern H.D.'s ambivalence about Shakespeare in subtle ways, too, by comparing the holograph to the printed version. The first page of the original holograph employs the phrases "my Love" and "our Love" in place of "Shakespeare"; she has struck through these affectionate phrases and uses "Shakespeare" in the final version. H.D. Papers.

14. H.D. was well aware of the significance of St. George; Delia Alton in *Sword* declares after the war that "Saint George had killed the dragon. He had become in my imagination, a symbol of England," 150.

15. Letter from H.D. to Bryher is dated July 18, [1945]. Bryher Papers. See chapter 7 of Collecott's *H.D. and Sapphic Modernism* for a discussion of H.D., Knight, and his volume on sexuality in Shakespeare.

16. Knight, *Olive*, 4. Knight is not the only one to reexamine Shakespeare during the war period; Crown's treatment of *By Avon River* confirms that "[l]iterary London, following the fashion set by Osbert and Edith Sitwell's obsession with all things Elizabethan, turned in wartime to Shakespeare as a symbol of nationalism and patriotism." "Two Judith Shakespeares," 82. In H.D.'s *White Rose and the Red*, William Morris counsels Godfrey, the character who represents British dominion over India, that "having Shakespeare makes us too important," 151.

17. Knight, *Olive*, 3, 86, 87, 26, 87, 88, emphasis in the original.

18. Ridley, Preface to *The Tempest*, xiv. A letter to May Sarton penned during the composition of *The Gift* suggests that by the early 1940s H.D. is already reading about early modern English voyages to and settlements in the New World. May Sarton Papers.

19. Letter from H.D. to Pearson is dated September 21, [1947]. Norman Holmes Pearson Papers. In her reading of the text, Chedgzoy writes that H.D. "is not explicitly concerned with *The Tempest* as an intervention into colonial discourse at all," *Shakespeare's Queer Children*, 108. But I will argue here that H.D. is quite interested in the politics of empire.

20. H.D., *By Avon River*, 60.

21. Ibid., 60, 67.

22. Hogue and Vandivere, Introduction to H.D., *Sword*, xliii.

23. Garrett, "That Four-Flusher," 41, 38. Bryher, with their close friend Robert Herring, ran *Life and Letters Today*, and H.D. read and contributed to it. H.D. also owned a pamphlet, *Shakespeare Survey*, edited by Herring that compiled Garrett's essay with two by William Empson.

24. H.D., *By Avon River*, 104, 53.

25. Ibid., 96. Ever attentive to wrongs done to poets, H.D. interjects here that Quarles's

estate was expropriated by the Commonwealth during the Interregnum, and his books were burned.

26. Ibid., 55.

27. Here I disagree with the otherwise compelling argument made by Chedgzoy when she asserts, "The troublesome marriage with the African king is here endowed with positive associations by being linked with the Song of Songs and with the plants celebrated in esoteric lore." *Shakespeare's Queer Children*, 111. She views H.D. as "resisting *The Tempest*'s inscription as a wholly political text," 129. My own reading is that any positive associations are disrupted by the allusion to arranged marriage. H.D.'s comment to Bryher, in a letter dated June 6, [1949], comparing Claribel to Desdemona in *Othello* also bespeaks a darker vision. Bryher Papers.

28. H.D., *By Avon River*, 52, 55.

29. Julien, *History of North Africa*, 143–144.

30. Ibid., 282.

31. Perkins, *History of Modern Tunisia*, 105–107. Pearson wrote to H.D. on May 14, 1943, about the eventual defeat of the Axis powers that invokes the theme of marriage: "Ah, these new warm days have brought a new life to me! The may [trailing arbutus] is in full flower, and their white sprinkled over the countryside green gives a bridal effect to the world. Maybe it's a marriage to hope we can now celebrate, after the splendid mutual effort in Tunisia." Quoted in Hollenberg, *Between History*, 24.

32. Orgel, Introduction to *The Tempest*, 30–31.

33. H.D., *By Avon River*, 60, 67.

34. Ibid., 59.

35. Friedman, "'Remembering Shakespeare,'" 48.

36. H.D., *By Avon River*, 54, 90, 83.

37. Ibid., 84, 126, 129. In the holograph, H.D. had initially described *Nymphidia* as "that somewhat tedious *reductio ad absurdum* of Mercutio's invocation to Queen Mab," but she strikes through it. She may have omitted this harsh judgment in the final version so as not to detract from the act of Shakespeare's plagiarism. H.D. Papers.

38. H.D., *By Avon River*, 88–89, 128, 126.

39. The Tower of London bears the taint of conquest and colonization, as it was thought to have been built by Caesar and was called "Caesar's Tower" until the eighteenth century.

40. H.D., *By Avon River*, 101, 77, 76.

41. See my introduction to *By Avon River* for a discussion of this anthology as H.D.'s source, 33n29. On Braithwaite, see Szefel, who traces Braithwaite's dogged advocacy of American verse and his "utopian vision of a harmonious, democratic, race-blind community devoted to beauty." "Beauty and William Braithwaite," 574. According to Szefel, Braithwaite was sympathetic with the anti-materialism of the Poetry Society of the America, though his democratic approach to the arts was later decried by Jessie B. Rittenhouse, an officer in the Society. "Encouraging Verse," 45, 50.

42. Braithwaite, Introduction to *Anthology of Magazine Verse*, xxiv.

43. Braithwaite, Introduction to *Book of Elizabethan Verse*, [n.p.].

44. H.D. began reading about the monarchs of the early modern period in the late 1930s, when she asked Bryher for both a good biography of Elizabeth I and current gossip about the Windsors; see letter dated [July 17, 1938]. In a letter dated [August 24, 1938], she tells Bryher that she is "soaking up rather third rate historical novels—after Henry VIII and Edd. VIII, have delved and am now, on a vol[ume] of Mary Queen of Scots." Bryher Papers. In the 1940s, she continued her research, which included her friend Edith Sitwell's *Fanfare for Elizabeth* and films such as *The Private Lives of Elizabeth and Essex* and *The Chronicle History of King Henry the Fifth with His Battell Fought at Agincourt in France*. Later in life, she clipped articles about the coronation of Queen Elizabeth II. H.D. Papers. Bryher was fascinated by the period and was a good source of information as well.

45. Knight, *Olive*, 95, 91.

46. H.D., *By Avon River*, 71, 101.

47. Ibid., 109. Interestingly, the end of this sentence refers to Shakespeare's death as scandalous. In the holograph version, she defends Shakespeare from this "accusation," pointing out that dying at the age of fifty-two was not uncommon in this period, or was "almost a good, old age"; in the printed version, however, she omits this defense of Shakespeare. Earlier in the manuscript, she refers to the vicar who makes the "accusation" as "shameless," but strikes through this characterization. H.D. Papers.

48. Janes, *Losing Our Heads*, 24.

49. Quoted in Owens, *Stages of Dismemberment*, 124.

50. H.D., *By Avon River*, 105.

51. Ibid., 83, 111, 83, 116, 114.

52. Ibid., 89, 75, 130–132.

53. Friedman, "'Remembering Shakespeare,'" 68.

54. H.D., *By Avon River*, 125.

55. Boughn, "Elements of the Sounding," 175.

56. H.D., *By Avon River*, 57.

57. Cf. an article by Jeffrey Twitchell-Waas, which contends, "In 'The Guest,' written in the immediate aftermath of World War II, H.D. suggests that much of the poetic genius of the Elizabethan age was stunted and dissipated because of various poets' engagement with the public sphere, whereas Shakespeare's genius achieved fulfillment because he resisted the lures of immediate history." "Seaward," 469. I see her view of Shakespeare's self-imposed isolation within the private sphere as more complicated.

58. H.D., *By Avon River*, 81, 92, 80–81, 98, 94–95.

59. Ibid., 111.

60. This note is located in some notes on Dante (H.D. Papers).

61. H.D. *By Avon River*, 119.

62. Brennan, "National Longing for Form," 59.

63. H.D., *By Avon River*, 109. Knight lauds the speech, exclaiming that it is "more suited to our time than to Shakespeare's." *Olive*, 15–16.

64. Knight, *Olive*, 4.

65. H.D., *By Avon River*, 78.

66. Knight, *Olive*, 60.

67. H.D., *By Avon River*, 121.

68. Ibid., 120. This theory of courtly love and "Our Lady" is derived largely from her reading of Denis de Rougemont. She read copies both in English and in the original French. See Friedman for more on the importance of de Rougemont's book *Love in the Western World*, which H.D. referred to as "MY BIBLE." "'Remembering Shakespeare,'" 58n25.

69. H.D., *By Avon River*, 124.

Chapter 5. Disappearing Bodies in *White Rose and the Red*

Epigraph source: H.D., *White Rose*, 238.

1. Johnson, "Savage City," 131.

2. Work on imperialism and gender can be found, for instance, in Paxton, *Writing under the Raj*; the fourth chapter of Gikandi, *Maps of Englishness*; the collection *Narratives of Nostalgia*; and Garrity, *Step-Daughters of England*.

3. The origins of the "Sepoy Mutiny" or Indian Rebellion are complicated, but H.D.'s understanding of it was the popular one, that it was sparked by a British plan to issue cartridges greased with beef tallow to Sepoy soldiers, for whom exposure was a violation of their religious beliefs. The rebellion spread throughout several regions of northern India and involved not just the military but private citizens. H.D. had learned about it by 1944, when she wrote Pearson that she had consulted Bryher about the significance of the cartridges. Hollenberg, *Between History*, 40–41.

4. H.D., "H.D. by Delia Alton," 194.

5. See Laity, who reads the text biographically as an examination of male Imagists who imaginatively "transport male modernity back to the maternal feminine" before they began to embrace "destructive, even fascistic extremes." H.D., 119. The only other comprehensive discussion of the novel is by Halsall, whose introduction to *White Rose* argues persuasively that it "mythologizes the struggles endured by nineteenth-century women in the artistic sphere" from the perspective of a woman treated as an object of art, ix.

6. Halsall, Introduction to H.D.'s *White Rose*, xviii.

7. Letter from H.D. to Pearson is dated September 22, [1949], quoted in Hollenberg, *Between History*, 92. In this vein, in a letter to May Sarton about *White Rose*, dated April 6, [1948], H.D. comments, "It is refreshing (if sad) to feel that the 'impractical' Victorian romantics had already predicted to-days [sic] problems." May Sarton Papers.

8. Letter from H.D. to Aldington is dated September 16, [1948], quoted in Zilboorg, *Richard Aldington & H.D.*, 127.

9. Letters from H.D. to Bryher are dated August 18, [1948] and August 19, [1948]. Bryher Papers.

10. Letter from H.D. to Pearson is dated August 20, [1944]; see Hollenberg, *Between History*, 40–41.

11. Letter from H.D. to Bryher is dated August 14, [1949]. Bryher Papers.

12. Letter from H.D. to Pearson is dated August 16, [1949]. Norman Holmes Pearson Papers.

13. M. Miller's article, "Enslaved," observes that the characters that populate the 1926 "Secret Name" are invested in an ancient Egypt utterly divorced from the modern European world from which they have come. About the late epic *Helen in Egypt*, Edmunds argues similarly that "H.D. indirectly enforces the suppression of the contemporary 'memory' of modern Egypt's struggle for independence from imperial Britain." *Out of Line*, 6. My article "H.D., India" is a version of this chapter that treats in more detail her representation of India in *Majic Ring* and *Sword*.

14. While writing *Majic Ring*, H.D. read a version of theosophy in a series of books by Homer and Harriette Curtiss that condensed and adapted a wide range of theosophist and occult ideas, including theories of a lost *ur*-human race that once lived in Atlantis. India seems to have taken the place of Atlantis in *Majic Ring*. I am grateful to Jane Augustine for alerting me to the importance of these volumes.

15. As discussed in Chapter 3, H.D. owned many of Lang's "fairy books," and about *White Rose* she tells Aldington in a letter dated March 9, [1948] that she "wander[s] into my own fairy-book." H.D. Papers. A letter from H.D. to Bryher dated January 31, [1938?] reflects on how the Indian tales influenced her view of the East: "I must have got a lot of my feeling for the east from those collected tales." Bryher Papers.

16. H.D., *End to Torment*, 23. H.D.'s library contained a book of Indian poetry, *The Garden of Kama* (1917).

17. H.D. and Bhaduri were close for a time, and she made a small provision for him in a wartime will. H.D. Papers. In 1942, H.D. wrote several Americans friends about finding work in the States for Bhaduri, though she was concerned about the racism he would encounter in the U.S.; see, for instance, letters to May Sarton dated January 24, 1942, May Sarton Papers, and Hattie Howard dated September 20, [1943], H.D. Papers.

18. Welby's xenophobic memoir consistently portrays most Indians as childlike and thus harmless. Welby reassures his English audience in 1933 that "1857 excites no feelings among the general population of the area of that terrible outburst" and that "no Indian has regarded or now regards the Mutiny as a national effort or cherishes any bitterness about the sometimes very drastic methods used in its suppression," 133–135. H.D.'s depiction of the Rebellion, then, runs counter to Welby's in her suggestion that it was in fact a significant event.

19. Cherberton describes India in some detail in a letter dated June 17, [1947]; in a letter dated July 19, [1947], she apologizes for disappointing H.D. by not writing even more about India. H.D. Papers.

20. See, for instance, a letter from H.D. to Bryher dated August 1, 1947, in which H.D. responds to Bryher's reporting of news of Indian independence. Bryher Papers.

21. It must be said that scholars of Pre-Raphaelitism disagree sharply about the gender politics of Rossetti's depictions of women. The most influential condemnatory view, perhaps, is voiced in Cherry and Pollock, "Woman as Sign"; usefully complicating this perspective are Andres, *Pre-Raphaelite Art*, and Bullen, *Pre-Raphaelite*

Body. While I find the latter view compelling to a point, I would maintain that H.D.'s perspective on Rossetti's mid-career paintings of women is more in line with that of Cherry and Pollock.

22. H.D., *White Rose*, 98.
23. Rossetti, *Collected Poetry and Prose*, 314.
24. Bradley, "Elizabeth Siddal," 136.
25. J. Hunt, *Pre-Raphaelite Imagination*, 187.
26. H.D., *White Rose*, 46, 142, 248.
27. Pearce, *Woman/Image/Text*, 54.
28. Pfordresher, "Dante," 120.
29. Welby, *Victorian Romantics*, 16, 33. Interestingly, this is the same Welby whose memoir, *One Man's India*, H.D. owned.
30. Rossetti, *Collected Poetry and Prose*, 314.
31. H.D., *White Rose*, 73, 174.
32. H.D. explains that "her personal war-terrors are intensified because of a nightmare obsession with an actual murder that took place in her neighbourhood when she was a child." "H.D. by Delia Alton," 196.
33. H.D., *White Rose*, 12, 74, 76, 86, 96.
34. H.D. conducted research for this novel, consulting Aldington frequently not just for sources on the Pre-Raphaelites but for facts, resources, and explanations of the political situation of the times as well; this letter dated December 31, 1947, for instance, contains a lengthy description of the war and political situation. H.D. Papers.
35. H.D., *White Rose*, 284.
36. Ibid., 73, 229.
37. Letter from H.D. to Pearson is dated December 3, [1948], quoted in Hollenberg, *Between History*, 84. See Halsall on H.D.'s refusal to reprint Siddall's purported suicide note. "H.D. and the Victorian," 128. Reprinting the note may have diverted our attention from "war-phobia" toward a more personal rationale.
38. See letters from H.D. to Pearson dated August 16, [1949], and September 22, [1949]. Norman Holmes Pearson Papers. That she sees the Crimean War as a clear cognate of modern wars is apparent when she refers to "MY post-war" as "post-Crimea" in a letter to Dobson dated October 28, [1949?], Silvia H. Dobson Papers, and when she calls the Korean War a "new 'Crimea'" in a letter to Pearson dated July 26, [1950], quoted in Hollenberg, *Between History*, 95.
39. H.D. *White Rose*, 13, 16.
40. Ibid., 312.
41. H.D.'s brief foreword to *White Rose* stresses Lushington's fictional status: "The character of Godfrey Lushington, as outlined in this romance, is presented in a purely symbolic manner," 7.
42. H.D. transcribed Pound's comment in some notes on Dante. H.D. Papers.
43. H.D., *White Rose*, 188, 197, 270, 273, 233, 234.
44. Ibid, 201. As noted in the Introduction, H.D. was aware of the importance of

the eagle to Nazism; see letter to Viola Jordan, dated March 30, [1941?]. Viola Baxter Jordan Papers.

45. H.D., *White Rose*, 203. This may explain, too, why H.D. restores and re-Anglicizes Elizabeth Siddall's name, 11; Rossetti's character spells it Siddal, the French form.

46. See, for instance, H.D.'s *Trilogy*, in which words are transfused in an alchemical process to yield a new word. *Sword* also engages in this kind of wordplay.

47. H.D., *White Rose*, 264, emphasis in the original.

48. Ibid., 18–19. H.D. began reading and translating Dante's *La Vita Nuova* while working on *White Rose and the Red*. She wrote to Aldington on May 14, [1948], that she had to read Dante before she could continue writing *Rose*. H.D. Papers.

49. H.D., *White Rose*, 299. H.D.'s sense of the vexed relationship between love, religion, and war derives in part from her reading of the works of Denis de Rougemont. In her copy of Rougemont, *Passion and Society*, she marked a passage that makes clear the Virgin Mary was a symbol, not "a woman of flesh and blood," 99, and another that asserts that troubadour poetry only *purported* to address real women, 102. She marks in Rougemont's *Love in the Western World* a passage that makes the same claim, 88.

50. H.D. *White Rose*, 271.

51. Gikandi, *Maps of Englishness*, 121, 122.

52. Garrity, *Step-Daughters of England*, 2.

53. Fuchs suggests that during World War II H.D. aligns "the author's personal body and London's topographical landscape." "Mapping Catastrophe," 310.

54. Said, *Orientalism*, 54; D. Gregory, *Colonial Present*, 17.

55. Gikandi, *Maps of Englishness*, 166.

56. Adams, *Colonial Odysseys*, 2.

57. D. Gregory, *Colonial Present*, 18.

58. Yaeger, "Introduction," 4.

59. H.D., *White Rose*, 310.

60. Ibid., 238.

61. Bickley, *Pre-Raphaelite Comedy*, 225, 224, 229. Her notes are located in the H.D. Papers.

62. Letter from H.D. to Aldington is dated March 19, [1948]. H.D. Papers.

63. H.D., *White Rose*, 185, 69.

64. Springer, "Violence Sits in Places," 90, 93.

65. Baucom, *Out of Place*, 3.

66. H.D., *White Rose*, 322. Here I would quibble with Halsall, "H.D. and the Victorian," which I find otherwise persuasive. Halsall argues that this bit of poetry is included by H.D. to humanize Siddall. I would contend that the focus on a body part, her face, accomplishes precisely the opposite, and that the ending is thus laden with irony.

67. This letter to Bryher is dated June 14, [1947]. Bryher Papers. She remarks further that she is "over-excited . . . by the Ganges discovery of Campione on the water-edge."

68. Adams, *Colonial Odysseys*, 47.

Chapter 6. The Mystery

Epigraph source: H.D, *The Mystery*, 70.

1. Letter from H.D. to Bryher is dated October 12, [1946], Bryher Papers, and Bryher's response is dated October 14, 1946, H.D. Papers.

2. Letter from H.D. to Bryher is dated February 16, [1947]. Bryher Papers.

3. Letters from H.D. to Bryher are dated June 11, [1947] and August 19, [1947]. Bryher Papers.

4. H.D., *Magic Mirror, Magic Mirror*, 32.

5. Letters from Bryher to H.D. about the condition of London are too numerous to list; one of the many letters about resident status is dated June 1, 1949. H.D. Papers. Letters from H.D. to Silvia Dobson confirm this claim. Dobson records in her memoir that though H.D. wished to retain her flat in London, Bryher felt otherwise. Silvia H. Dobson Papers.

6. Letters from H.D. to Bryher are dated May 2, [1949], and September 21, [1949]. Bryher Papers.

7. Letter from H.D. to Pearson is dated October 4, [1951], quoted in Hollenberg, *Between History*, 108. Augustine's Introduction to *The Mystery* also remarks the transitional nature of this novella: "This novel in its condensation and oblique approach resembles her imagist poetry more than the lengthy word-associative prose of her immediately preceding novels, signaling its importance as a transitional work in both form and content," xxiii. Augustine goes on to argue that "[t]he literary act frees her from dominance by male spiritual authority but lets her accept insights from her male mentors," xxxii. In this chapter, I tie its transitional nature to her recovery from postwar trauma rather than to the end of a spiritualist period, though those frameworks most certainly overlap; in Chapter 8, I touch on the ways in which H.D. continues to navigate her male mentors.

8. In H.D.'s *The Mystery*, Saint-Germain makes explicit this observation about Elizabeth de Watteville, 130.

9. Augustine, Introduction to *The Mystery*, xxv.

10. H.D., *The Mystery*, v.

11. Ibid., 70, 34, 28, 29, 32, 34, 32.

12. Ibid., 64, 76, 18, 73, 46, 62, 76, 33, 71, 74.

13. Letters from H.D. to Pearson noting this possible title are dated April 16, [1951] (see Hollenberg, *Between History*, 101), and April 18, [1951]. Norman Holmes Pearson Papers.

14. Augustine, Introduction to H.D.'s *The Mystery*, xxx.

15. Ibid., 62.

16. H.D., *The Mystery*, 18, 21, 17, 71.

17. See Augustine's introduction and notes to *The Mystery*, for a further discussion of the Faustian elements of the novella. H.D. apparently did not actually read Goethe's *Faust* until after she was nearly finished drafting *The Mystery* (see letter from H.D. to Bryher dated July 18, [1951], Bryher Papers).

18. H.D., *The Mystery*, 73.

19. H.D. read the anti-Moravian tracts of Henry Rimius. Her notes on these texts reveal her interest in Rimius's conspiracy theories about Zinzendorf, whom he accuses of manipulating his followers into participating in a secret plot. H.D. Papers.

20. My gratitude to Matte Robinson for sharing with me his copy of this rare book.

21. H.D. was influenced not only by Éliphas Lévi, *The History of Magic*—as Augustine notes—but also by Chaboseau, by *The Return of the Magi* by Maurice Magre, and by several works by her friend Eliza Butler on Faust and the figure of the magus, which she and Bryher discuss in letters as early as May 6, 1948. H.D. Papers. According to a letter to Bryher dated July 18, [1951], she also relied on Hermann Hesse's *The Glass Bead Game*. Bryher Papers. Works by Butler, Lévi, and Magre contained extended discussions of Saint Germain and Cagliostro.

22. Butler, "Goethe and Cagliostro," 3.

23. Butler, *Myth of the Magus*, 2.

24. Letter from H.D. to Pearson is dated June 16, [1951]. Norman Holmes Pearson Papers.

25. Butler, *Myth of the Magus*, 3, 4. Butler observes, "Women are not totally absent from the legendary tales about magicians; but in general they play a small and atrophied part . . . [L]ove-interest plays no great part in the lives of magicians, who had more urgent things on their minds . . . [L]ove did not, except in one or two instances, make the magician's world go round."

26. The list changes at various points: see, for instance, H.D., *Compassionate Friendship, Magic Mirror*, 96, 102, 103, 122, 141–142. In the *Hirslanden Notebooks*, she refers to Bhaduri as the "determinative" (in the Freudian sense) of the "genial magician," 8.

27. H.D., *Hirslanden Notebooks*, 8; H.D., *Compassionate Friendship, Magic Mirror*, 96.

28. H.D., *The Mystery*, 63.

29. In *Majic Ring*, H.D. tells the story of Rodeck (fictionalized as Peter van Eck) in the first and second sections of Part II; see also H.D., *Tribute to Freud*, 154–166; and H.D., "Pontikonisi (Mouse Island)," *Narthex*, 38. About Rodeck, she writes in 1951, "This mystery was experienced by me but I could not record it." "H.D. by Delia Alton," 202. In *Tribute to Freud*, she also recounts the story of a woman in 1918 Cornwall who saw her son materialize the very instant that she learns he has died in the West Indies, 173. In her introduction to *The Mystery*, Augustine argues that H.D. sees physical illness as a necessary prelude to an experience of the otherworldly, citing Delia's physical illness preceding her apocalyptic vision, Saint-Germain's illness upon being caught between two dimensions, and Dante's reported illness before he sees Beatrice in *La Vita Nuova*, 127, 167, 180–181. The third chapter of Adalaide Morris's *How to Live* compellingly discusses the Rodeck episode as an instance of projection.

30. H.D., *Sword*, 203. Flammarion is also the author of *Lumen*, the science fiction novel discussed in Chapter 2.

31. Flammarion, *Death and Its Mystery*, 36, 25.

32. H.D., *Sword*, 129.

33. Flammarion, *Death and Its Mystery*, 30.

34. Certeau, "Mysticism," 15.

35. In her introduction to *The Mystery*, Augustine notes this claim about Zinzendorf. She goes so far as to suggest that H.D.'s experience of bi-location motivated her to write *The Mystery*: "These legends of bi-location inspired the novel's plot centered on the 'Visitor,'" xxvii.

36. H.D., *The Mystery*, 49.
37. Grotstein, "Autoscopy," 259, 265.
38. Freud, "The Uncanny," 253, 238, 241.
39. Grotstein, "Autoscopy," 297.
40. H.D., *The Mystery*, 63, 69, 63, 65.
41. Grotstein, "Autoscopy," 297.
42. Kristeva, *Powers*, 4, 14, 5, 15, 10, 9.
43. H.D., *The Mystery*, 82, 17, 21.
44. Augustine, Notes to *The Mystery*, 127.
45. H.D., *The Mystery*, 49.
46. Detloff, *Persistence of Modernism*, 80, 82.
47. H.D., *The Mystery*, 74.
48. Grotstein, "Autoscopy," 267.
49. Davis, *Haunted Subjects*, 9, 117.
50. Wolfreys, *Victorian*, 1.
51. On this aspect of ghostliness, see Thurston, "Double-crossing," on Elizabeth Bowen's ghost stories, which H.D. read.
52. Botting, "Stories, Spectres, Screens," 107.
53. Thurston, "Double-crossing," 7.
54. H.D. possessed a pamphlet on Zinzendorf that stresses the inclusiveness of this vision, recounting his founding, as a teenager, of a group dedicated "to the high principles of tolerance and love of one's neighbor" and his subsequent dedication to a belief "that there were different ways of apprehending Christian truths." The pamphleteer avers that "[i]t was this very obliviousness to the distinctions between class and class that alarmed his aristocratic contemporaries. Zinzendorf's democratic spirit was shocking to those of his day." H.D. Papers. In her introduction to *The Mystery*, Augustine argues that H.D. was drawn to these aspects of Zinzendorf's vision: "She saw the Moravian church as propagating a universal eternal spirituality transcending human division—competing sects, warring nations, the personal opposition of male and female," xxx.

Part III. Re-formations: Postwar Ethics and Identity

Epigraph sources: Light, "Outside History," 256; letter from H.D. to Clifford Howard is dated March 17, [1942], H.D. Papers.

Chapter 7. Facing the Past, Becoming *l'autre*

Epigraph source: H.D., *Vale Ave*, 33.

1. Harrison, "When," 85.

2. Letter from H.D. to Howard is dated September 29, [1940]. H.D. Papers.

3. Letter from H.D. to Aldington is dated December 13, [1946], quoted in Zilboorg, *Richard Aldington & H.D.*, 81.

4. Lévi, *History of Magic*, 435.

5. Augustine, Notes to *The Mystery*, 122.

6. Morris, "Relay," 494"; the fourth chapter of Morris's *How to Live* is an updated version of this important article.

7. Hoberman, *Gendering Classicism*, 2.

8. E. Gregory offers a helpful timeline of these key dates. *H.D. and Hellenism*, 60–62. Gregory's study uncovers that H.D. drew upon accounts of Hipparchia by Diogenes Laertius, Plutarch, Pausanias, Appian, and Arrian.

9. H.D., *Palimpsest*, 4, 29, 9, 11–12, 17, 20, 9, 12.

10. Friedman, *Penelope's Web*, 241.

11. H.D., *Palimpsest*, 3.

12. Ibid., 65, 32, 65, 66.

13. Ibid., 65–66.

14. Levinas, *Totality and Infinity*, 39.

15. Levinas, "Paradox of Morality," 170.

16. Levinas, *Humanism of the Other*, 33.

17. H.D., *Palimpsest*, 75.

18. Shaw, *Forms of Historical Fiction*, 34.

19. Hutcheon, *Poetics of Postmodernism*, 110.

20. Benjamin, *Illuminations*, 255. This assertion echoes one H.D. found in Flammarion's *Lumen*, discussed in Chapter 2. The protagonist of that novel, Lumen, is able to occupy a position outside of time in order to view history in its entirety. Lumen explains that "[e]ach event is bound in an indissoluble manner with the past and the future," 68.

21. Hindrichs, "H.D.'s Palimpsest," 94.

22. H.D., *Thorn Thicket, Magic Mirror*, 165, 169, 172.

23. H.D., *Sword*, 8, 32, 104, 61, 33, 112, 90, 121.

24. H.D., *Thorn Thicket, Magic Mirror*, 161.

25. Hogue, "(Re)Storing Happiness," 855.

26. H.D., *Sword*, 223.

27. H.D., *Thorn Thicket, Magic Mirror*, 174.

28. H.D., *Sword*, 151.

29. Butler, *Precarious Life*, 20.

30. Gardiner, "Alterity and Ethics," 129.

31. Silverman, *Threshold*, 2.

32. H.D., *Sword*, 91, 214.

33. Silverman, *Threshold*, 24.

34. Friedman, *Penelope's Web*, 241.

35. H.D., *Palimpsest*, 29, 6, 22, 25, 31.

36. H.D., *Magic Mirror, Magic Mirror*, 70, 31.

37. H.D., *Vale Ave*, 52.

38. H.D., *Helen in Egypt*, 303.
39. H.D., *Vale Ave*, 45.
40. Freud, *Standard*, Vol. XVIII, 105.
41. Silverman, *Threshold*, 91.
42. Levinas, *Totality and Infinity*, 173, 172.
43. H.D., *Sword*, 30–31, 43, 44, 29.
44. H.D., *Thorn Thicket, Magic Mirror*, 180.
45. H.D., *Compassionate Friendship, Magic Mirror*, 89–90.
46. Gardiner, "Alterity and Ethics," 130.
47. H.D., *Sword*, 64.
48. Benjamin, *Illuminations*, 255.
49. H.D., *Magic Mirror, Magic Mirror*, 62.
50. H.D., *Magic Mirror, Magic Mirror*, 104.
51. Letter from H.D. to Aldington is dated December 13, [1946]. H.D. Papers.
52. H.D., *Magic Mirror, Magic Mirror*, 7.
53. H.D., "H.D. by Delia Alton," 192.
54. H.D., *Sword*, 62.
55. Silverman, *Threshold*, 86. It is an interesting coincidence that Silverman turns to Sergei Eisenstein for an extended example of the approach to filmmaking best-suited to inducing heteropathic identification. H.D. and Bryher greatly admired Eisenstein, whose theories influenced their own approach to filmmaking and film reviewing. For a discussion of Eisenstein's impact on H.D., Bryher, and other modernists, see McCabe, *Cinematics of Modernism*.
56. H.D., *Magic Mirror, Magic Mirror*, 3, 33.
57. Ibid., 55; H.D., *Thorn Thicket, Magic Mirror*, 170.
58. Ibid., 55–56, 61.
59. Shaw, *Forms of Historical Fiction*, 34; Levinas, *Totality and Infinity*, 87, 46.
60. H.D., *The Mystery*, 33.

Chapter 8. The Invisible Other: The Psychoanalyst as Spy

Epigraph source: H.D., *Vale Ave*, 49.

1. H.D., *Tribute to Freud*, 18, 101.
2. See Debo, *American H.D.*, for instance, for an argument about how the Cold War had an impact on H.D.'s *Helen in Egypt*, 110–115.
3. Letter from H.D. to Francis Wolle is dated June 10, [1944]. H.D. Papers. My profuse thanks to Cynthia Hogue and Julie Vandivere for first suggesting to me the possible relevance of Perdita's war work with the OSS. See their introduction to *Sword* for a brief discussion of Bryher and Perdita's wartime activities, xlviiin48.
4. Letter from H.D. to Clifford Howard is dated September 23, [1939]. H.D. Papers.
5. Letter from H.D. to Plank is dated July 2, [1940]. George Plank Papers.
6. Letter from Bryher to H.D. is dated November 16, [1939]. H.D. Papers.
7. See, for instance, letters from H.D. to Bryher dated April 26, [1940] and May 10,

[1940]. H.D. describes an evening of "search-lights" and the injuries due to "flying glass" after a bombing: "I do hope the CENSOR will understand this very mild comment," she pleads. A frustrated H.D. records her argument with censors in a letter to Bryher dated April 15, [1940]. Bryher Papers.

8. See, for instance, letters from Bryher to H.D. dated November, 20, [1939] and April 23, 1940. H.D. Papers.

9. Letter from H.D. to Dobson is dated October 15, 1946. Silvia H. Dobson Papers.

10. Melley, *Covert Sphere*, 43.

11. See, for instance, letters from H.D. to Bryher dated September 21, 1946, and September 28, 1946. Bryher Papers.

12. Letter from H.D. to Bryher, misdated March 11, [1929]. Bryher Papers. Of *The Heat of the Day*, H.D. tells Bryher, "I think that the 'Day' has been too much for the reviewers in England, as Liz Bowen does not mince matter about Dunkirk and so on, though it is her hero-villain who does the holding-forth, it is very eloquent; the spy-traitor was wounded at Dunkirk and was not so much against England as against the whole 'racket,' as he calls it." Bryher's letter to H.D. is dated June 18, 1951. H.D. Papers.

13. Letter from Bryher to H.D. is dated June 14, 1951. H.D. Papers.

14. It is clear in their letters that H.D. and Bryher's political views begin to diverge after the war. Bryher's distaste for West's book is recorded in her letter to H.D. dated September 16, 1949: "I don't like Rebecca West and she avows herself a member of the Labor party." H.D. Papers. H.D. responds, conversely, that the book is "a fascinating revelation": "I am so excited about Rebecca West. I read the last part first, am now going over the pre-war ground inch by inch and it is wonderful how lucid she is and what a study she has made of William Joyce, London and the baffling contradictions of the thirties" (see letters dated September 19, [1949], and September 20, [1949], Bryher Papers). H.D. also recommends it to Pearson as "very good" in a letter dated September 22, [1949]. Norman Holmes Pearson Papers.

15. Letter from Bryher to H.D. is dated June 11, 1951. H.D. Papers.

16. Letter from Bryher to H.D. is dated June 18, 1951. H.D. Papers.

17. Ibid.

18. H.D., *Compassionate Friendship, Magic Mirror*, 86.

19. Letter from Bryher to H.D. is dated June 18, 1951. H.D. Papers.

20. Letter from H.D. to Pearson about Dowding is dated August 5, [1948]; see Hollenberg, *Between History*, 80.

21. H.D., *By Avon River*, 81. The holograph is located in the H.D. Papers.

22. H.D., *Compassionate Friendship, Magic Mirror*, 104, 144.

23. H.D., *Magic Mirror, Magic Mirror*, 82; *Compassionate Friendship, Magic Mirror*, 143.

24. H.D., *Magic Mirror, Magic Mirror*, 21.

25. H.D., *Compassionate Friendship, Magic Mirror*, 144, 118.

26. H.D., *Magic Mirror, Magic Mirror*, 42.

27. H.D., *Compassionate Friendship, Magic Mirror*, 146.

28. Ibid., 109. H.D. writes, for instance, "This *Little Mermaid* is England, an England that Erich cannot comprehend."

29. H.D., *Magic Mirror, Magic Mirror*, 42, 43.
30. H.D., *Compassionate Friendship, Magic Mirror*, 145.
31. H.D., *Magic Mirror, Magic Mirror*, 42.
32. H.D., *Compassionate Friendship, Magic Mirror*, 144.
33. Ibid., 146–148.
34. H.D., *Compassionate Friendship, Magic Mirror*, 118; *Magic Mirror, Magic Mirror*, 43.
35. H.D., *Magic Mirror, Magic Mirror*, 42, 43.
36. H.D., *Compassionate Friendship, Magic Mirror*, 143, 147. A letter from H.D. to Pearson dated January 29, [1959], refers to this group as "imaginary," reassuring him that she intends this reference to be strictly "symbolic." Quoted in Hollenberg, *Between History*, 236.
37. H.D., *Magic Mirror, Magic Mirror*, 26.
38. H.D., *Compassionate Friendship, Magic Mirror*, 104–105, 145.
39. H.D., *Magic Mirror, Magic Mirror*, 20.
40. H.D., *Compassionate Friendship, Magic Mirror*, 104.
41. H.D., *Magic Mirror, Magic Mirror*, 29.
42. H.D., *Compassionate Friendship, Magic Mirror*, 104, 84.
43. H.D., *Magic Mirror, Magic Mirror*, 45.
44. H.D., *Compassionate Friendship, Magic Mirror*, 145.
45. H.D., *Magic Mirror, Magic Mirror*, 42.
46. H.D., *Compassionate Friendship, Magic Mirror*, 147, 149, 146.
47. H.D., *Magic Mirror, Magic Mirror*, 56.
48. Ibid., 72.
49. Ibid., 31.
50. Freud, *Standard*, Vol. XI, 100, 51.
51. Freud, *Standard*, Vol. XII, 108.
52. Ibid., 159, 161, 163, 166.
53. Ibid., 115. Freud also warns future analysts against revealing confidences or personal information to patients; while it may encourage the patient's necessary emotional attachment, it may also hinder resolving transference, 118. In 1910, he argued that an analyst must root it out lest the therapeutic process suffer. *Standard*, Vol. XI, 144–145. He called for a rigorous self-analysis on the part of analysts, insisting that "[a]nyone who fails to produce results in a self-analysis of this kind may at once give up any idea of being able to treat patients." He was so convinced of the inappropriateness of counter-transference that he later called for third-party intervention into the process of self-analysis, 145n1.
54. Freud, *Standard* Vol. XII, 165, 166.
55. Ibid., 123.
56. Ibid., 168, 169.
57. DuPlessis, "Romantic Thralldom."
58. Hepburn, *Intrigue*, 29.
59. Friedman, *Psyche Reborn*, 18–19.
60. H.D., *Tribute to Freud*, 16. In another passage, 146–147, Freud expresses his displeasure at being cast in a maternal role in the transferential process.

61. Freud, *Standard*, Vol. XII, 100.

62. Silverman, *Threshold*, 24.

63. Freud, *Standard*, Vol. XVIII, 105.

64. Carlston, *Double Agents*, 5.

65. G. Smith, "National Security," 311.

66. H.D., *Magic Mirror, Magic Mirror*, 34. As discussed in Chapter 6, Saint-Germain in H.D.'s *The Mystery* is also a magician.

67. Hepburn, *Intrigue*, 5.

68. The second chapter of Friedman's *Psyche Reborn* discusses Freud's approach to dreams.

69. H.D., *The Mystery*, 53, 43.

70. Siddiqi, *Anxieties*, 2.

71. Redding, *Turncoats*, 3.

72. Hepburn, *Intrigue*, 52.

73. H.D., *Magic Mirror, Magic Mirror*, 34.

74. Hepburn, *Intrigue*, xv.

75. Diamond, "Existential Psychotherapy," 305.

76. Massey, "Humanistic," 706.

77. Other aspects of Boss's work with which H.D. would undoubtedly have sympathized include his expansive notion of space and time and his openness to extra-sensory perception. I focus here on Boss because he was Heydt's teacher, but H.D. also owned Rollo May's *Existence: A New Dimension in Psychiatry and Psychology*.

78. Boss, *Analysis of Dreams*, 82, 108.

79. Boss, "Dreaming," 235–236, 240.

80. Boss, "The Ego?" 219, 220.

81. Boss, *Analysis of Dreams*, 113.

82. Boss, "Dreaming," 237.

83. Diamond, "Existential Psychotherapy," 305.

84. Boss, *Psychoanalysis and Daseinsanalysis*, 123.

85. Granted, there are obvious ethical problems to such an approach to a therapeutic relationship; my point here, though, is that it is a strikingly different paradigm from that to which H.D. was accustomed.

86. Christodoulides, Introduction to *Magic Mirror*, xxxvi.

87. From a legal standpoint, this is quite literally true. According to Abramov, "While on a mission, during his time 'in the cold' the spy is legally 'un-representable,' radically abandoned to non-regulation." "Kleist's Spy Writing," 423–424.

88. Abramov, "Kleist's Spy Writing," 427.

89. Bennett, "Secrets and Lies," 95.

90. Melley, *Covert Sphere*, 5–6.

91. Hepburn, *Intrigue*, 10.

92. H.D.'s *Tribute to Freud* relates that she did in fact lie on a couch during her sessions, with Freud positioned behind her, 35 (and elsewhere).

93. Ibid., 110, 73.

94. See, for instance, the violence of her response in her memoir, *Thorn Thicket, Magic Mirror*, 161–162.

95. H.D., *Tribute to Freud*, 80.

96. Ibid., 83. My focus here is on the trope of conquering, but this is one of several problematic passages that associate Freud with money; on H.D. and Jewishness, see Harrison and Freedman, Chapter 5.

97. H.D., *Sword*, 206.

98. Ibid., 62. For all of her fond memories of Pound, H.D.'s anger at him is documented in *End to Torment*, 34; see the coda to this book. Repeated references make it clear that Pearson had pushed her to write this memoir.

99. This note from Heydt is in the Barbara Guest Papers.

100. Letter from H.D. to Aldington is dated November 11, [1958]. H.D. Papers.

101. H.D., *Magic Mirror, Magic Mirror*, 10.

102. Indeed, the first mention of Heydt in letters from H.D. to Plank refers to him simply as "the German." The letter is dated October 5, [1953]. George Plank Papers.

103. H.D., *Magic Mirror, Magic Mirror*, 46.

104. Carlston, *Double Agents*, 9.

105. Hepburn, *Intrigue*, 4.

106. R. West, *Meaning of Treason*, 21.

107. Hepburn, *Intrigue*, 11.

108. Bowen, *Heat of the Day*, 301, 308, emphasis in the original.

109. Letter from H.D. to May Sarton is undated. May Sarton Papers.

110. *Close Up*, 136.

111. Letter from H.D. to Plank is dated [September, 1942]. George Plank Papers.

112. H.D., *Magic Mirror, Magic Mirror*, 18.

113. H.D., *Hirslanden Notebooks*, 41.

114. H.D., *Magic Mirror, Magic Mirror*, 19. *Magic Mirror* stresses the international nature of the group. In a letter from H.D. to Plank dated February 26, [1958], she wrote that it was "the world, our old microcosm in makrocosm." George Plank Papers. H.D. referred to the "wonderful polyglot crowd here" in a letter to Pearson dated May 27, [1949], quoted in Hollenberg, *Between History*, 74; and to the "huge international" nature of her fellow residents in a letter to Aldington dated December 9, [1949]. H.D. Papers. To Barbara Guest, Heydt emphasizes H.D.'s embrace of the diversity of the group when he recounts that H.D. enjoyed spending time at the dining table with other patients from different parts of the world. Barbara Guest Papers.

115. H.D., *The Mystery*, 74.

116. H.D., *Tribute to Freud*, 71.

117. Detloff observes, "The compelling, apocalyptic language of *Trilogy* is not without its costs, however, for in its redemptive turn, the poem redescribes loss as something triumphant, character-building, transformative." *Persistence of Modernism*, 80.

118. R. West, *Meaning of Treason*, 71; Bowen, *Heat of the Day*, 347.

119. H.D., *Hermetic Definition*, 54.

120. H.D., *Bid Me to Live*, 181.

121. H.D., *Hirslanden Notebooks*, 69; these words constitute the final entry in a 1961 diary.
122. H.D., *Magic Mirror, Magic Mirror*, 23.
123. H.D., *End to Torment*, 56.
124. H.D., *Hermetic Definition*, 7.

Coda

Epigraph sources: Nora, "Between Memory and History," 7; H.D., *End to Torment*, 19.

1. See the second chapter of Debo, *American H.D.*
2. H.D., *End to Torment*, 46. As Debo puts it, "This memoir, by recording the friendship between major American modernist poets, represented for Pearson another avenue toward solidifying H.D.'s position in the American canon." *American H.D.*, 116.
3. Korg, *Winter Love*, 161.
4. In her study of the book's questions, Jean Kerblat-Houghton observes, "H.D. hesitates and shifts from past to present without transition, as she can never be sure of reality or truth." "'But am I,'" 260.
5. H.D., *End to Torment*, 47. On Bryher's objections, see Hollenberg, *Between History*, 198.
6. H.D., *End to Torment*, 47, 11.
7. Ibid., 11, 46, 47, 16, 20, 48.
8. Ibid., 45, 12, 55, emphasis in the original.
9. H.D.'s letters to Pearson make clear that she is only "pro-Ezra" in her memories of him as an American, in Pennsylvania when they were young; as Debo asserts, "H.D. remained fond of Pound, but of the early Pound, the Pound of her youth." *American H.D.*, 116. It is clear from H.D.'s correspondence, however, that she does send financial support over the course of several years to Dorothy, as well as to Olga Rudge and her and Pound's daughter Mary.
10. H.D. had already been made aware of Pound's connection to Kasper in the previous year when Aldington sent her articles about it. Letters from Pearson to H.D. dated March 10, 1957, and March 31, 1957, confirm what she had read; see Hollenberg, *Between History*, 203–205.
11. As Debo observes, readers could not miss the negative portrayal of Pound because she refers to it "no less than eighteen times over the course of the sixty-page memoir." *American H.D.*, 125.
12. H.D., *End to Torment*, 34. A letter from H.D. to Pearson dated January 16, [1959], indicates that this passage was added to the manuscript after Pearson had seen a draft, and she is concerned that Pearson will object; see Hollenberg, *Between History*, 235. The letters between them indicate some degree of tension around her desire to please Pearson by writing a book that would establish both her and Pound as key American modernists and her need to express her own "torment" over Pound's actions.
13. H.D., *End to Torment*, 48, 45, 37, 38, 36.
14. Quoted in Hollenberg, *Between History*, 197.

15. H.D., *End*, 12. As Friedman and DuPlessis argue, "H.D. visualized Ezra less as sympathetic companion than as judge." "'I had,'" 223.

16. H.D., *End*, 49, 44, 56, 35, emphasis in the original.

17. Letters between H.D. and Pearson on July 8 and July 12 of 1958 confirm that H.D. did not authorize the gift; see Hollenberg, *Between History*, 228–230. H.D. silently omits from her book Pearson's request that she forgive him the imposition. Pearson had taken a similar liberty a few months earlier when he wrote that she should not refuse if he offered greetings to Pound on her behalf; see Hollenberg, *Between History*, 212.

18. H.D., *End to Torment*, 60–62, 50–51.

19. Nora, "Between Memory and History," 8.

Works Cited

Abbott, H. Porter. "Autobiography, Autography, Fiction: Groundwork for a Taxonomy of Textual Categories." *New Literary History* 19.3 (1988): 597–615.
Abramov, Tamar. "Kleist's Spy Writing, or the Autobiography of the Dash." *The German Quarterly* 85.4 (2012): 420–438.
Adams, David. *Colonial Odysseys: Empire and Epic in the Modernist Novel*. Ithaca: Cornell UP, 2003.
Agamben, Giorgio. *Homo Sacer: Sovereign Power and Bare Life*. Stanford: Stanford UP, 1998.
Aldington, Richard. "Violet Hunt." *Egoist* 1.1, January 1, 1914, 17–18.
Ambelain, Robert. *Dans l'Ombre des Cathédrales*. Paris: Éditions Adyar, 1939.
——. *La Kabbale Pratique*. Paris, Niclaus, 1951.
Anderson, Elizabeth. *H.D. and Modernist Religious Imagination: Mysticism and Writing*. New York: Bloomsbury, 2013.
Andres, Sophia. *The Pre-Raphaelite Art of the Victorian Novel: Narrative Challenges to Visual Gendered Boundaries*. Columbus: Ohio State UP, 2005.
Ashby, Lillian, and Roger Whately. *My India: Recollections of Fifty Years*. Boston: Little, Brown, 1937.
Augustine, Jane. Introduction and Notes to *The Mystery*, by H.D., xxiii–xxxii; 101–217. Gainesville: UP of Florida, 2009.
——. "Preliminary Comments on the Meaning of H.D.'s *The Sword Went out to Sea*." *Sagetrieb* 15.1/2 (1996): 121–132.
Bacchilega, Cristina. *Postmodern Fairy Tales: Gender and Narrative Strategies*. Philadelphia: U of Pennsylvania P, 1997.
Baccolini, Raffaella. "Remembering and Rewriting Shakespeare: H.D.'s *By Avon River*." In *Shakespeare e la sua eredità*, edited by Grazia Caliumi, 247–260. Parma, Italy: Zara, 1993.
Barthes, Roland. *Image-Music-Text*. London: Fontana, 1977.
Baucom, Ian. *Out of Place: Englishness, Empire, and the Locations of Identity*. Princeton: Princeton UP, 1999.
Bausinger, Hermann. "Concerning the Content and Meaning of Fairy Tales." *The Germanic Review* 62.2 (1987): 75–82.
Beebee, Thomas O. *The Ideology of Genre: A Comparative Study of Generic Instability*. University Park: Pennsylvania State UP, 1994.

Works Cited

Benjamin, Walter. *Illuminations*. Edited by Hannah Arendt. New York: Schocken Books, 1968.

Bennett, Bruce. "Secrets and Lies: Secret Agents and the Search for Truth." *Atenea* 26.2 (2006): 95–105.

Benson, Stephen. *Cycles of Influence: Fiction, Folktale, Theory*. Detroit: Wayne State UP, 2003.

Benstock, Shari. "Authorizing the Autobiographical." In *The Private Self: Theory and Practice of Women's Autobiographical Writings*, edited by Shari Benstock, 10–33. Chapel Hill: U of North Carolina P, 1998.

Boss, Medard. *The Analysis of Dreams*. New York: Philosophical Library, 1958.

———. "Dreaming and the Dreamed in the Daseinsanalytical Way of Seeing." *Soundings: An Interdisciplinary Journal* 60.3 (1997): 235–263.

———. "The Ego? Human Motivation?" *Acta Psychologica* 19 (1961): 217–222.

———. *Psychoanalysis and Daseinsanalysis*. New York: Basic Books, 1963.

Bottigheimer, Ruth B. "Fairy-Tale Origins, Fairy-Tale Dissemination, and Folk Narrative Theory." *Fabula* 47 3/4 (2006): 211–221.

Botting, Fred. "Stories, Spectres, Screens." In *Modernism, Postmodernism, and the Short Story in English*, edited by Jorge Sacido, 99–123. New York: Rodopi, 2012.

Boughn, Michael. "Elements of the Sounding: H.D. and the Origins of Modernist Prosodies." *Sagetrieb* 6.2 (1987): 101–122.

Bowen, Elizabeth. *The Heat of the Day*. New York: Knopf, 1949.

Bradley, Laurel. "Elizabeth Siddal: Drawn into the Pre-Raphaelite Circle." *Art Institute of Chicago Museum Studies* 18.2 (1992): 136–145, 187.

Braithwaite, William S. Introduction to *Anthology of Magazine Verse and Yearbook of American Poetry*, ix–xii. Boston: Small, Maynard, 1917.

———. Preface to *The Book of Elizabethan Verse*, n.p. London: Chatto and Windus, 1908.

Brennan, Timothy. "The National Longing for Form" In *Nation and Narration*, edited by Homi K. Bhabha, 44–70. New York: Routledge, 1990.

Briggs, Julia. "'Almost Ashamed of England being so English': Woolf and Ideas of Englishness." In *At Home and Abroad in the Empire: British Women Write the 1930s*, edited by Robin Hackett, Freda Hauser, and Gay Wachman, 97–118. Newark: U of Delaware P, 2009.

———. *Night Visitors: The Rise and Fall of the English Ghost Story*. London: Faber, 1977.

Bryher. Bryher Papers. General Collection, Beinecke Rare Book and Manuscript Library, Yale University, New Haven, Connecticut.

———. *Days of Mars: A Memoir, 1940–1946*. New York: Harcourt Brace, 1972.

Bullen, J. B. *The Pre-Raphaelite Body: Fear and Desire in Painting, Poetry, and Criticism*. Oxford: Clarendon Press, Oxford UP, 1998.

Burling, William J. "Reading Time: The Ideology of Time Travel in Science Fiction." *KronoScope* 6.1 (2006): 5–30.

Buss, Helen M. *Repossessing the World: Reading Memoirs by Contemporary Women*. Waterloo, ON: Wilfrid Laurier UP, 2002

Butler, E. M. *The Myth of the Magus*. New York: Macmillan, 1948.
Butler, Judith. *Precarious Life: The Powers of Mourning and Violence*. New York: Verso, 2004.
Cacicedo, Alberto. "'You must remember this': Trauma and Memory in *Catch-22* and *Slaughterhouse-Five*." *Critique* 46.4 (2005): 357–368.
Carlston, Erin G. *Double Agents: Espionage, Literature, and Liminal Citizens*. New York: Columbia UP, 2013.
Caruth, Cathy. "Unclaimed Experience: Trauma and the Possibility of History." *Yale French Studies* 79 (1991): 181–192.
Caserio, Robert L. "Abstraction, Personality, Dissolution." In *Modernism and Autobiography*, edited by Maria DiBattista and Emily O. Wittman, 197–210. New York: Cambridge UP, 2014.
———. "James, Cather, Vollmann, and the Distinction of Historical Fiction." *symploke* 12.1–2 (2004): 106–129.
Cavaliero, Glen. *The Supernatural in English Fiction*. Oxford UP, 1995.
Certeau, Michel de. "Mysticism." Translated by Marsanne Brammer. *Diacritics* 22.2 (1992): 11–25.
Chaboseau, Jean. *Le tarot: essai d'interprétation selon les principes de l'Hermétisme*. Paris: Éditions Niclaus, 1946.
Chedgzoy, Kate. *Shakespeare's Queer Children: Sexual Politics and Contemporary Culture*. Manchester: Manchester UP, 1995.
Cherry, Deborah, and Griselda Pollock. "Woman as Sign in Pre-Raphaelite Literature: A Study of the Representation of Elizabeth Siddall." *Art History* 7.2 (1984): 206–227.
Chisholm, Dianne. "H.D.'s Autoheterography." *Tulsa Studies in Women's Literature* 9.1 (1990): 79–106.
Christodoulides, Nephie J. Introduction to *Magic Mirror, Compassionate Friendship, Thorn Thicket: A Tribute to Erich Heydt*, by H.D., xxiii–xxxvii. Victoria, BC: ELS, 2012.
Close Up: Cinema and Modernism, 1927–1933. Edited by James Donald, Anne Friedberg, and Laura Marcus. London: Cassell, 1998.
Cohen, Ralph. "History and Genre." *New Literary History* 17.2 (1986): 203–218.
Collecott, Diana. *H.D. and Sapphic Modernism 1910–1950*. Cambridge: Cambridge UP, 1999.
Conilleau, Claire. "'What's in a Name?': H.D.'s Re-vision of Shakespeare," *Transatlantica* 1 (2010). Accessed December 1, 2013. http://transatlantica.revues.org/4801.
Connor, Rachel. *H.D. and the Image*. Manchester: Manchester UP, 2004.
Cosslett, Tess. "'History from Below': Time-Slip Narratives and National Identity." *The Lion and the Unicorn* 26.2 (2002): 243–253.
Crown, Kathleen. "Two Judith Shakespeares: Virginia Woolf, H.D., and the Androgynous Brother-Sister Mind." In *Virginia Woolf; Texts and Contexts*, edited by Beth Rigel Daugherty and Eileen Barrett, 81–86. New York: Pace University Press, 1996.
Curti, Lidia. *Female Stories, Female Bodies: Narrative, Identity and Representation*. New York: New York UP, 1998.

Dahlen, Beverly. "Homonymous: A Meditation on H.D.'s *Trilogy*," *Sagetrieb* 6.2 (1987): 166–171.
Daly, Ann. *Done into Dance: Isadora Duncan in America*. Bloomington: Indiana UP, 1995.
Dane, Clemence. "Fairy-Tale." *The North American Review* 242.1 (1936): 143–152.
Davis, Colin. *Haunted Subjects: Deconstruction, Psychoanalysis and the Return of the Dead*. New York: Palgrave, 2007.
de Lauretis, Teresa. *Alice Doesn't: Feminism, Semiotics, Cinema*. Bloomington: Indiana UP, 1984.
Debo, Annette. *The American H.D.* Iowa City: U of Iowa P, 2011.
———. Introduction to *Within the Walls and What Do I Love?*, by H.D., 1–104. Gainesville: UP of Florida, 2014.
Dekker, George. *The American Historical Romance*. Cambridge: Cambridge UP, 1987.
DeKoven. Marianne. "History, the Twentieth Century, and a Contemporary Novel." *Novel: A Forum on Fiction* 42.2 (2009): 332–336.
Deleuze, Gilles, and Félix Guattari. *Anti-Oedipus: Capitalism and Schizophrenia*. Translated by Robert Hurley, Mark Seem, and Helen R. Lane. New York: Penguin, 1977.
de Man, Paul. "Autobiography as De-facement." *MNL* 94.5 (1979): 919–930.
Dembo, L. S. "Norman Holmes Pearson: An Interview." *Contemporary Literature* 10.4 (1969): 435–446.
Derrida, Jacques. "The Law of Genre." *Critical Inquiry* 7.1 (1980): 55–81.
Detloff, Madelyn. *The Persistence of Modernism: Loss and Mourning in the Twentieth Century*. New York: Cambridge UP, 2009.
Diamond, Stephen A. "Existential Psychotherapy." In *Encyclopedia of Psychology and Religion*, Vol. 2, edited by David A. Leeming, Kathryn Madden, Stanton Marlan, 304–308. Springer, 2010.
DiBattista, Maria, and Emily O. Wittman. Introduction to *Modernism and Autobiography*, xi–xix. New York: Cambridge UP, 2014.
Dillon, Sarah. *The Palimpsest: Literature, Criticism, Theory*. London, England: Continuum, 2007.
Dobson, Silvia. Silvia H. Dobson Papers. Beinecke Rare Book and Manuscript Library, Yale University, New Haven, Connecticut.
Doty, Mark. *Firebird: A Memoir*. New York: Harper Collins, 1999.
DuPlessis, Rachel Blau. "Romantic Thralldom in H.D." *Contemporary Literature* 20.2 (1979): 178–203.
Dustin, Lheisa. "'Now It Will Soon Be Over': Apocalyptic Redemption in *The Sword Went Out to Sea*." *Genre* 45.3 (2012): 395–422.
Eakin, Paul John. *Living Autobiographically: How We Create Identity in Narrative*. Ithaca: Cornell UP, 2008.
Edmunds, Susan. *Out of Line: History, Psychoanalysis, & Montage in H.D.'s Long Poems*. Stanford: Stanford UP, 1994.
Eliot, T. S. *Selected Essays, 1917–1932*. New York: Harcourt, Brace, 1932.
Emmitt, Helen V. "Forgotten Memories and Unheard Rhythms: H.D.'s Poetics as a Response to Male Modernism." *Paideuma* 33.2/3 (2004): 131–53.

Works Cited

Esty, Joshua. *A Shrinking Island: Modernism and National Culture in England*. Princeton: Princeton UP, 2004.

Flammarion, Camille. *Death and Its Mystery*. New York: Century, 1922.

———. *Lumen*. Translated by Brian Stableford. Middletown, CT: Wesleyan UP, 2002.

Fleishman, Avrom. *The English Historical Novel: Walter Scott to Virginia Woolf*. Baltimore: Johns Hopkins UP, 1971.

Folkenflik, Robert. "The Self as Other." In *The Culture of Autobiography: Constructions of Self-Representation*, edited by Robert Folkenflik, 215–234. Stanford: Stanford UP, 1993.

Forter, Greg. "Freud, Faulkner, Caruth: Trauma and the Politics of Literary Form." *Narrative* 15.3 (2007): 259–285.

Freedman, Ariela. *Death, Men, and Modernism: Trauma and Narrative in British Fiction from Hardy to Woolf*. New York: Routledge, 2003

Freud, Sigmund. *The Standard Edition of the Complete Psychological Works of Sigmund Freud*. Vols. XI, XII, XVII, XVIII. Translated and edited by James Strachey. London: Hogarth, 1971.

Friedman, Susan Stanford. "Exile in the American Grain: H.D.'s Diaspora." *Agenda* 25.3–4 (1987): 27–50.

———. *Penelope's Web: Gender, Modernity, H.D.'s Fiction*. Cambridge: Cambridge UP, 1990.

———. *Psyche Reborn*. Bloomington: Indiana UP, 1981.

———. "'Remembering Shakespeare Always, But Remembering Him Differently.'" *Sagetrieb* 2.2 (1983): 45–70.

———, ed. *Analyzing Freud: Letters of H.D., Bryher, and Their Circle*. New York: New Directions, 2002.

Friedman, Susan Stanford, and Rachel Blau DuPlessis. "'I had two loves separate': The Sexualities of H.D.'s HER." In *Signets: Reading H.D.*, edited by Susan Stanford Friedman and Rachel Blau DuPlessis, 205–232. Madison: U of Wisconsin P, 1990.

Frow, John. "'Reproducibles, Rubrics, and Everything You Need': Genre Theory Today." *PMLA* 122.5 (2007): 1626–1634.

Fuchs, Miriam. "H.D.'s The Gift: 'Hide-and-Seek' with the 'Skeleton-Hand of Death.'" In *Redefining Autobiography in Twentieth-Century Women's Fiction: An Essay Collection*, edited by Janice Morgan and Colette T. Hall, 85–102. New York: Garland, 1991.

———. "Mapping Catastrophe: Topography, Tropology, and Testimony in H.D.'s *The Gift*." In *Mapping the Self: Space, Identity, Discourse in British Auto/Biography*, edited by Frédéric Regard, 297–310. Saint-Etienne, France: Université de Saint-Etienne, 2003.

Gardiner, Michael. "Alterity and Ethics: A Dialogical Perspective." *Theory Culture Society* 13 (1996): 121–143.

Garrett, George. "That Four-Flusher Prospero." *Life and Letters Today* 16.7 (1937). Reprinted in *Shakespeare Survey*, edited by Robert Herring. London: Brendin, 1937.

Garrity, Jane. *Step-Daughters of England: British Women Modernists and the National Imaginary*. New York: Manchester UP, 2003.

Gavaler, Christopher P. "'I Mend a Break in Time': An Historical Reconstruction of H.D.'s Wunden Eiland Ceremony in *The Gift* and *Trilogy*." *Sagetrieb* 15.1/2 (1996): 94–120.

Gikandi, Simon. *Maps of Englishness: Writing Identity in the Culture of Colonialism*. New York: Columbia UP, 1996.

Gilmore, Leigh. *Autobiographics: A Feminist Theory of Women's Self-Representation*. Ithaca: Cornell UP, 1994.

———. "Limit-Cases: Trauma, Self-Representation, and the Jurisdictions of Identity." *Biography* 24.1 (2001): 128–139.

Girard, René. *Violence and the Sacred*. Translated by Patrick Gregory. Baltimore: Johns Hopkins UP, 1977.

Goodspeed-Chadwick, Julie. *Modernist Women Writers and War: Trauma and the Female Body in Djuna Barnes, H.D., and Gertrude Stein*. Baton Rouge: Louisiana State UP, 2011.

Gregory, Derek. *The Colonial Present*. Malden, MA: Blackwell, 2004.

Gregory, Eileen. *H.D. and Hellenism: Classic Lines*. New York: Cambridge UP, 1997.

Grotstein, James S. "Autoscopy: The Experience of Oneself as a Double." *Hillside Journal of Clinical Psychiatry* 5.2 (1983): 259–304.

Guest, Barbara. Barbara Guest Papers, Yale Collection of American Literature, Beinecke Rare Book and Manuscript Library, New Haven, Connecticut.

———. *Herself Defined: The Poet H.D. and Her World*. New York: Doubleday, 1984.

Guthrie, Ramon. "Ezra Pound in Paris and Elsewhere." *The Nation*, November 16, 1957, 345.

Halsall, Alison. "H.D. and the Victorian Spectres of *White Rose and the Red*." *College Literature* 38.4 (2011): 115–133.

———. Introduction to *White Rose and the Red*, by H.D., xvii–xlviii. Gainesville: UP of Florida, 2009.

Hansen, Jim. "Samuel Beckett's *Catastrophe* and the Theater of Pure Means." *Contemporary Literature* 49.4 (2008): 660–682.

Harris, Paul A. "Deleuze's Cinematic Universe of Light: A Cosmic Plane of Luminance." *SubStance* 39.1 (2010): 115–124.

Harrison, Victoria. "When a Gift Is Poison: H.D., the Moravian, the Jew, and World War II." *Sagetrieb* 15.1/2 (1996): 69–93.

Hart, Kevin. "Fields of *Dharma*: On T. S. Eliot and Robert Gray." *Literature & Theology* 27.3 (2013): 267–284.

Hay, Simon. *A History of the Modern British Ghost Story*. New York: Palgrave, 2011.

H.D. *Bid Me to Live (A Madrigal)*. Edited by Caroline Zilboorg. Gainesville: UP of Florida, 2011.

———. *By Avon River*. Edited by Lara Vetter. Gainesville: UP of Florida, 2014.

———. *Collected Poems 1912–1944*. Edited by Louis L. Martz. New York: New Directions, 1986.

———. *End to Torment*. New York: New Directions, 1979.

———. *The Gift*. Edited by Jane Augustine. Gainesville: UP of Florida, 1998.

———. "H.D. by Delia Alton." Edited by Adalaide Morris. *Iowa Review* 16.3 (1986): 174–221.

———. H.D. Papers. Yale Collection of American Literature, Beinecke Rare Book and Manuscript Library, New Haven, Connecticut.

———. *Hedylus*. Redding Ridge, CT: Black Swan Books, 1980.

———. *Helen in Egypt*. New York: New Directions, 1961.

———. *Hermetic Definition*. New York: New Directions, 1972.

———. *HERmione*. New York: New Directions, 1981.

———. *Hirslanden Notebooks*. Edited by Matte Robinson and Demetres P. Tryphonopoulos. Victoria, BC: ELS, 2015.

———. "A Letter from England." *Bryn Mawr Alumnae Bulletin* 21.7 (1941): 22–23.

———. *Magic Mirror, Compassionate Friendship, Thorn Thicket: A Tribute to Erich Heydt*. Edited by Nephie J. Christodoulides. Victoria, BC: ELS, 2012.

———. *Majic Ring*. Edited by Demetres P. Tryphonopoulos. Gainesville: UP of Florida, 2009.

———. *The Mystery*. Edited by Jane Augustine. Gainesville: UP of Florida, 2009.

———. *Narthex & Other Stories*. Edited by Michael Boughn. Toronto: BookThug, 2013.

———. *Nights*. New York: New Directions, 1986.

———. "A Note on Poetry." Edited by Diana Collecott. *Agenda* 25.3/4 (1987): 71–76.

———. *Notes on Thought and Vision*. London: Peter Owen, 1982.

———. *Paint It To-day*. Edited by Cassandra Laity. New York: New York UP, 1992.

———. *Palimpsest*. Carbondale: Southern Illinois UP, 1968.

———. *Pilate's Wife*. Edited by Joan A. Burke. New York: New Directions, 2000.

———. *The Sword Went Out to Sea: Synthesis of a Dream, by Delia Alton*. Edited by Cynthia Hogue and Julie Vandivere. Gainesville: UP of Florida, 2007.

———. *Tribute to Freud*. New York: New Directions, 1984.

———. *Trilogy*. Edited by Aliki Barnstone. New York: New Directions, 1998.

———. *Vale Ave*. New York: New Directions, 2013.

———. *White Rose and the Red*. Edited by Alison Halsall. Gainesville: UP of Florida, 2009.

———. *Within the Walls and What Do I Love?* Edited by Annette Debo. Gainesville: UP of Florida, 2014.

Hepburn, Allan. *Intrigue: Espionage and Culture*. New Haven: Yale UP, 2005.

Hesse, Hermann. *The Fairy Tales of Hermann Hesse*. Translated by Jack Zipes. New York: Bantam, 1995.

———. *The Glass Bead Game (Magister Ludi)*. Translated by Richard and Clara Winston. New York: Picador, 1990.

Hindrichs, Cheryl. "H.D.'s *Palimpsest*: The Work of the 'Advance-Guard' in a History of Trauma." *The Space Between 1914–1945* 2.1 (2006): 87–112.

Hines, Sara. "Collecting the Empire: Andrew Lang's Fairy Books (1889–1910)." *Marvels & Tales* 24.1 (2010): 39–56.

Hoberman, Ruth. *Gendering Classicism: The Ancient World in Twentieth-Century Women's Historical Fiction*. New York: State U of New York P, 1997.

Works Cited

Hogue, Cynthia. "(Re)Storing Happiness: Toward an Ecopoetic Reading of H.D.'s *The Sword Went Out to Sea (Synthesis of a Dream)*, by Delia Alton." *ISLE (Interdisciplinary Studies in Literature and Environment)* 18.4 (2011): 840–860.

Hogue, Cynthia, and Julie Vandivere. Introduction to *The Sword Went Out to Sea: Synthesis of a Dream, by Delia Alton*, by H.D., xv–liii. Gainesville: UP of Florida, 2007.

Hollenback, Jess Byron. *Mysticism: Experience, Response, and Empowerment*. University Park: Pennsylvania State UP, 1996.

Hollenberg, Donna Krolik, ed. *Between History and Poetry: The Letters of H.D. and Norman Holmes Pearson*. Iowa City: U of Iowa P, 1997.

———, ed. "'Within the World of Your Perceptions': The Letters of Denise Levertov and H.D." *Paideuma* 33.2/3 (2004): 247–271.

Hollywood, Amy. *Sensible Ecstasy: Mysticism, Sexual Difference, and the Demands of History*. Chicago: University of Chicago Press, 2002.

Hunt, John Dixon. *The Pre-Raphaelite Imagination, 1848–1900*. Lincoln: U of Nebraska P, 1968.

Hunt, Violet. *Tales of the Uneasy*. Leipzig: Bernard Tauchnitz, 1911.

———. *The Wife of Rossetti: Her Life and Death*. London: John Lane, The Bodley Head, 1932.

Hutcheon, Linda. *A Poetics of Postmodernism: History, Theory, Fiction*. New York: Routledge, 1988.

Jacobs, Naomi. *The Character of Truth: Historical Figures in Contemporary Fiction*. Carbondale: Southern Illinois UP, 1990.

James, David. "Localizing Late Modernism: Interwar Regionalism and the Genesis of the 'Micro Novel.'" *Journal of Modern Literature* 32.4 (2009): 43–64.

Jameson, Fredric. "Modernism and Imperialism." In *Nationalism, Colonialism and Literature*, edited by Terry Eagleton, Fredric Jameson, and Edward Said, 43–68. U of Minnesota P, 1990.

Janes, Regina. *Losing Our Heads: Beheadings in Literature and Culture*. New York: New York UP, 2005.

Jantzen, Grace M. *Power, Gender and Christian Mysticism*. Cambridge: Cambridge UP, 1995.

Johnson, Alan. "The Savage City: Locating Colonial Modernity." *Nineteenth-Century Contexts* 25.4 (2003): 315–332.

Jordan, Viola. Viola Baxter Jordan Papers. Beinecke Rare Book and Manuscript Library, Yale University, New Haven, Connecticut.

Julien, Charles-André. *History of North Africa: Tunisia, Algeria, Morocco*. Translated by John Petrie. Edited by C. C. Stewart. New York: Praeger, 1970.

Keller, Joseph. "Mysticism and Intersubjective Creativity." *Studia Mystica* 8.4 (1985): 36–46.

Kerblat-Houghton, Jeanne. "'But am I wrong?': A Study of Interrogation in *End to Torment*." *H.D.: Woman and Poet*, edited by Michael King, 259–277. Orono, ME: National Poetry Foundation, University of Maine, 1986.

Knight, G. Wilson. *The Olive and the Sword: A Study of England's Shakespeare*. New York: Oxford University Press, 1944.

Works Cited

Korg, Jacob. *Winter Love: Ezra Pound and H.D.* Madison: U of Wisconsin P, 2003.

Kristeva, Julia. *The Powers of Horror: An Essay on Abjection*, translated by Leon S. Roudiez. New York: Columbia UP, 1982.

LaCapra, Dominick. "History and Psychoanalysis." *Critical Inquiry* 13.2 (1987): 222–251.

Laity, Cassandra. *H.D. and the Victorian Fin de Siècle: Gender, Modernism, Decadence.* Cambridge: Cambridge UP, 1996.

Lassner, Phyllis. *British Women Writers of World War II: Battlegrounds of their Own.* New York: Palgrave, 1998.

Lejeune, Philippe. "Autobiography in the Third Person." *New Literary History* 9.1 (1977): 27–50.

———. *On Autobiography*, edited by Paul John Eakin. Translated by Katherine Leary. Minneapolis: U of Minnesota P, 1989.

Levi, Primo. *The Drowned and the Saved.* New York: Random House, 1989.

Levinas, Emmanuel. *Humanism of the Other.* Translated by Nidra Poller. Urbana: U of Illinois P, 2003.

———. *Totality and Infinity: An Essay on Exteriority.* Pittsburgh: Duquesne UP, 1979.

Levinas, Emmanuel, Tamra Wright, Peter Hughes, and Alison Ainley. "The Paradox of Morality: An Interview with Emmanuel Levinas." Translated by Andrew Benjamin and Tamra Wright. In *The Provocation of Levinas: Rethinking the Other*, edited by Robert Bernasconi and David Wood, 168–180. New York: Routledge, 1988.

Light, Alison. "Outside History? Stevie Smith, Women Poets and the National Voice." *English* 43.177 (1994): 237–259.

Lim, Shirley Geok-lin. "The Troubled and Troubling Genre Life On-Going Writing or On-Going Life Writing." *Prose Studies* 31.3 (2009): 300–315.

Lindsay, Clarence. "H. G. Wells, Viktor Shlovsky, and Paul de Man: The Subversion of Romanticism." In *The Scope of the Fantastic: Theory, Technique, Major Authors*, edited by Howard D. Pearce and Eric S. Rabin, 125–133. Westport, CT: Greenwood, 1985.

Mackay, Marina. "The Lunacy of Men, the Idiocy of Women: Woolf, West, and War." *NWSA Journal* 15.3 (2003): 124–144.

———. *Modernism and World War II.* Cambridge: Cambridge UP, 2007.

Mandel, Charlotte. "The Redirected Image: Cinematic Dynamics in the Style of H.D. (Hilda Doolittle)." *Literature Film Quarterly* 11.1 (1983): 36–45.

Mandelbrote, Scott. "History, Narrative, and Time." *History of European Ideas* 22.5/6 (1996): 337–350.

Manzoni, Alessandro. *On the Historical Novel.* Translated by Sandra Bermann. Lincoln: U of Nebraska P, 1984.

Marx, John. *The Modernist Novel and the Decline of Empire.* Cambridge: Cambridge UP, 2005.

Massey, Sharon Davis. "Humanistic, Interpersonal, and Existential Psychotherapies: Review and Synthesis." In *The Comprehensive Handbook of Psychotherapy, Interpersonal/Humanistic/Existential*, edited by Robert F. Massey and Sharon Davis Massey, 699–718. New York: Wiley, 2002.

McCabe, Susan. *The Cinematics of Modernism: Modernist Poetry and Film*. New York: Cambridge UP, 2009.

McGinn, Bernard. "Mystical Consciousness: A Modest Proposal." *Spiritus* 8 (2008): 44–63.

McIntosh, Mark A. *Mystical Theology: The Integrity of Spirituality and Theology*. Oxford: Blackwell, 1998.

Melley, Timothy. *The Covert Sphere: Secrecy, Fiction, and the National Security State*. Ithaca: Cornell UP, 2012.

Messent, Peter B. Introduction to *Literature of the Occult: A Collection of Critical Essays*, 1–16. Englewood Cliffs, NJ: Prentice-Hall, 1981.

Miller, Meredith. "Enslaved to Both These Others: Gender and Inheritance in H.D.'s 'Secret Name: Excavator's Egypt.'" *Tulsa Studies in Women's Literature* 16.1 (1997): 77–105.

Miller, Tyrus. *Late Modernism: Politics, Fiction, and the Arts between the World Wars*. Berkeley: U of California P, 1999.

Morris, Adalaide. "Autobiography and Prophecy: H.D.'s *The Gift*." In *H.D.: Woman and Poet*, edited by Michael King, 227–236. Orono, ME: National Poetry Foundation, University of Maine, 1986.

———. *How to Live/What to Do: H.D.'s Cultural Poetics*. Urbana: U of Illinois P, 2008.

———. "A Relay of Power and of Peace: H.D. and the Spirit of the Gift." *Contemporary Literature* 27.4 (1986): 493–524.

Moss, Anita. "Crime and Punishment—or Development—in Fairy Tales and Fantasy." *Mythlore: A Journal of J.R.R. Tolkien, C. S. Lewis, Charles Williams, and the Genres of Myth and Fantasy Studies* 8.1 [27] (1981): 26–28.

Murphy, Richard. "History, Fiction, and the Avant-Garde: Narrativisation and the Event." *Phrasis* 48.1 (2007): 83–103.

Myers, Tony. "Modernity, Postmodernity, and the Future Perfect." *New Literary History* 32.1 (2001): 33–45.

Narratives of Nostalgia, Gender, and Nationalism. Edited by Jean Pickering and Suzanne Kehde. New York: New York UP, 1997.

Neuman, Shirley. "The Observer Observed: Distancing the Self in Autobiography." *Prose Studies* 4.3 (1981): 317–336.

Nikolajeva, Maria. "Fairy Tale and Fantasy: From Archaic to Postmodern." *Marvels & Tales: Journal of Fairy-Tale Studies* 17.1 (2003): 138–56.

Nora, Pierre. "Between Memory and History: *Les Lieux de Mémoire*." *Representations* 26 (1989): 7–24.

Orgel, Stephen. Introduction to *The Tempest*, by William Shakespeare, 1–88. Oxford: Clarendon UP, 1987.

Owens, Margaret E. *Stages of Dismemberment: The Fragmented Body in Late Medieval and Early Modern Drama*. Newark: U of Delaware P, 2005.

Paige, Nicholas. "Permanent Re-Enchantments: On Some Literary Uses of the Supernatural from Early Empiricism to Modern Aesthetics." In *The Re-Enchantment of the World: Secular Magic in a Rational Age*, edited by Joshua Landy and Michael Saler, 159–80. Stanford: Stanford UP, 2009.

Works Cited

Passmore, John. *The Perfectibility of Man*. New York: Scribner's, 1970.
Paxton, Nancy L. *Writing under the Raj: Gender, Race, and Rape in the British Colonial Imagination, 1830–1947*. New Brunswick, NJ: Rutgers UP, 1999.
Pearce, Lynne. *Woman/Image/Text: Readings in Pre-Raphaelite Art and Literature*. U of Toronto P, 1991.
Pearson, Norman Holmes. Norman Holmes Pearson Papers, Yale Collection of American Literature, Beinecke Rare Book and Manuscript Library, New Haven, Connecticut.
Perkins, Kenneth J. *A History of Modern Tunisia*. Cambridge: Cambridge UP, 2004.
Pfordresher, John. "Dante Gabriel Rossetti's 'Hand and Soul': Sources and Significance." *Studies in Short Fiction* 19.2 (1982): 103–132.
Phillips, Kathy J. "Seeing the War through Cut-Off Triangles: H.D. and Gertrude Stein." In *Back to Peace: Reconciliation and Retribution in the Postwar Period*, edited by Aránzazu Usandizaga and Andrew Monnickendam, 217–229. Notre Dame: U of Notre Dame P, 2007.
Plank, George. George Plank Papers. Yale Collection of American Literature, Beinecke Rare Book and Manuscript Library, New Haven, Connecticut.
Poznar, Susan. "Judith Hawkes' *Julian's House* and the Possibilities of the Postmodern Ghost Story." *Para-doxa* 17 (2002): 210–234.
Preston, Carrie J. *Modernism's Mythic Pose: Gender, Genre, and Solo Performance*. Oxford UP, 2011.
Proust, Marcel. *A la Recherche du Temps Perdu*, Vol. 3, edited by Jean-Yves Tadié. Paris: Gallimard-Pléiade, 1987–89.
Radford, Jean. "Late Modernism and the Politics of History." In *Women Writers of the 1930s: Gender, Politics, and History*, edited by Maroula Joannou, 33–45. Edinburgh: Edinburgh UP, 1999.
Rado, Lisa. *The Modern Androgyne Imagination: A Failed Sublime*. Charlottesville: U of Virginia P, 2000.
Randall, Bryony. *Modernism, Daily Time and Everyday Life*. New York: Cambridge UP, 2007.
Rattray, David. "Weekend with Ezra Pound." *The Nation* (November 16, 1957): 343–349.
Redding, Arthur. *Turncoats, Traitors, and Fellow Travelers*. Jackson: UP of Mississippi, 2008.
Renza, Louis A. "The Veto of the Imagination: A Theory of Autobiography." *New Literary History* 9.1 (1977): 1–26.
Ridley, M. R. Preface to *The Tempest*, by William Shakespeare, vii–xix. London: Dent, 1935.
Riquelme, John Paul. "Modernist Transformations of Life Narrative: From Wilde and Woolf to Bechdel and Rushdie." *MFS* 59.3 (2013): 461–479.
Robinson, Matte. *The Astral H.D.: Occult and Religious Sources and Contexts for H.D.'s Poetry and Prose*. New York: Bloomsbury, 2016.
———. "H.D. and Robert Ambelain: Doubles in H.D.'s Late Work." *Caliban* 35 (2014): 51–65. Accessed May 25, 2015. doi: 10.4000/caliban.238.
———. Introduction to *Hirslanden Notebooks*, by H.D., edited by Matte Robinson and Demetres P. Tryphonopoulos, ix–xxix. Victoria, BC: ELS, 2015.

Rossetti, Dante Gabriel. *Collected Poetry and Prose*. Edited by Jerome McGann. New Haven: Yale UP, 2003.
Rossetti, William Morris. *Dante Gabriel Rossetti: His Family-Letters with a Memoir. The Complete Writings and Pictures of Dante Gabriel Rossetti: A Hypermedia Archive*. Edited by Jerome J. McGann. Accessed June 16, 2014. https://archive.org/details/dantegabrielrosso1rossuoft.
Said, Edward W. *Culture and Imperialism*. New York: Vintage, 1993.
——. *Orientalism*. New York: Pantheon, 1978.
Saint-Amour, Paul K. "Air War Prophecy and Interwar Modernism." *Comparative Literature Studies* 42.2 (2005): 130–161.
Sarker, Sonita. "Virginia Woolf in the British Commonwealth." In *Virginia Woolf and the Common(wealth) Reader*, edited by Helen Wussow and Mary Ann Gillies, 65–76. Clemson: Clemson UP Digital Press, 2014.
Sarton, May. May Sarton Papers. Berg Collection of British and American Literature, New York Public Library, New York, New York.
Schiff, Sarah Eden. "Recovering (from) the Double: Fiction as Historical Revision in Octavia E. Butler's *Kindred*." *Arizona Quarterly* 65.1 (2009): 107–136.
Serres, Michel, with Bruno Latour. *Conversations on Science, Culture, and Time*. Translated by Roxanne Lapidus. Ann Arbor: U of Michigan P, 1995.
Shaw, Harry E. *The Forms of Historical Fiction: Sir Walter Scott and his Successors*. Ithaca: Cornell UP, 1983.
Siddiqi, Yumma. *Anxieties of Empire and the Fiction of Intrigue*. New York: Columbia UP, 2008.
Silverman, Kaja. *The Threshold of the Visible World*. New York: Routledge, 1996.
Silverstein, Louis. "H.D. Chronology." *H.D. (Hilda Doolittle)*. Accessed June 3, 2015. http://www.imagists.org/hd/hdchron.html.
Slusser, George, and Danielle Chatelain. "Conveying Unknown Worlds: Patterns of Communication in Science Fiction." *Science Fiction Studies* 29.2 (2002): 161–185.
——. "Spacetime Geometries: Time Travel and the Modern Geometrical Narrative." *Science Fiction Studies* 22.2 (1995): 161–186.
Smith, Geoffrey S. "National Security and Personal Isolation: Sex, Gender, and Disease in the Cold-War United States." *International History Review* 14.2 (1992): 307–337.
Smith, Sidonie. "Performativity, Autobiographical Practice, Resistance." *Auto/Biography Studies* 10.1 (1995): 17–33.
Smith, Stevie. *In Search of Stevie Smith*. Edited by Sanford Sternlicht. Syracuse: Syracuse UP, 1991.
Smol, Anna. "The 'Savage' and the 'Civilized': Andrew Lang's Representation of the Child and the Translation of Folklore." *Children's Literature Association Quarterly* 21.4 (1996): 177–183.
Springer, Simon. "Violence Sits in Places? Cultural Practice, Neoliberal Rationalism, and Virulent Imaginative Geographies." *Political Geography* 30 (2011): 90–98.
Stace, W. T. *Mysticism and Philosophy*. Philadelphia: J. P. Lippincott, 1960.

Steinmetz, Horst. "History in Fiction—History as Fiction: On the Relations between Literature and History in the Nineteenth and Twentieth Centuries." In *Narrative Turns and Minor Genres in Postmodernism*, edited by Theo d'Haen and Johannes Willem Bertens, 81–103. Atlanta, GA: Rodopi, 1995.

Stewart, Victoria. *Women's Autobiography: War and Trauma*. New York: Palgrave, 2003.

Stonebridge, Lyndsey. *The Writing of Anxiety: Imagining Wartime in Mid-Century British Culture*. New York: Palgrave, 2007.

Stoneburner, Tony. "Notes on Prophecy and Apocalypse in a Time of Anarchy and Revolution: A Trying Out." *TriQuarterly* 23–24 (1972): 246–282.

Sword, Helen. *Engendering Inspiration: Visionary Strategies in Rilke, Lawrence, and H.D.* Ann Arbor: U of Michigan P, 1995.

———. *Ghostwriting Modernism*. Ithaca: Cornell UP, 2002.

Szefel, Lisa. "Beauty and William Braithwaite." *Callaloo* 29.2 (2006): 560–586.

———. "Encouraging Verse: William S. Braithwaite and the Poetics of Race." *New England Quarterly* 74.1 (2001): 32–61.

Thurston, Luke. "Double-Crossing: Elizabeth Bowen's Ghostly Short Fiction." *Textual Practice* 27.1 (2013): 7–28.

Tiffin, Jessica. *Marvelous Geometry: Narrative and Metafiction in Modern Fairy Tale*. Detroit: Wayne State UP, 2009.

Todorov, Tzvetan. "The Origin of Genres." *New Literary History* 8.1 (1976): 159–170.

Twitchell-Waas, Jeffrey. "Seaward: H.D.'s *Helen in Egypt* as a Response to Pound's *Cantos*." *Twentieth Century Literature* 44.4 (1998): 464–483.

———. "'Set in Eternity but Lived In': H.D.'s *Vale Ave*." *Sagetrieb* 15.1/2 (1996): 203–227.

Vetter, Lara. "H.D., India, and Gendered Narratives of Imperialism." *Review of English Studies* 67.278 (2016): 146–164.

———. Introduction to *By Avon River*, by H.D., 1–42. Gainesville: UP of Florida, 2014.

———. *Modernist Writings and Religio-scientific Discourse: H.D., Loy, and Toomer*. New York: Palgrave Macmillan, 2010.

———. "Representing 'a sort of composite person': Autobiography, Sexuality, and Collaborative Authorship in H.D.'s Prose and Scrapbook." *Genre* 36.1/2 (2003): 107–129.

———. Review-essay. *English Studies* 94.1 (2013): 57–63.

Wesseling, Elisabeth. "Historical Fiction: Utopia in History." In *International Postmodernism: Theory and Literary Practice*, edited by Hans Bertens and Douwe Fokkema, 203–211. Philadelphia: John Benjamins, 1997.

Whittier-Ferguson, John. *Mortality and Form in Late Modernist Literature*. Cambridge UP, 2014.

Wilde, Alan. "Surfacings: Reflections on the Epistemology of Late Modernism." *Boundary 2* 8.2 (1980): 209–227.

Williams, William Carlos. *Kora in Hell: Improvisations*. Boston: The Four Seas Company, 1920.

Willis, Elizabeth. "A Public History of the Dividing Line: H.D., the Bomb, and the Roots of the Postmodern." *Arizona Quarterly* 63.1 (2007): 81–108.

Works Cited

Wolfreys, Julian. Introduction to *Victorian Hauntings: Spectrality, Gothic, the Uncanny, and Literature*, edited by Julian Wolfreys, 1–24. New York: Palgrave, 2002.

Wolle, Francis. Francis Wolle Papers. University of Colorado Library, Special Collections, Boulder, Colorado.

Women Writers of the 1930s: Gender, Politics, and History. Edited by Maroula Joannou, Edinburgh: Edinburgh UP, 1999.

Woolf, Virginia. *Three Guineas*. New York: Harcourt Brace Jovanovich, 1966.

Yaeger, Patricia. "Introduction: Narrating Space." In *The Geography of Identity*, edited by Patricia Yaeger, 1–38. Ann Arbor: U of Michigan P, 1996.

Ziarek, Ewa Plonowska. "Bare Life on Strike: Notes on the Biopolitics of Race and Gender." *South Atlantic Quarterly* (2008): 107.1: 89–105.

Zilboorg, Caroline, ed. *Richard Aldington & H.D.: The Later Years in Letters*. New York: Manchester UP, 1995.

Ziolkowski, Theodore. *The Novels of Hermann Hesse: A Study in Theme and Structure*. Princeton UP, 1965.

Zipes, Jack. *Breaking the Magic Spell: Radical Theories of Folk and Fairy Tales*. Austin: U of Texas P, 1979.

———. "Hermann Hesse's Fairy Tales and the Pursuit of Home." In *The Fairy Tales of Hermann Hesse*, translated by Jack Zipes, ix–xxvii. New York: Bantam, 1995.

Works Mentioned that H.D. Owned and/or Read

This portion of the bibliography lists writings mentioned in this book that H.D. owned and/or read. It is drawn from references in her prose writings and her correspondence, and from her library (as documented in the H.D. Papers) and Bryher's library (now located in East Hampton, New York).

Ager, John C. *Emanuel Swedenborg; Who He Was; What He Did*. N.p.: Commemorative Pamphlet, 1938.
Aldington, Richard. *David Herbert Lawrence*. Hamburg: Rowohlt, 1961.
Almedingen, E. M. *Frossia*. London: Bodley Head, 1943.
Anderson, Margaret. *My Thirty Years' War: An Autobiography*. New York: Covici, Friede, 1930.
Angeli, Helen Rossetti. *Dante Gabriel Rossetti: His Friends and Enemies*. London: Hamish Hamilton, 1949.
———. *Pre-Raphaelite Twilight: The Story of Charles Augustus Howell*. London: Richards, 1954.
Arnold-Forster, Mary. *Basset Down an Old Country House*. London: Country Life Limited, n.d
Bainbridge, John. *Garbo*. Garden City, NY: Doubleday, 1955.
Bainton, George, ed. *The Art of Authorship: Literary Reminiscences*. London: James Clarke, 1890.
Balchin, Nigel. *A Sort of Traitors*. London: Collins, 1949.
Batchelor, Paula. *Angel with Bright Hair*. London: Methuen, 1957.
Beach, Sylvia. *Shakespeare and Company*. New York: Harcourt, Brace, 1959.
Beauclerk, Helen. *Mountain and the Tree*. New York: Coward-McCann, 1936.
Beerbohm, Max. *Mainly on the Air*. London: William Heineman, 1946.
Bell, Charles. *Portrait of the Dalai Lama*. London: Collins, 1946.
Berenson, Bernard. *Sketch for a Self-Portrait*. New York: Pantheon, 1949.
Bickley, Francis. *The Pre-Raphaelite Comedy*. New York: H. Holt, 1933.
Blackwood, Algernon. *The Centaur*. London, Macmillan, 1911.
Blake, Leonardo. *The Last Year of War and After*. London: Andrew Dakers, 1940.
Bottome, Phyllis. *Search for a Soul*. London: Faber & Faber, 1947.

Bowen, Catherine Drinker and von Meck, Barbara. *"Beloved Friend": The Story of Tchaikowsky and Nadeja von Meck*. New York: Random House, 1937.
Bowen, Elizabeth. *Bowen's Court*. London: Longmans, Green, 1942.
Bowen, Stella. *Drawn from Life*. London, Collins Publishers, n.d.
Boyle, Kay. *Primer for Combat*. New York: Simon & Schuster, 1942.
Brinnin, John Malcolm. *Dylan Thomas in America*. Boston: Little, Brown, 1955.
Brooke, Jocelyn. *Mine of Serpents*. London: Bodley Head, 1949.
Brunner, Theodor. *Erinnerungen an Ludwig Snell, 1785–1854*. Stäfa: T. Gut, 1954.
Bullock, George. *Marie Corelli*. London: Constable, 1940.
Burdekin, Katharine. *Burning Ring*. London, T. Butterworth, 1927.
———. *Proud Man*. New York: Feminist Press, 1993 [1934].
———. *The Rebel Passion*. London, T. Butterworth, 1929.
———, as Murray Constantine. *Swastika Night*. London, V. Gollancz, ltd., 1937
Burdekin, Katharine, and Margaret Goldsmith. *Venus in Scorpio*. London: Bodley Head, 1940.
Burlingham, Dorothy, and Anna Freud. *Young Children in War-Time*. London: George Allen, 1942.
Burroughs, Betty, ed. *Vasari's Lives of the Artists*. New York: Simon & Schuster, 1946.
Burton, Jean. *Heyday of a Wizard: Daniel Home, the Medium*. London, G.G. Harrap, 1948.
Butler, E. M. "Goethe and Cagliostro." *Publications of the English Goethe Society* n.s. 16 (1947): 1–28.
———. *Paper Boats: An Autobiography*. London: Collins, 1959.
———. *Silver Wings*. New York: G. P. Putnam's Sons, 1953.
Byron, Robert. *Byzantine Achievement: An Historical Perspective, A.D. 330–1453*. London: George Routledge & Sons, 1929.
Chakhotin, Sergei. *The Rape of Masses: The Psychology of Totalitarian Political Propaganda*. London: E. W. Dickes, 1940.
Chambers, P. Franklin. *Juliana of Norwich*. London: Victor Gollanoz, 1955.
The Chronicle History of King Henry the Fifth with His Battell Fought at Agincourt in France. Dir. Laurence Olivier. Perf. Laurence Olivier, Robert Newton, and Leslie Banks. Eagle Lion, 1944. Film.
Cladel, Judith. *Rodin: A Biography*. London: Kegan Paul, Trench, Trubner & Co., n.d.
Cline, C. L. *Byron, Shelley and Their Pisan Circle*. London: John Murray, 1952.
Clodd, Edward. *Memories*. London: Chapman and Hall, 1916.
Collier, Basil. *Leader of the Few: The Authorised Biography of Air Chief Marshall, the Lord Dowding of Bentley Priory, G.C.B., G.C.V.O., C.M.G.* London: Jarrolds, 1957.
Cooper, Diana. *Trumpets from the Steep*. London: R. Hart-Davis, 1960.
Corvo, Baron [Frederick Rolfe]. *The Desire and Pursuit of the Whole*. London: Cassell, 1934.
Couperus, Louis. *The Comedians*. Translated by J. Menzies Wilson. London: Jonathan Cape, 1926.
Cournos, John. *Autobiography*. New York: G. P. Putnam's, 1935.
Courtenay, Jennifer. *Several Faces*. London: Victor Gollancz, 1930.

Cunard, Nancy. *Grand Man: Memories of Norman Douglas*. London: Secker and Warburg, 1954.
Delarue-Mardrus, Lucie. *Petite Thérèse de Lisieux*. Paris: Fasquelle, 1937.
Douglas, Norman. *Alone*. London: Chapman & Hall, 1921.
———. *Looking Back. An Autobiographical Excursion*. 2 vols. London: Chatto and Windus, 1933.
———. *Together*. London: Chapman & Hall, 1923.
Draper, Muriel. *Music at Midnight*. New York: Harper, 1929.
Duncan, Isadora. *My Life*. New York: Boni and Liveright, 1927.
du Maurier, Daphne. *The Infernal World of Branwell Bronte*. London: Victor Gollancz, 1960.
Ede, H.S. *Savage Messiah*. London: William Heinemann, 1931.
Ehrlich, Leonard. *God's Angry Man*. New York: Simon and Schuster, 1932.
Eshleman, Lloyd Wendell. *Victorian Rebel: The Life of William Morris*. New York: Scribner's, 1940.
Farson, Negley. *Bomber's Moon*. London: Vector Gollancz, 1941.
Fenby, Eric. *Delius as I Knew Him*. London: G. Bell, 1937.
Ffrench, Yvonne. *Ouida: A Study in Ostentation*. London: Cobden-Sanderson, 1938.
Forster, E. M. *Nordic Twilight*. London: Macmillan, 1940.
Front Line, 1940–1941. London: His Majesty's Stationary Office, 1942.
Ghéon, Henri. *Secret of the Little Flower*. Translated by Donald Attwater. London: Sheed & Ward, 1940.
Glaspell, Susan. *Fugitive's Return*. London: Victor Gollancz, 1929.
———. *The Road to the Temple*. London: Ernest Benn, 1926.
Glyn, Elinor. *Romantic Adventure Being the Autobiography of Elinor Glyn*. London: I. Nicholson and Watson, 1936.
Godwin, Edward F., and Stephani Godwin. *Warrior Bard: The Life of William Morris*. London: G.G. Harrap, 1947.
Goldring, Douglas. *South Lodge*. London: Constable, 1943.
Green, Roger Lancelyn. *Andrew Lang*. London: Edmund Ward, 1946.
Halliday, W. R. *Indo-European Folk-Tales and Greek Legend*. Cambridge: Cambridge UP, 1933.
Harding, Bertita. *Golden Fleece: The Story of Franz Joseph and Elisabeth of Austria*. London: G. G. Harrap, 1937.
Hathaway, Katharine Butler. *Little Locksmith*. New York: Coward-McCann, 1943.
Henrey, Robert. *The Incredible City*. London: Dent, 1944.
Hope, Laurence. *The Garden of Kama: And Other Love Lyrics from India*. London: Heinemann, 1917.
Hoult, Norah. *There Were No Windows*. London: Heinemann, 1944.
Hughes, M.V. *London at Home*. London: Dent, 1931.
Huxley, Aldous. *Grey Eminence*. London: Chatto and Windus, 1941
Jones, Ernest. *The Life and Work of Sigmund Freud Life & Work*. 3 vols. New York: Basic Books, 1953–1957.

Jones, Peter, ed. *Life & Journals of Kah-ke-wa-Quo-va-by*. Toronto: Wesleyan Printing, 1860.
Jucker, Ninetta. *Curfew in Paris, A Record of the German Occupation*. London: Hogarth Press, 1960.
Knight, G. W. *Lord Byron's Marriage*. London: Routledge, 1957.
Lang, Andrew, ed. *The Blue Fairy Book*. London: Longmans, Green, 1937.
———, ed. *The Crimson Fairy Book*. London: Longmans, Green, 1937.
———, ed. *The Grey Fairy Book*. London: Longmans, 1937.
———, ed. *The Pink Fairy Book*. London: Longmans, 1936.
———, ed. *The Red Fairy Book*. London: Longmans, Green, 1937.
———, ed. *The Violet Fairy Book*. London: Longmans, 1937.
———, ed. *The Yellow Fairy Book*. London: Longmans, Green, 1937.
Lee, Vernon. *The Snake Lady and Other Stories*. New York: Grove, 1954.
Lévi, Éliphas [Alphonse Louis Constant]. *The History of Magic*. Translated by Arthur Edward Waite. London: Rider & Son, 1922.
Lowndes, Mrs. Belloc. *Where Love and Friendship Dwelt*. London: Macmillan, 1943.
Lubbock, Percy. *Portrait of Edith Wharton*. London: Jonathan Cape, 1947.
Luhan, Mabel Dodge. *Edge of Taos Desert*. New York: Harcourt, Brace, 1937.
———. *Lorenzo in Taos*. London: Martin Secker, 1933.
Lutyens, Lady Emily. *Candles in the Sun*. London: Rupert Hart-Davis, 1957.
Mackenzie, Faith Compton. *Always Afternoon*. London: Collins, 1943.
———. *Napoleon at the Briars*. London: Jonathan Cape, 1943.
Maclean, Catherine Macdonald. *Dorothy Wordsworth: The Early Years*. London: Chatto & Windus, 1932.
Macqueen-Pope, W. *Goodbye Piccadilly*. London: Michael Joseph, 1960.
Magre, Maurice. *The Return of the Magi*. Translated by Reginald Merton. London: Philip Allan, 1931.
Mantz, Ruth Elvish, and J. Middleton Murry. *Life of Katherine Mansfield*. London, Constable, 1933.
May, Rollo. *Existence: A New Dimension in Psychiatry and Psychology*. Edited by Rollo May, Ernest Angel, and Henri F. Ellenberger. New York: Basic Books, 1958.
Merrild, Knud. *A Poet and Two Painters*. New York: Viking, 1939.
Meynell, Esther. *Portrait of William Morris*. London: Chapman and Hall, 1947.
Moore, George. *Confessions of a Young Man*. London: Heinemann, 1917
Moore, Harry. *D H. Lawrence: The Intelligent Heart*. New York: Farrar, Straus and Young, 1954.
Morley, Iris. *The Proud Paladin*. New York: William Morrow, 1936.
Murray, D. L. *Folly Bridge: A Romantic Tale*. London: Hodder and Stoughton, 1945.
Norman, Charles. *The Muses' Darling Christopher Marlowe*. New York: Macmillan, 1960.
Oldenbourg, Zoé. *The World is Not Enough*. London: Victor Gollancz, 1949.
Orioli, G. *Adventures of a Bookseller*. Florence: Privately printed for subscribers by G. Orioli, 1937.

Painter, George Duncan. *Marcel Proust: A Biography*. London, Chatto & Windus, 1959–1965.
Patmore, Derek. *The Life and Times of Coventry Patmore*. New York: Oxford, 1949.
Pope-Hennessy, James. *Queen Mary 1867–1953*. London: George Allen and Unwin, 1959.
Pound, Ezra. *Indiscretions*. Paris: Three Mountains P, 1923.
Powell, Nicholas. *The Hills Remain*. London: Bodley Head, 1947.
The Private Lives of Elizabeth and Essex. Dir. Michael Curtiz. Perf. Bette Davis and Errol Flynn. Warner Brothers, 1939. Film.
Read, Herbert. *The Innocent Eye*. London: Faber and Faber, 1933.
Reed, Clarence. *Great Prophecies about the War*. London, Faber and Faber, 1941.
Reid, Ian. *Prisoner at Large*. London: Victor Gollancz, 1947
Renault, Mary. *The King Must Die*. London: Longmans, Green, 1958.
Rimius, Henry. *A Candid Narrative of the Rise and Progress of the Herrnhuters, Commonly Called Moravians or Unitas Fratrum*. London: A Linde, 1753.
———. *A Second Solemn Call on Mr. Zinzendorf, Otherwise Call'd Count Zinzendorf, &c., the Author and Advocate of the Sect of Herrnhuters, Commonly Known by the Name of Moravians or Unitas Fratrum*. London: A. Linde, 1757.
Rose, Sir Francis. *Saying Life*. London: Cassell & Co., 1961.
Rougemont, Denis de. *Love in the Western World*. Translated by Montgomery Belgion. New York: Pantheon, 1956.
———. *Passion and Society*. Translated by Montgomery Belgion. London: Faber & Faber, 1940.
Sachs, Hanns. *Caligula*. Translated by Hedvig Singer. London, E. Mathews & Marrot, 1931.
Sackville-West, V. *The Eagle and the Dove*. London: Michael Joseph, 1943.
———. *Pepita*. London, 1939.
Sencourt, Robert. *Carmelite and Poet*. London: Hollis and Carter, 1943.
Sender, Toni. *Autobiography of a German Rebel*. New York: Vanguard P, 1939.
Shakespeare, William. *The Tempest*. Edited by M. R. Ridley. London: Dent, 1935.
Sitwell, Edith. *Fanfare for Elizabeth*. New York: Macmillan, 1946.
Smyth, Ethel. *As Time Went On*. New York: Longmans, Green, 1936.
———. *Impressions That Remained: Memoirs by Ethel Smyth*. New York: Longmans, Green, 1923.
———. *What Happened Next*. New York: Longmans, Green, 1940.
Spender, Stephen. *The Back-ward Son*. London: Hogarth P, 1940.
Spring, Howard. *All the Day Long*. London: Collins, 1959.
St. John, Christopher, et al. *Ethel Smyth*: A Biography. New York: Longmans, Green, 1959.
Symons, A.J.A. *The Quest for Corvo*. New York: Macmillan Co., 1934.
Tardieu, Jean. *Charles d'Orléans*. Paris: Egloff, 1947.
Thomas, Helen. *As It Was . . . World without End*. London: Heinemann, 1946.
Waln, Nora. *The House of Exile*. Boston: Little, Brown, 1933.

Warmington, E.H. *The Commerce between the Roman Empire and India*. Cambridge: Cambridge UP, 1928.

Welby, T. Earle. *One Man's India*. London: Lovat Dickson, 1933.

———. *The Victorian Romantics, 1850–70: The Early Work of Dante Gabriel Rossetti, William Morris, Burne-Jones, Swinburne, Simeon Solomon and Their Associates*. Hamden, CT: Archon Books, 1966.

Welch, Denton. *A Voice through a Cloud*. London: John Lehmann, 1950.

Wellesley, Dorothy. *Far Have I Travelled*. London: James Barrie, 1952.

West, Edward Sackville. *A Flame in Sunlight*. London: Cassell, 1936.

West, Rebecca. *The Meaning of Treason*. New York: Viking, 1947.

Wharton, Edith. *A Backward Glance*. New York: D. Appleton, 1934.

Wilder, Thornton. *Woman of Andros*. London: Longmans, Green, 1930.

Williams, Valentine. *Crouching Beast: A Clubfoot Story*. London: Hodder and Stoughton, 1933.

Wolle, Francis. *Fitz-James O'Brien*. Boulder: U of Colorado, 1944.

Wright, Constance. *Chance for Glory*. New York: Holt, 1957.

Young, Stark. *So Red the Rose*. New York: Scribners, 1934.

Zugsmith, Leane. *Summer Soldier*. New York: Random House, 1938.

Index

Abbott, H. Porter, 49, 207n52
Abramov, Tamar, 187, 231n87
Adams, David, 135, 137
Agamben, Giorgio, 70, 113, 122
Agamemnon, 83
"Albertopolis," 17
Aldington, Richard: on *By Avon River*, 217n12; as character, 45, 166, 167, 168, 211n74; on the Crimean War, 131, 222n34; as "initiator," 147, 212n84; on Pound, 194, 196, 233n10; on *The Sword Went Out to Sea*, 82, 213n6; on women writers, 34–35. *See also* H.D.: and marriage to Aldington
Almedingen, E. M., 84
Ambelain, Robert, 148
Anderson, Elizabeth, 23
Anderson, Margaret, 40
Andres, Sophia, 221n21
Arthur of England, 3, 86, 96
Ashby, Lillian, 127
astral projection, astral plane, 56, 62, 207n59; in *The Mystery*, 148–49, 150; in *The Sword Went Out to Sea*, 33, 64–73, 78, 148. *See also* bi-location
Aucassin et Nicolette, 86
Augustine, Jane: on illness and visions, 75, 225n29; on *Majic Ring*, 221n14; on *The Mystery*, 27, 143, 144, 151, 158, 224nn7,17, 225n21, 226nn35,54; on *The Sword Went Out to Sea*, 24, 212n88

Bacchilega, Cristina, 87, 89, 95, 100, 214n54, 216n85

Baccolini, Raffaella, 216n7
Bacon, Francis, 117, 118, 121
Baker, Gretchen Wolle, 2, 200n47
Balchin, Nigel, 14
Bally, G., 178
Barnes, Djuna, 20
Barthes, Roland, 35
Baucom, Ian, 136
Bausinger, Hermann, 89
Beach, Sylvia, 41, 195
Beauclerk, Helen, 84
Beckett, Samuel, 20, 70
Beebee, Thomas O., 25
Beerbohm, Max, 14
Benjamin, Walter, 89, 164
Bennett, Bruce, 187
Benson, Stephen, 90, 93, 214n40
Benstock, Shari, 38
Berenson, Bernard, 40
Bhabha, Homi, 123
Bhaduri, Arthur, 46, 127, 147, 165, 221n17, 225n26
Bickley, Francis, 136, 223n61
bi-location, 147–49, 152, 225n29, 226n35
Blackwood, Algernon, 49
Blake, Leonardo, 14
Bontemps, Arna, 87
Boss, Medard, 174, 178, 179, 185–87, 231n77
Bottigheimer, Ruth B., 215n54
Botting, Fred, 51, 153
Bottome, Phyllis, 41
Boughn, Michael, 118–19
Bowen, Elizabeth, 13, 175, 176, 190, 191, 226n51, 229n12

Index

Boyle, Kay, 14
Bradley, Laurel, 128
Braithwaite, William S., 115–16, 121, 218n41
Brennan, Timothy, 121
Briggs, Julia, 19, 48
British Museum, 16
Brooke, Jocelyn, 40
Brown, Hannah, 130
Bryher (Winifred Ellerman), 6, 36, 160, 179; *Days of Mars*, 1, 2, 15; and the early modern period, 219n44; on espionage, 175–77; and film, 228n55; and H.D.'s postwar illness, 9–12, 97, 141–42, 174, 175, 224n5; in *Hedylus*, 163; on Heydt, 179; and historical fiction, 83, 84, 87; on India, 127–28, 220n3, 221n20; library of, 40, 56, 210; on the magus, 225n21; and national identity, 16; in *Paint It To-day*, 7, 57; on politics, 13–15, 141, 202nn74,76, 224n5, 229n14; on Pound, 189, 194, 233n5; and science fiction, 210; suicide attempt of, 11; on Woolf, 201n54; and World War II, 9, 54, 174, 175, 199n1, 228n3
Bullen, J. B., 221n21
Burdekin, Katharine (Murray Constantine), 83–84, 210n46
Burgess, Guy, 176
Burling, William J., 71, 211n70
Burlingham, Dorothy, 14
Buss, Helen M., 38
Butler, E. M., 41, 146, 147, 179, 206n38, 225n21, 225n25
Butler, Judith, 41, 166
Butts, Mary, 87
Byron, George Gordon, 40
Byron, Robert, 128, 132

Cacicedo, Alberto, 62
Capper, Jessie (Jennifer Courtenay), 40
Carlston, Erin G., 183, 190
Caruth, Cathy, 73
Caserio, Robert L., 8
Catharism, 56, 86, 121
Cather, Willa, 87
Cavaliero, Glen, 50

Certeau, Michel de, 61, 64, 148
Chaboseau, Jean, 47, 146, 225n21
Chakhotin, Sergei, 14
Chatelain, Danielle, 66, 93
Chedgzoy, Kate, 107, 217nn7,19, 218n27
Cherberton, Una, 128, 221n19
Cherry, Deborah, 221n21
Chisholm, Dianne, 35
Christodoulides, Nephie J., 187
Chronicle History of King Henry the Fifth with His Battell Fought at Agincourt in France, The, 219n44
Churchill, Winston, 13, 14, 141, 202n76
Clares, Order of Saint, 113, 122, 123
Close Up, 191, 206n41
Cohen, Ralph, 25
Cold War, 168–69, 174, 175, 183–84, 228n2
Coleridge, Samuel, 84
Collecott, Diana, 108, 217n15
Conilleau, Claire, 216n7
Connor, Rachel, 24, 206n41
Conrad, Joseph, 87
Cooper, Diana, 40
Cornforth, Fanny, 128
Cosslett, Tess, 72, 211n71
Couperus, Louis, 84
Cournos, John, 41, 147
Crimean War, 18, 27, 126, 127, 130–31, 133, 137, 143, 222nn34,38
Crown, Kathleen, 216n7, 217n16
Crusades: in *By Avon River*, 65, 121, 122; in *White Rose and the Red*, 17, 27, 125, 126, 132, 133
Curti, Lidia, 25–26, 86
Curtiss, Homer and Harriette, 22n14

Dahlen, Beverly, 58, 72
Dalai Lama, 40
Daly, Ann, 6
Dane, Clemence, 79
Dante Alighieri, 128, 129, 133, 150, 219n60, 222n42, 223n48, 225n29
Davis, Colin, 49, 152
Davison, Francis, 115

256

Index

Debo, Annette: on H.D.'s national identity, 15, 202n78; on H.D.'s postwar illness, 12, 201n67; on *Helen in Egypt*, 228n2; on Pearson, 193, 206n22, 233n2; on Pound, 232nn9,11
Dekker, George, 86
DeKoven, Marianne, 87
Delarue-Mardrus, Lucie, 210n43
de Lauretis, Teresa, 73
Deleuze, Gilles, 151
Delius, Frederick, 40
Delsarte, François, 6, 200n31
de Man, Paul, 38, 39
de Medici, Catherine, 112
De Quincey, Thomas, 40
de Rachewiltz, Mary, 233n9
Derrida, Jacques, 25, 211n64
Detloff, Madelyn, 48, 60, 151, 191, 201n50, 232n117
Diamond, Stephen A., 185, 187
DiBattista, Maria, 8, 35
Dillon, Sarah, 35
Dobson, Silvia, 10, 11, 42, 175, 201n54, 202n85, 224n5
Doolittle, Charles, 57
Doolittle, Eric, 47, 57
Doolittle, Gilbert, 57
d'Orléans, Charles, 40
Doty, Mark, 31
Douglas, Norman, 41
Dowding, Hugh, 12; and espionage, 177; as "initiator," 147, 212n84; in *Magic Mirror*, 46; in *Majic Ring*, 42; in *The Sword Went Out to Sea*, 34, 45–47, 166
Drake, Francis, 132–33
Draper, Muriel, 40
Drayton, Michael, 114, 118, 218n37
du Maurier, Daphne, 40
Duncan, Isadora, 40, 200n31
DuPlessis, Rachel Blau, 46, 182, 234n15
Durán, Josepha, 40
Durand, Lionel, 46, 47, 75
Dustin, Lheisa, 205n19, 211n81
Dyer, Edward, 115

Eagleton, Terry, 19
Eakin, Paul John, 51–52
Edmunds, Susan, 127, 221n13
Edward VIII of England, 219n44
Egypt, 57, 58, 127, 221n13
Ehrlich, Leonard, 84
Einstein, Alfred, 64, 209n18
Eisenstein, Sergei, 228n55
Eleanor of Aquitaine, 123
Eliot, T. S., 20–21, 34, 35, 100, 137, 196, 206n22
Elisabeth of Austria, 40
Elizabeth (Queen Mother of Elizabeth II), 216n6
Elizabeth I of England, 40, 111, 115, 117, 219n44; and marriage, 112–13; and New World exploration, 18, 92, 106, 114, 115; in *The Sword Went Out to Sea*, 42, 72, 85, 189; writings of, 116, 121
Elizabeth II of England, 106, 216nn5,6
Elizabeth of Bohemia (Elizabeth Stuart), 106, 110–11, 117
Emmitt, Helen V., 17
Empson, William, 217n23
espionage, 28–29, 146, 169, 173–97, 229nn12,14, 231n87
Essex (Robert Devereux), 42, 85, 115, 117, 120, 189
Esty, Joshua, 20–23, 80, 100, 137, 203nn96,103
ethics, 18, 24, 26, 28–29, 83, 102; and bilocation, 152; and espionage, 173, 174, 177–80, 187–92; and infidelity, 157–69, 172; and mysticism, 63–64; and psychoanalysis, 180–88
Euripides, 42, 83, 135

Farson, Negley, 14–15
Faulkner, William, 87
Faust (book), 76, 224n17
Faust (character), 76, 146, 147, 224n17, 225n21
Felton, Monica, 176, 177
Flammarion, Camille, 64–65, 148, 210n46, 225n30, 227n20

Fleishman, Avrom, 88, 90, 213n28, 214n39
Fletcher, John, 114
Folkenflik, Robert, 43
Ford, Ford Madox, 87
Ford, Thomas, 120
Forster, E. M., 14, 20, 21, 99, 137
Forter, Greg, 73
Freedman, Ariela, 201n50
French Revolution, 65, 84, 143
Freud, Anna, 14
Freud, Sigmund, 40, 75, 80, 170, 174, 191, 232n96; and analysis with H.D., 3, 13, 37, 180, 182, 188–89, 231n92; on dreams, 185, 186, 231n68; on identification and transference, 168, 181–84, 187, 188, 190, 230nn53,60; as "initiator," 147; on paranoia, 76–77; on repetition compulsion, 47–48; on the uncanny, 149–50, 151. *See also* Psychoanalysis; *Tribute to Freud*
Friedman, Susan Stanford, 24, 29, 83, 185, 203n87, 207n54; on *By Avon River*, 107, 108, 109, 113, 118, 216nn3,7, 220n68; on Freud, 174, 183; on national identity, 2, 15; on *Palimpsest*, 161, 167; on Pound, 234n15; on *The Sword Went Out to Sea*, 24, 203n106
Front Line, 15
Frow, John, 25
Fuchs, Miriam, 36, 207n51, 223n53

Garbo, Greta, 40
Gardiner, Michael, 166–67, 169
Garrett, George, 110, 217n23
Garrity, Jane, 134, 220n2
Gates, Thomas, 109
Gaudier-Brzeska, Henri, 40
Gavaler, Christopher P., 36
Ghéon, Henri, 210n43
Gikandi, Simon, 20, 134–35, 220n2
Gilmore, Leigh, 39, 44, 47
Girard, René, 55
Glasgow, Ellen, 9
Glaspell, Susan, 40
Glyn, Elinor, 40
Godfrey of Bouillon, 132

Goethe, Johann Wolfgang von, 76, 197, 224n17
Goldwyn, Samuel, 33
Goodspeed-Chadwick, Julie, 201n50
Graves, Robert, 87
Greece (ancient), 21, 56, 105, 157, 169, 172; drama of, 43, 118; in "Hipparchia," 28, 160–64; in historical fiction, 84; and Imagism, 135, 205n8; in "Secret Name," 58; in *The Sword Went Out to Sea*, xi, 42, 82–86, 91, 95–96, 166–67, 172
Greece (modern), 7, 16, 137, 202n86
Green, Roger Lancelyn, 215n59
Greenacre, James, 27, 126, 130–31, 136
Greene, Robert, 177
Gregory, Derek, 134
Gregory, Eileen, 35–36, 161
Grey, Cecil, 147
Grimm, Jacob and Wilhelm, 86, 95, 97, 100
Grotstein, James S., 149–50, 152
Guattari, Félix, 151
Guest, Barbara, 189, 232n114
Guthrie, Ramon, 195

Halliday, W. R., 86, 95, 214n38
Halsall, Alison, 126, 220n5, 222n37, 223n66
Hannibal, 188–89
Hansen, Jim, 70, 113
Harris, Paul A., 64
Harrison, Victoria, 157, 232n96
Hart, Kevin, 55
Hathaway, Anne, 118
Hathaway, Katharine Butler, 40
Hawkins, Richard, 132
Hay, Simon, 51
H.D.
—"Aegina," 59
—*Bid Me to Live (A Madrigal)*, xi, 27, 167, 192, 200n40, 204n116, 206n24
—*By Avon River*, 9, 16, 26–27, 105–24, 134, 216n3, 217n25; assessments of, 216n7, 217nn12,19, 218n27, 219n57; and biography, 44, 177, 196; and Braithwaite's anthology, 115–16, 218n41; composition of,

Index

xi, 13, 177, 204n129, 217n13, 218n37, 219n47; and drama, 41; and genre, 101; German language version of, 96; and imperialism, 18, 85, 133, 157; and *The Mystery*, 142, 143, 144; and time, 65
—*Compassionate Friendship*, 9, 28, 47, 169, 201n63, 206n38; composition of, xii; and espionage, 176–80, 188; and "initiators," 225n26; and paranoia, 173
—death of, xii
—"Death of Martin Presser, The," 59
—and drama, 41–42, 45, 73, 78
—"Ear-ring, The," 8
—*End to Torment*, xii, 29, 189, 193–97, 232n98
—and film, 7, 38, 54, 206n41, 228n55
—*The Gift*, 41, 60, 134, 201n50, 217n18; as autobiographical fiction, 36, 44, 101, 207n51; and Moravianism, 143, 157
—"Guardians, The," 59, 60
—"H.D. by Delia Alton," 4, 208n4, 225n29; on autobiographical fiction, 36, 37, 41, 171; on *The Sword Went Out to Sea*, 23, 24, 66, 170; on *White Rose and the Red*, 126, 222n32; on World War II, 67
—*Hedylus*, 160
—*Helen in Egypt*, 29, 37, 80, 135; and the Cold War, 228n2; composition of, xi, 216n3; and imperialism, 221n13; and violence, 168
—*Hermetic Definition*, xii, 192
—*HERmione*, 36–37, 57, 110
—"Hesperia," 58, 59, 60
—"Hipparchia," 8, 26, 28, 37, 159–67, 170, 171, 172
—*Hirslanden Notebooks*, xii, 3, 46, 75, 191, 201n65, 225n26
—"Jubilee," 59
—"The Last Time," 59
—"A Letter from England," 13
—"Loss," 1
—*Magic Mirror*, xii, 28, 46–47, 141, 165, 167, 169–80, 189–92, 232nn94,114
—*Majic Ring*, 16, 36, 42, 82–83, 101, 202n86; and bi-location, 147, 225n29; and India, 127, 137, 221n13; and spiritualism and the occult, 7, 48, 50, 65–66, 72, 210n50, 221n14
—and marriage to Aldington, 15, 45–47, 57, 67, 127, 160–72
—*Moment, The* (book), 58, 66. See also "Aegina"; "The Death of Martin Presser;" "The Guardians"; "Hesperia"; "Jubilee"; "The Last Time"; "The Moment"
—"Moment, The" (short story), 66
—"Murex," 35, 37, 164, 209
—*The Mystery*, 27–28, 102, 137, 141–53, 172, 191, 213n66, 216n6; and bi-location, 65, 147–51, 226n35; composition of, xi, 44; and espionage, 177, 184, 187; and genre, 101, 224n7; and Goethe, 76, 224n17; and Hesse, 225n21; and illness, 145, 151, 225n29; and imperialism, 18; and Moravianism, 158, 226n54; and time, 65
—and naming, 42–44
—"Narthex," 37, 54, 57, 225n29
—national identity of, 1–2, 15–16, 21, 28, 157–58, 172, 202nn78,85,86, 203n87
—*Nights*, 26, 57
—"Note on Poetry, A," 14
—*Notes on Thought and Vision*, 5–6, 58
—*Paint It To-day*, 5–6, 7, 8, 9, 36, 37, 57
—*Palimpsest*. See "Hipparchia"; "Murex"; "Secret Name"
—*Pilate's Wife*, 105, 160
—"Pontikonisi (Mouse Island")*,* 26, 225n29
—"Pygmalion," 6
—postwar illness of, 10–12, 74–75, 173–74, 179, 201nn63,65
—and reading, 106, 127, 216n3, 217n23; Dante's writings, 223n48; about the early modern period, 110, 217n18, 219n44; English literary canon, 204n129; about espionage, 176–77, 190; fairy tales, 86, 95, 96, 127; Freud's writings, 76, 149, 151; Goethe's writings, 224n17; historical fiction, 83–84; life writing, 40–41; about Moravianism, 225n19; about mysticism, 210n43; about politics, 14–15, 141; about

259

H.D.—*continued*
  Pound, 194, 233n10; about Pre-Raphaelitism, 128, 129, 136; Rougemont's writings, 220n68, 223n49; science fiction, 64–65, 210n46; about spirituality and the occult, 56, 64, 146, 147, 148, 151, 158, 206n38, 209n14, 221n14; supernatural tales, 226n51; about trade, 132–33
—*Sagesse*, xii
—*Sea Garden*, 4–5
—"Sea Lily," 4–5
—"Sea Rose," 4
—"Secret Name," 58, 66, 148, 221n13
—*Sword Went Out to Sea, The*, 4, 24–28, 105, 158–60, 165–72, 182, 191, 200n40, 206n33, 211n73, 212n90, 215n59, 223n46; and arranged marriage, 110; assessments of, 205n19, 212nn81,88; and autobiography, 33–53, 71, 74, 80–82, 88, 100, 158; and bilocation, 148, 149; composition of, xi, 13; and espionage, 177, 184, 189; and fairy tale, 79, 86–102, 211n71; and form, 23, 124, 170, 194; and St. George, 217n14; and H.D.'s postwar illness, 11–12, 201n65; and historical fiction, 79, 83–102; and imperialism, 9, 17–18, 21; and India, 127, 221n13; and *The Mystery*, 142–45, 151–52; and mysticism, 54–78; and science fiction, 64–78, 107; and supernatural tale, 44, 48–52, 153; and time, 211n70; and war, 3, 8, 10, 143, 228n3
—*Thorn Thicket*, xii, 47, 165, 169
—*Tribute to Freud*, 204n116; and bilocation, 147–48, 225n29; composition of, xi; and fairy tale, 80, 213n2; and Freud, 107, 183, 188, 189, 217n7, 230n60, 231n92; and time, 208n4; and trauma, 201n50; and war, 58
—*Trilogy*, 2, 27, 77, 84, 152, 223n46; assessments of, 5, 60, 72, 105, 151, 170, 232n117; composition of, 3, 8, 15, 105; and history, 15, 66, 71, 95, 122, 135; and "the Lady," 123, 126, 130, 142, 144; and spiritual vision, 58, 120; and time, 80, 81; and trauma, 201n50
—*Vale Ave*, xii, 60, 79, 157, 167, 168, 173

—*Walls Do Not Fall, The*. See *Trilogy*
—*What Do I Love?*, 15
—*White Rose and the Red*, 26–27, 28, 125–37, 141, 200n40, 211n66, 216n6, 222n41, 223n48; assessments of, 220n5, 223n66; composition of, xi, 41, 44, 207n47; and espionage, 177; and fairy tale, 221n15; and gender, 123, 142–43, 223n45; and genre, 101, 143; and imperialism, 9, 105, 157, 217n16; and medievalism, 17, 86, 121; and time, 62, 65; and the Victorians, 220n7; and war, 8, 9, 18, 77, 143
—*Winter Love*, xii
—*Within the Walls*, 13, 54, 99–100, 199n1, 208n4
—and World War I, 7, 8, 13, 16, 28, 60, 142; and *Bid Me to Live*, 37, 200n40; H.D.'s experience of, 2–3, 16, 47, 57; and Hesse, 97, 98; in *Palimpsest*, 163, 164; in *The Sword Went Out to Sea*, xi, 45, 48, 67, 80–81
—and World War II, 26, 29, 42, 55, 101, 191, 202nn74,76, 212n90; and *By Avon River*, 107, 219n57; in *Compassionate Friendship*, 201n63; and *End to Torment*, 193–97; and *The Gift*, 36, 101, 201n50; in "H.D. by Delia Alton," 66; H.D.'s experience of, 1–4, 11, 14–16, 38, 142, 199nn1,10, 200n47, 201n48, 202n67, 211n57, 213n12, 229n7; in "A Letter from England," 13; in *Magic Mirror*, 47, 159, 170; and *Majic Ring*, 7, 82; and mysticism, 56, 60, 62, 64; in *The Sword Went Out to Sea*, xi, 9, 34, 43, 45, 48–52, 67–69, 74, 77; and *Tribute to Freud*, 201n50; and *Trilogy*, 71, 85, 151, 201n50; and *White Rose and the Red*, 125–27, 137; in *Within the Walls*, 54
—and World War III, 57–58, 74–75, 80, 169, 191, 212n81
Henrey, Robert, 14
Henry II of England, 119
Henry VIII of England, 40, 117. See also *Chronicle History*
Hepburn, Allan, 182, 184–85, 188, 190
Hermes, 25, 63, 147, 187, 209n14

Herrick, Robert, 47, 115
Herring, Robert, 10, 16, 217n23
Hesse, Hermann, 86, 96–100, 127, 137, 215nn67,68, 225n21
Heydt, Dori, 165
Heydt, Erich, 174, 182, 183, 189, 191, 231n77, 232nn102,114; in *Compassionate Friendship* and *Magic Mirror*, xii, 47, 158, 166, 177–80, 185, 188, 190, 191, 194; in *End to Torment*, 194; and illness, 75; as "initiator," 46, 147
Hindrichs, Cheryl, 7, 28, 165
Hines, Sara, 95
Hipparchia of Thrace, 161, 227n8
Hoberman, Ruth, 86–87, 91, 92, 95, 160
Hogue, Cynthia, 41, 61–62, 67, 110, 166, 206n33, 228n3
Hollenback, Jess Byron, 64, 209n14, 210n41
Hollywood, Amy, 210n39
Home, Daniel, 40
Howard, Clifford, 155, 157, 175, 199n10
Howard, Hattie, 213n12, 221n7
Howell, Charles Augustus, 40
Hughes, Molly, 9, 10, 16
Hunt, John Dixon, 128
Hunt, Violet, 35, 40, 49, 125, 147
Hutcheon, Linda, 87, 89, 90, 92, 100, 164

Imagism, 4–5, 7, 61, 105, 115, 135, 224n7; and *White Rose and the Red*, 126, 220n5
imperialism, 15, 16–19, 21–22, 24, 159, 160, 161, 191; and *By Avon River*, 26–27, 102, 105–6, 108–9, 112–15, 117–19, 123, 157, 217n19; and "The Ear-Ring," 8; and *End to Torment*, 195; and fairy tale, 95, 97–98, 215n62; and "Hipparchia," 161–63, 164; and late modernism, 19–22, 100, 220n2; and *Nights*, 26; and *The Sword Went Out to Sea*, 53, 56, 62, 68–69, 72, 79, 85, 88, 96, 166, 172, 211n70; and *White Rose and the Red*, 26–27, 102, 105, 125–28, 132–37, 157. See also "Albertopolis"
India, 27, 137, 221nn15–19, 223n67; in *Majic Ring*, 65, 127, 221nn13,14; in *The Sword Went Out to Sea*, 127; in *White Rose and the Red*, 18, 125, 127–28, 132–37, 177, 217n16, 221n13
infidelity, 46, 57, 160; in *Palimpsest*, 161–63, 164–65, 167; in *The Sword Went Out to Sea*, 159, 165–69, 172
Iphigenia, 83

Jacobs, Naomi, 88, 89
James, David, 17
James, William, 209n7
James I of England, 110–11, 113, 114, 117
Jameson, Fredric, 20, 214n40
Jameson, Storm, 13
Janes, Regina, 117
Jantzen, Grace M., 63, 210n39
Joannou, Maroula, 22
John of the Cross, 40
Johnson, Alan, 125
Jonson, Ben, 114, 117, 118, 123
Jordan, Viola Baxter, 202n86
Joyce, William, 229n14
Jucker, Ninetta, 15
Juliana of Norwich, 40
Julien, Charles-André, 112
Julius Caesar, 106, 218n39; and the eagle, 18, 77; in *The Sword Went Out to Sea*, 28, 72, 85, 91, 95, 96, 166; in *Tribute to Freud*, 188–89

Kasper, John, 195, 233n10
Keller, Joseph, 63
Kerblat-Houghton, Jeanne, 233n4
Knight, G. Wilson: *The Olive and the Sword*, 108–9, 116, 120–23, 217n16, 219n63; on Shakespeare's sexuality, 217n15
Korg, Jacob, 194
Kristeva, Julia, 150

LaCapra, Dominick, 48
Laity, Cassandra, 200n27, 220n5
Lang, Andrew, 40, 86, 95, 96, 97, 127, 215nn59,62, 221n15

Lassner, Phyllis, 13, 22, 23
late modernism, 19–23, 29–30, 31, 137, 197, 203n103; and *By Avon River*, 124; and *The Sword Went Out to Sea*, 38, 52, 53, 69–70, 81, 89, 100, 101, 170; and women writers, 80, 190
Lawrence, D. H., 37, 40, 45, 147, 167
Leclerc du Tremblay, François, 40
Lee, Vernon, 49
Lejeune, Philippe, 40, 42–43, 207n48
Lévi, Éliphas, 147, 158, 225n21
Levi, Primo, 46
Levinas, Emmanuel, 152, 159, 162–63, 167, 168, 172
Lewis, Wyndham, 20, 47
Life and Letters Today, 217n23
Light, Alison, 22, 155
Lim, Shirley Geok-lin, 35, 49
Lindsay, Clarence, 71
Lowell, Amy, 5
Lowndes, Marie Belloc, 40
Loy, Mina, 8
Lucy, Thomas, 114
Lutyens, Emily, 40
Lyly, John, 117

Mackay, Marina, 8, 13, 19, 20, 203nn98,105
Mackenzie, Faith Compton, 41
Maclean, Donald, 176, 177
Macpherson, Kenneth, 147, 206n41
Macqueen-Pope, W. J., 40
Magre, Maurice, 147, 225n21
Mandel, Charlotte, 206n41
Mandelbrote, Scott, 101
Mansfield, Katherine, 40
Manzoni, Alessandro, 88
Marlowe, Christopher, 40, 114, 115, 116, 123, 177; *The Jew of Malta*, 114
Martinelli, Sheri, 194, 196
Marx, John, 20
Mary I of England (Mary Tudor, Bloody Mary), 117
Mary I of Scotland (Mary Stuart, Queen of Scots), 111, 219n44

Mary of Teck, 40
Massey, Sharon Davis, 185
May, Rollo, 231n77
McCabe, Susan, 206n41, 228n55
McGinn, Bernard, 63
McIntosh, Mark A., 63
Melley, Timothy, 175, 187–88
Messent, Peter B., 50
Millais, John Everett, 136
Miller, Meredith, 127, 221n13
Miller, Tyrus, 20–23, 31, 52, 53, 69, 81, 89, 101
Mithridatic Wars, 161
monarchy, 40, 70, 219n44; in *By Avon River*, 26–27, 106, 108, 113–20, 122
Monnier, Adrienne, 195
Montfort, Simon de, 121
Moore, George, 40
Moravianism, 24, 28, 56, 157, 159, 203n87, 216n6, 225n19, 226n54; in *The Mystery*, xi, 18, 143, 158, 216n6. *See also* Zinzendorf, Nicolaus
Morley, Iris, 84
Morris, Adalaide, 24, 28, 35, 159, 200n40, 205n3, 212n2, 225n29
Morris, Jane, 128
Morris, William, xi, 26, 40, 68, 86, 125; in *White Rose and the Red*, 128–33, 136, 217n16
Mortimer, Raymond, 176
Moss, Anita, 99
Murphy, Richard, 92
Murray, D. L., 84
Myers, Tony, 89

Nashe, Thomas, 115, 120, 177
nationalism, 160, 192; and *By Avon River*, 102, 105, 107, 108, 121; and the early modern period, 108–9, 116, 120, 121, 217n16; and existential psychotherapy, 188; and Hesse's writings, 97; and "Hipparchia," 163, 164; and late modernism, 19–23, 30, 100, 203n105; and *Magic Mirror* and *Compassionate Friendship*, 187–92; and modernist women writers, 22; and

science fiction, 72; and *The Sword Went Out to Sea*, 21, 22, 29, 72, 172
Neuman, Shirley, 43
Nikolajeva, Maria, 93
Nora, Pierre, 193, 197
Normandy, xi, 37, 69, 74, 82, 85, 86, 88, 91, 92, 96, 112, 172

O'Brien, Fitz-James, 40
Oldenbourg, Zoé, 84
Olivier, Laurence, 41
Orgel, Stephen, 112–13
Orioli, G., 40
Ouida, 40
Owens, Margaret E., 117

Paige, Nicholas, 50–51
Passmore, John, 63–64
Patmore, Coventry, 40
Paxton, Nancy L., 220n2
Pearce, Lynne, 129
Pearson, Norman Holmes, 3, 86, 205n8, 218n31; and *End to Torment*, 194, 195, 197, 213n17, 232n98, 233n12, 234n17; as H.D.'s executor and promoter, 37, 193, 196, 205n22, 232n98, 233nn2,12; and *The Mystery*, 147; and Perdita, 174; and *White Rose and the Red*, 127, 131
Peele, George, 177
Peloponnesian War, 88, 92
Pericles, 42, 85, 88, 95, 96
Perkins, Kenneth J., 112
Plank, George, 1–2, 11, 175, 191
Pfordresher, John, 129
Phillips, Kathy J., 8
Pollock, Griselda, 221n21
Portinari, Beatrice, 128, 133, 150, 225n29
Pound, Dorothy Shakespear, 196, 197, 233n9
Pound, Ezra, 37, 41, 121, 127, 132, 147, 206n22, 212n84; and Imagism, 4; at St. Elizabeths, 169, 178, 189, 193–97, 232n98, 233nn9,10,11,12, 234n17. See also *End to Torment*
Powell, Nicholas, 14

Poznar, Susan, 52
Pre-Raphaelitism, xi, 17, 26, 41, 125–37, 204n129, 221n21, 222n34
Presser, Martin, 59–60
Preston, Carrie J., 200n31
Private Lives of Elizabeth and Essex, The, 219n44
Proust, Marcel, 33, 35, 40
Psychoanalysis, 171, 180; existential, 28–29, 174, 180, 185–88, 231nn77,85; Freudian, 28–29, 174, 180–84, 186–88, 230n53, 231nn68,92

Quarles, Francis, 111, 217n25

Rackwitz, Irmgard, 192
Radford, Jean, 80
Rado, Lisa, 207n67
Raleigh, Walter: in *By Avon River*, 115, 116, 117, 119, 120, 123; in *White Rose and the Red*, 132–33
Randall, Bryony, 7, 38, 48
Rattray, David, 195, 196
Read, Herbert, 40
Redding, Arthur, 184
Reed, Clarence, 15
Reid, Ian, 15
Renault, Mary, 84
Renza, Louis A., 35
Richard I of England (Richard the Lionheart), 106, 119, 121, 123
Richard III of England, 109
Richardson, Ralph, 41
Riding, Laura, 87
Ridley, M. R., 109, 217n18
Rimius, Henry, 225n19
Riquelme, John Paul, 35
Robinson, Matte, 24, 26, 148, 207n59, 225n20
Rodeck, Peter, 146, 148, 225n29
Rodin, Auguste, 40
Rolfe, Frederick (Baron Corvo), 41
"romantic thralldom," 46, 167, 182, 188
Rome, ancient, 21, 28, 95, 109, 166; in *By*

Avon River, 122–23; in "Hipparchia," 159, 161–64, 167; in historical fiction, 84; in *Paint It To-day*, 6; in *The Sword Went Out to Sea*, xi, 69, 72, 74, 82–86, 91–92, 96, 166

Rose, Francis, 40

Rossetti, Dante Gabriel, xi, 26, 40, 41, 125, 216n6; paintings of, 128–30, 221n21; in *White Rose and the Red*, 126, 130–33, 136, 137, 223n45

Rossetti, William Michael, 130

Rougemont, Denis de, 86, 220n68, 223n49

Rudge, Olga, 233n9

Sackville-West, Vita, 210n43

Said, Edward W., 26, 134

Saint-Amour, Paul K., 2

Sarker, Sonita, 203n96

Sarton, May, 15, 201nn48,54, 217n18, 220n7, 221n17

Schaffner, Perdita, 6, 11, 47, 174, 201n58, 228n3

Scheler, Max, 167

Schiff, Sarah Eden, 69

Schmideberg, Walter, 10, 147, 179

Schreber, Daniel, 75–76

Seidel, Elizabeth, 216n6

Sender, Tori, 40

Sepoy Rebellion, 18, 27, 126, 127, 128, 132, 133, 135, 143, 177, 220n3

Serres, Michel, 25, 63

Shakespeare, William, 6, 16, 106, 107, 112, 113, 216n16, 219n63; *Antony and Cleopatra*, 122; *As You Like It*, 110; in *By Avon River*, xi, 9, 18, 26–27, 41, 107–24; *Cymbeline*, 112; *The Merchant of Venice*, 114; *Midsummer Night's Dream*, 114; *Richard II*, 121; *Romeo and Juliet*, 114; *The Tempest*, xi, 41, 65, 106–14, 217n19, 218n27; *The Winter's Tale*, 6

Shaw, Harry E., 163, 172, 214n39

Shelley, Percy, 40

Shirley, James, 120

Siddall, Elizabeth, xi, 26, 40, 125, 126, 128, 136, 216n6, 222n37; in *White Rose and the Red*, 9, 27, 125–26, 128–37, 222n32, 223n45, 223n66

Siddiqi, Yumma, 184

Sidney, Philip, 112, 115, 117, 118

Silverman, Kaja, 159, 167, 168, 170–71, 183, 228n55

Sitwell, Edith, 217n16, 219n44

Sitwell, Osbert, 201n48, 217n16

Slaughterhouse-Five, 62

Slusser, George, 66, 93

Smith, Geoffrey S., 184

Smith, Sidonie, 41, 42

Smith, Stevie, 13, 22

Smol, Anna, 215n62

Smyth, Ethel, 41

Snell, Ludwig, 40

Somers, George, 109

Sophia of Hanover, 106

Southwell, Robert, 115

Spartali, Marie, 128

Spender, Stephen, 40, 176

Spenser, Edmund, 115, 118, 123

Spring, Howard, 84

Springer, Simon, 136

Stace, W. T., 209n7

Stebbins, Genevieve, 6, 200n31

Stein, Gertrude, 47

Steinmetz, Horst, 87, 93

Stewart, Victoria, 39–40

Stonebridge, Lyndsey, 22, 203n103

Stoneburner, Tony, 60, 212n82

Swedenborg, Emanuel, 40

Sword, Helen, 24, 51, 61

Szefel, Lisa, 218n41

Tchaikovsky, Peter Ilyich, 40

Teresa of Ávila, 40, 64, 196, 210n43

Theocritus, 215n59

Thomas, Dylan, 40

Thomas, Edward, 40

Thurston, Luke, 152, 153

Tiffin, Jessica, 86, 87, 89, 90, 94, 100, 214n30, 215n70

Todorov, Tzvetan, 25

Index

trauma, 24, 26, 39–40, 56, 65, 159–60, 166, 172, 201n50; in *End to Torment*, 193–95; and existential psychotherapy, 29, 185; and H.D.'s postwar illness, 10–12, 173–74, 212n81; and Hesse, 98–99; and late modernism, 19, 22; in *Magic Mirror* and *Compassionate Friendship*, 168–69; in *The Mystery*, 145, 149, 150–51, 224n7; in *Palimpsest*, 164, 165; and religion and mysticism, 55, 61; and supernatural tale, 51; in *The Sword Went Out to Sea*, 44–53, 66, 68–74, 77, 100–102, 168; and World War I, 2, 57, 60; and World War II, 2–3, 7–8, 15, 33, 38, 56, 60
Trojan War, 83
Tryphonopoulos, Demetres, 24, 26, 210n50
Tunisia, 27, 65, 106, 110, 112, 122, 218n31
Twitchell-Waas, Jeffrey, 46–47, 219n57

Uncle Tom's Cabin, 41
Underhill, Evelyn, 209n7
U.S. Civil War, 133
U.S. Revolutionary War, 127

van der Leeuw, J. J., 75, 212n84
Vandivere, Julie, 41, 61–62, 67, 110, 201n51, 206n33, 228n3
Veidt, Conrad, 147
Venice, Italy, 61, 65, 91, 112, 122, 204n132
Vetter, Lara, 7, 36, 54, 200n31, 206n24, 210n46
Victoria and Albert Museum (South Kensington Museum), 16–17

Waller, Edmund, 115
Waln, Nora, 40
Warmington, E. H., 127–28, 132
War of the Roses, 119
Welby, T. Earle, 40
Welch, Denton, 40
Wellesley, Dorothy, 40
Wesseling, Elisabeth, 94

West, Rebecca, 15, 176, 190, 191, 229n14
Wharton, Edith, 41
Whittier-Ferguson, John, 23, 38, 47, 81, 203n103
Widing, Alice, 128
Wilde, Alan, 19
Wilder, Thornton, 84
William I of England (William of Normandy, William the Conqueror), 72, 85
Williams, Valentine, 84
Williams, William Carlos, 29
Willis, Elizabeth, 3
Wittman, Emily O., 8, 35
Wolfreys, Julian, 152
Wolle, Francis, 9, 10, 11, 200n47, 202n86
Woolf, Virginia: *Between the Acts*, 79, 87; and late modernism, 20, 21, 23, 100, 137; suicide of, 10, 201n54; *Three Guineas*, 8, 18–19, 22, 27
Wordsworth, Dorothy, 40
World War I, 13, 16, 19, 38, 97–98, 115, 215n67. *See also* H.D.: and World War I
World War II, 62, 70, 77, 84, 131, 217n16; and Bowen, 191; and espionage, 174, 184; and Glasgow, 9; and late modernism, 8, 13, 19, 20, 47, 203n105; and Perdita, 228n3; and Woolf, 10, 79. *See also* H.D.: and World War II
Wotton, Henry, 111
Wright, Constance, 84

Yaeger, Patricia, 135
Yorke, Dorothy, 45
Young, Stark, 84

Ziarek, Ewa Plonowska, 121
Zinzendorf, Nicolaus, 143, 146, 149, 152, 153, 216n6, 225n19, 226nn35,54
Ziolkowski, Theodore, 96
Zipes, Jack, 97, 215n68
Zugsmith, Leane, 14

LARA VETTER is professor of English at the University of North Carolina at Charlotte. She is the author of *Modernist Writings and Religio-scientific Discourse: H.D., Loy, and Toomer*, as well as the editor of several books, including an annotated edition of H.D.'s *By Avon River* and (with Annette Debo) *Approaches to Teaching H.D.'s Poetry and Prose*.

www.ingramcontent.com/pod-product-compliance
Lightning Source LLC
Chambersburg PA
CBHW031432160426
43195CB00010BB/699